SCREENING LOVE AND WAR IN
TROY: FALL OF A CITY

Imagines – Classical Receptions in the Visual and Performing Arts

Series Editors: Filippo Carlà-Uhink and Martin Lindner

Other titles in this series

Ancient Greece and Rome in Videogames: Representation, Play, Transmedia, by Ross Clare

Ancient Violence in the Modern Imagination: The Fear and the Fury, edited by Irene Berti, Maria G. Castello, and Carla Scilabra

Art Nouveau and the Classical Tradition, by Richard Warren

Classical Antiquity in Heavy Metal Music, edited by K. F. B. Fletcher and Osman Umurhan

Classical Antiquity in Video Games, edited by Christian Rollinger

A Homeric Catalogue of Shapes, by Charlayn von Solms

Orientalism and the Reception of Powerful Women from the Ancient World, edited by Filippo Carlà-Uhink and Anja Wieber

Representations of Classical Greece in Theme Parks, by Filippo Carlà-Uhink

The Ancient Mediterranean Sea in Modern Visual and Performing Arts, edited by Rosario Rovira Guardiola

SCREENING LOVE AND WAR IN
TROY: FALL OF A CITY

Edited by Antony Augoustakis and Monica S. Cyrino

BLOOMSBURY ACADEMIC
LONDON • NEW YORK • OXFORD • NEW DELHI • SYDNEY

BLOOMSBURY ACADEMIC
Bloomsbury Publishing Plc
50 Bedford Square, London, WC1B 3DP, UK
1385 Broadway, New York, NY 10018, USA
29 Earlsfort Terrace, Dublin 2, Ireland

BLOOMSBURY, BLOOMSBURY ACADEMIC and the Diana logo are trademarks
of Bloomsbury Publishing Plc

First published in Great Britain 2022

Copyright © Antony Augoustakis, Monica S. Cyrino and Contributors, 2022

Antony Augoustakis and Monica S. Cyrino have asserted their right under the Copyright,
Designs and Patents Act, 1988, to be identified as Editors of this work.

For legal purposes the Acknowledgments on p. xvi constitute an extension of this
copyright page.

Series cover design: Clare Turner.
Logo design: Ainize González and Nacho García.
Cover image © Wild Mercury Productions Company Ltd.

All rights reserved. No part of this publication may be reproduced or transmitted
in any form or by any means, electronic or mechanical, including photocopying,
recording, or any information storage or retrieval system, without prior
permission in writing from the publishers.

Bloomsbury Publishing Plc does not have any control over, or responsibility for, any
third-party websites referred to or in this book. All internet addresses given in
this book were correct at the time of going to press. The author and publisher
regret any inconvenience caused if addresses have changed or sites have
ceased to exist, but can accept no responsibility for any such changes.

A catalogue record for this book is available from the British Library.

Library of Congress Cataloging-in-Publication Data
Names: Augoustakis, Antony, editor. | Cyrino, Monica Silveira, editor.
Title: Screening love and war in Troy: fall of a city / [edited by Antony Augoustakis and
Monica S. Cyrino].
Other titles: Imagines – Classical receptions in the visual and performing arts.
Description: London ; New York : Bloomsbury Academic, 2022. | Series: Imagines: classical
receptions in the visual and performing arts | Includes bibliographical references and index.
Identifiers: LCCN 2021026842 (print) | LCCN 2021026843 (ebook) |
ISBN 9781350144231 (hardback) | ISBN 9781350257009 (paperback) |
ISBN 9781350144255 (ebook) | ISBN 9781350144262 (epub)
Subjects: LCSH: Troy: fall of a city (Television program) | Troy (Extinct city–On television.
Classification: LCC PN1992.77.T776 S37 2022 (print) | LCC PN1992.77.T776 (ebook) |
DDC 794.45/72—dc23
LC record available at https://lccn.loc.gov/2021026842
LC ebook record available at https://lccn.loc.gov/2021026843

ISBN: HB: 978-1-3501-4423-1
PB: 978-1-3502-5700-9
ePDF: 978-1-3501-4425-5
eBook: 978-1-3501-4426-2

Series: IMAGINES – Classical Receptions in the Visual and Performing Arts

Typeset by RefineCatch Limited, Bungay, Suffolk

To find out more about our authors and books visit www.bloomsbury.com
and sign up for our newsletters.

CONTENTS

List of Illustrations   vii
Notes on Contributors   ix
Foreword by Derek Wax, Executive Producer, *Troy: Fall of a City*   xiii
Editors' Acknowledgments   xvi
List of Episodes   xvii

Introduction: Screening Love and War in *Troy: Fall of a City*
Antony Augoustakis and Monica S. Cyrino   1

Part I Epic Narrative

1. **Binge for Me, O Muse: Episodes, Books, and Cycles** *Dan Curley*   13
2. **Delineating the Divine: Gods and Religion at Troy** *Lisa Maurice*   25
3. **From Judgment to Fall: Aphrodite and Paris** *Monica S. Cyrino*   37
4. **Sympathy for Troy's Jezebel: Helen as Antihero** *Meredith E. Safran*   51
5. **The Curse of Troy: Odysseus' Story** *Emma J. Stafford*   65

Part II Cast and Character

6. **Racist Reactions to Black Achilles** *Rebecca Futo Kennedy*   79
7. **Pussy Politics: Women and Power in the Homeric Patriarchy**
   Kirsten Day   97
8. **Queering Troy: Freedom and Sexuality** *Thomas E. Jenkins*   111
9. **Heroic Hairstyles and Manless Amazons at Troy**
   Walter Duvall Penrose, Jr.   127
10. **Costume Changes: Dressing Helen of Sparta and Troy**
    Stacie Raucci   141

Part III Tragic Resonances

11. **Fallen Heroes: Recasting Ajax and the Greeks on Screen**
    Anastasia Bakogianni   155
12. **Family vs. Compassion: Odysseus and the Ethics of War**
    Meredith Prince   169

Contents

13 Bloody Brides: Iphigenia, Helen, and Ritual Exchange
    Amy L. Norgard   183

14 Kings of Men and Sacrificial Daughters   *Krishni Burns*   197

15 Lessons for Leaders: Destiny, Devotion, and Self-Deception
    Brian Cooke   211

Epilogue: *Troy: Fall of a City* and Its Ancient Sources   *Diana Burton* 223

Bibliography   233
Filmography   247
Index   251

ILLUSTRATIONS

I.1	Aeneas (Alfred Enoch) limps along the abandoned streets of the lower city of Troy in Episode 8, "Offering"	9
1.1	Paris (Louis Hunter) opens the chest that conceals Helen and brings closure to Episode 1, "Black Blood"	19
2.1	Hera (Inge Beckmann) approaches Zeus (Hakeem Kae-Kazim) in Episode 2, "Conditions"	29
3.1	Paris (Louis Hunter) gives Aphrodite (Lex King) the golden apple in the Judgment scene in Episode 1, "Black Blood"	40
3.2	Aphrodite (Lex King) on the Trojan plain before battle in Episode 2, "Conditions"	42
4.1	Hermione (Grace Hogg-Robinson) is ill-equipped to compete with Helen (Bella Dayne) for the attention of Paris (Louis Hunter) in Episode 1, "Black Blood"	57
5.1	Odysseus (Joseph Mawle) sails away from Troy at the end of Episode 8, "Offering"	65
6.1	Achilles (David Gyasi) in Episode 6, "Battle on the Beach," and Athena (Shamilla Miller) in Episode 1, "Black Blood"	80
7.1	Clint Eastwood as Blondie in Sergio Leone's *The Good, the Bad, and the Ugly* (1966) and the Amazon queen Penthesilea (Nina Milner) in Episode 6, "Battle on the Beach"	102
7.2	Lalo Alcaraz's political cartoon depicting Christine Blasey Ford and Brett Kavanaugh (2018) and Cassandra (Aimee-Ffion Edwards) in Episode 1, "Black Blood"	106
8.1	Helen (Bella Dayne) costumed like a bird in Episode 1, "Black Blood"	112
8.2	The reunion of Paris (Louis Hunter) and Helen (Bella Dayne) in Episode 6, "Battle on the Beach"	115
8.3	Achilles (David Gyasi), Patroclus (Lemogang Tsipa), and Briseis (Amy Louise Wilson) in Episode 6, "Battle on the Beach" (left), and Elena Gogou's Tumblr post of the scene reimagined (with permission from the creator)	119
9.1	Penthesilea (Nina Milner) in Episode 7, "Twelve Days"	127
10.1	Helen (Bella Dayne) and Paris (Louis Hunter) join hands in marriage in Episode 3, "Siege." Helen's signature bird ring and wrist cuff are visible	145
10.2	Helen (Bella Dayne) distributes food to the people of Troy in a stunning red dress in Episode 3, "Siege"	149
11.1	Ajax (Garth Breytenbach) goes into battle in Episode 2, "Conditions"	157

Illustrations

11.2	Thersites (Waldemar Schultz) reveals Astyanax and his nurse in Episode 8, "Offering"	160
12.1	Odysseus (Joseph Mawle) remembers leaving Penelope (Erica Wessels) in Episode 2, "Conditions"	170
12.2	Odysseus (Joseph Mawle) holds Astyanax at Troy's walls in Episode 8, "Offering"	177
13.1	Helen (Bella Dayne) and Paris (Louis Hunter) consummate their union at Troy in Episode 2, "Conditions"	187
13.2	Agamemnon (Johnny Harris) mourns a deceased, bloody Iphigenia (Lauren Coe) on the offering table in Episode 2, "Conditions"	188
14.1	Menelaus (Jonas Armstrong), Agamemnon (Johnny Harris), and Odysseus (Joseph Mawle) contemplate the sacrifice of Iphigenia in Episode 2, "Conditions"	197
15.1	Priam (David Threlfall) during the festivities at Troy in Episode 8, "Offering"	214
15.2	The Trojan Horse in Episode 8, "Offering"	218
E.1	Helen (Bella Dayne) and Achilles (David Gyasi) meet in Troy in Episode 3, "Siege"	226

CONTRIBUTORS

Antony Augoustakis is Professor of Classics at the University of Illinois at Urbana-Champaign in Urbana, Illinois, US. His research interests include Latin imperial epic, Roman comedy and historiography, women in antiquity, classical reception, and gender theory. He is the author of *Motherhood and the Other: Fashioning Female Power in Flavian Epic* (2010) and *Statius, Thebaid 8* (2016). He has edited or co-edited several volumes on Flavian poetry and Roman comedy, among which are two volumes on classical reception on screen: *STARZ Spartacus: Reimagining an Icon on Screen* (with Monica S. Cyrino, 2017) and *Epic Heroes on Screen* (with Stacie Raucci, 2018). He is the editor of *The Classical Journal*.

Monica S. Cyrino is Professor of Classics at the University of New Mexico in Albuquerque, New Mexico, US. Her academic research centers on the reception of the ancient world on screen, and the erotic in ancient Greek poetry. She is the author of *Aphrodite* (2010), *A Journey through Greek Mythology* (2008), *Big Screen Rome* (2005), and *In Pandora's Jar: Lovesickness in Early Greek Poetry* (1995). She is the editor of *Rome, Season Two: Trial and Triumph* (2015), *Screening Love and Sex in the Ancient World* (2013), *Rome, Season One: History Makes Television* (2008), and co-editor of *Classical Myth on Screen* (with Meredith E. Safran, 2015) and *STARZ Spartacus: Reimagining an Icon on Screen* (with Antony Augoustakis, 2017). She has published numerous articles and book chapters and often gives lectures around the world on the representation of classical antiquity on film and television. She has served as an academic consultant on several recent film and television productions.

*****

Anastasia Bakogianni is Senior Lecturer in Classical Studies at Massey University in Auckland, New Zealand. Her research and publications focus on the reception of Greek tragedy. She is the author of *Electra Ancient and Modern: Aspects of the Tragic Heroine's Reception* (2011), editor of *Dialogues with the Past: Classical Reception Theory and Practice* (2013), and co-editor of *War as Spectacle: Ancient and Modern Perspectives on the Display of Armed Conflict* (with Valerie M. Hope, 2015) and *Locating Classical Receptions on Screen: Masks, Echoes, Shadows* (with Ricardo Apostol, 2018).

Krishni Burns is Lecturer of Latin at the University of Illinois at Chicago in Chicago, Illinois, US. Her main areas of study are ancient religion and the lives of women in Republican Rome, as well as the expression of classical myth in children's popular culture. Her current book project is *Bringing Their Mother Home: Roman Multiculturalism and the Mother of the Gods*. She participates in the European Research Council project *Our*

Contributors

Mythical Childhood, and chairs the Committee on Ancient and Modern Performance (CAMP).

Diana Burton is Senior Lecturer in Classics at the Victoria University of Wellington, New Zealand. Her research interests and publications include early Greek poetry, Greek art and iconography, myth and religion, death, immortality, and the afterlife, and the areas where these intersect. She is being slowly and inexorably drawn into classical reception.

Brian Cooke is founder and leader of IRIS Learning, a consulting group that coaches high-performing leaders and teams throughout the world. Prior to founding IRIS Learning, Brian was a teacher, coach, and college advisor at Deerfield Academy and Milton Academy in Massachusetts, US. Brian is author of several books, including *Frank Boyden: The Vision and Politics of an Educational Idealist* (1991), *The Best We Can Be: A Guide for Leading Purposeful Change* (2009), and *Aim High—Notes for Leadership and Peak Performance* (2020).

Dan Curley is Associate Professor of Classics at Skidmore College in Saratoga Springs, New York, US. His teaching and research interests include ancient epic, tragedy, and the classical world in screen media. He is the author of the book *Tragedy in Ovid* (2013). He contributed a chapter "The Hero in a Thousand Pieces: Antiheroes in Recent Epic Cinema" to the volume *Epic Heroes on Screen* (2018), as well as "'Benefits of a Classical Education': The Dynamics of Classical Allusion in ABC's *Revenge*" to the collection *New Voices in Classical Reception Studies* (2020).

Kirsten Day is Professor and Chair of the Classics Department at Augustana College in Rock Island, Illinois, US. She is the author of *Cowboy Classics: The Roots of the American Western in the Epic Tradition* (2016), and has published a number of articles on classical reception and women in antiquity. She is also the editor of a special issue of *Arethusa* entitled *Celluloid Classics: New Perspectives on Classical Antiquity in Modern Cinema* (2008).

Rebecca Futo Kennedy is Associate Professor of Classics, Women's and Gender Studies, and Environmental Studies at Denison University in Granville, Ohio, US. She is the author of *Athena's Justice* (2009) and *Immigrant Women in Athens* (2014). She is the editor of *Brill's Companion to the Reception of Aeschylus* (2018), and co-editor of *The Routledge Handbook to Identity and the Environment in the Classical and Medieval Worlds* (with Molly Jones-Lewis, 2015) and *Race and Ethnicity in the Classical World: An Anthology of Primary Sources in Translation* (with C. Sydnor Roy and Max L. Goldman, 2013).

Thomas E. Jenkins is Professor of Classical Studies and Director of the Collaborative for Learning and Teaching at Trinity University in San Antonio, Texas, US. He has published widely on classical literature and its reception, including *Antiquity Now: The Classical World in the Contemporary American Imagination* (2015). His article on Lucian's *Mimes of the Courtesans* was awarded the inaugural Rehak Award for LBGTQ studies in

Classics (2005). His adaptation of Plautus' "The Haunted House" premiered at the Overtime Theater in San Antonio in 2013.

Lisa Maurice is Associate Professor in the Department of Classics at Bar-Ilan University, Ramat Gan, Israel. She is the author of *The Teacher in Ancient Rome* (2013) and *Screening Divinity* (2019). She is the editor of three volumes on the reception of the ancient world in popular culture, including most recently *Our Mythical Childhood*, a wide-ranging volume examining the use of classical mythology in formal education worldwide (2021).

Amy L. Norgard is Associate Professor of Classics in the Department of Classical and Modern Languages at Truman State University in Kirksville, Missouri, US. Her research interests include Roman satire, the body and senses in Latin literature, and modern receptions of classical antiquity, especially through horror film. She is currently working on a contribution to an edited volume on women in classical-themed video games.

Walter Duvall Penrose, Jr. is Associate Professor of History at San Diego State University in San Diego, California, US. His research focuses on the history of gender and sexuality in Ancient Greek, Hellenistic, and South Asian contexts. He is the author of *Postcolonial Amazons: Female Masculinity and Courage in Ancient Greek and Sanskrit Literature* (2016). He has published numerous journal articles and book chapters on issues of ancient Greek gender, sexuality, and disability, as well as the later reception of these topics.

Meredith Prince is Associate Professor of Classics at Auburn University in Auburn, Alabama, US. She teaches Greek, Latin, and courses in translation, including the ancient world in film. She has published on Augustan age poetry, especially Ovid's *Metamorphoses*, and has worked extensively on classical reception, with recent book chapters on STARZ *Spartacus* and HBO *Game of Thrones*. She is currently working on the reception of the Roman emperor Nero's wife Poppaea in nineteenth-century historical fiction and twentieth-century films.

Stacie Raucci is Frank Bailey Professor of Classics at Union College in Schenectady, New York, US. Her research focuses primarily on the reception of the ancient world in popular culture and Roman love elegy. She is the author of *Elegiac Eyes: Vision in Roman Love Elegy* (2011), co-author of *Rome: A Sourcebook on the Ancient City* (with Fanny Dolansky, 2018), and co-editor of *Epic Heroes on Screen* (with Antony Augoustakis, 2018).

Meredith E. Safran is Associate Professor of Classical Studies at Trinity College in Hartford, Connecticut, US. She is the editor of the volume *Screening the Golden Ages of the Classical Tradition* (2019), and co-editor of the volume *Classical Myth on Screen* (with Monica S. Cyrino, 2015), and co-editor of a special issue of *The Classical Journal* on Roman Comedy: Performance, Pedagogy, Research (with Laurel Fulkerson, Fall 2015). She has contributed chapters to *Screening Love and Sex in the Ancient World* (2013), *A Companion to Ancient Greece and Rome on Screen* (2017), and *Epic Heroes on Screen* (2018).

Contributors

Emma J. Stafford is Professor of Greek Culture at the University of Leeds, UK. She is author of numerous works on Greek myth, religion, and iconography, including the monographs *Worshipping Virtues* (2000) and *Herakles* (2012), and co-editor of a volume *Personification in the Greek World* (with J. E. Herrin, 2005). She is coordinator of the project *Hercules: A Hero for All Ages* (www.herculesproject.leeds.ac.uk) and co-editor of its four volumes published in Brill's *Metaforms* series (2020–2022).

FOREWORD

Derek Wax, Executive Producer, Troy: Fall of a City

In 2013, the writer David Farr and I developed an idea for a long-form drama about Troy. The BBC commissioned a first script, and we were greenlit and financed jointly by the BBC and Netflix in 2016. We started around six months of filming in 2017 and the series *Troy: Fall of a City* aired the year after.

In this Foreword, I hope to give some context for the inspiration behind the series, how we put it on the screen and dealt with some of the challenges that arose along the way.

From the outset our aim was to explore the accumulated myths and narratives that cover the Trojan War, to embrace the depth and complexity of elements not only in Homer's *Iliad* but also in the other ancient source material, and to reinterpret and illuminate these powerful stories for a modern audience. We were greatly inspired by the work of Michael Wood (*In Search of the Trojan War*, 1996) and Barry Strauss (*The Trojan War*, 2006), and supported by two superb historical advisors, Bettany Hughes and Nigel Tallis, who helped us considerably in understanding the culture of the Bronze Age.

We wanted to create an epic drama that felt grounded in heartbreaking emotions and psychological truth. A faithful adaptation of the *Iliad* would of course have been impossible, as Homer's classic covers only a period of a few weeks in the middle of the war, and David and I were determined to encompass a wider time-frame, to take it from the birth of Paris right through to the violent and tragic destruction of the city.

Several of the essays in the present volume reflect upon our "antiwar interpretation of the Trojan War" (Bakogianni, 165). Indeed, my thinking about modern warfare certainly informed my initial thinking about this project.

When I brought the idea to David, we felt that even though Homer's epic is nearly three thousand years old it still has much to say about the military conflicts of the twenty-first century, for example the 2003 US invasion of Iraq. In both, a flimsy pretext was used for disproportionately aggressive action, and diplomatic concerns were hastily brushed aside.

My time making *Occupation* (2009), a mini-series written by Peter Bowker for the BBC about the Iraq War, also made me keen to continue exploring how war affects people's lives in unforeseeable, devastating ways.

David Farr and I were drawn to this extraordinary story and to the fascinatingly complex characters, changed by war, riven by moral dilemmas. It is a world where both sides believe that the only way to justify the blood already shed is to keep on killing. The themes feel elementally rich, speaking to us urgently across the generations – intrigue and betrayal, love and loss, family rivalries. We were determined that any retelling of this story should feel fresh, passionate, and vivid.

Foreword

David grounded the storylines in psychological reality and nuance, and chose to tell the story from the Trojan point of view (as he said in a media interview), as he was "temperamentally driven to see things from the point of view of the attacked rather than the attacker," and to focus on "a peasant who finds out he's a prince, and a queen who is utterly unhappy in her marriage, who fall into a passionate affair and unleash demons" (*bbc.co.uk/mediacentre*, February 14, 2018). David also made the decision to bring the ancient gods into the story, honouring Homer and the other mythologies, which Petersen's *Troy* film (2004) had dispensed with.

David and I, along with our script editor Alice Pearse and head of production Ben Holt, travelled to Turkey in early 2017, to Hisarlik, the ancient site of the city of Troy, where we were captivated by the many cities built on top of each other over many thousands of years. We were struck by its extraordinary proximity to the First World War battlefields of Gallipoli, with the ancient and modern sites located side by side.

Having scoured southern Europe for places to film the series, we finally decided that South Africa gave us the best opportunities. Filming with a highly experienced camera crew in the countryside outside Cape Town, we were able to faithfully recreate the Bronze Age cities of Sparta and Troy.

Director Owen Harris brought an imaginative sweep, beauty, and detail to the way he approached the series, and designer Rob Harris stunned us with the grandeur and intricacy of his design for both the cities of Troy and Sparta, as well as the Greek camp.

Always we returned to Homer, trying to honour and acknowledge the beauty and terrible violence of the *Iliad*, ensuring that we saw the deaths in battle – for example Achilles' brutal killing of the young Trojan, Simoisius, with a spear at the end of Episode 2 "Conditions" – as extraordinarily painful. Homer expresses so graphically throughout the epic poem that war only rarely allows "heroic" deaths: more often death in battle is horrible, gruesome, macabre.

We were thrilled by the casting opportunities opened up to us – our only aim was to cast the best actor available for each role. But when the first photos of our cast, including the excellent actors David Gyasi as Achilles and Hakeem Kae-Kazim as Zeus, were released, several months before the series transmitted, we were both perplexed and disappointed by the racist reactions they provoked on social media. Trolls absurdly accused the show of being unfaithful to the supposed whiteness of Greek mythological characters. Some of my creative team received anonymous death threats and the racists branded us as "terrorists" online.

Various alt-right websites and individuals unleashed a campaign of abuse in this vein on social media platforms, with white supremacists posting videos encouraging people to condemn the series as a failure. Many posted one-star ratings well before the series had even been broadcast, in effect review-bombing the show, motivated only by their own warped and racist claims about the homogeneity of ethnicities in ancient Greece, which academics maintain are a complete historical fallacy. Such is the trolling of the social media age. It was appalling to see that 37,000 people had viewed one particular YouTube video that argued Achilles should have been cast with a white actor.

But many others praised the show's diverse casting choices. As Tim Whitmarsh, Professor of Greek Culture at the University of Cambridge, observed: "There's value

Foreword

disrupting the narrative in this way and making us think again what people would look like" (*RadioTimes.com*, February 24, 2018).

Reading the insightful essays in this volume, I was once again made aware of the many discussions and creative decisions we made when developing the series in the writers' room, where three other writers, Nancy Harris, Mika Watkins and Joe Barton, gave vital contributions and input to the arc of the narrative, helping to fill in the gaps that some of the sources had left. In particular, we wanted to give expressive voice to the exceptionally varied experiences of the women of the Trojan War narrative who deserved to have more facets of their characters explored, such as Hermione, Hecuba, Andromache, Cassandra, and Briseis.

I feel it's worth saying something about the way we treated Helen in the series, which owed much to Bettany Hughes' superb book about her (*Helen of Troy*, 2005), particularly in relation to what is being suggested in Meredith Safran's essay in this volume on Helen as an antihero (Chapter 4). I would argue that Helen tries to empower herself, and makes a bold, passionate decision to leave an oppressive and coercive marriage, but tragically she is trapped, deceived by manipulative, controlling, and aggressive men. I would agree with the view of Diana Burton, who observes in this volume's Epilogue: "The women in *TFOAC*, including Helen, serve more than any other characters to illustrate the costs of the war" (Burton, 228). That they are ultimately treated as "powerless commodities" (Burton, 228) is, I would argue, a comment on the terrible damage that war inflicts on its victims. Helen allows the Greeks into the city of Troy because she believes that striking this bargain is the only way to save the life of Paris, the man she loves: it's a tragic dilemma and of course Menelaus doesn't respect the agreement. Helen may be naive, but she is empathetic and at the end does have both nobility and tragic dignity. She stands up to Menelaus, and refuses to be cowed.

I was fascinated to read these critical essays, which are full of imaginative and penetrating insights into our series. I hope this volume will encourage those who have not yet watched *Troy: Fall of a City* to do so, and will inspire viewers to return to the series in a richer and deeper way.

London, June 2021

EDITORS' ACKNOWLEDGMENTS

We would like to thank the individual authors for their enthusiasm in embracing this collective project right from the outset and for their inspiring contributions to the present volume: we are so profoundly appreciative of their collegiality and perseverance during the many unprecedented challenges of the past several months. Special thanks are owed to Alice Wright at Bloomsbury for her unwavering support of this volume from the very beginning, and to her assistant editor, Lily Mac Mahon, for her expert assistance throughout the production process, as well as the *Imagines* series editors, Filippo Carlà-Uhink and Martin Lindner, for their encouragement from start to finish. We have greatly benefitted from the feedback provided by the two anonymous reviewers: their comments and suggestions made this into a stronger and much improved volume. Finally, we would like to thank our families, students, and colleagues who continue to inspire us to explore classics and popular culture. This volume is dedicated to them.

EPISODES

Readers may consult https://www.netflix.com/title/80175352 and www.theguardian.com/tv-and-radio/series/troy--fall-of-a-city--episode-by-episode for a synopsis of each episode.

Episode 1: "Black Blood," written by David Farr, directed by Owen Harris. Original air date: February 17, 2018

Episode 2: "Conditions," written by David Farr, directed by Owen Harris. Original air date: February 24, 2018

Episode 3: "Siege," written by Nancy Harris, directed by Owen Harris. Original air date: March 3, 2018

Episode 4: "Spoils of War," written by Mika Watkins, directed by Mark Brozel. Original air date: March 10, 2018

Episode 5: "Hunted," written by David Farr, directed by Mark Brozel. Original air date: March 17, 2018

Episode 6: "Battle on the Beach," written by Joe Barton, directed by Mark Brozel. Original air date: March 24, 2018

Episode 7: "Twelve Days," written by David Farr, directed by John Strickland. Original air date: March 31, 2018

Episode 8: "Offering," written by David Farr, directed by John Strickland. Original air date: April 7, 2018

INTRODUCTION
SCREENING LOVE AND WAR IN *TROY: FALL OF A CITY*

Antony Augoustakis and Monica S. Cyrino

This new edited collection brings together a wide range of perspectives on the original television series *Troy: Fall of a City* (2018)—abbreviated throughout this volume as *TFOAC*. A co-production between BBC One and Netflix, created and written by David Farr, the series was commissioned by BBC One and first aired in the United Kingdom in February 2018, and was later streamed in the United States and internationally by Netflix in April 2018. Shot on location in and around Cape Town, South Africa, eight carefully crafted hour-long episodes tell the celebrated ancient Greek tale of the Trojan War, starting with the illicit love affair of Paris and Helen, followed by the devastating ten-year siege of the city that leads to the inevitable fatal consequence described in the series title. While the series was not a ratings blockbuster, *TFOAC* was praised by critics and fans alike for its faithful adaptations of the ancient mythological, artistic, and literary (both epic and tragic) sources; for the steady pacing of the plot that allowed a finely nuanced development of characters; for its evocative portrayal of the Greek gods; and for its high-quality acting, costuming, and set design.

Every episode of *TFOAC* begins with a title card that proclaims: "Inspired by Homer and the Greek myths." In responding to this claim, the contributors to this volume all engage on some level with the keen awareness that the Trojan War as a legendary ancient conflict has in the popular imagination become paradigmatic of all wars, and thus the myth of Troy offers a powerful and compelling way to contemplate various aspects of the human condition. As historian Naoise Mac Sweeney explains in her exuberant new survey of the ancient site's persistent cultural significance, *Troy: Myth, City, Icon*:

> The unique fame of Troy comes from its myth—the myth of the Trojan War. It is a story best known from Homer's epic poem, the *Iliad*, composed in ancient Greek in the eighth century BCE. The poem explores love and anger, duty and heroism, setting these against the backdrop of a bloody and ongoing war. This war was, of course, the decade-long conflict between the massed armies of the Achaean Greeks on one side and the Trojans and their allies on the other, resulting in the eventual defeat and destruction of Troy. Throughout history, the name of Troy has been synonymous with this myth of the Trojan War, and the story of Troy has always been bound up with the story of this conflict.[1]

In his 1985 BBC documentary television series and accompanying book *In Search of the Trojan War*, historian and broadcaster Michael Wood also emphasized the centrality of the Homeric epic poems alongside the immense storehouse of mythological material available to the ancient Greek bards:

> Homer of course is the starting point, with the *Iliad* and the *Odyssey*. But it is as well to make clear at the start that he was drawing on a vast cycle of stories which dealt with the Trojan War. The *Iliad* in fact deals with only one episode covering a few weeks in the tenth year of the war. In classical times a great series of epics, now lost or in fragments, told those parts of the story ignored by the earlier Homeric poems, and some of these, like the epics known as the *Kypria* or the *Sack of Ilios*, were evidently of great scope and power ... These successors to Homer may have written down their epics, but it is clear from the surviving fragments that they, like Homer, were drawing heavily on a long oral tradition.[2]

In a series of spirited conversations in their recent book, *Homer's* Iliad *and the Trojan War: Dialogues on Tradition*, Mac Sweeney and classicist Jan Haywood unpack the variety of ways the *Iliad* has throughout history shaped numerous receptions of the Trojan War, which in turn respond by dynamically transforming the epic source texts they conjure:

> For while it is impossible for us to imagine the Trojan War without taking some kind of recourse to the *Iliad*, it is no less difficult to imagine the *Iliad* bereft of the monumental, tentacular series of cross-cultural dialogues that have emerged from this wider tradition.[3]

Entering into this vibrant transmedia dialogue on the time-honored myth of Troy, the series *TFOAC* introduces an original episodic version of the ancient epic war that draws on many of its predecessors on the big screen, such as Robert Wise's midcentury film *Helen of Troy* (1956), and the more recent feature film directed by Wolfgang Petersen, *Troy* (2004).[4] Yet *TFOAC* has also been influenced by the recent wave of premium cable television series set in the ancient world, such as HBO *Rome* (2005–7)[5] and STARZ *Spartacus* (2010–2013),[6] upon which *TFOAC* draws extensively for its portrayal of ancient warfare, society, politics, kinship, race, gender, religion, and sexuality. Moreover, like other series set in the historical or legendary past, *TFOAC* takes advantage of its more measured episodic pace to reject the corner-cutting and composite character strategies employed by earlier feature films. In this new and fundamentally reimagined epic and tragic portrayal of the Trojan War, viewers are invited to appreciate how the story weaves together a nexus of complicated relationships among heroic warriors, kings, queens, families, servants, and captives, while considering the depiction of siege warfare and the domestic and social politics of the royal houses. *TFOAC* offers an original representation of the Trojan War, as the ancient epic story is recast for a modern twenty-first-century audience ready to stream—and perhaps even binge-watch—an extended episodic retelling of what happened before, during, and after the war at Troy.

Introduction

About This Volume

This collection of essays on *Troy: Fall of a City* engages with an exciting and provocative range of topics focused on the various characters, themes, and issues arising from the series. The individual chapters in this volume are written by scholars and thought-leaders in the fields of classics, history, classical reception, and film studies, who cover numerous subjects such as society, politics, warfare, gender, race, religion, genre, media, and production design. In addition to drawing connections between this new episodic version of the story and previous cinematic and media receptions of the epic and tragic strands of the Trojan War tale, the contributors to the present volume all assess the greater creative and narrative freedoms afforded to the showrunners in producing eight gripping and original hours of television drama. Thus assembled, the individual chapters work together to offer consciously and intentionally differing perspectives on certain characters, narratives, and themes; readers of the volume as a whole will find numerous cross-references to signal purposeful links between contributions, while also discovering their own connections among the diverse analyses presented here. As the first volume of essays published on the series, *Screening Love and War in Troy: Fall of a City* offers a vigorous scholarly contribution to the area of onscreen classical receptions, and the *TFOAC* series will no doubt continue to attract extensive academic and pedagogical interest and discussion in the years to come.

This volume is organized into three sections, each of which groups together contributions addressing specific topics and themes, followed by an epilogue that deftly gathers the various strands of Trojan Cycle receptions into a comprehensive survey of ancient sources. The first section of this volume, "Epic Narrative," considers the ways in which the *TFOAC* series engages with its ancient epic sources, foundations, and precedents. In the first chapter, "Binge for Me, O Muse: Episodes, Books, and Cycles," Dan Curley explores storytelling formats in Homeric epic poetry and televised serials, illustrating how the conventions of one can illuminate the other. Curley argues that the episodic structure of *TFOAC* evokes the so-called books of the *Iliad* and the *Odyssey*, inasmuch as discrete storytelling segments collectively contribute to an extended narrative. If it is possible that the Homeric epics came to be divided into books after negotiations between singers and scribes, Curley suggests, the brainstorming sessions of modern showrunners and their writing teams come very close to such ancient practices. In addition, epic cycles include prequels and sequels, allowing the poems to allude routinely to events outside their scope. But while audiences of Homeric performances were more likely to hear self-contained scenes instead of complete books, the varied interests of modern viewers are served by digital platforms, which can access the story at any conceivable point, a totalizing experience available to few if any ancient audiences.

In the second chapter, "Delineating the Divine: Gods and Religion at Troy," Lisa Maurice explores the conspicuous depiction of the gods in *TFOAC*. While the ancient gods have been variously portrayed in cinema, Maurice reveals how the series *TFOAC* utilizes a distinctive technique: the gods are visible, and their power is obvious, but they are usually unseen by the mortals whom they invisibly influence (the notable exception being the Judgment of Paris scene, discussed in the next chapter). Maurice analyzes this novel method as one that engages with contemporary understandings of, and relationships with, divinity. Equally ground-breaking is the physical depiction of these gods, Maurice notes, with the casting of British-Nigerian actor Hakeem Kae-Kazim, in particular, as the supreme god Zeus, which raised a considerable storm among viewers and critics. Ultimately, *TFOAC* interacts with recent cinematic and television traditions for the portrayal of the divine, while also reflecting wider twenty-first-century attitudes toward religion and the divine.

In the third chapter, "From Judgment to Fall: Aphrodite and Paris," Monica S. Cyrino explores the depiction of the goddess Aphrodite (Lex King) and her close relationship with her mortal favorite, Paris (Louis Hunter) in *TFOAC*. Through an analysis of several key scenes in the series, Cyrino argues that Aphrodite's intimate engagement with Paris, the Trojan shepherd-turned-prince, forms the emotional through-line of the series, as this chain of sequences shared between goddess and mortal punctuate the epic story and delineate the passage of narrative time. From the opening dramatization of the infamous Judgment of Paris scene as the foundational myth of the Trojan War, to the closing sequence of the charred city in eponymous ruins, the onscreen presence of Aphrodite and her constant intervention in the life of her favorite Paris drives the main plot and serves as a compelling structural and temporal framework for the entire series. Cyrino demonstrates how the narrative, dialogue, camera work, and visual imagery of the series function to bond Paris and Aphrodite together as the principal agents of the city's destruction.

In the fourth chapter, "Sympathy for Troy's Jezebel: Helen as Antihero," Meredith E. Safran discusses how Helen (Bella Dayne) reflects the entertainment industry's embrace of the American-style antihero and is shaped after the current vogue for sympathetic protagonists. The antihero's success is abetted by powerful charisma that leads to admiration by both internal and external audiences: charisma and cunning assist the antihero in evading attempts by the unenchanted to convince others of the threat they pose. Yet the antihero is no victim, but the author of their own story: Helen engineers her own escape from a loathsome forced marriage to Menelaus (Jonas Armstrong); proves assertive in inserting herself into the Trojan royal family to protect her own interests; and clings doggedly to her claims of love for Paris, up to the moment when her actions lead to his brutal killing. However, as Safran points out, Helen's moral hollowness contrasts with her repeatedly emphasized intelligence. With this depiction, *TFOAC* offers an essentially misogynistic portrayal of Helen even as the series condemns the Greeks for their misogyny.

In the fifth chapter, "The Curse of Troy: Odysseus' Story," Emma J. Stafford offers a comparative discussion of the character of the wily Ithacan hero Odysseus (Joseph Mawle) in *TFOAC* alongside his predecessors as depicted in film and television. Since Odysseus is a key character throughout the eight-episode trajectory of *TFOAC*, the series appears to end on an ominous note with Odysseus and allusions to future suffering, rather than on the traditional and potentially more hopeful indication of Aeneas' escape and the foundation of Rome. Stafford considers Odysseus' *TFOAC* story arc from his first appearance in the series to the end, discussing how the portrayal of Odysseus invites questions about his heroic status and motivations, as well as foreshadowing the length of the war. Odysseus' initiative and stratagems drive much of the action, and viewers of *TFOAC* see more of the character of Odysseus throughout these episodes than in any of his screen predecessors, making this series very much Odysseus' story.

The second section of the volume, "Cast and Character," surveys several issues surrounding decisions made by the showrunners in terms of casting talent as well as the development and portrayal of specific characters. This section opens with the sixth chapter, "Racist Reactions to Black Achilles," where Rebecca Futo Kennedy analyzes the substantial backlash in response to casting the leading character of Achilles with British-Ghanaian actor David Gyasi, along with a few other key roles played by actors of color, including Zeus (Hakeem Kae-Kazim), Athena (Shamilla Miller), Patroclus (Lemogang Tsipa), and Aeneas (Alfred Enoch). In her discussion of casting strategies—colorblind, color-conscious, and diversity casting—Kennedy points out that the showrunners of *TFOAC* intentionally sought to cast African and Black British actors for roles, while not specifically casting for other races/ethnicities. In addition, Kennedy examines racist claims for the Whiteness of classical antiquity, and why people are so invested in the Whiteness of Achilles, and less so in other characters cast as Black; how this backlash is a response to diversity casting more generally; and whether the practice of diversity casting encourages this type of investment in identity when used in a color-conscious time.

In the seventh chapter, "Pussy Politics: Women and Power in the Homeric Patriarchy," Kirsten Day explores how the portrayal of strong, independent women in *TFOAC* satisfies contemporary expectations about women in society, while the female characters also exert power more subtly, through cunning and deception, or by capitalizing on their sexuality. Day argues that each of these characterizations represents a deviation from ancient tradition while also nodding to it; each denotes an attempt by these women to exert influence in a patriarchal world; and each offers a revealing glimpse into how the series attempts to connect with the Trojan War cycle while simultaneously resonating with the experiences of women today. Yet the presentation of women as strong and independent is ultimately undercut by the patriarchal framework. Like casting decisions, as Day notes, these narrative choices represent political moves on the part of the showrunners; but while the intention seems to be to showcase a progressive stance on depictions of race and gender, in the latter case, it serves to demonstrate how far we have to go.

In the eighth chapter, "Queering Troy: Freedom and Sexuality," Thomas E. Jenkins considers the frequent use of anachronistic political terms like "freedom" in cinematic and televisual recreations of the mythic and historical past, and argues that such terms are often directly correlated with specific characters' sexuality. In *TFOAC*, Jenkins observes that the series presents a kind of Orientalism in reverse: that is, the west (Sparta) is depicted as authoritarian and sexist, while the east (Troy) emerges as politically enlightened and sexually progressive. This idea of "freedom" propels the narrative arcs of both Helen (Bella Dayne) and Achilles (David Gyasi): but while the supposedly freeing romance of Helen and Paris (Louis Hunter) ultimately fails, with Helen herself seemingly trapped in a "Hollywood Helen" role, the sexual freedom and queer polyamory of Achilles and his lovers, Patroclus (Lemogang Tsipa) and Briseis (Amy Louise Wilson), stands out as one of the show's most noteworthy innovations. As Jenkins demonstrates, *TFOAC* pushes the envelope of using classical antiquity as a medium for interrogating contemporary sexual roles and stereotypes.

In the ninth chapter, "Heroic Hairstyles and Manless Amazons at Troy," Walter Duvall Penrose, Jr. discusses the depiction of the Amazons in the series, and in particular, the notable portrayal of their queen, the androgynous Penthesilea (Nina Milner), who seeks revenge against Achilles (David Gyasi) for the loss of her warrior sisters. While the ancient sources relate the story of their interaction in a heteronormative manner, Penrose describes how *TFOAC* has queered the narrative: a bisexual Achilles shows no desire for Penthesilea, but turns only to his grief for his slain male lover, Patroclus (Lemogang Tsipa); and although she briefly flirts with Aeneas (Alfred Enoch), Penthesilea maintains that she does not sleep with men. Like Amazons portrayed in some media versions of the myth, she is "manless," has a short pixie haircut, and brashly refuses to wear a helmet. With reference to the recent feature film *Wonder Woman* (2017), Penrose examines the ways in which the series portrays the Amazons in a twenty-first-century vision of all women united in feminist sisterhood.

In the tenth chapter, "Costume Changes: Dressing Helen of Sparta and Troy," Stacie Raucci traces the various transformations in the costumes of Helen (Bella Dayne) over the episodic course of *TFOAC*, scrutinizing Helen's dresses, hair pieces, and various adornments and comparing them to those of other key female characters in the series. Raucci proposes that Helen's wildly varying costumes transform her into a different performer for each new audience she encounters in each new scene. As Helen moves from Sparta to Troy, her changing costumes reflect her transitions in social and narrative roles, from Helen, Queen of Sparta, to her assimilation as an uncertain member of the Trojan royal family, to her marker as the downfall of the city of Troy. While her changing outward appearance blends with her shifting circumstances, Raucci argues that the internal Helen remains stable: Helen's dresses may vary throughout the series, but a few visual elements of her persona remain constant to reflect her unwavering inner state.

The third section of this volume, "Tragic Resonances," weighs the series against the backdrop of the ancient genre of tragedy, and delves into the various dramatic elements that permeate the narratives of damaged heroes and shattered familial bonds. In the eleventh chapter, "Fallen Heroes: Recasting Ajax and the Greeks on Screen," Anastasia Bakogianni examines how the series *TFOAC* presents its Greek warriors, focusing on two minor characters in the series, Ajax (Garth Breytenbach) and Thersites (Waldemar Schultz), who nevertheless serve to reaffirm the overwhelmingly negative interpretation of the Greek side's motives and actions in the Trojan War. Bakogianni filters her analysis through a corrective tragic lens, one that both reflects and refracts the tragic arc that the series superimposes on the story of the war at Troy. To appreciate fully the complexity of the series' reception of the Greek army at Troy, Bakogianni argues, requires an examination of the repurposing of the tragic narratives centered on the Trojan War to promote a liberal, antiwar agenda on stage and screen. This comparative perspective enriches our understanding of these complex ancient heroes, allowing us both to contemplate the very processes of reception and to interrogate the current state of our relationship with this ancient story.

In the twelfth chapter, "Family vs. Compassion: Odysseus and the Ethics of War," Meredith Prince considers how *TFOAC* uses the character of Odysseus (Joseph Mawle) to confront the dilemma of maintaining one's humanity during war, by foregrounding his involvement in the series' most agonizing moments: the sacrifice of Iphigenia (Lauren Coe), and the murder of the infant Astyanax. While Odysseus' displays of compassion toward women and children derive from love of his own family, in contrast to the other Greeks, Prince argues that his overwhelming desire to return to or protect his family collides with and overrides his moral code, leading to an ethical power struggle with Agamemnon (Johnny Harris) and his agency in the deaths of Iphigenia and Astyanax. Against the background of Greek tragedy, Prince observes, the series rehabilitates the shady tragic villain and instigator of killing children and merges those acts with his well-known epic desire for home. Yet the series finale suggests the trials of his homecoming are self-inflicted sufferings caused by incompatible attempts to keep both his humanity intact and his family safe during war.

In the thirteenth chapter, "Bloody Brides: Iphigenia, Helen, and Ritual Exchange," Amy L. Norgard explores the interplay between the characters Helen (Bella Dayne) and Iphigenia (Lauren Coe) in *TFOAC*, as the series both evokes the tragic source material in its portrayal of Iphigenia's sacrifice, while also positing new implications of the maiden's death as a trade-off for Helen's second marriage to Paris (Louis Hunter). Norgard demonstrates how scenes from Iphigenia's gruesome marriage-turned-sacrifice are intercut with shots of Helen performing actions typical of a bride: as Iphigenia makes her way to the sacrificial altar, Helen applies cosmetics and adorns herself with fine clothes, and even makes passionate love to her bridegroom. As Norgard argues, Iphigenia in the series becomes the sacrificial exchange to facilitate Helen's second chance at life, suggesting that women are ultimately exploited as commodities—interchangeable with monetary wealth, objects, and even the lives of other women—with no inherent value on their own.

In the fourteenth chapter, "Kings of Men and Sacrificial Daughters," Krishni Burns establishes how *TFOAC* asks each of its foremost Greek kings, Odysseus (Joseph Mawle), Agamemnon (Johnny Harris), and Menelaus (Jonas Armstrong), to sacrifice a daughter, literally or figuratively, for the sake of the war, as the ramifications of these individual decisions motivate all of their subsequent actions. In the case of the sons of Atreus, Agamemnon and Menelaus, the choice to sacrifice a daughter is unambiguously coded as wrong and leads inexorably to the father's downfall: Agamemnon's grief drives his transformation from leader into monster, while Menelaus loses first his authority and ultimately his integrity. As a moral foil to these two kings, Odysseus chooses instead to save his daughter, a nameless female baby contrived by the series to replace the boy Telemachus under Odysseus' plow: as Burns notes, given the show's comparative fidelity to its source material, this creative choice is striking and expressive of the theme of fathers and daughters.

The final chapter, "Lessons for Leaders: Destiny, Devotion, and Self-Deception," de-centers the academy and the specialized readings of the previous chapters by deploying onscreen reception studies for a broader audience. Brian Cooke explores the series *TFOAC* as a source of practical lessons for effective coaches to share with leaders interested in the timeless questions that influence success, wellbeing, and advancement. First, Cooke considers the concept of destiny to assess the extent to which experience and performance are determined by forces beyond our control. Second, Cooke poses the questions of devotion and duty, in particular to whom and for what reasons we are obligated and motivated to live, work, and fight, while he also looks at the critical risks of self-deception for leaders, as illustrated by the cautionary narrative of Priam (David Threlfall) and the Trojan Horse in the series. Cooke concludes by addressing the contemporary relevance of classical reception for developing leadership today.

In the volume's epilogue, "*Troy: Fall of a City* and its Ancient Sources," Diana Burton shows how the series draws on a broad range of ancient authors, artists, and mythographical sources to deploy in its mythmaking, and how the series often fills out storylines for which such sources provide only a quick sketch. In addition, Burton demonstrates that *TFOAC* stays relatively close to its ancient sources, compared to recent feature films supposedly based on Greek epic and mythology. As Burton points out, the series is particularly successful in underscoring the effects of war and its aftermath, making convincing use of the Greek tragic texts that explore the consequences of the events at Troy for its participants and bystanders. In the spirit of classical art and mythmaking, *TFOAC* exhibits both tradition and originality in its rendering of the cosmic and human misfortune of the Trojan War.

The closing shots of the eighth and final episode of the series, "Offering," advance the reception of the myth of Troy as an enduring cultural sign with a propulsive chain of interconnected and memorable images. After the Greek ships are shown sailing away from the beach, viewers see a wounded Aeneas (Alfred Enoch) rise from a tangle of corpses in the ruins of the Trojan royal palace, and then watch as he limps along the abandoned streets of the lower city (Fig. I.1): there in the empty dirt road littered with slaughtered Trojans, Aeneas is met by two refugees inside the broken gate, the local boy Evander (Woody Norman) and his brother Hesion (Deon Lee-Williams). Soon they are joined by Briseis (Amy Louise Wilson), once a captive prize of the Greeks, but throughout the series a fighting figure of survival and resistance, who embraces the child and tells him, "You're alive": the camera lingers for a moment on this ragtag band of survivors, who together symbolize the continuing spirit of the Trojan people. The shot moves through the ruptured gate and reveals the supreme god Zeus (Hakeem Kae-Kazim) standing solemnly outside the smoking ruins of Troy: the camera follows his brooding gaze as he looks up toward the storm clouds he has gathered in the grey sky, intending both to wash the ravaged city clean and to harass the victorious Greeks as they try to sail home. And the final image is Odysseus (Joseph Mawle), upright and motionless on his ship well under sail away from Troy, his hooded eyes looking back at the dark expanse of water separating him from his dubious actions in the war, but also hinting at the perilous ten-year journey that awaits him before reaching his longed-for island home. While this

Introduction

Figure I.1 Aeneas (Alfred Enoch) limps along the abandoned streets of the lower city of Troy in Episode 8, "Offering."

final proleptic sequence of images—Aeneas and his fellow Trojan emigrants, the divine mythological machinery at work, and the wanderings of Odysseus—seems to promise a sequel or two, the series *TFOAC* leaves viewers with the inescapable feeling that Troy will follow us all our life.

Notes

1. Mac Sweeney 2018: 3.
2. Wood 1996: 19. The critically acclaimed six-part documentary series, written and presented by Wood and directed by Bill Lyons, was first broadcast in 1985 on BBC Two.
3. Haywood and Mac Sweeney 2019: 6.
4. See the essays in Winkler 2007a.
5. See the essays in Cyrino 2008 and 2015.
6. See the essays in Augoustakis and Cyrino 2017.

PART I
EPIC NARRATIVE

CHAPTER 1
BINGE FOR ME, O MUSE: EPISODES, BOOKS, AND CYCLES
Dan Curley

A 2018 co-production of the British Broadcasting Company and Netflix, *Troy: Fall of a City* reached television audiences in two distinct phases.[1] First, from February 28 onward, new episodes were broadcast weekly on BBC One in the prestigious Saturday prime-time slot. Second, after the final broadcast on April 7, all eight episodes became available to stream on Netflix and, later, other digital platforms like Amazon Prime. Both phases underscore the seriality of *TFOAC*, its status as a series of self-contained installments that collectively tell the larger story of the Trojan War made famous in Homer.[2]

This chapter places the seriality of *TFOAC* in dialogue with the seriality of ancient epic. Along the way it draws analogies between the production of episodic media in antiquity and modernity, and between the reading and viewing (or consumer) cultures of both. Enabling the latter analogy is the era of complex television in which we now live, an era that demands viewers pay attention to the poetics of the medium, of which seriality is an indispensable feature.[3] In other words, it is an era whose sophistication is comparable to that of literary communities in Greco-Roman antiquity. Most important, the dialogue is meant to be two-sided. Just as the traditions of ancient epic inform considerations of screen epic, so the reverse ought to be true.

Episodes

We begin with the episode, the building-block of serial media. The origins of the term can be traced back to the putative godfather of screenwriting, Aristotle, and his epoch-making treatise on drama, the *Poetics* (fourth century BC).[4] Although concerned with the genre of tragedy, Aristotle also has much to say about epic, as represented by Homer's *Iliad* and *Odyssey*. The philosopher finds considerable common ground among the two genres, but draws a hard line between their ideal lengths. The *Iliad*, which depicts the rage of Achilles in the ninth year of the Trojan War, is a long poem. But, as Aristotle notes, it could have been longer:

> Homer's inspired superiority is evident, because of his refusal to attempt to make a poem about the entire war … Such a plot would be too bulky, and could not be perceived as a unity; or, if moderate in size, would be too intricately detailed.[5]

As though taking Aristotle's verdict as a dare, screen adaptations of the Trojan cycle delight in ranging beyond the poem and incorporating past episodes, such as the meeting of Paris and Helen; or future ones, such as building the Trojan Horse and sacking the city. These and other extra-Homeric incidents are so common as to constitute traditional features of Iliadic screen epic, from Borgnetto and Pastrone's *La caduta di Troia* (1911) onward. As we will have occasion to observe, *TFOAC* is fully invested in aligning with these traditions.

The extreme length of an epic poem, as opposed to a tragic play, depends on the number of episodes as well as their impact on the plot. To explain this idea, Aristotle cites the *Odyssey*:

> Now, in drama the episodes are concise, while epic gains extra length from them. The main story of the *Odyssey* is short. A man is abroad for many years, is persecuted by Poseidon, and is left desolate. Further, circumstances at home mean that his property is consumed by suitors, and his son is a target for conspiracy. But the man survives shipwreck to reach home again, reveals his identity to certain people, and launches an attack. His own safety is restored, and he destroys his enemies. This much is essential; the rest is episodes.[6]

On the one hand, Aristotle's minimalist synopsis shows how straightforward the premise of the *Odyssey* is, such that he can reduce it to a few spare clauses. On the other hand, he is pitting the concision of tragedy against the expansiveness of epic poetry. Epic is prone to adding on—the word for episode, *epeisodion*, is prefixed by *epi-*, "in addition"—and this tendency helps to explain the size of poems like the *Odyssey* and the *Iliad*. As in tragedy, some episodes will be integral to the plot, such as the altercation between Achilles and Agamemnon in *Iliad* Book 1. Other episodes, like the Catalog of Ships in Book 2, will digress from it and prolong the poem.[7] To call epic "episodic" is to draw attention as much to the sheer accumulation of episodes, as to their potential to stray from the main business of the text. Their discursiveness is more design feature than flaw.[8]

An Aristotelian sense of episode, denoting an "incidental narrative or digression in a poem, story," and other literary kinds, prevailed through the nineteenth century.[9] Examples from this period and earlier mostly derive from works of classical scholarship and reception, where Aristotle's theories had ongoing purchase. Not until the early twentieth century, with the widespread distribution and broadcast of dramatic media, does episode finally signify an installment "into which a film, television or radio drama ... is divided for transmitting as a series."[10] This shift in semantics reflects a larger shift in the reception of dramatic media, in which episodes become principal, not ancillary, texts in the delivery of plot. As such—and this is key—they become conflated with the plot itself. The conflation was apparently underway before Aristotle, in the gradual marginalization of the Chorus from Athenian tragedy and comedy, which would have rendered these genres episodic in a sense rather close to current usage.[11] Nonetheless, it is in recent modernity that the episode has come into its own, the primary vehicle by which dramatic media—and even news programs and podcasts—have been parceled out for serial consumption.

Binge for Me, O Muse: Episodes, Books, and Cycles

This brief history of episodes has bearing on *TFOAC* as televised screen epic. Producing a series on Troy obviously mandates an episodic approach, or by definition it could not be a series. Less obvious, perhaps, are the benefits of such an approach. One advantage, if not *the* advantage, is the spaciousness afforded by the episodes themselves, which allow the plot to unfold at length. As noted above, Iliadic screen epics traditionally ignore Aristotle's advice and range well beyond Homer. When these epics are feature films, their totalizing ambitions can be at odds with their run times. For example, *Helen of Troy* and *Troy* (1956 and 2004, respectively) both have sequences set in Sparta, where Helen and Paris first meet. While the first movie covers everything from Helen (Rossana Podestà) finding Paris (Jacques Sernas) shipwrecked and unconscious, to their arrival at the Trojan harbor, the second presents an affair *in medias res* and with far less nuance. The differences are striking: over forty minutes of screen time incorporating many scenes of dialogue between the two lovers, versus less than nine with only one dialogue scene— which cuts to the chase and whisks Helen (Diane Kruger) and Paris (Orlando Bloom) out of the banquet hall and into the bedroom. Even as it devotes nearly two-and-a-half hours to a complete Iliadic saga, the 2004 film *Troy* ends up spreading itself too thin where Helen is concerned. Rather than a protagonist, Kruger's heroine is treated like "a minor character" (as one classicist-critic puts it), "poorly realized and insubstantial."[12]

Helen of Troy faces the inverse challenge. Because it is heavily invested in the Helen– Paris origin story, the film is half over, and the war not yet begun, by the time the lovers reach Troy. Extra-Homeric material on the front end exacts a toll on the best-known Homeric material later on. In *Iliad* 22, Achilles and Hector duel to the death; Hector is killed, and Achilles drags his corpse around the city walls and back to his camp. In Book 24, Priam visits Achilles and persuades him to return his son's body for burial. These episodes are integral to the theme of Achilles' rage, initially directed at Agamemnon and his fellow Greeks, and later toward Hector and the Trojans. Returning the body to Priam signals a resolution to Achilles' anger, and the poem ends, appropriately, with Hector's funeral. *Helen of Troy* compresses and eliminates such iconic episodes. After Achilles (Stanley Baker) kills Hector (Harry Andrews) and begins to mutilate his corpse, Paris delivers a fatal arrow to Achilles' heel. The warrior's death, which is foreshadowed in the *Iliad* yet lies outside its scope, obviates Priam's intercession on behalf of his son and allows the movie to spend its final twenty minutes enacting the fall of Troy.

Comprised of eight hour-long episodes, *TFOAC* is structurally equipped to fulfill the totalizing agendas of its cinematic predecessors. According to producer-writer David Farr, "Longform television allows you to settle the pace and really suits a story about a city."[13] From the birth of Paris in the very first moments of "Black Blood" (Episode 1), the series advertises its engagement with extra-Homeric material. From here, the episode spends roughly half an hour relocating the now-grown Paris (Louis Hunter) from the pastoral vales of Ida to the urbane palace of Troy, and another half-hour in Sparta matching him with Helen (Bella Dayne), as promised by Aphrodite. Like *Helen of Troy* before it, "Black Blood" foregrounds the interpersonal dynamics of Paris and Helen, especially the give-and-take between their social obligations and their clandestine desire. Like *Troy*, it couches that desire in explicit sexuality and nudity, taking advantage of its

Mature Audiences (MA) rating. And all of this in the first hour, with seven left to follow, during which the pair will be tested by the vicissitudes of the war. In those remaining hours, *TFOAC* also has room to develop Homeric material. In contrast with *Helen of Troy*, here the final books of the *Iliad* receive substantial treatment: the duel between Achilles (David Gyasi) and Hector (Tom Weston-Jones) in "Battle on the Beach" (Episode 6), and the reconciliation of Achilles and Priam (David Threlfall) in "Twelve Days" (Episode 7). The show's episodic structure ensures balance—a kind of Aristotelian unity, even—between the Homeric and extra-Homeric across its run, while constituting a work of duly epic proportions.

Books

Helpful as they are for evaluating the length and inclusiveness of *TFOAC*, analogies between episodes in the *Poetics* and in modern serial media go only so far. The reason is one of scale: the episodes of *TFOAC* themselves contain the equivalents of smaller, Aristotelian episodes. A closer analog for the television episode is therefore the epic book, a unit of text that collates episodes/scenes of various length.

So ingrained in classical studies is the concept of the book, that scholars tend to take its origins and its capacity to organize ancient literature for granted. For most people, the term "book" signifies the volume itself—cover to cover, so to speak—whether fiction or non-fiction, and regardless of print, digital, or audio format. Any modern translation of Homer is in this sense a book. In its classical sense, book refers to a major division within the volume. While novels are divided into chapters, the *Iliad* and the *Odyssey* are each divided into twenty-four books, which allow the poems to be read in serial fashion, if desired.[14] This usage of book is not confined to Greco-Roman tradition. It also applies to the Bible, where the convention is arguably more familiar and, because its books are (at least in English) named after events, persons, prophets, or authors, certainly more intuitive. Popular screen texts are sometimes styled as books: *Oh, God! Book II* (1980), for example, the sequel to the blockbuster film *Oh, God!* (1977); or the cable series *Avatar: The Last Airbender* (2005–8), whose three seasons each occupy a single book ("Water," "Earth," and "Fire").[15] Such usage is aspirational, a gesture toward the solemnity or grandeur associated with literature from antiquity. For *TFOAC* to have followed suit would have been too on the nose, perhaps. All the same, its episodes can be construed in terms of epic books, both as organizational units and indices of the series' production.

On the production side, the greenlighting of *TFOAC* as an eight-episode series has precedent in the enumeration of Homeric books. The question of how the *Iliad* and the *Odyssey* were divided up is nearly as fraught as the question of whether or not there was a Homer. It is widely agreed that the book-divisions post-date the origins of both poems by several centuries, and that the twenty-four letters of the Ionian alphabet provided a convenient system for labeling them.[16] Although Alexandrian scholars of the third century BC are often credited with this work, the Panathenaic festivals of the sixth century, where Homer's epics were recited in their entirety, present an earlier, if not more plausible context.¹⁷ It is true that the divisions of the *Iliad* and the *Odyssey* were originally called *rhapsodiae* ("recitation units"); the term book, though appropriate for later epic, is anachronistic. These units were named after the *rhapsodes* ("song-stitchers"), professional performers of Homeric verse. *Rhapsodes* at the Panathenaea were ostensibly assigned lettered portions of the *Iliad* and *Odyssey*, which over time became the bases of the canonical books. The result, no matter how the divisions came about, was to systematize the distribution and consumption of Homer's poetry. Such nascent corporate interventions are precursors to every network's business model, and particularly that of Netflix, which in less than twenty years evolved from renting DVDs by mail to financing original series like *TFOAC*. Netflix has become notorious for limiting its shows to three seasons of ten episodes or fewer, the better to minimize production costs and maximize viewer engagement.¹⁸ The eight episodes of *TFOAC* are in keeping with the company's current practice, though that number was not a given: executive producer Derek Wax reportedly "pushed hard" for more than six installments.¹⁹

The active negotiation of episodes calls to mind the notion of authorship, which is fundamental for the production of ancient and screen epic. Epic poetry from the beginning is cast as the work of an author, who with help from the muse narrates the story. The author is present at every turn, giving voice to the largest themes and the smallest details. Later epics, although they maintain the conceit of oral performances, are written texts under the editorial control of their poets. The arrangement and division of books consequently becomes a legible function of epic authorship. Establishing authorship in collaborative media such as film and television is a thornier task. In film the status of author (or *auteur*) is often ascribed to the director, whose control over the finished work grants "authorship by responsibility," while in television the producer has been traditionally granted "authorship by management."²⁰ However, television authorship for decades has been shifting to the so-called showrunner, who usually creates the program and, after it is greenlit, serves as producer and head writer.²¹ In each of these capacities, the showrunner exerts authorial control over the show, but as head writer they most resemble the figure of the epic author, and vice versa. Just as the author becomes responsible for dividing the epic into books, so it falls to the showrunner to make a series, or a season thereof, by parceling out the storyline into episodes. Such was the work facing the showrunner of *TFOAC*, David Farr. Tasked with fleshing out Wax's vision for a Trojan War series, Farr was not only an executive producer, but also the head writer, with sole credit on five of the eight episodes.²²

Shaped by authorial intent, epic books and episodes repay close scrutiny, especially in regard to design and patterning. The *Argonautica* of Apollonius Rhodius (third century BC), which tells the story of Jason, Medea, and the Golden Fleece, offers a clear instance of symmetry in later Greek epic: Books 1 and 2 cover the Argonauts' outward journey; Books 3 and 4, the taking of the Fleece and the journey home. Vergil's *Aeneid*, the quintessential Latin epic (first century BC), likewise divides into halves, which themselves constitute structural allusions to Homer: Books 1–6, the wanderings of Aeneas after the fall of Troy, pay homage to the *Odyssey*; Books 7–12 recall the conflicts and intrigues of the *Iliad*, as the Trojans find themselves under siege once more.²³ The episodic structure

17

of *TFOAC* yields similar patterns. On the one hand, ring composition seems important to the architecture of the series. The central episodes, "Spoils of War" and "Hunted" (4 and 5, respectively) focus on the victimization that comes with war, while those left and right of center, "Siege" and "Battle on the Beach" (Episodes 3 and 6) foreground warfare itself. "Conditions" and "Twelve Days" (Episodes 2 and 7) showcase negotiations, whether between gods and mortals or Trojans and Greeks. The outermost episodes, "Black Blood" and "Offering" (Episodes 1 and 8) bookend destructive acts of sacrifice. On the other hand, smaller patterns abound. In "Conditions" (Episode 2), for example, Agamemnon (Johnny Harris) must sacrifice his daughter, Iphigenia (Lauren Coe), in order to summon favorable winds for sailing to Troy. This perversion of the father–child relationship is echoed two episodes later in "Spoils of War" (Episode 4), when Agamemnon rapes Chryseis (Jamie-Lee Money). The two incidents are separated by years of diegetic time, but their relative proximity within alternating episodes facilitates their comparison.

A reliable feature of complex television is the balance between the stand-alone episode and the large story arc, commonly known as the mythology, an elaborate backstory that emerges as a series progresses.[24] Because its mythology has been told and retold over the course of 2,500 years, *TFOAC* relies on other strategies to maintain viewer interest, strategies predicated less on what happens than on when—that is, in which episode. Here, too, ancient epic recommends itself as a model in the use of books, or the transitions between them, to mark the passage of time. The genre favors diachronic narrative, in which time moves forward in linear fashion. (*Odyssey* 9–12, the "flashback" to the wanderings of Odysseus, are a famous exception.) In the *Iliad*, book transitions are often seamless, with little or no time elapsing in between; so, for instance, the sequence of Books 4–7, a single day of fighting after a truce is broken. Sometimes, however, the transition between books coincides with the transition from night to day, as in Books 7–8 and 18–19, and in most books of the *Odyssey*. On such occasions, gaps in the narrative are most pronounced and, in turn, highlight the seriality of the poem as a sequence of books. Later epics operate in similar fashion, although Ovid's *Metamorphoses* (early first century AD) raises book transitions to new levels of artifice due to its vast chronological sweep. A common Ovidian tactic is to remain in place but switch characters, as in Books 14–15, which see the rule of Rome pass from Romulus to Numa. Alternatively, the conclusion of a narrative in one location might overlap with the beginning of another somewhere else, as in Books 2–3, where the rape of Europa unexpectedly gives way to Cadmus' search for his lost sister. The epic's most audacious transition is also its first: Books 1–2 completely elide Phaëthon's journey, by no means brief or easy, to the house of the Sun. The variety of Ovid's book transitions, while appropriate to an epic preoccupied with change, are also instructive to the reader, who learns not only to expect the unexpected, but also to take pleasure in it.[25]

TFOAC vaunts its status as screen epic with an almost Ovidian flair for episode transitions. Since the series revolves around Troy and its environs, most episodes begin and end there, apart from "Black Blood" (Episode 1), which concludes at sea (Fig. 1.1), and "Spoils of War" (Episode 2), which opens with a brief return to Sparta. Although they have little geographic variation, transitions between episodes almost always correspond

Figure 1.1 Paris (Louis Hunter) opens the chest that conceals Helen and brings closure to Episode 1, "Black Blood."

to significant leaps forward in time. Intervals range from the familiar Homeric gap between night and day, as in "Twelve Days" and "Offering" (Episodes 7 and 8), to an entire year, as in "Conditions" and "Siege" (Episodes 2 and 3). Only "Hunted" and "Battle on the Beach" (Episodes 5 and 6) buck the trend, the latter beginning with the immediate aftermath of Paris' apparent suicide at the end of the former. Chronological jumps, even as they allow the Trojan War to be collapsed into eight episodes, also "give a sense of what it was like to be under siege for years."[26] With each installment dedicated to a new point in the war, *TFOAC* resembles the groundbreaking *La caduta di Troia*, which is comprised of seventeen distinct scenes—or episodes in the Aristotelian sense.[27] Whereas the silent film uses placards to signpost its transitions, the television series relies on subtle dialogue and visual cues, by which viewers calculate where in the overall saga the current episode resides. Farr remarks, "Sometimes we do something bold, like maybe a year or two years will pass ... and the unexpectedness of that is enjoyable." Farr's emphasis on enjoyment, while acknowledging that *TFOAC* is first and foremost popular entertainment, nevertheless links the show's appeal to its seriality: "Dickens famously wrote ... in chapters, and what that gives you is the moment where the page turns for viewers and for storytellers."[28] Dickens might well agree, but so would the generations of epic poets and audiences accustomed to turning the page—if only figuratively.

Cycles

What are the limits of seriality? So far this chapter has shown how the eight episodes of *TFOAC* function as repositories of smaller episodes that, according to Aristotle, constitute the bulk of epic poetry. And it has located those same episodes, on analogy with epic books, within the series as a whole. What remains, by way of conclusion, is to consider the series itself as part of a larger continuum of screen epic. As before, this line of inquiry takes its bearings from traditions of Greco-Roman epic, some of which we have previously encountered, and some of which will move us further along. At issue once again are the totalizing ambitions of epic, its capacity to attract other stories, and even other epics, into its orbit.

Those who would answer the above question could do worse than point to the *Odyssey*. Composed in imitation of the *Iliad* and set ten years after the end of the Trojan War, the poem is a sequel in all the senses that matter to the entertainment industry. Not only was it produced in the wake of a successful first installment, and not only does it blend familiar characters with new ones in the service of advancing the story, but it also comes from the original creative team, so to speak. The last point is particularly important. With the *Aeneid*, Vergil created a Roman sequel to both the *Iliad* and the *Odyssey*, while Apollonius Rhodius created an Alexandrian prequel with the *Argonautica*. In our litigious era, these works could be considered infringements of copyright (unless they were dismissed as fan fiction). Attaching Homer's name to the *Odyssey*, however, gives the poem an author as well as authorization. The question of whether *TFOAC* will receive a sequel is, as of this writing, still open. Some conditions for a second season are favorable, including support from the show's creators. Even before BBC One broadcast the first episode of *TFOAC*, Farr had publicly speculated about future installments: "There is obviously the *Odyssey*, there is also the great story of Agamemnon coming back to Clytemnestra ... and having to feel the consequences of his actions."[29] The most important condition, however, will be the show's success on streaming platforms—its ability to transcend the lukewarm reception surrounding its initial release and to reach new audiences.[30]

TFOAC Season 2, real or hypothetical, activates new possibilities for theorizing epic seriality. Sequels and prequels, with their connotations of following and preceding, are inherently serial concepts. Yet they cannot by themselves capture the nuances that might apply, say, to a second season on Netflix. Another slate of eight episodes, for example, would be seen as a deliberate parallel with Season 1, both as artistic patterning and as corporate standardization—much like how the twenty-four books of the *Odyssey* were made to parallel those of the *Iliad*. Furthermore, a Season 2 would build the brand for everyone involved: producer and showrunner, who would continue the story; actors, who would reprise their roles; and, above all, Netflix itself, which would have made continuation possible in the first place. Viewers would experience the company's branding first-hand when navigating the menus on the *TFOAC* landing page, dominated by the Netflix logo and laid out to facilitate navigation. The very act of browsing from one season to the next would implicate the viewer in verifying that additional content exists: two seasons and counting, both courtesy of Netflix.

Just beyond brand recognition and standardization lurks the notion of the franchise, and its promise of a massive and interconnected story-world. An example of ancient 'franchising' is the Epic Cycle (seventh and sixth centuries BC), whose Troy poems were composed in response to the *Iliad* and the *Odyssey*, but designed to fill the gaps before, after, and between them.[31] Cyclic poems about Troy include: the *Cypria* (eleven books), an *Iliad* prequel about the rape of Helen and the beginning of the war; the *Aethiopis* (five books), an *Iliad* sequel that depicted the deaths of the Amazon Penthesilea and Achilles; the *Iliou persis* (two books), the "sack of Troy" in the wake of the Trojan Horse; and the

Nostoi (five books), an *Odyssey* prequel on the homecomings of Greek heroes from the war. Efforts were made to bring these later epics in line with their Homeric precursors, most notably by assigning their authorship to Homer (i.e., more branding). In addition, as the Cycle grew in popularity, the *Iliad* and the *Odyssey* were edited in order to make them consistent with their successors (more standardization). The Epic Cycle represents one apex of epic totalizing. Collectively, the Troy poems "retcon" (or impose retroactive continuity on) the *Iliad* and the *Odyssey*, drawing them into a franchise whose scope surpasses anything Homer might have intended.

Of course, *TFOAC* in its current form cannot match the scale of the Epic Cycle. For a recent screen epic that does, we might look instead to the Marvel Cinematic Universe, with its various phases of production in film and on television.[32] Yet *TFOAC* embraces the point of the Cycle by incorporating its material in order to contextualize Homer. The *Iliad* finds ample representation in "Spoils of War," "Hunted," "Battle on the Beach," and "Twelve Days" (Episodes 4–7), which rehearse the major plot points, from the initial quarrel in the Greek camp (Book 1) to the funeral of Hector (Book 24). Preceding this Homeric core are "Black Blood" and "Conditions" (Episodes 1–2), which draw inspiration from the *Cypria*. Following it are the second half of "Twelve Days" and "Offering" (Episode 8), which recall the *Aethiopis* and the *Iliou persis*, respectively. As discussed earlier, much of this material is also traditional in earlier Iliadic screen epic, to which *TFOAC* is a worthy successor. Nevertheless, the series' episodic structure seems especially attuned to the serial nature of the Epic Cycle, which parcels out the Trojan saga epic by epic, book by book. Within its relatively limited remit, *TFOAC* offers an alternative model of epic totalizing: a cycle for the twenty-first century under the auspices of a single, branded series. Whether this cycle will be expanded and perfected by way of the *Nostoi*, the *Odyssey*, and other myths remains to be seen.

Epic cycles . . . and re-cycles? Books and episodes enable the sequential consumption of epic. Yet they are only guides. Audiences of Homeric performances were just as likely to hear self-contained episodes (such as the *teichoskopeia* or "Helen at the Walls" in Book 3) as they were complete books. The varied interests of modern viewers are likewise well served by digital platforms, which can access the story at any conceivable point. Conversely, the opportunity to binge-watch the entire series is the sort of totalizing experience available to few if any ancient audiences—apart from attendees of the Panathenaea and other festivals featuring complete Homeric performances, or readers with the stamina to tackle twenty-four books in one sitting. Here streaming services like Netflix are capable surrogates for the Homeric *rhapsodes*. In *Iliad* 2, just before launching into the Catalog of Ships, the narrator despairs over the enormity of the task, lacking the ten tongues, tireless voice, and lungs of bronze that would still not be enough to mention all the soldiers by name.[33] The digital platform, however, is indefatigable. It is ready to play all, or just a little. It holds our place, yet lets us navigate at will. It asks, if we are watching too much, whether we are still enjoying ourselves. When the series is finished, it recommends something new—such as *Blood of Zeus* (2020–) or even Wolfgang Petersen's *Troy*—and allows us to compile our own epic cycle. If nothing else, it gives us the option to start all over again.

Let the digital bard have the last word, or nearly so. Here is the summary of *TFOAC* from its landing page on Netflix:

> Searching for the woman promised to him by Aphrodite, herdsman Paris learns his true identity and falls for Helen of Sparta, igniting the Trojan War.

To bring this chapter to an Aristotelian *telos*, add: This much is essential; the rest is episodes.

Notes

1. My thanks to the editors, Antony Augoustakis and Monica Cyrino, for their encouragement and advice. Special thanks to Fiona Macintosh, Professor of Classical Reception at the University of Oxford and Curator of the Ioannou Centre for Classical and Byzantine Studies, for sponsoring my visitorship at the Centre (August 2018), where the groundwork for this chapter began.
2. Homer (and Homeric): shorthand for the authorial forces that shaped the *Iliad* and the *Odyssey*, and a nod to the cultural hero constructed in antiquity, but never a reference to an actual person. See Nagy 1996: 20–1.
3. Complex television: the concern of Mittell 2015, to whom this chapter owes a tremendous debt.
4. Aristotle and screenwriting: Hiltunen 2002, Tierno 2002.
5. *Poetics* 23 (my ellipsis). This and other excerpts of the *Poetics* derive from the translation of Halliwell 1987.
6. *Poetics* 17.
7. Catalog of Ships: At *Poetics* 23, Aristotle mentions this as one of many episodes responsible for expanding the *Iliad*.
8. Helpful discussions of episodes in Aristotle, including their nature as well as their impact on tragedy and epic, include Heath 1989: 49–55, Belfiore 1992: 121–31, and Finkelberg 2006.
9. *Oxford English Dictionary* (*OED*) "episode" 2.
10. *OED* "episode" b.
11. On the decline of the dramatic Chorus, see Csapo and Slater 1994: 349–54. See also *Poetics* 18, where Aristotle credits the tragedian Agathon (late fifth century BC) with reducing choral odes to interludes (*embolima*) having no connection to the plot.
12. Roisman 2008: 128 and 148 and likewise Blondell 2013b. Cyrino 2007 offers a somewhat more sympathetic reading of Kruger's Helen.
13. Farr, quoted in Tate 2018.
14. Ancient books also contained collections of smaller poems, as well as historical narratives (sometimes further subdivided into chapters).
15. *The Book of Boba Fett*, slated for December 2021, is perhaps the most recent exemplar of the trend.
16. Heiden 1998, who proposes that the book-divisions of the *Iliad* were in place from the start, is a notable exception.

17. Alexandrian scholars: Griffin 2010: 14. Panathenaic festivals: Nagy 1996: 80–2 and West 2010: 140–1.
18. Clark 2019.
19. Tate 2018.
20. Authorship by responsibility/management: the terminology of Mittell 2015: 87–9, who also employs "authorship by origination" for the "literary model of singular authors."
21. Mittell 2015: 89–92 details the typical showrunning process.
22. Tate 2018. Farr 2018 gives a full account of his intentions as showrunner.
23. *Oxford Classical Dictionary* (*OCD*) "books, poetic" notes "subdivision encourages patterning."
24. Mittell 2015: 19, with reference to the *X-Files* (1993–2002) and its notoriously impenetrable mythology.
25. Compare Fowler 1989: 97: "There is in fact immense variety in the effects of closure Ovid elicits from his book-ends, and they all deserve to be seen as a resource of his art, not an inconvenience."
26. Farr 2018.
27. Seventeen distinct scenes: based on the film's 2005 restoration by the Italian Museo Nazionale del Cinema.
28. Both quotations from Preece 2018 (my ellipses).
29. Van Vorhis 2018 (original ellipsis).
30. Lukewarm reception: the series currently holds a 71% Fresh critics' rating on rottentomatoes.com, the leading review-aggregator, but only a 23% Fresh rating among general audiences.
31. Epic Cycle: Davies 2001, to which this paragraph is indebted.
32. Marvel Cinematic Universe as franchise: Burke 2018 makes an excellent starting point.
33. *Iliad* 2.484–93.

CHAPTER 2
DELINEATING THE DIVINE: GODS AND RELIGION AT TROY
Lisa Maurice

"And there are gods. Living, breathing gods. Zeus. Hera. Aphrodite. I felt it was vital to keep that other force in play," explained David Farr in an interview just before the release of *Troy: Fall of a City*.[1] As the writer of the series, it was important to him to include the gods, whom he saw as, in the words of Derek Wax, "a sort of disconcerting parallel reality to our human world."[2] This stands in contrast with the series' perhaps most important recent predecessor, Petersen's *Troy* (2004), in which the gods were removed entirely, and thereby highlights how *TFOAC*'s approach to depicting the gods and incorporating them into the plot is distinctive.. In this chapter, I discuss how the Greek gods are portrayed in this series, how the humans think of and relate to the deities, and what this reveals about the attitudes toward both divinity and religion in *TFOAC*.

The Physical Depiction of the Gods

Traditionally, the Greek gods on screen share a common stereotypical depiction, in that they are usually clad in long white robes, often trimmed with gold, and featuring elements such as peplum-style skirts, and chiton-like tunics, often decorated with traditional classical motifs. They have invariably been Caucasian, with Zeus and Poseidon shown as elderly bearded men, and the goddesses as beautiful women.[3] The divinities also appear with their individual iconography, including symbols, standardized characteristics, and the presence of particular animals.[4] Such a portrayal is epitomized by Ray Harryhausen's deities in *Jason and the Argonauts* (1983) and *Clash of the Titans* (1981).[5]

Recently, there has been a move away from this kind of portrayal, just as there has been a parallel departure from the gleaming, white marble and bright, shining technicolor of a perfect and sparklingly clean ancient world in favor of a gritty, "realistic" look.[6] Greek gods on screen in recent years have been portrayed more like ancient heroes, in armor rather than flowing robes; Tarsem Singh's deities in *Immortals*, for example, are young, muscled, and clad in costumes with as many fantastic elements as classical ones.[7] *TFOAC* takes a different approach that is colored by these more recent twenty-first-century depictions, but also novel in its own right. In keeping with the contemporary attitude toward portraying the ancient world in a "natural" manner, the luminous snowy white has given place to homespun, earthy colors. The clothes of the deities are more reminiscent of African tribes and decorated with natural elements such as shells and the teeth of animals, perhaps a nod to the idea that the time and society was, at least superficially, primitive. In muted colors, made of materials with a rough finish, they are a far cry from the polished and neatly finished garments, and exquisitely-worked gold jewelry of many earlier depictions. Zeus wears a rough brown tunic and long, hooded cloak in darker brown, made from materials that look simple and unfinished, and the necklace he wears contains three ornamental beads on a thick cord. He is marked by none of the symbols often associated with Zeus on screen, such as a venerable beard, a crown, or lightning bolt, although an eagle, the bird associated with the deity, does sometimes indicate his presence. Even less elaborate is Hermes, who is almost invariably featured in other productions with winged helmet, sandals, and caduceus, but here appears dressed in plain woolen cloak and tunic, and with none of the traditional symbols of the god.[8]

With the goddesses there is more conformity to traditional iconography. Hera wears a black cloak that seems to be made of feathers and her hair is bound with a turquoise ribbon, both elements that hint to the peacock that was the bird associated with the goddess, and that has on occasion provided elements that have featured in her screen appearances.[9] Similarly, Athena has a full-length cloak, but, in a nod to her classical attributes, her tunic is much shorter, more like that of a man. Her dress looks vaguely armor-like, with a bodice shaped like a breastplate during the golden apple scene, and material crossed over her chest in the episode in which she walks among the battle lines prior to the battle. Aphrodite's clothing, on the other hand, does not draw on classical depictions; her costume, a short green two-piece, reminiscent of a swimsuit, topped occasionally by a long green cloak, is entirely twenty-first century, although the sea-green body art decorating her arms and torso may hint to the story of her birth from the sea after the castration of Uranus.[10] In all cases, the clothes of the goddesses, like those of the male gods, are unsophisticated in style, and with natural fabrics of muted colors, and ragged unfinished hems.

Beyond the costume design, the casting of the gods was also somewhat of a departure from tradition. Although Lex King's red-headed Aphrodite is reminiscent of images by Botticelli and pre-Raphaelite painting, the choice of actors cast as some of the other gods was more contentious in the minds of certain viewers. In perhaps the only occasion on which Athena has been portrayed in a mainstream screen production by a non-Caucasian actress, the goddess was played by South African actress, Shamilla Miller, who brought an extraordinary authority to the role, with her dark beauty and piercingly powerful gaze. Even more controversial was the choice of fifty-five-year-old British-Nigerian actor, Hakeem Kae-Kazim for Zeus. The selection of Kae-Kazim, like that of David Gyasi who played Achilles, provoked a range of reactions among viewers, some of whom accused the production team of "blackwashing" the story, although others rightly dismissed these charges as ludicrous.[11] Far more important than his skin color was the power that Kae-Kazim brought to the role, as his formidable voice echoed resonantly in a godlike manner, and his commanding presence dominated, as he sat broodingly aloof, watching the insignificant mortals act out their petty war.

Delineating the Divine: Gods and Religion at Troy

The Nature of the Gods

In Homer's depiction, the anthropomorphic Olympian gods have much in common with mortals.[12] They live in houses on Olympus, eat and drink their divine ambrosia and nectar, and have quarrels and love affairs with both other deities and humans.[13] Defined principally by their power rather than by their virtue, they are larger than life, but neither omnipotent nor omniscient. Yet despite this resemblance with mortals, the gods are immortal, never ageing, and eternally beautiful. This creates a sense of remoteness from the worries and fears of humankind.

The gods of *TFOAC* are in many ways very human in their reactions, display human emotions, acting and reacting like mortals; as the website *Drama Quarterly* puts it: "The gods, strikingly, are played by local actors and integrated as carefully as possible: there will be no declaiming in togas or brandishing fistfuls of lightning."[14] This was a conscious decision on the part of David Farr, who explained: "As for the gods, I never saw them as anything that different to humans. They're equally capricious, passionate and volatile. They're just part of the brew."[15] Yet the deities are also very Homeric in many ways. Zeus is firmly in authority over all the other gods, including Hera, who is clearly subservient to him. The queen of the gods is also a jealous goddess, as she was in the ancient world; when Paris chooses Aphrodite and hands her the golden apple, she lets out an echoing shriek of rage, and disappears in a flurry of her cloak, leaving Paris with his hands clapped to his ears in terror. Athena, like Hera and Aphrodite, blesses and protects individual favorite heroes, and, in fact, this personal protection and favor is her sole distinguishing feature in this production.

It is also striking that, as in Homer, *TFOAC* depicts the gods as being very much involved with the affairs of humankind. Aphrodite in particular is inextricably intertwined with the human tale. This is obvious from the very outset, with Paris' birth immediately preceding the Judgment of Paris and awarding of the golden apple to Aphrodite, the act that causes the entire war, and continues throughout the series. During the one-on-one fight between Menelaus and Paris, it is Aphrodite who intervenes, urging Paris to run. Later, it is she who appears to Paris, Hector, and Hecuba, telling them that the curse has been lifted. Finally, at the very end of the series she is seen in the ruins of Troy, mourning Paris' death, and watched by Hera and Athena. This appearance links her symbolically with the city's destruction, emphasizing her role in its fall.

Despite this interaction with the human world, the intervention of the gods is largely unseen by mortals. Even in Homer, gods sometimes intervene in human affairs without actually appearing to the humans involved, as an unseen influence, as they inspire individuals with courage or prevent them from spilling blood.[16] Nevertheless, in ancient myth deities regularly appear to heroes, assisting them, and recognized by them. In *TFOAC* this is rare, and although the divinities may encourage the humans, their presence is not consciously registered by the recipients. Such a depiction may sit more comfortably in the modern world, where theophany is an outlandish idea, but where the idea of a power in the form of a deity, or even deities, unseen by humans, is acceptable. It is also in keeping with the realism that was one of the stated aims of the production;

Derek Wax explained, that he wanted this tale of Troy to be "grounded and authentic" and to "wipe away the dust that may have accrued on it for some people, and mine the urgent, raw reality."[17] This was not a fantasy production in the mode of *Immortals* (2011) or *Percy Jackson* (2010, 2013), in which the mingling of the divine and human realms was a key feature.

Yet it was also not a retelling that removed the gods entirely, as *Troy* (2004) or *Hercules* (2014) had done; the gods act as the driving force for the action, as one blog pointed out: "The gods are not there to emphasize the severity of war and present a stark contrast between the casual life of immortals and tragic lives of humans, as in the *Iliad*, but are simply there just [sic] push the plot along."[18] This is rather to understate the case, for the gods and the truth of their existence is actually fundamental for the plot, unlike in some recent films, such as *Noah* (2014) and *Exodus: Gods and Kings* (2014), where it is left open as to whether the theophany was genuine, or might actually have been a mere figment of imagination. In *TFOAC* this could not be the case, as is clear from the only example in which direct interaction with the gods does occur, namely the Judgment of Paris. Because *TFOAC* places Paris as the central focus, the presentation of the Judgment of Paris as a true experience is essential for plot purposes. Without this, there is no justification for Paris and Helen's flight (leaving aside the question of whether it is abduction or elopement), and his subsequent acts would be misguided and wrong. Thus there could be no doubt here as to the existence of the gods, or the genuineness of humans' belief in them, as Barney Reisz, the series producer, explains: "the key is that we know the humans are completely invested in them and fundamentally believe in them. People do extraordinary acts because they've been told to by the gods."[19] Hence, the presentation of the Judgment is critical, both as the primary propellant of whole plot, and for the presentation of Paris and Helen as heroes.

Yet the Judgment of Paris scene stands out in *TFOAC* for its uniqueness in portraying such direct interaction between mortal and divine. By positioning this scene at the very beginning of the series, five minutes into Episode 1, and following on from the prophetic visions of Cassandra regarding Paris' birth, the scene is given prominence but also allowed to act as an introduction for the entire narrative, almost standing apart from the production as a whole. For the entirety of the rest of the series the gods are rarely seen by the mortals, although they continue to influence events, sometimes in prominent ways. Thus in Episode 6 Aphrodite's communication with Hector, Hecuba, and Paris allows for Paris' return to Troy and acceptance there. Similarly, Zeus causes the storm in the first episode that prevents Paris from sailing home, and in Episode 2 Artemis appears to the Greek priest, Calchas, to tell him the price that must be paid in the form of Iphigenia. Even in this case, however, Calchas' reaction of shock at the theophany is so noticeable that it actually emphasizes the unusual nature of the event, and the fact that divine appearance to mortals was beyond normal human expectations. In fact, the gods in *TFOAC* are most commonly depicted as unseen, observing the human action with calm detachment, often from above, on hilltops or trees. Moreover, it is stressed that this is the correct way of the world, and that the immense power of the gods should actually be limited with regard to their interaction in the mortal world. As Reisz put it, "they're a presence, without interacting too

Figure 2.1 Hera (Inge Beckmann) approaches Zeus (Hakeem Kae-Kazim) in Episode 2, "Conditions."

directly with the humans. They're around and influencing things, but not in charge as they'd like to be."[20] When Hera approaches Zeus asking him to show loyalty "to Greece and to me," Zeus' response is that Athena had already demanded this, but that he "will not take sides" (Fig. 2.1). Similarly, in Episode 7, when Aphrodite declares that she doesn't trust the Greeks to keep their side of this agreement, Zeus orders firmly, "No meddling from any of you. Let the truce happen. Clear?"

The reason for these restrictions seems to be that the gods are also subject to natural laws of fate.[21] Again this was a conscious decision on the part of Farr, who approached the gods as a means to explore the concepts of destiny and fate, as he explained:

> Destiny. Even now in our more agnostic age, how many of us truly feel we are in charge of our lives, that "fate" never plays a part? It's a vital element of Homer's story that I wanted to honour.[22]

Thus when Aphrodite argues that the curse on Paris has been lifted, Zeus reminds her reprovingly, "You don't decide fate, Aphrodite. None of us do." Such an attitude is reminiscent of the words of the king of the gods at *Iliad* 16.438–49; paradoxically, Zeus is subject to the dictates of his own daughters, the Fates. So important is the role of fate that Hera even accuses Zeus of setting up the whole situation in order to cause the omens to be fulfilled, although Zeus denies this, declaring that he merely gave Paris "a chance to seize his own destiny."[23] Since his taking this chance inevitably caused the fated events to occur, this argument is rather ingenuous, but the following line in which Zeus declares that "forgiveness isn't our way," again underscores the remoteness of the gods, whose intervention in the mortal world is direct only on very rare occasions, and then purely in order to ensure that the laws of fate prevail.

Prayer

Homeric-style direct interaction between gods and mortals is not the only form of communication between mortal and divine in *TFOAC*, and rather more common methods are shown: perhaps the most familiar to contemporary viewers is the act of prayer. Throughout the series, various figures are seen praying. On some occasions, this is a private affair, taking place within the domestic setting, and these prayers are in the form of requests made to an individual god. In such cases, a format is followed, and the appeal to the deity is made before a small idol, a figurine that provides the focus for the petitioner. This can be seen on two occasions on which Hector prays to Aphrodite, once in Episode 4 after he wakens from a nightmare, and again in Episode 6 when he is despairing of finding food for the citizens of Troy. Both follow the same formulaic pattern. In each case, he appears to carry out a set ritual, first lighting a lamp and then sitting down before the statuette and addressing the deity. In the first example, his petition is short and to the point, as, hands spread in supplication, he pleads, "Aphrodite, tell me what to do." The second is more expansive. Again Hector follows the same procedure, and after sitting he visibly readies and composes himself, before uttering the following prayer:

> Aphrodite. Allow me to find a way through the darkness . . . to hold the walls of my city together. Let the children of Troy play in the sun again. Let them taste bread. Let fathers grow old with their young ones, with their wives . . . their brothers.

Helen similarly demonstrates set actions in the third episode, when she prays, again to Aphrodite, for Paris' safe return. Although there is no lighting of a lamp (possibly because the scene occurs during daylight hours), the small idols feature once again. In this case there are two figurines and a garment of Paris' lies before the statues on the table. She stands, with her head bent and her eyes down, her hands lowered, until she lifts Paris' cloak and inhales its scent. Her prayer on this occasion runs, "Aphrodite, if you did choose me, protect Paris now. Give him the caution he lacks. Bring him home."

The prayers of both Helen and Hector are those of petition and are marked by an air of sincerity and piety, with the figurine representing the deity becoming the focus of the request, and the medium through which the god is addressed. These statues themselves look to be about fifteen centimeters in height, and with their spread arms, and elaborate headdresses they evoke bronze-age, near-Eastern cult figures, particularly fertility goddesses such as Anat, Astarte, and the Minoan snake goddess. The form of prayer, in front of the cult statue, seems also perhaps to have been influenced by HBO-BBC's *Rome* (2005–2007), in which similar figures, in the form of the household gods, are depicted in rituals that are similar to those seen in *TFOAC*.[24] Where in *Rome* the petitions and addresses to deities seem slightly exotic, however, with formalistic language and style that is in fact closer to ancient prayers, those in *TFOAC* are colloquial, allowing the viewers to identify with their message and appreciate its genuine and heartfelt nature, as their sympathy with the Trojan petitioners increases.

Delineating the Divine: Gods and Religion at Troy

Other prayers in the series, uttered by, or on behalf of, a group are rather less personal, and are consequently more formal and ritualistic. In the third episode, the Cilicians are seen in a ritual procession, the men and women, some holding bunches of flowers, walking behind the priest and all chanting in unison, "Apollo. Giver of Truth and Light. Hear our prayers." Similarly, in Episode 4, they are depicted as carrying out a ritual, whereby the priest, Litos, after having mixed a libation that appears to be composed of milk and oil, intones, "Son of Zeus, and Leto, great Apollo, Eros, help us to feed the people of Troy." Eetion, King of the Cilicians, then anoints the lips of the men who file past him, repeating each time the petition, "Bless our cause. Help us to feed the people of Troy." The processions that feature in both cases reflect authentic ancient religion, in which they commonly figured,[25] and the use of sacrificial elements and their participants are presented as being sincere in their motivations, as they carry out the simple rituals.

This sincerity is an important element, with the devotion of the believers to their religion portrayed as praiseworthy, an aspect that stands in contrast to that of the Greeks, none of whom are depicted as praying either individually or communally. The sole exception is that of Calchas, who formally petitions the gods in his role as priest, in order to discover the reason for the delayed winds at Aulis. Standing before an altar on the cliff overlooking the sea, he is shown with his eyes almost closed and his arms spread as he petitions the goddess, saying, "Artemis, accept these pledges of regret for our forgetfulness. Huntress, abate your anger. Please, show mercy. Tell us your will. Whatever you desire, we will perform." The placement in a religious setting of an altar, stance of the petitioner, and ceremonial language on behalf of an entire group all mark this out as a very different form of request from those sincere addresses voiced by the individual Trojans.

Sacrifices

In addition to prayer, sacrifice, the central religious act of the ancient world, is also shown as a vital element in *TFOAC*. The importance of sacrifice in the ancient world is summarized by Kearns, who explains that the ancient Greeks very often performed animal sacrifice along with prayer:

> ...whether to bolster up their request or to make good a promise, or even as a pious preliminary to eating. The centrality of animal sacrifice to Greek religious practice is abundantly clear from other sources, and in the epic it is indicated from an Olympian perspective by the keenness of the Gods to receive sacrifice, wherever it may be performed and—other things being equal—their regard for those who offer it.[26]

Within *TFOAC*, two main scenes of sacrifice occur, of which the most important and powerful is that of Iphigenia. In a graphic scene that provoked a shocked response from some viewers,[27] Agamemnon, in obedience to Artemis, slits the throat of his daughter, who was decked out in the bridal finery she had donned for what she thought was her marriage to Achilles. Howling in despair, Agamemnon roars out his pain, and is then seen carrying his daughter's heavily bloodstained body in his arms.

Despite the brutality of the scene, it is striking that emphasis is placed on the fact that it is carried out as a result of a definite lack of piety toward Artemis, as the conversation between Odysseus, Agamemnon, and Menelaus reflects. Odysseus asks Agamemnon if he made offerings to the goddess, and Agamemnon admits that "in the haste of anger, rituals may have been neglected." Odysseus, who is consistently presented as the voice of reason and intelligence, declares that Artemis is offended, and, despite Menelaus' angry protest that "the offence is against us," his brother quickly acknowledges the truth of Odysseus' words and acts to rectify the fault, giving orders to "Get the priest and the seers. Make offerings of birds to the goddess. Now!," and adding, with somewhat less confidence, "surely Artemis will understand." While the goddess is implacable and without mercy, it is made clear that the responsibility lies with Agamemnon himself through his negligence toward the gods.

The other major sacrifice scene involves Paris' offering up of a horse as part of a funeral rite for Andromache's father, Eetion. As Priam explains to Paris:

> Andromache believes that no one has performed her father's funeral rites. Your brother wants to hold the ceremony here, to permit Eetion safe passage into Elysium.

Since Eetion's body is "inaccessible," they decide to offer "a holy vessel in his place," the vessel in this case being a horse. On hearing this, Paris resolves to offer his own horse, a gift he had received from Eetion himself. This is clearly a difficult decision; as he rides around on the horse, Helen asks him doubtfully whether he is sure about it, and his rather morose reply is telling: "You make sacrifices for the people you love. Even if it makes you hate yourself." Although it is not entirely clear why he hates himself—perhaps a somewhat anachronistic guilt at killing an innocent animal?—the level of loss he feels, and his sincerity, are not in doubt. Influenced by Christian tradition, sacrifices in *TFOAC*, whether that of Agamemnon or of Paris, are portrayed as painful, and it is for this reason that they work.[28]

As with Iphigenia, the painful nature of the offering is highlighted by the graphic brutality with which it is portrayed. The horse, a censer of incense tied to his bridle, is led between the rows of silently watching citizens up to the priest, who is also holding an incense burner and murmuring some ritual words under his breath. Under the eyes of the watching crowd, the knife is shown being sharpened, sparks flying from it, and then the slashing noise is heard and the priest's body is seen in motion, swinging the knife to carry out the killing blow. A second later, blood gushes out, spattering liberally over him in a moment reminiscent of the scene of sacrifice at Caesar's triumph in the first episode of HBO-BBC's *Rome*, and the death throes of the dying horse are heard. Clearly sickened by the act, both Helen and Paris' feelings are written clear on their faces. The corpse of the animal is then burnt as an offering, and Andromache intones the prayer, "May you cross over Father." In contrast with the Iphigenia scene, where the acceptance of the sacrifice is evident immediately, as the winds change, here there is no indication that the offering has accomplished its aim, and in fact, when Helen tells Paris that he has done a good thing, his only reaction is a silent and somewhat bitter shake of his head in denial, creating an impression of uncertainty regarding the whole act.

Omens, Visions, and Prophecy

Another form of divine communication presented in the series is through signs and omens. In the ancient world, these were regarded as a fact of life, and divination, the interpretation of the mysterious and enigmatic messages of the gods, was an integral and essential skill practiced by experts. Such professionals were able to infer the messages and will of the gods, and their support or otherwise for human endeavors. The interpretation was carried out through commonly accepted techniques and signs, including augury, the observation of natural conditions and phenomena, interpretation of dreams, and the examination of the entrails of animals after they had been sacrificed to a deity.[29]

Within the series, Cassandra's visions and dreams play a prominent role. The veracity of these revelations is unquestioned in the production and demonstrate graphically the danger that Paris represents to the city. At his birth, Cassandra is a child, and dreams of black blood seeping under the door, before seeing a vision of the gates of Troy opening to reveal the city on fire. She experiences the same visions at Paris' return, despite seemingly not having been subject to such revelations in the intervening years, and another, yet more vivid, when touching the Trojan Horse on its entry into Troy. It is striking that in contrast with the ancient tradition by which Cassandra was a true seer whose forecasts of doom are disregarded by others, in *TFOAC* her prophecies are believed. Litos, Priam, and Hecuba are so convinced of their truth that they agree to expose the baby Paris at birth, but thereafter pretend that Cassandra is disturbed and her visions insane ravings, a condition which requires her to be isolated, maintaining this fiction even to Hector. It is clear that Cassandra is mentally fragile and confused, doubting her own sanity, and lacking in social skills and awareness, while at the same time acknowledging the truth of her visions and feelings, but this condition seems to have been brought about as much by the way her parents have treated her as the supernatural experiences themselves. As Aimee-Ffion Edwards, the actress who played Cassandra, explained:

> She foresees the downfall of Troy. She is kept hidden and protected, her claims of the curse dismissed until Paris returns as an adult, by which time she is fragile and confused. Her feelings are real to her but there is a part of her that also doubts her own sanity having been told for so long that she's not well. It was this emotional conflict and confusion which drew me to the character the most.[30]

Thus the veracity of the visions in this production is taken for granted, but the effect of the revelation on the recipient in the mortal world is the aspect examined in most detail.

Despite the inclusion of the supernatural in *TFOAC*, the focus remains firmly on the human and the real world rather than the fantastical.

This is the also the case with the omens, which are conveyed throughout the series through a form of animal sacrifice carried out by the priest Litos. At the end of Episode 1, in the flashback to Paris' birth, he is shown cutting the throat of a dove and letting the blood flow into water, whereupon it turns black. In the third episode, viewers are then told that this phenomenon has returned since Paris was restored to the Trojan royal household: "This is what happened at his birth. And every day since he returned, the blood runs black. And you know what that means." In the following episode this is explained further:

> I cut the doves at your birth. The blood ran black. The gods have cursed you, Alexander. They place your life on the scales, and Troy on the other end ... The prophecy. For Troy to live, you have to die.

The meaning is clear and underscored by Litos himself; the Trojans ignored the direct message of the gods, and in so doing will bring down destruction upon their own heads. The Trojan disobedience in this case was Priam and Hecuba's inability to kill their own son. In contrast, Agamemnon, who does submit to Artemis' command and sacrifices Iphigenia, reaps the rewards of obedience with his ultimate sack of Troy. The message is difficult for modern viewers to comprehend, in that it is the child killers who are victorious, and indeed this infanticide is decreed by the deities themselves. This unavoidable fact does not, however, result in the attitude seen in a number of recent screen depictions of religion and gods, whereby the gods and their followers are depicted as at best misguided, and at worst fanatically closed-minded and dangerous.[31] Litos, while implacable and showing no mercy toward Paris, is both devoted to his city, whose fate he is attempting to avert, and ultimately correct; neither his beliefs nor his actions are condemned in the series.[32]

Summing Up Gods and Religion in *TFOAC*

In some ways, the portrayal of the gods in the series is in keeping with other recent trends of reception of antiquity on screen, depicting them in a naturalistic manner that parallels the modern portrayal of the ancient world as a colorful and somewhat grubby place, in rejection of the traditional gleaming pillars and pristine white and purple togas. It is also clear that these deities, while close in essence to the Homeric depiction, are far removed from modern Judeo-Christian perceptions of divinity. The portrayal of ancient Mediterranean religion, with its idols and sacrifices, lends an air of mystery and strangeness to antiquity. Yet reverence toward the gods, dutiful practice of religion, and utilization of heartfelt prayer are all used as an indicator of virtue for the individual characters. Hector and Helen pray with sincerity, Paris makes a noble sacrifice, and Odysseus is aware that the correct rites must be followed; all of these contribute to the positive portrayal of these characters with whom viewers are intended to identify. Agamemnon, however, has neglected his religious duties and thereby brought upon himself the terrible situation whereby he is forced to sacrifice his own daughter.

Although Artemis is portrayed as implacable from this point of view, it is striking that the blame is placed squarely on Agamemnon, rather than on the goddess herself. Unlike in many recent productions,[33] the deities themselves are not shown as cruel or vindictive; while playing a central role in the action of the Trojan War, they are in fact also somewhat helpless, with their powers constrained by the natural laws of the world and by fate. The message seems to be not that the gods are evil, but rather that the world is a harsh place in which unstoppable events occur. Wise people recognize this and adapt themselves to the situation by carrying out religious rites; nowhere are religious belief or priests presented in any way other than positively, and showing respect for these strange, yet also very human, anthropomorphic gods is presented as virtuous. This behavior cannot protect against fate, however, and it is perhaps the greatness of this tragedy that shines through in this production; the Trojans are god-fearing and noble, but even this cannot prevent the inevitable: Troy, the city, must still fall.

Notes

1. Farr 2018.
2. Farr 2018.
3. Maurice 2019: 32, 41–3, 7, 93–126.
4. See Maurice 2019: 23.
5. See Llewellyn-Jones 2007, 2009, and 2013b.
6. See Maurice 2016.
7. Maurice 2019: 75–6.
8. Maurice 2019: 76–8.
9. Most notably in *Hercules: The Legendary Journeys* (1995–1999) syndicate. See Maurice 2019: 96.
10. There may also be an unconscious connection to Ursula Andress who played Aphrodite in Harryhausen's *Clash of the Titans* (1981), and who was inseparably connected in the minds of many viewers with her iconic swimsuit in *Dr. No* (1962). See Cyrino 2010: 138 and Maurice 2019: 120.
11. Ling 2018a and 2018b, Johnson 2018, Clarke 2018. See Kennedy in this volume.
12. See Maurice 2019: 7.
13. See Morford, Lenardon, and Sham 2013: 140–2.
14. In the video "So Farr, so Good," March 20, 2018 (www.dramaquarterly.com).
15. www.bbc.co.uk/mediacentre/mediapacks/troy/david-derek; www.bradfordzone.co.uk/troy-fall-of-a-city-interview-with-writer-david-farr-and-executive-producer-derek-wax.
16. E.g., Hera influences Agamemnon to spur on the Achaeans (*Iliad* 8. 218–19). See Kearns 2006: 65.

17. www.bbc.co.uk/mediacentre/mediapacks/troy/david-derek.
18. Trusty 2018.
19. See n15 above.
20. See n15 above.
21. See n15 above.
22. See n1 above.
23. In Episode 5: Hera: "None of this need have happened. You set the whole thing up. The competition, Helen, all just to satisfy the omens." Zeus: "No. I gave the boy a chance to seize his own destiny, and he took it."
24. See, e.g., Season 1, Episode 3, where Vorenus prays before the statue of Venus, and Episode 4, where he and his family do so before the bust of Janus.
25. See Kindt 2012: 69–70.
26. Kearns 2006: 64.
27. See Daly 2018.
28. Whereas Christianity linked the self-sacrifice of Jesus with his suffering, thereby making pain an integral element of sacrifice, it is not at all clear that ancient Greek, Roman, or Jewish religions integrated this idea within sacrifice. See Knust and Várhelyi 2011: 3–31, Heim 2016: 255–69.
29. See Johnston 2008.
30. www.tvarchive2018.bradfordzone.co.uk/2018/02/14/troy-fall-of-a-city-interview-with-aimee-ffion-edwards-cassandra.
31. Maurice 2019: 202.
32. It should also be noted that Litos bears a disturbing resemblance to the eponymous character in Goscinny and Uderzo's *Asterix and the Soothsayer*!
33. See Maurice 2019: 200–2.

CHAPTER 3
FROM JUDGMENT TO FALL: APHRODITE AND PARIS
Monica S. Cyrino

Among the most striking and singular aspects of how the series *Troy: Fall of a City* (2018) makes use of the ancient mythological and literary sources is its vivid onscreen depiction of the ancient Greek gods.[1] Just a few years ago, Wolfgang Petersen's feature film *Troy* (2004) banished the major gods from its reels, allowing only a brief appearance by the sea goddess, Thetis, in an early establishing scene with her son, the semi-divine hero, Achilles.[2] In direct and audacious contrast to the divine stinginess of the earlier film, the series skillfully and robustly portrays the actions and words of several Olympian deities throughout its multiple episodes, utilizing imagery, dialogue, and costuming that are at the same time both realistic and impressionistic. *TFOAC* offers tangible and suitably gorgeous glimpses of numerous divinities, including Zeus, Hermes, Artemis, Hera, and Athena; and, most prominently for an epic storyline that starts and ends with her, the series lets us see and hear Aphrodite, the goddess of love and beauty.

Ancient Greek mythology and literature confirm the notion that Aphrodite is actively and frequently engaged in the human sphere and she can be remarkably intimate with her favorite mortals.[3] More often than other Greek deities, Aphrodite is constantly present on the terrestrial plane, persistently mixing it up with mortals in her attentive familiarity with their affairs: she can be intensely solicitous and protective of her mortal favorites, but equally demanding and petulant when defied. With her profound involvement in the human condition, Aphrodite is depicted in early Greek epic poetry, as Lorenzo F. Garcia, Jr. aptly describes her, "as being enmeshed in human temporality" through her close connection to embodied human existence in the act of love: whenever she intervenes in the mortal realm, as Garcia argues, the goddess Aphrodite is made vulnerable to the physical risks and damages of time as experienced by humans.[4] In the Greek epic tradition, Aphrodite is most closely affiliated with her mortal favorite Paris, Prince of Troy, and she both instigates and oversees his illicit love affair with Helen, Queen of Sparta, which is the primary cause of the Trojan War.[5] So too in *TFOAC*, Aphrodite's intimate engagement with Paris, the Trojan shepherd-turned-prince, forms the emotional through-line of the series, as a sequence of compelling scenes shared between goddess and mortal punctuate the epic story and delineate the passage of narrative time. From the opening dramatization of the infamous Judgment of Paris scene as the foundational myth of the Trojan War, to the closing sequence of the charred city in eponymous fallen ruins, the onscreen presence of Aphrodite drives the main plot and serves as a compelling structural and temporal framework for the entire series.

Screening Love and War in *Troy: Fall of a City*

Aphrodite and Paris

This chapter explores the series' extraordinary depiction of the goddess Aphrodite, played by Lex King, a British-South African actor and model who had appeared in a few television and movie roles before her performance as Aphrodite.[6] King had a part in the American apocalyptic fantasy television series *Dominion* (2015) on the SyFy network, and appeared in the British military thriller *Eye in the Sky* (2016), a feature film starring Helen Mirren and Alan Rickman: both of these productions were shot in South Africa, as was *TFOAC*. King then decided to focus on her education and enrolled in a Master's program studying Psychology and Neuroscience at King's College London before being cast as Aphrodite; she subsequently completed this MS degree with Distinction in December 2020.[7] Following her appearance in the *TFOAC* series, King appeared as Callie on the short-lived Lifetime comedy-drama series *American Princess* (2019), a send-up of contemporary Renaissance Faire culture. Recently, King played nineteenth-century German journalist Ottilie Assing, the (assumed) mistress of American abolitionist Frederick Douglass (Daveed Diggs), in the acclaimed Showtime historical drama series *The Good Lord Bird* (2020). King currently lives in Los Angeles to focus on her acting career.

Although King initially met with *TFOAC* casting and production personnel in London to audition for the role of Helen, the showrunners later contacted her about playing Aphrodite: King had previously worked with one of the series directors, Owen Harris, whose familiarity with her distinctive personality and physicality tipped the scales in favor of the role of the goddess.[8] The actor explains: "As a tall, athletic redhead, I struggle to find roles that are right for me, so it was a huge compliment to be approached to play the Goddess of Love and Beauty. I put a scene on tape and sent it to the UK and within a few weeks I was on a plane to South Africa to shoot for six months!"[9] King's childhood training in dance and her earlier career as a model helped prepare her to assume the alluring persona of Aphrodite, and she worked conscientiously to imbue her performance with the right amount of divine glamour, silky speech, and supple movement: "I wanted Aphrodite to feel like the embodiment of grace and femininity, and so I tapped into a way of feeling and moving my body that helped bring that to life. Her voice and interaction with other characters naturally developed from that point."[10] The actor's lissome gestures and mellifluous line delivery persuasively evoke the Homeric Aphrodite who engages with both her Olympian family members and her mortal favorite, Paris.

From the outset, the series *TFOAC* highlights the intense and evocative bond between the goddess Aphrodite and the Trojan prince Paris, played by Louis Hunter, a theater-trained Australian actor.[11] Born and raised in Sydney, Hunter's first lead role was as a teenager on the Australian serial murder mystery *Out of the Blue* (2008–2009),[12] and soon after he appeared as Prince Edward in the play *The War of the Roses* for the Sydney Theater Company (2009) alongside Cate Blanchett. The actor made his American debut in a recurring role as Nick Armstrong on the supernatural teen drama *The Secret Circle* (2011–2012) on The CW network, and then appeared in a recurring role as Nick Stratos on the award-winning LGBT family drama *The Fosters* (2013–2018) on the Freeform cable channel.[13] Hunter's most recent appearance was as Lachlan O'Leary in the critically acclaimed Australian boxing mini-series *On the Ropes* (2018) on the public television network SBS. Hunter currently lives in Los Angeles.

Paris is unmistakably one of the main human characters of the series *TFOAC*, and the casting of the laddish, scruffily bearded, and outdoorsy-handsome actor Hunter in the role immediately sets up a visual distinction with earlier onscreen Parises, who were typically more smooth-skinned and palace-adjacent, such as Orlando Bloom in Petersen's feature film *Troy* or Matthew Marsden in the *Helen of Troy* mini-series that screened on the USA Network (2003).[14] As television critic Sarah Hughes notes of Hunter's casting and performance in the role: "Most versions of this story tend to cast Paris as something of a useless pretty boy, but here he's a rough-around-the-edges outsider with a chip on his shoulder. That not only helps us understand why he might take the risk of seducing Helen, but also explains why she would leave everything behind for him."[15] This new Paris starts out in *TFOAC* as a Patagonia fleece-wearing herdsman, free-spirited and a tough fighter, and becomes rather more gentrified only later in the series as the experiences of politics, love, and war polish away his coarser edges. Likewise, it is this Paris, both shepherd and prince, who inspires a fierce loyalty and divine favoritism from the goddess Aphrodite. During the shoot, *TFOAC* showrunners deliberately emphasized the intimate bond between goddess and mortal favorite, as actor King elucidates:

> From reading the scripts, it was clear to me that most of Aphrodite's action in this storyline is in relation to Paris. From her perspective, everything is about Paris, and any interactions with other characters are only relevant in how they affect her relation to Paris … So, for Aphrodite, I focused on interacting with everyone on set with love, kindness and grace. It was important to me that right from meeting Louis (who played Paris), I was just going to love and adore him, in a protective and motherly way. Doing this means that when it comes to shooting, the way I engage with him on screen will feel natural, and I will have to do less "pretending."[16]

With the fortunate discovery that they enjoyed a natural rapport, the actors playing Aphrodite and Paris were able to concentrate all the energy of their performances more authentically on their characters' special attachment throughout several episodes of the series:

> So much of acting is figuring out the dynamic between your scene partner(s), and sometimes you get lucky and there is a natural understanding. There was no disagreement or power struggle needed to establish the dynamic between me as Aphrodite and Louis as Paris. And when it's working, it's better to not overtalk it, because you risk forcing something and destroying the natural connection … Thankfully, the connection between me and Louis was instant, and I think we both understood our characters' bond without having to discuss it extensively.[17]

In the following analysis, we explore how *TFOAC* stages several key scenes in which the close relationship between Aphrodite and Paris is deployed to create a structural and temporal framework for the entire narrative trajectory of the series. We start by considering the celebrated Judgment tale and the acquisition of Helen shown in the early episodes of the series, events that were told in the lost Greek epic *Cypria*;[18] and then we move on to the devastating Fall of Troy sequence, derived considerably from Book 2 of Vergil's *Aeneid*,[19] that draws the storyline to an agonizing conclusion in the series finale. Throughout this exploration, the actor who plays Aphrodite in the series, Lex King, generously offers her insightful personal commentary on the making and meaning of the scenes in which she performed, adding an exclusive and illuminating dimension to the usual academic discourse about onscreen classical reception.

Judgment

In the first episode, "Black Blood," the pre-title sequence of the ill-omened birth of Paris cuts immediately to the most crucial event of the young man's life: his deliberate and decisive selection of the goddess Aphrodite in the notorious Judgment. Right away the viewer recognizes the destiny-marked Trojan shepherd in the opening scenes as he makes love to the nymph Oenone (Lise Slabber) and tends his flocks on the edges of the wild woods. Paris then sees a wolf as he is drawn into the sacred grove on Mount Ida, known to the ancient Greeks as "mother of beasts."[20] We catch a glimpse of Aphrodite, as she is the first embodied deity to appear on screen in the series. There in the grove Paris is met by a reluctant Hermes (Diarmaid Murtagh), who tells him he's been chosen "to resolve a dispute."

Aphrodite appears as a pale willowy redhead clad in deep forest-green robes, rather than the cerulean blues and golds usually associated with the goddess: the dark verdant color of her dress may have been a costuming choice both to reflect the lush natural

Figure 3.1 Paris (Louis Hunter) gives Aphrodite (Lex King) the golden apple in the Judgment scene in Episode 1, "Black Blood."

surroundings of the wooded grove and also to contrast strikingly with the actor's strawberry-cream coloring (Fig. 3.1). The goddess touches Paris tenderly on the arm and reminds him, "You know me, of course—from your dreams." Actor King describes the process of performing one of Aphrodite's most celebrated moments of persuasion from Greek mythology:

> While this is the first time that we see Aphrodite and Paris together on screen, her words indicate that the connection between the two characters has been previously established, albeit in the dream world. For me, Aphrodite entered the scene with an existing love and care for Paris, although perhaps more sexual than the maternal love it later becomes, and without the guilt that she carries after these events begin to create turmoil in Paris' life.[21]

The scene is remarkable for its convincing evocation of a range of ancient artistic and mythological imagery. From the moment Hermes pulls the burning golden apple from the campfire and hands it to Paris, who then bestows it upon the triumphant Aphrodite with the words "I choose you," the series underscores the agency and culpability of Paris and his choice of love as the direct cause of Troy's fiery downfall. With the solemn presence of Zeus (Hakeem Kae-Kazim) throughout the entire Judgment sequence, the event is suffused with enormous magnitude and impact, as the king of the gods intones gravely, "The mortal has spoken."[22] The look of sheer exultation and conquest on Aphrodite's face as she accepts the apple from Paris, alongside the shrieking gusts of rage of rejected goddesses Hera (Inge Beckmann) and Athena (Shamilla Miller), forcefully signal the importance of this mythological scene as the pivotal inflection point in the story that carries through the series, as actor King makes clear:

> Aphrodite's manipulation to get the golden apple is selfishly motivated: she wants to win the power struggle against Hera and Athena and establish herself as superior … I wanted to portray a feeling of absolute triumph and powerfulness when Aphrodite gets the apple, because this moment of her perceived win is actually the catalyst for her eventual great loss, after the ensuing discord between Troy and Sparta leads to the Trojan war and Paris' death.[23]

According to King, the showrunners filmed the critical (and logistically complicated) Judgment scene twice. First, it was shot at the beginning of filming: this was at the end of a very long shoot day, where the cast and crew were rushing for time and kept shooting until early morning. Yet given how important the Judgment scene is to setting the tenor and narrative of the entire series, the producers decided to reshoot the crucial scene, dedicating an entire day to get it right:

> What was amazing was getting the chance to revisit the scene after having worked with the other actors and gaining a clearer understanding of the relevance of the action in the scene. We shot in a beautiful forest, and we had a helicopter flying

right above us to create the wind chaos and shaking trees after Paris gives the apple to Aphrodite, so it felt wonderfully dramatic![24]

Later in the same episode, the newly discovered Prince Paris celebrates his reintegration into the Trojan royal family, and in a drunken flash he locks eyes with Aphrodite during the revels in the great hall upon the Trojan citadel. A quick cut shows the furtive wolf from the forest grove of the Judgment scene darting into the palace, as the black blood of the episode title flows under the door: the terrifying images indicate that the liaison between love goddess and new prince will bring danger and eventually death to the palace. Actor King emphasizes the darker and more intimidating aspects of the goddess' brief appearance in the Trojan great hall, noting how the scene evokes her more aggressive traits and cements her fateful attachment to Paris and the city of Troy:

> In this quick flash I felt Aphrodite's presence was twofold: first, a reminder that Paris is now inseparably intertwined with the goddess, but also secondly, through Aphrodite's gaze, a mirror is held up to Paris indicating the immaturity and foolishness of his actions. It's definitely foreboding. To evoke Aphrodite's more dangerous aspects I leaned into her sexuality—she is not dangerous because she is bad or evil, but rather inside her she contains a formidable power over desire and this can be very destructive.[25]

Thus, the opening episode immediately introduces and establishes the way the series will represent the gods: they are implacable, cruel, terrifying, and awe-inspiring in the most literal ways. As critic Hughes observes: "Human beings are little more than pawns in their wider game and they can—and do—destroy lives on a whim."[26] Just as Zeus later

Figure 3.2 Aphrodite (Lex King) on the Trojan plain before battle in Episode 2, "Conditions."

raises the storm that keeps Paris from sailing home to Troy, thereby facilitating the disastrous attainment of Helen, Paris' glimpse of Aphrodite among the revelers occurs just before he embarks upon his fatal love affair. Thus, from the very first episode of the series, the narrative, dialogue, and visual imagery work to bond Paris and Aphrodite together as the principal agents of the city's destruction.

Several other scenes depicting Aphrodite in the series reinforce her portentous and ultimately lethal attachment to the Trojan people. In the second episode, "Conditions," Aphrodite joins Hera and Athena in a fantasy-league catalog of troops, as each goddess appears to walk among the warriors on the Trojan battlefield, and each one calls out to and "blesses" her champions arrayed on the plain of war (Fig. 3.2).[27] Critic Hughes describes the serious menace of the goddesses' swaggering manifestation in the catalog montage: "They are truly otherworldly beings, they are not easily placated and cannot simply be bought off with a passing dove. Instead they feed on sacrifice, violence, and blood as this episode made horribly clear."[28] During the catalog of heroes scene, Aphrodite names the Trojan warriors Aeneas (Alfred Enoch) and Hector (Tom Weston-Jones), but she does not mention her favorite Paris, whom she no doubt wishes to protect from the violence of battle. Actor King conveys her motivation in the scene:

> It's a beautiful scene showing the connection between goddesses and warriors, from both sides. While having full faith in her Trojan warriors, Aphrodite, the Goddess of Love, does not desire war, and so this scene indicates that things are starting to go wrong for Aphrodite, and she begins to experience the consequences of her selfish actions. I wanted to begin to portray the heaviness of her heart in this scene, the weight of the battle on her shoulders, along with her continued stubbornness and refusal to lose to Hera and Athena, who align themselves with the Greeks.[29]

Indeed, right after Athena names Achilles (David Gyasi), the greatest Greek hero, marking a conspicuous moment of climax within the catalog of warriors, Aphrodite is shown in an astonishing long shot running in front of the Trojan line between the two armies—this image unequivocally emphasizes her direct agency in the conflict, as actor King agrees: "Charging into the battle displays the responsibility Aphrodite is willing to take for her actions. Even though she doesn't want war, she is not going to absolve herself of responsibility and hide in the shadows. She has power and integrity to lead the fight."[30] This impressive scene was filmed in a number of different ways, with some of the takes shot on location and some in front of a green screen, with the whole sequence ingeniously put together in post-production. Actor King recalls the very real dangers of shooting this scene on location with the rest of the cast equipped as troops:

> We also did a take where I charged directly into the Greek army. We had marked it with the stunt team, and all seemed safe, but before my shot the smoke machines had made such thick smoke that I actually couldn't see very far in front of me. So, I was sprinting from one side and the Greeks were charging at me from the other

with spears—props, but still made of metal and wood—and I remember hearing their feet before I could see them and realizing they were right on top of me. I collided with one of the soldiers and fell to the ground, everyone else around me crashing and tumbling too. I remember the medic and director came running over to me to check if I was injured. Thankfully I just had some scrapes on my legs, but I was otherwise okay. I shudder to think if one of the spears had connected with my face! Anyway, needless to say, the director refused to do another take, so that is the one that made it into the show—obviously cut before the collision![31]

King's graphic recollection of filming this scene brings to mind the Homeric Aphrodite's perilous encounter with the Greeks on the Trojan battlefield in Book 5 of the *Iliad*, where the goddess eagerly rushes into the fray to save her son Aeneas from danger, but is attacked and wounded by the fierce Greek warrior Diomedes;[32] the scene also confirms Aphrodite's vulnerability to human risk and pain with her relentless inclination toward intervening in the mortal realm, even in the midst of deadly combat.

The fourth episode, "Spoils of War," presents the famous *monomachia* sequence from Book 3 of the *Iliad*, where Paris and Menelaus engage in a hand-to-hand duel for the possession of Helen; in the epic, Menelaus is clearly the victor, and Paris is only saved by the intervention of Aphrodite.[33] During the duel scene in the *TFOAC* series, the Trojan high priest, Litos (Jonathan Pienaar), is brought forward to describe the dove sacrifice at the birth of Paris. Since doves are sacred to Aphrodite, the priest's memory narration links the goddess to the first newborn breaths of her mortal favorite, while the bloody white birds are an ominous proleptic image of the eventual slaughter of Trojans in the palace. As critic Hughes cheekily confessed: "It's a little worrying that I care more about the fate of the doves . . . than that of the Trojan royal family."[34] After the priest dramatically reveals the original curse on Paris, an infuriated Menelaus (Jonas Armstrong) reinforces the doom-laden words: "Your own family tried to kill you. You have brought them nothing but death." When Menelaus knocks Paris down and is about to deliver the deathblow, Paris closes his eyes in submission to his fate; but then Aphrodite appears, presumably seen and heard only by Paris, and her voice-over urges him with the single disembodied word: "Run." Actor King explains the impassioned word spoken off-camera: "Aphrodite's voice in this scene is to demonstrate that she has taken the role of protector to Paris. Even when he feels alone, she is there looking over him and ensuring his safety."[35] And Paris does exactly what his ever-present divine protector tells him to do with her one-word command: he runs. Like her epic literary counterpart, the goddess is not yet ready to surrender her favorite: in this instant, the notoriously capricious Aphrodite displays a stubborn side.

Fall

Just as Aphrodite does in the duel sequence, where she saves Paris from certain death under the sword of Menelaus, the series portrays the goddess as repeatedly acting to propel or even change the course of the plot—she refuses to accept the fated downfall of Troy (even though it is right there in the series title). In the sixth episode, "Battle on the Beach," Aphrodite continues to favor and protect Paris, now a fugitive from the city, as he is rescued from leaping off a cliff and trying to drown himself by a group of Amazon warriors on their way to fight for Troy. When Paris tells the Amazons his sad story about how he is dogged by a divine birth curse, their queen Penthesilea (Nina Milner) shrugs breezily: "There always is with boys like you."[36] Nevertheless, the Amazons attempt to convince a dubious Paris to make the journey with them back to Troy.

Later in the episode, Aphrodite appears in a vivid simultaneous three-way waking dream to Paris, who is still on the lam with the Amazons, and at the same time to Hector and Hecuba (Frances O'Connor) in the Trojan royal palace: this imaginative sequence allows Aphrodite's voice to spill over between interwoven shots of the three actors, as if she is speaking to them instantaneously in an enveloping stream.[37] During the dream sequence, Aphrodite persuades all three of the Trojans that the birth curse is conveniently broken (on a technicality) and the city is now safe: whether this is wishful thinking on the part of the goddess or an intentional deception, the result is that the members of the Trojan royal family foolishly fall for her divine assurance, which leads Hector to his fatal fight against Achilles, as critic Hughes surmises:

> Not only was his suicide attempt thwarted by a passing bunch of Amazons, who chose to adopt him as a sort of bearded pet and help him get back to Troy rather than doing the sensible thing and leaving him to drown in his own self-importance, but Aphrodite also personally assured him that pesky curse business was now lifted and the men, women, and children of Troy would survive and thrive.[38]

With these scenes, then, the series seems to suggest that Aphrodite is engineering an inherently unfair exchange of Hector's life for that of her favorite, Paris. In the dream sequence, Aphrodite focuses on Paris, asking him, "Do you remember choosing me?" as she prompts him to pledge that he would choose her "a thousand times more": this indicates that their relationship—and in particular his devotion to her—now supersedes all other considerations. Actor King, however, indicates that she performed the scene with a sense of transparency of purpose, noting that even though the goddess is trying to guide the runaway Paris back to the palace, she truly cares for Hector and wants to save the Trojan royal family:

> I took Aphrodite's intentions here to be pure—I don't think she is trying to deceive them, I think she genuinely believes that the curse is in fact broken. Maybe on some level she knows it's a bit of a cheat, as the curse being broken rests on the technicality of Paris having died and being brought back by the women warriors, but I think at this point Aphrodite is just desperate to believe anything that might rewrite the fate that Troy will fall, and she will lose Paris . . . I don't think Aphrodite intends to sacrifice Hector to Achilles, but I think her sole focus is on keeping Paris safe, so whatever happens as a consequence of that happens. Perhaps it's more of a

passive sacrifice—but I don't think she's happy about that either, Hector was her greatest fighter.[39]

As the series moves inexorably toward the destruction of the people and city of Troy, twice in the final episodes a troubled Aphrodite appeals directly to the supreme god Zeus: these scenes evoke an intimate level of persuasion and a familiarity with the king of the gods that blurs Aphrodite's kinship lines—is she Zeus' daughter or is she something else, a seductive but not quite equal power?[40] The actors playing Aphrodite and Zeus deliberated together about how they would portray the essential connection between them, as King explains:

> Hakeem (Zeus) and I discussed the relationship between Zeus and Aphrodite and decided that a paternal relationship felt right. But as ruler of the gods Zeus is a kind of father to all, so we didn't get hung up on the biology of it, which I don't think really applies to gods anyway. They're beyond genetics and appropriate familial relations![41]

In the fifth episode, "Hunted," Aphrodite and Zeus are watching the fugitive Paris at night by a campfire, and she softly but firmly reproaches the great god for setting Paris up for failure. "No," Zeus replies gravely, "I gave the boy a chance to seize his destiny"—referring to Paris' transition from shepherd to prince. Aphrodite then caresses and kisses Zeus, coaxing him to spare her favorite: "Forgive him ... for me." When Zeus holds the divine line with "Thing is ... forgiveness isn't our way," Aphrodite threatens the supreme god, "I won't let you take him." Their gripping exchange in this scene hints at the more powerful figure of the primordial Aphrodite, and not merely the obedient Olympian daughter, as the goddess moves effortlessly from using seduction in her attempt at inducement and then turns rebellious when her desires are thwarted. Actor King characterizes the expression of Aphrodite's power in this scene with Zeus:

> I interpreted the seduction scene as Aphrodite using her feminine wiles to get what she wants. She's not considering whether Zeus is her father and whether that is appropriate, those are more mortal concerns: she just knows that she can manipulate men (or male gods) with her sexuality, and she's going to use whatever she can to save Paris. Her response that she won't let Zeus take him echoes that of a defiant child, but again I think it relates more to Zeus' status as the ruler of the gods and less to him being her father. She knows Zeus is more powerful than she is, and when he sees through her manipulative tactics and calls her out on it, her only option is to be defiant.[42]

Later, in the seventh episode, "Twelve Days," Aphrodite remains defiant as she stands in the bright sunshine before the storied gates of Troy alongside both Hera and Zeus, and he sharply informs her even the gods are ruled by Fate: "You don't decide Fate, Aphrodite ... None of us do." As viewers might have suspected, Aphrodite's persuasive falsehood

From Judgment to Fall: Aphrodite and Paris

that the curse has been lifted in the previous episode was only her aspirational attempt to get her beloved Paris safely back inside the Trojan royal palace. In this stark sunlit moment, with the weight of the coming disaster upon her, Aphrodite realizes that she and the other gods can undeniably aid those they support, but they cannot change the course of fate—Paris is alive (for now), but Troy, as the gods (and we viewers) have always known, will fall:

> Here Aphrodite is realizing that her plans to rewrite fate have failed. I think she's beginning to see that she has been in denial about Troy and Paris, and this is causing her frustration. She cares and feels responsible for Paris and has done everything within her power to control the outcome, but Zeus makes her aware that she cannot control fate. I don't think Aphrodite likes to feel the limits of her power, and she's having to face that in this scene.[43]

The final episode, "Offering," is ostensibly named for the infamous Trojan Horse, but the title also suggests the divinely-witnessed sacrifice of the people and city of Troy. In the last few scenes of the episode, the series uses imagery and camera work to link the last appearance of Aphrodite to two of the traditional human survivors of the war, Helen and Aeneas, even as the goddess grieves the loss of her beloved Paris in the smoking ruins of the Trojan palace. When the victorious Greeks take Helen down to their waiting ships, viewers follow her focalization as she gazes mournfully back to the smoldering city of Troy where her lover Paris lies dead. The camera quickly cuts to their ravaged palace bedroom and reveals Aphrodite's shocked and tear-stained face as she contemplates the body of her slain favorite, and then moves to Hera and Athena, the other two goddesses from the Judgment in the first episode, standing quietly there too, in a fine visual ring composition of culpability. The very next image is Aeneas rising from a pile of bloody bodies in the great hall of the palace, as he limps toward his uncertain future.

These concluding moments of the last episode poignantly underscore a network of accountability and suffering for both the mortal and divine protagonists in the tale of the Trojan War. As the three goddesses exchange leaden glances in the ruined palace, it is doubtful that any sort of divine reconciliation occurs; while Hera and Athena do not openly exult over Aphrodite's devastating loss, it appears anger and mutual jealousy endure among them. Actor King shares the burden of emotion that infuses this scene, emphasizing her nonverbal projection of Aphrodite's sense of grief and responsibility:

> In this final moment Aphrodite, facing the death of Paris, feels immense pain and guilt. On some level, she knows this was because of her and the game she played to get the apple. However, she projects this blame onto Hera and Athena. Even in these final moments, Aphrodite cannot acknowledge that her ego and power games led to this loss. Athena and Hera also refuse to take any responsibility for their parts, and instead use this as an opportunity to gloat and rub salt into the wound. But I think the great tragedy amongst the goddesses is that this is not the outcome any of them would've desired. This scene shows the consequence of

the games the gods play with mortals. It is what Zeus could see unfolding from the start and what he constantly warns the goddesses about throughout the story, yet they remain too selfish and immature to heed his warnings.[44]

Thus, Aphrodite's somber presence in the closing frames of the series links her thematically and visually to the titular "fall of the city," while perhaps signaling her continued involvement in any potential onscreen exploration of future narratives for Helen, or more likely, for Aeneas. In the final lines of Book 2 of Vergil's *Aeneid*, after the propulsive first-person account of his last night in the burning city, Aeneas' heartrending narration describes the Morning Star, Venus, the heavenly body associated with Aphrodite, as it rises over Mount Ida to signal a promised new dawn after the total destruction of Troy . . . and perhaps the hint of a sequel.

> It startled me to find how many more
> Had streamed there—mothers, men in their best years,
> Young men, gathered pathetically for exile.
> They came from everywhere, supplied, resolved,
> To sail with me to any land I chose.
> The Dawn Star rose past Ida's highest slopes
> And brought the day. The Greeks held every gate
> To the city. There was nothing left to help us.
> I picked my father up and sought the mountains.[45]

Notes

1. A version of this paper was delivered on April 5, 2019 at the annual meeting of the Classical Association of the Middle West and South at the University of Nebraska in Lincoln. On the depiction of the gods in the series, see Maurice in this volume; for the ancient mythological and literary sources utilized by the series, see Burton in this volume.
2. This is the scene where Thetis (Julie Christie) issues the famous warning to her son Achilles (Brad Pitt) that he will not survive the war at Troy. On the Petersen film, see the contributions in the volume edited by Winkler 2007.
3. On Aphrodite's intimacy with mortals as a defining characteristic of her divinity, see Cyrino 2010: 79–103.
4. Garcia 2019 analyzes how Aphrodite experiences human time, both to influence and to suffer from its progression. See also Purves 2006 for the experience of other Homeric gods "falling into time."
5. See Cyrino 2010: 83–8 on Aphrodite's special relationship with Paris and Helen. Note, however, the series *TFOAC* chooses not to stage the goddess' traditional interactions with her semi-divine avatar, Helen (Bella Dayne), or even her half-mortal son, Aeneas (Alfred Enoch), which has the effect of putting all the narrative emphasis in the series on Aphrodite's single-minded devotion to Paris.
6. Information from IMDb ~ Lex King (www.imdb.com).

From Judgment to Fall: Aphrodite and Paris

7. In an Instagram post [@lex_in_pictures] dated December 2, 2020, King posted a screenshot of herself in character as Aphrodite together with an image of her diploma: "Mighty Aphrodite. I used the money I made on this show to pay tuition for my master's degree. It's been a tough few years, but this education is the best thing I've ever given myself. Yesterday my MS in Psychology and Neuroscience was officially conferred. Felt only right to give thanks to the Goddess of Love for enabling this accomplishment. #troyfallofacity."
8. King had a small role in *The Gamechangers* (2015), a television film Harris directed for the BBC.
9. From interview conversations between the author and actor Lex King in November and December 2020.
10. Author's interview with Lex King, December 2020.
11. Information from IMDb ~ Louis Hunter (www.imdb.com).
12. The series was commissioned by the BBC and first screened on BBC One, then soon shifted to BBC Two; the series was shown on Network Ten in Australia.
13. At the time of the series, Freeform was known as the ABC Family Channel, and is still owned by the ABC Family Worldwide subsidiary of Walt Disney Television.
14. On these earlier and more debonair Paris roles, see Cyrino 2005b. In Ovid's *Heroides* 5.9–16, Oenone alludes to Paris' process of gentrification, as she reminds her former lover that he was once a rustic herdsman: I thank Noah Holt for this reference.
15. Hughes 2018a.
16. Author's interview with Lex King, December 2020.
17. Author's interview with Lex King, December 2020.
18. For the lost epic *Cypria* as the source of pre-Iliadic events in the tale of Paris and Helen, see Cyrino 2007: 132–6, 138–41. See also Burton in this volume.
19. See Ahl 2007: 171–2 and 184 on the influence of Vergil's *Aeneid* in later receptions of the narrative of the Fall of Troy.
20. *Homeric Hymn to Aphrodite* 68.
21. Author's interview with Lex King, December 2020.
22. British-Nigerian actor Hakeem Kae-Kazim is known as the "Man with a Beautiful Voice" and has also done extensive voice-over work ranging from television and radio to video games. On the casting of Kae-Kazim, see Kennedy in this volume.
23. Author's interview with Lex King, December 2020.
24. Author's interview with Lex King, December 2020.
25. Author's interview with Lex King, December 2020.
26. Hughes 2018a.
27. The scene evokes the Catalog of Ships in Book 2 of the *Iliad*, where the various leaders of the Greek contingents that sailed to Troy are named (2.494–759), followed by a shorter catalog of Trojans and their allies (2.816–77).
28. Hughes 2018b.
29. Author's interview with Lex King, December 2020, who adds: "This was actually the scene I sent for my audition!"
30. Author's interview with Lex King, December 2020.
31. Author's interview with Lex King, December 2020.

32. *Iliad* 5.311–430. On Aphrodite's controversial association with warfare, see Cyrino 2010: 49–52.
33. *Iliad* 3.314-382. See Cyrino 2007: 138–39 for the Homeric duel scene as a sort of narrative "flashback" to events that occurred at the start of the war that serves to reintroduce the theme of the illicit love affair of Paris and Helen.
34. Hughes 2018e.
35. Author's interview with Lex King, December 2020, who notes that the theme of protection in Aphrodite's bond with Paris is reiterated later in the series as the goddess protects him when he jumps from the cliff.
36. On the portrayal of the Amazons in the series, see Penrose in this volume.
37. Actor King recalls how director Brozel encouraged the actors to be inventive as they filmed the shots that would be edited into the dream sequence: "I love this scene! . . . It felt like a real creative collaboration between director and actors, instead of just being a vehicle for the director's vision." Author's interview with Lex King, December 2020.
38. Hughes 2018f.
39. Author's interview with Lex King, December 2020.
40. In the earliest ancient Greek sources, Aphrodite has two distinct birth stories: she is often referred to as "the daughter of Zeus" whose mother is the goddess Dione (e.g., Homer's *Iliad* 5.370–1); but the more famous story is that she is born directly from the sea, as a primordial power (Hesiod's *Theogony* 188–206). On Aphrodite's birth stories and kinship connections, see Cyrino 2010: 11–18.
41. Author's interview with Lex King, December 2020.
42. Author's interview with Lex King, December 2020.
43. Author's interview with Lex King, December 2020.
44. Author's interview with Lex King, December 2020.
45. Vergil's *Aeneid* 2.795-804. Translated by Ruden 2008.

CHAPTER 4
SYMPATHY FOR TROY'S JEZEBEL: HELEN AS ANTIHERO
Meredith E. Safran

Troy: Fall of a City joins numerous film and television productions that have aimed to create a novel interpretation of this ancient story for viewers "today."[1] That interpretive work includes determining how to characterize Helen, whose departure from Sparta sparks the war that made her Western cultural history's most famous runaway wife.[2] Twentieth-century "sword and sandal" or peplum films that shaped the Western popular imagination of the classical world in general offered two options.[3] Robert Wise's 1956 film *Helen of Troy* featured a sympathetic romantic heroine overmatched by men; so too latter-day peplums, John Kent Harrison's 2003 television mini-series *Helen of Troy* and Wolfgang Petersen's 2004 film *Troy*, presented similarly fair-skinned blonde Helens as doomed romantic heroines.[4] By contrast, Michael Cacoyannis' 1971 film adaptation of Euripides' post-war tragedy *Trojan Women* styles its Helen as a vampy villain whose sexual power enables her to manipulate men, aligning viewers emotionally with the fair-complected titular captives who condemn the dark-haired, dark-eyed Helen who seduces her cuckolded husband into taking her back, unpunished.

TFOAC showrunner David Farr and his team take a novel approach in their depiction of Helen. In a "race-blind" British production intended for global distribution, Helen is a dark-haired, dark-eyed romantic heroine whose escape from marital captivity viewers are initially encouraged to cheer.[5] The series devotes considerable screen time to Helen's experiences during the war, especially her struggle for acceptance and fear of being sent back. During its eight-episode run, however, *TFOAC* also repeatedly tests viewers' tolerance for choices that erode the nobility of Helen's cause. As the collateral damage of her quest for self-determination mounts not only on the battlefield but, unusually, in the palace, *TFOAC* reveals Helen to be far less than heroic—yet not quite a villain. This chapter traces how *TFOAC*'s Helen reflects the entertainment industry's embrace of the American-style antihero as a signature element of "Quality TV" in the current golden age of television, building especially on the work of Margrethe Bruun Vaage.

Antiheroes, "Quality TV," and the New Golden Age of Television

Media critics broadly agree that the period since the late 1990s constitutes a new golden age of television due to the variety, ambition, and exponential increase in production during an industry-wide paradigm shift related to digital technologies. The programming most associated with this development has been dubbed "Quality TV," a stylistic designation that recognizes a series' ambitions, whether or not those goals are realized.[6] This style differs from television's dominant "Least Objectionable Programming" model by aiming to attract "affluent, highly educated, urban viewers."[7] The resultant niche programming is aesthetically well crafted, populated with high-quality talent, and situated in a morally compromised world that normalizes the unconventional behavior of its protagonist(s). As the slogan adopted by a primary driver of this programming explained, "It's not TV. It's HBO."

Greater freedom to program transgressive content enabled pay cable channels to promote the most boundary-breaking "Quality TV" early on, exemplified by HBO's watershed series *The Sopranos* (1999–2007), *The Wire* (HBO, 2002–8), and *Dexter* (Showtime, 2006–2013). Basic cable and network channels chased this trend within their regulatory boundaries, with series like *The Shield* (FX, 2002–8), *Lost* (ABC, 2004–2010), *Mad Men* (AMC, 2007–2015), and *Breaking Bad* (AMC, 2008–2013), followed by streaming services like Netflix, *TFOAC*'s distributor in the United States. The critical acclaim and popularity of "Quality TV" influenced not only American but global popular culture, particularly through the symbolic value of iconic protagonists like suburban mafioso in therapy Tony Soprano, advertising executive living under an assumed identity Don Draper, and terminally ill chemistry teacher turned international drug lord Walter White.

"Quality TV" often features a distinctive type of protagonist: the antihero, a fascinating underdog battling larger forces that threaten his security, who struggles with the bad things he must do to achieve ends that the series urges viewers to see as worthy—until those choices create such collateral damage that the antihero must face a moral reckoning.[8] This antihero has come to dominate storytelling globally, given the worldwide impact of the US entertainment industry and culture generally. Series like *TFOAC*, co-produced by the BBC and the American company Netflix, highlight the cultural dimension of the "special relationship" between the United Kingdom and the United States, which is also one of the world's largest entertainment markets. This antihero boom has also attracted attention from scholars of moral psychology who study viewers' reported enjoyment of onscreen antisocial behavior and its real-world implications.[9]

Series facilitate viewer enjoyment of the antihero by offering morally plausible justifications for transgressive behavior: commonly, the protection of family.[10] For the predominantly male antiheroes of "Quality TV,"[11] this justification assumes patriarchal protection of women and children, even as the antihero's behavior endangers them. The antihero convinces himself that he can manage these risks, so viewers believe that too and align against characters who obstruct him—especially his wife, whose reasonable concerns are framed as a threatening constraint.[12] It is important to underscore that while female antiheroes can behave like male predecessors in some respects, persistent ideas about women's "traditional" or "natural" social roles can complicate what viewers will tolerate.[13] *TFOAC* presents the rare female antihero with no vocation and thus no identity beyond the domestic sphere, drawing unusual focus to Helen's trade-off: abandon her family to gain personal freedom. Although the series initially seems progressive in dramatizing this gendered bind, the antihero's arc toward moral reckoning reflects the revanchist conservatism underpinning the classical epic tradition and American-style male-centered antihero series.

Promoting Allegiance to the Antihero

Although Paris and Helen's relationship culminates in the titular "fall of a city," viewers must root for "star-crossed" lovers in such narratives; otherwise, the emotional center will not hold. *TFOAC* facilitates this partiality by establishing the lovers as protagonists, aligning viewers with their experiences and perspectives.[14] The series capitalizes on this alignment by deploying characterization strategies that build allegiance to Helen: third-party validation, aesthetic appeal, backstory, and relative morality.[15] Such strategies cushion subsequent revelations that may deter viewers from bonding to an antihero by offering permission to forgive deviations from conventional morality.

TFOAC initially aligns viewers with Paris, a favorable lens for encountering Helen. After dramatizing his cursed birth, Episode 1 ("Black Blood") announces a jump to "20 years later" and introduces Paris as a scruffy ne'er-do-well shepherd. Although hesitant to judge the divine contest, he does so in exchange for the "prize" promised by Aphrodite: "the most beautiful woman in the world . . . You'll know her when you see her." His search drives Paris to crash the Trojan princes' training and beat them in a race; they take him to the city games, where Queen Hecuba and King Priam save him from mortal combat by recognizing their long-lost son. But this louche outsider chafes at the social constraints imposed by his new royal identity, such that viewers may join King Priam's family in questioning his decision to send Paris on an embassy to Sparta.[16]

After encouraging viewers to anticipate Helen's advent, *TFOAC* teases disappointment to enhance the pleasure of seeing her. Paris rubs at the whitewashed wall of his Spartan guest quarters to reveal the image of a dark-haired woman with large naked breasts, but at dinner he sees an empty chair next to King Menelaus. "Is the queen not joining us?" Paris eventually asks. Menelaus explains, "Helen is unwell tonight" and asks to hear Paris' wondrous story. As he begins, a noise at the doorway draws focus to Helen, her heavily made-up face crowned with an intricate headdress and held high above a densely feathered gown, while birds flit around her. All rise for Helen as the camera cuts to a wide shot of the queen processing past her subjects, then toward Menelaus, who remarks on her recovery. "Curiosity defeated my tiredness," she quips, capturing the starry-eyed Paris with a glance.

Helen's entrance illustrates her spectacular appeal and skill in deploying the charismatic power attributed to her since antiquity; antiheroes benefit from this amoral characterization strategy, since aesthetic appeal and display of charismatic influence over others make a character enjoyable to watch.[17] Assuming that the queen styles herself, Helen also uses her feathered outfit to communicate what words cannot: her feeling of captivity, like a bird in a gilded cage.[18] Helen's self-representation is underlined when Paris asks about her pet birds. Helen avers that her father had allowed them to fly free in the palace, spurring Menelaus to snidely comment, "one of his little indulgences." Shots of the birds' wooden cages, and their flight from the palace upon Helen's escape, underline the symbolic relationship.

Helen's sympathetic backstory also encourages viewers to support her flight. When Paris asks Menelaus how he and his wife "got together," viewers learn how Menelaus' brother Agamemnon won Helen for him in a contest, making her a literal trophy wife. That Menelaus narrates this story while Helen sits silently beside him, eyes downcast, underlines her suppressed agency—as does her small smile, when Paris points out that Menelaus did not win Helen himself, spurring Menelaus to declares his wife "tired" and end the interview. As Helen later explains to Paris, women "don't get to select our fate"; now that Paris is royal, she cautions him, "duty will be your master, too." In this light, Helen being "tired" and "unwell" resonates with a contemporary archetype: the depressed housewife trapped in an unhappy marriage.[19]

TFOAC gives viewers further permission to support Helen's escape by establishing relative morality, when morally worse or simply unsympathetic characters cast the antihero in a comparatively favorable light.[20] Menelaus' revelation that he did not "win" his own wife diminishes his worth relative to the prize, the winner, and even Paris, whose story of defeating the Trojan princes impresses Helen. Although he is always courtly and appreciative of Helen, Menelaus' sneering manner toward Paris and controlling attitude toward Helen compound his presentation as unworthy of his wife. Considering its alignment with the free-spirited Paris and sympathy for the captive Helen, *TFOAC* encourages viewers to build allegiance to Helen and cheer her eventual escape.

Introducing the Antihero's Moral Complexity

Among characterization strategies, moral complexity differentiates hero from antihero. The antihero knows right from wrong, selectively violates those categories, yet retains the sympathy of viewers who agree that these violations are justified; in fact, dismissing conventional good/bad moral polarity creates enjoyable suspense because viewers cannot predict the antihero's behavior.[21] *TFOAC* creates this ambiguity through another spectacle that imbricates Helen's cultural identity in her captivity narrative. Later that night, a sleepless Paris follows the sound of reedy, percussive music to a room draped with colorful fabric. He covertly observes a gathering of women loosely draped in white cloth, some lounging on the floor while others gyrate languidly. Hair unbound, robe loosened, Helen presides over this nocturnal court while smoking from a communal opium pipe and laughing sensually. Then she turns her head and sees the peeping Paris, who startles, caught in her gaze. Only when she breaks eye contact does he back away.

This scene crystallizes *TFOAC*'s complication of Helen by presenting her as Other, playing on the enduring, and problematic, power of Orientalism in the Western (post-) colonial imagination. While *TFOAC*'s production design is generically primitivistic and orientalizing, only Helen is situated in explicit visual quotations of nineteenth-century European colonial fantasies; here, of the harem as a secluded space where feminine sensuality is on display for male consumption.[22] Actress Bella Dayne's dark hair and eyes differentiate her look from the series' other non-Black actors, as does the German actress' pronunciation, compared to her British castmates. *TFOAC* even puts an orientalizing spin on Helen as "unhappy housewife" by making her "mother's little helper" an opium pipe, recalling the drug-addicted Cleopatra in HBO's *Rome* (2005–2007).[23] Helen's Spartan wardrobe, laden with feathers and seashells, reflects what Menelaus derisively calls Sparta's "wilderness." "I've done my best to tame it," he confides to Paris, after waxing nostalgic for the "real culture" of his hometown. All the while, Menelaus is shadowed by a slave carrying a parasol, like Batiatus at the salt mines in *Spartacus* (1960). Although Otherness is frequently correlated with diminished moral standing, within *TFOAC*'s relative morality Helen's depiction as an oppressed Other, combined with her aesthetic appeal, renders her preferable to the colonizer Menelaus.

The feminine submissiveness entailed in the harem fantasy intersects with *TFOAC*'s interest in Helen's suppressed agency. Paris' voyeurism reserves control for the desiring male subject and diminishes the woman into the object of his intrusive gaze. The colonial fantasy of the harem amplifies those dynamics by fetishizing female vulnerability as the Other's cultural norm. But Helen up-ends those expectations when, rather than raise the alarm upon spotting Paris, she commits the small rebellion of allowing this outsider to invade her intimate space, even holding him in her gaze. The series ascribes similar power to her later in Episode 1, in another sexualized orientalizing setting: the hammam. In a sequence staged for viewers' visual pleasure, Helen's hypnotic chanting becomes voice-over for a montage sequence that intercuts shots of a sexually frustrated Paris in bed with shots of Helen's naked body in a soft-core bathing scene that recalls nineteenth-century colonialist paintings, and the 1971 Helen's seductive introduction.[24]

TFOAC promptly balances its complicating nocturnal revelation with assurances that Helen recognizes conventional morality. The next day, Helen uses the myth of Actaeon—a man torn to pieces for spying on a bathing goddess—to warn Paris privately against seeing what is forbidden and to assert her power over him. But Paris suggests that Actaeon's punishment was "worth it," calling Helen's bluff: expose and punish him, or remain complicit by concealing his violation. By saying nothing, she implicitly chooses complicitly, but at dinner she retaliates by giving Paris the silent treatment before again confronting him privately. Within minutes, however, she is quivering to accept his kiss, because he alone has seen her: not just her body, but her yearning for freedom. Only a messenger announcing the death of Menelaus' father breaks the spell of desire, and Helen reverts to her "dutiful wife" persona.

TFOAC's first episode concludes with Helen staking out these moral extremes. After Menelaus departs for his father's funeral Helen withdraws from view, to Paris' frustration. After a Zeus-driven storm prevents his premature departure, Helen summons Paris to a secluded bower, where she soliloquizes on her lovesickness before inviting him to have sex. The next morning, she abandons him there after nearby voices risk their discovery and withdraws again, spurring the enraged Paris' departure—but not before Helen's slave entrusts him with a giant wooden chest: a gift for his mother, supposedly. Paris' quizzical look indicates that he has not been included in what viewers can see is Helen's escape plan, despite his clearly being willing. Viewers may admire Helen's authorship and agency, even if she uses underhanded tactics—can you blame her, in such a complicated situation? Antihero series continually ask viewers to assess that question.

Reality Checks and Re-allegiance in Sparta

By presenting Helen's freedom-loving rule-breaking as not only excusable but admirable, *TFOAC* authorizes viewers to enjoy vicariously the carnivalesque thrill of the antihero's transgression, or "fictional relief."[25] This escapist fantasy is literalized in Helen's flight from patriarchal captivity and motivated by her hunger for self-determination, a value that viewers are likely to share. But personal autonomy is not the only value that matters. An antihero's choices will thus periodically trigger a "reality check" that challenges viewers' allegiance.[26] For the series to continue, viewers must have reasons to morally accommodate such behavior, resulting in "cyclical re-allegiance."[27] *TFOAC* deploys its first reality check in Episode 1, the day after Paris' nocturnal voyeurism, by revealing that Helen has a teenage daughter named Hermione. Prior Trojan War screen adaptations disregarded this well-attested but inconvenient character, whom the series ages up from her traditional pre-war infancy such that the twenty-year-old Paris may be closer in age to teenage Hermione than her mother.

This novel love triangle engages with contemporary discourses around sexual relationships between older women and younger men. As the mother flirting with her teenage daughter's gentleman caller, viewers may perceive Helen as a "cougar," a term that pathologizes older women's desire for younger men as predatory even when women reclaim it.[28] Paris' pursuit renders Helen a "MILF" ("mother I'd like to fuck"). This type, popularized in the United States by the teen sex comedy *American Pie* (1999) and Fountains of Wayne's hit pop song and video "Stacy's Mom" (2003), ignores women's subjectivity while expanding the range of acceptable objects for male desire to include the formerly taboo.[29] Jo Littler has explicitly critiqued the British version of the MILF, the "yummy mummy," as the product of popular conservatism.[30]

Using Hermione to generate a reality check also raises the question of what maternity means to Helen. Revealing Helen's daughter as Paris' intended wife not only complicates Helen and Paris' romance, it puts Hermione in unwinnable competition against her mother during her own courtship (Fig. 4.1). Helen appears indifferent to this demoralizing asymmetry, as she is to Hermione in general. Helen shows neither affection toward her daughter, regarding her impassively and barely touching her, nor empathy for her daughter's vulnerability, despite Helen's own difficult courtship; as Hermione tells Paris, "She refused all offers until her father forced her to take a husband." Nor does Helen refrain from overshadowing her daughter in extravagant, breast-revealing outfits and deploying her "skill" with men, as the comparatively ordinary Hermione terms her mother's *modus operandi*.

Helen pays attention to her daughter only when Paris provokes her, and not to Hermione's benefit. At the dinner where Helen ignores him, Paris retaliates by suggesting that he get better acquainted with Hermione. Menelaus directs his daughter to show

Sympathy for Troy's Jezebel: Helen as Antihero

Figure 4.1 Hermione (Grace Hogg-Robinson) is ill-equipped to compete with Helen (Bella Dayne) for the attention of Paris (Louis Hunter) in Episode 1, "Black Blood."

their guest the "Chamber of Silks."[31] As Hermione recounts to Paris, "these were a gift from an Indian king. He tried to buy my mother's hand. She turned him down." Surrounded by manifestations of her mother's worth, Hermione has just confessed her feelings of inadequacy to Paris when Helen makes another entrance. She banishes a resentful Hermione for "mak[ing] a fool of yourself," then rebukes Paris for "playing games" with a girl. Is she motivated by protective maternal instinct? Or by jealousy, as Paris transparently intended? When Menelaus insists that Paris stay while he attends his father's funeral, Helen withdraws to her chambers, leaving her daughter to host the sullen Paris. After Helen and Paris have sex in her bower, she again uses Hermione to deflect his pressure to run away: "I have a daughter. I can't just walk away. She doesn't deserve that."

As when she confronted Paris over his voyeurism, *TFOAC* reassures viewers that Helen understands conventional morality; here, maternal duty to prioritize her child's good. Even during post-coital pillow talk with Hermione's would-be fiancé, Helen shies away from publicly violating social expectations, even if it means staying in a forced marriage with an unworthy man. In family melodrama, suffering for a beloved child validates a mother's honor. But Helen frames maternal care through the lens of deserts, not affective bonds, and such maternal self-sacrifice has come under pressure from feminism's critique of patriarchal structures and ethics, fueled by Western liberalism's emphasis on the rights of the individual, including the pursuit of happiness. While some welcome challenges to misogynist structures that functionally imprison women in gendered service to others, others regard women's liberation as cause for moral panic, decrying abandonment of their "natural" role as selfless caregiver.

Screening Love and War in *Troy: Fall of a City*

The series' unusual decision to position Helen in this love triangle necessarily provokes controversy around her choice as a mother. *TFOAC* signals its awareness of feminist critique in Paris' response to her self-abnegating rhetoric: "What do *you* deserve?" In Helen's situation, this discourse of deserts signals the influence of Oprah Winfrey's media empire and the women's self-care industry it has fostered. Winfrey's core audience, formed during her career in daytime television, consists of women likely to identify with this gendered moral bind. As Marjorie Jolles summarizes in her study of Winfrey's "What I Know for Sure" column in *O Magazine*, such pop culture versions of American feminist thought draw from modern liberal theory that celebrates self-determination as the superior path to selfhood.[32]

Jolles also notes a dark side to Winfrey's paradigm of empowerment. The reward for achieving self-knowledge and autonomy is the romantic love that all women deserve, but potentially at the cost of defying social expectations, even detaching from relationships that hinder self-actualization. When Menelaus asks in Episode 2 what he did to deserve such treatment, Helen responds flatly, "Nothing. I found love. That's all. One day, perhaps, you'll understand." In Episode 3, she opines that Hermione will be better off without her, observing "Not all women are designed for motherhood . . . I never found it easy to be a mother." As Jolles notes, feminist theorists have rejected this pop culture view that being true to oneself requires rejecting all ties and commitments. Still, a woman who rejects maternity to pursue personal ends still risks being demonized—especially those who become "walk-away moms."[33]

Viewers who recognize women's right to the goods of contemporary Western liberal ideology may applaud Paris' promotion of freedom and happiness, and Helen's bravery in taking her chance at both. *TFOAC* also justifies Helen's alienation from her daughter by casting an actress who looks nothing like Helen but resembles Menelaus, who affectionately praises Hermione as "beautiful . . . with brains to match." When this "daddy's girl" mentions obliquely how her mother's "skill" has impacted other male visitors, viewers may dismiss sourpuss Hermione as a moody teenager going through the phase of hating her mother, perhaps even rationalizing that Hermione is old enough for Helen to leave. The plot's momentum toward Paris and Helen's union, supported by viewers' narrative alignment with Paris' desires and by sympathy for Helen's bind, obscures Helen's disregard for her daughter's needs. When Episode 2 begins by juxtaposing an unsympathetic Hermione tattling to her father with romantic rebels Paris and Helen clasping hands, *TFOAC* indicates where viewers' sympathy should reside.

Reality Checks and Re-allegiance in Troy

Helen's new beginning in Troy is promptly troubled by *TFOAC* deploying the obvious reality check: her presence endangers the city. Helen needs political support to stay, and *TFOAC* foregrounds the complicating role of gender in her attempt to secure it, pointedly pitting Helen against another woman. In the private royal chambers, Hecuba pragmatically assesses Paris and Helen's choice as a foolish, selfish risk to Trojan security and tells Priam "she must go back." At this moment, Helen makes an entrance, in a flowing white gown and dripping with cowrie shells—and against the king's express orders. Helen ignores Hecuba's outrage at her "nerve" and makes her case in explicitly gendered terms:

> I hear, my queen, that you rule Troy alongside your husband. That in this city, man and woman are equal in respect and power. I *humbly* claim that respect now. I was married at 14 against my will to a man I had not met and would never love. Not for one moment have I been happy with Menelaus. I didn't choose him and never would have. I do choose to be with your son. I'm not a possession. I'm a woman.

How can Hecuba send Helen back to a hated marriage she was forced into as a girl and still uphold Troy's principle of women's equality?[34] After Hecuba's downcast eyes show the chastening effect of Helen's rhetorical performance, the camera follows Helen out of the room, reinforcing allegiance to her and against the hypocritical Hecuba, who valued national security over the women's rights that she herself enjoys.

TFOAC's portrayal of Trojans as supporting women's self-determination puts a contemporary twist on the post-Vergilian convention of rendering them, rather than the Greeks, as sympathetic protagonists. The "good" (proto-Roman) Trojans who defend women against "bad" Greeks map onto Western societies that championed the rights of women in Middle Eastern countries that the United States proposed to invade after the 9/11 terrorist attacks.[35] Helen shares similar appearance, backstory, and goals with another contemporary refraction of this "War on Terror" archetype: the Yemeni woman Hanin in Season 1 of Amazon's *Jack Ryan* (2018–). Like Helen, Hanin's father married her off young to a "bad guy" in their warrior society, an anti-US militant. When she flees her controlling husband's compound, his relentless pursuit is hampered after Hanin comes under the protection of the United States, personified by White male CIA agent Jack Ryan. Hanin's flight is also complicated by maternity. When her son remains loyal to his father, like "daddy's girl" Hermione, an anguished Hanin flees with her daughters. Her maternal devotion likely enhances her moral status with viewers, rendering Hanin a sympathetic Other in this "white savior" narrative.[36]

TFOAC reskins this narrative for Helen's world but, unlike Hanin, Helen tries to erase her maternity, which generates reality checks suggesting her monstrosity. In Episode 2, Andromache points out to her husband, "She left her own daughter, Hector. What kind of a woman does that?" Although traditionally imagined as a mother due to her appearance with baby Astyanax in *Iliad* Book 6, *TFOAC*'s Andromache begins the series desperately childless, uniquely positioning her to recognize Helen's selfishness. When she tries to befriend Helen in Episode 3 by asking about her daughter, Helen speaks of Hermione in the past tense and coldly shrugs off their separation as better for her daughter. Through her disgust, Andromache recognizes the manipulative power of Helen's "charm" and departs in anger. Even though Helen has shared a pregnancy-inducing wine, Andromache is not transactional, so she cannot overlook Helen's moral violation. Such moral integrity counts against a character who threatens the antihero's success, and *TFOAC* undermines Andromache's credibility by rendering her an unlikeable messenger, like Hermione: plain, anxious, and defective as a woman in her own eyes.

TFOAC stages another reality check by asserting that Helen's happiness comes at the expense of another family, when Agamemnon seeks divine favor for the war by sacrificing his daughter Iphigenia.[37] She and her mother Clytemnestra believe that Agamemnon has summoned her to marry Achilles, similar to Hermione's strategic alliance with Paris—and equally doomed. A montage sequence intercuts shots of Clytemnestra's anguished rage upon realizing what is happening and Agamemnon repeatedly screaming "why?" over his daughter's corpse with Helen enjoying sex with Paris and proclaiming herself "happy." This visual rhetoric implies that the cost of daughter-discarding Helen "living her best life" is paid with Clytemnestra's maternity, Agamemnon's sanity, and the life of another marriageable girl.

TFOAC attempts to rebalance Helen's standing by deploying relative morality, presenting Helen in a metaphorically maternal role that shows up the Trojans' insufficient care for their subjects. Once the Greeks' siege depletes Troy's grain supply (Episode 3), Priam and the courtier Pandarus enact strict rationing and punishment to deter scofflaws. Making one of her now-signature disruptive entrances, Helen schools the Trojans on her father's theory of good and bad royal families, declaring that she will distribute her share of grain to the people. When the crowd hesitates to accept her gift, she acknowledges that she too thinks she is the cause of Troy's troubles. A woman steps forth to call what she did "brave" and name her "Helen of Troy," authorizing others come forward, to Helen's delight. This kind of charity work echoes Princess Margaery's maternal populism in *Game of Thrones* 3.1 ("Valar Dohaeris"), which references Princess Diana's highly publicized charity work.[38] What's the sacrifice of a few, when Helen feeds a whole city?

From Rubicon to Reckoning: Accountability for the Antihero

Eventually, the antihero commits a transgression that becomes the point of no return, leading to unforgivable collateral damage. When moral judgment overtakes viewers' partiality for the antihero, a reckoning becomes inevitable.[39] Helen's Rubicon moment restages her "original sin" in Sparta. Achilles infiltrates Troy and ambushes Helen alone in her chambers, even threatening sexual assault while he interrogates her (Episode 3). Helen admirably maintains self-control during Achilles' attack, then shames him with her charismatic rhetoric until he leaves—as witnessed by one slave, with whom Helen makes eye contact. Yet she does not alert the Trojans to Achilles' infiltration of the city or interrogation of her.

Unfortunately, Helen unwittingly revealed the location of a secret military operation: Andromache's hometown Cilicia, which is preparing to supply the besieged Troy through a tunnel. Achilles later reveals that he left without Helen because he gained this information. Helen's silence thus renders her complicit in a major disaster, for both Troy and Andromache personally. News of Cilicia's destruction raises fear of a traitor in the palace; still, Helen says nothing (Episode 4). She tries to bribe the slave who witnessed Achilles' departure from her chambers but he returns the bauble, unwilling to be complicit in treason: another reality check on Helen's moral drift (Episode 5).

Helen's self-preservation instinct drives her to conspire with yet another Greek who infiltrates Troy, Odysseus' slave Xanthius. After Achilles charges him with watching over Helen, Xanthius murders the loyal Trojan slave (Episode 5). He later explains his mandate to Helen and warns her about Pandarus' investigation, but she angrily rejects his help—while also not revealing the presence of this second Greek spy. When she realizes Pandarus has evidence against her, Helen enjoins Xanthius to expel him from the city without hurting him but refuses to let the Greek into the palace: "that would be treason." Xanthius states bluntly that Pandarus will find out the truth if she doesn't, so Helen complies, enabling him to not only kill Pandarus but also to frame the loyal man as the traitor (Episode 5). Should viewers overlook Helen's indirect responsibility for these crimes, *TFOAC* raises the stakes when Xanthius is captured (Episode 7). Helen contrives to watch Paris interrogate him, allowing viewers to observe her mute terror at the possibility of being exposed. To cover her tracks, Helen helps Xanthius to murder the guard and escape (Episode 7).

TFOAC's screen predecessors provide an avenue by which Helen may yet prove herself worthy of viewers' allegiance: surrender herself to the Greeks, as Helen claimed to have attempted in Euripides' *Trojan Women* (955–8). While they also adopt Thucydides' *realpolitik* view of Agamemnon's true motive being imperialistic avarice, what matters for characterization is Helen's belief that her self-sacrifice would end the war.[40] The 1956 Helen makes a serious attempt, meeting the Greek leaders by day with an official Trojan escort, until Agamemnon's unexpected demand for crushing reparations scuttles the deal; by contrast, the 2004 Helen sneaks away alone by night only to be intercepted by Hector, who assures her of the futility of the gesture before sending her back to Paris. Episode 2 of *TFOAC* ends with a distressed Helen trying to surrender after the first bloody day of war, until Paris catches her crossing the battlefield. "I can't be responsible" for more deaths, she cries, only to be turned around by Paris' plea that love "is worth fighting for." Episode 3 begins with Helen and Paris' wedding, and Hecuba's reassurance that Helen's sacrifice would have been fruitless.

Unusually, Helen makes a second attempt to surrender. After Paris recoils from her suggestion that they run away and abandon the city to its doom, proving correct Xanthius' observation that the Trojan prince no longer values her only, she helps the spy escape so that he can convey her surrender to Menelaus (Episode 7). She sets one condition: "no one else in the city is to be harmed." While her self-possession and care for others remain admirable, Helen's belief that she can extract concessions from a man whom she has so publicly humiliated may strike some viewers as delusional—much as Helen's earlier assurance to Paris that "this will be over without war . . . I have to believe it" (Episode 2). Self-delusion to justify improper behavior is a common quality among antiheroes.[41] By attempting to broker a peace on her own, Helen betrays Troy and Paris—whatever her intent.

Helen's reckoning arrives with the horse effigy that the Trojans find on the beach instead of the Greek army—the day after she agreed to surrender (Episode 8). Once again, Helen knows information that would undermine the explanation offered by Thersites, the spy whom the Greeks "left behind" as a "sacrifice," along with the last of their supplies stored in the horse. When Paris pokes the belly, grain falls out: a callback to Helen's "maternal" charity in Episode 3. Helen observes in silence as the Trojans wonder at the horse, drag it into the city, and celebrate the war's end. When Thersites sidles up during the festivities to inform her that it's time to go, Helen breathes, "I can't. Please, get me out of this," as she had to Paris in Episode 2 when she feared expulsion from Troy: "Help me. Get me out. I can't go back." Helen's attempt to renege on her deal with Menelaus and save herself, at the expense of Troy and Paris, should further erode viewers' allegiance—especially after Thersites smirks that he's too "thick-skinned" for her "charm."

The failure of Helen's charismatic manipulation marks the beginning of her end. Once more, costuming guides viewers' perception: Helen's scarlet gown identifies her as a Jezebel, pilloried for flaunting her sexuality against patriarchal norms and leaving a path of destruction in her wake, in the tradition of Bette Davis in *Jezebel* (1938) and Scarlett O'Hara in *Gone with the Wind* (1939).[42] Helen complies with Thersites by first distracting the horse's guards so that Odysseus can quietly kill them, then ordering other guards to open the gates. When she meets Menelaus, Helen fails to perceive his acquiescence to her terms as a lie. Once the gates are open, she is surprised to see the Greek army. After the Greeks storm the city, she is forced to witness the consequences of her actions upon people she claimed to care for: Paris, gutted by Menelaus on their conjugal bed after learning how she betrayed Troy; Andromache's longed-for infant, crushed by Odysseus; Troy's smoking hulk, which Helen regards despondently from the deck of Menelaus' ship before bowing her head in defeat.

Conclusion: Sympathy for Troy's Jezebel?

After this brutal reckoning, whither viewers' sympathy for this Jezebel of Troy? According to Jason Mittell, an antihero series' conclusion must "offer (or actively refuse) a moral position toward the characters' behaviors."[43] Some series redeem an antihero and allow him to escape punishment (e.g., *Mad Men*'s Don Draper), while others subject an antihero to constraints he sought to avoid (e.g., *The Shield*'s Vic Mackey). Helen's return to Sparta places her in the second category. While offering viewers the option to pity the grime-stained woman, by characterizing Helen as an antihero *TFOAC* denies her the nobility of the 1956 Helen, whose "true love" for Paris assumes a salvific quality that allows her to transcend her bodily captivity. *TFOAC* Helen's styling in the last episodes also highlights her Otherness by darkening her make-up, just as the now-widowed Andromache publicly accuses Helen of treason. What saves Helen from villainy is her lack of intent to do harm and belief that all she does is necessary, if grievous, as the series' many shots of her prettily distraught visage communicate.

As for the popular-feminist causes that Helen and Troy latterly embodied, viewers may perceive the downfall of both as invalidating those principles. The Helen who stakes her asylum claim on the moral necessity of women's self-determination is delegitimized by harming countless other women in pursuing her self-gratification. Only when Paris refuses to abandon his family and city to run away with her does Helen suddenly care about Hermione, whose abandonment she throws in Paris' face. Indeed, Helen's most significant reality checks come as and/or from other women, inciting *TFOAC*'s gendered tensions, even as the series condemns the Greeks for their misogyny. Yet, tellingly, *TFOAC* refrains from portraying Menelaus as overtly abusive of his wife in Sparta, denying its Helen the moral leverage that all three prior screen epics deployed, domestic violence being the sword that cuts the Gordian knot of patriarchal authority.

The series that began with Paris' cursed birth ends by framing Helen as the cause of his death and Troy's fall. The disproportionate value she places on her own happiness at the expense of others, her skillful manipulations through charisma and deceit, her betrayal of those who help her and participation in murder, all mark Helen's behavior as sociopathic. Narcissism, Machiavellian intelligence, and psychopathy—the "dark triad" of antisocial personality traits—figure prominently in antihero behavior, and Helen is no exception.[44] Paris provided encouragement and opportunity, but even her manner of escape showed that she never took this young naif as a true partner, despite her professed love for him. Her moral hollowness contrasts with her repeatedly emphasized intelligence: if Helen failed to predict the outcome of her choice to leave Sparta, it was because she chose not to. Although Helen's comeuppance should entail a larger restoration of moral order, the series' ultimately tragic worldview has no place for moral certitude, let alone women's agency—much like the populist patriarchal authoritarianism that has swept the globe on the heels of the American-style antihero.

Notes

1. Thank you to Monica Cyrino and Antony Augoustakis for including this chapter in their volume, and to audiences at the annual meetings of Film & History (2018), the Classical Association of the Middle West and South (2019), the Classical Association of the Atlantic States (2019), and the Southwest Popular and American Culture Association (2020) for their feedback on various aspects of this project.
2. Maguire 2009, Blondell 2013a.
3. Günsberg 2004: 97–132.
4. Cyrino 2007, Winkler 2009: 210–50, Blondell 2009, Vivante 2013, Nikoloutsos 2015.
5. See Kennedy in this volume.
6. Thompson 1997, McCabe and Akass 2007, Newman and Levine 2012.
7. Vaage 2016: xii.
8. Mittell 2015: 142–63, Vaage 2016.
9. Vaage 2016: 1–38 and *passim*.
10. Vaage 2016: *passim*.
11. Lotz 2014, Vaage 2016: *passim*.

12. Vaage 2016: 150–81.
13. Tally 2016.
14. Vaage 2016: 39–63.
15. Mittell 2015: 142–63, Vaage 2016: 90–119.
16. On Priam's leadership, see Cooke in this volume.
17. Blondell 2013a: 1–26, Mittell 2015: 144–5, Vaage 2016: 105–6.
18. See the chapters by Jenkins and Raucci in this volume.
19. Wollersheim 2015.
20. Mittell 2015: 143.
21. Vaage 2016: 103–5.
22. Yeazell 2000.
23. Thanks to Emma Scioli and Jaclyn Neel for these observations.
24. Pasin 2016, Vivante 2013: 40–2.
25. Vaage 2013 and 2016: *passim*.
26. Vaage 2013 and 2016: *passim*.
27. García 2016.
28. E.g., Gibson 2002, *Cougar Town* 2009–2015; Alarie and Carmichael 2015.
29. Friedman 2014.
30. Littler 2013.
31. On Menelaus and Hermione, see also Burns in this volume.
32. Jolles 2007.
33. Seidel 2013, Drexler 2011, 2013.
34. See the chapters by Jenkins and Day in this volume.
35. Ayotte and Husain 2005.
36. Ngangura 2018.
37. See the chapters by Burns and Norgard in this volume.
38. British viewers may see broader influence of Diana Spencer's public career in *TFOAC*'s depiction of a royal wife who walks away from a controlling marriage.
39. Mittell 2015: 147–8.
40. Rabel 1984.
41. Mittell 2015: 160–2.
42. On the White Jezebel as a "belle gone bad," see Fra-Lopéz 2010; on its epigonal "Lady in Red" trope, see www.tvtropes.org/pmwiki/pmwiki.php/Main/LadyInRed.
43. Mittell 2015: 148.
44. Jonason *et al.* 2012.

CHAPTER 5
THE CURSE OF TROY: ODYSSEUS' STORY
Emma J. Stafford

Well before *Troy: Fall of a City* (2018) had finished airing on the BBC and landed on Netflix in April 2018, speculation was rife about a possible sequel based on the *Odyssey*, already commissioned from writer David Farr.[1] A strong hint is provided in the final episode of the series, which ends with a twenty-five-second shot of Odysseus gazing back at Troy from the stern of his ship as it sails away, the camera panning from a full back-view to dwell for the final eight seconds on a close-up on his bloodstained, ravaged face (Fig. 5.1).

He already seems to be bearing the curse that Andromache has pronounced on him— "May Troy be the curse that follows you all your life." The series thus ends on an ominous note, rather than on the potentially more hopeful indication of Aeneas' escape with Briseis, young Evander and Hesion, after Paris has exhorted him, "You have to live, for all of us." In this chapter, I will consider the story arc which leads Odysseus to this point, making comparisons with other onscreen adaptations of the character. According to Verreth's brief survey, Odysseus was one of the first Greek heroes to feature in film, in Georges Méliès' four-minute *L'île de Calypso* (1905), and has subsequently appeared in more than eighty movies, some telling parts of the Trojan War myth, others inserting the hero into stories of modern invention.[2] Here I refer in particular to three of the films which cover more or less the same narrative as *TFOAC*. Wolfgang Petersen's *Troy* (2004) is an obvious comparator, its Iliadic story framed by a pair of voice-overs by Sean Bean's

Figure 5.1 Odysseus (Joseph Mawle) sails away from Troy at the end of Episode 8, "Offering."

Screening Love and War in *Troy: Fall of a City*

Odysseus (2004), his character and role recently analyzed by Louden.[3] Also useful is the Hallmark mini-series *The Odyssey* (1997), directed by Andrei Konchalovsky and starring Armand Assante: the first half-hour in fact relates the pre-*Odyssey* part of the story, from Odysseus' summons from Ithaca to the fall of Troy. Robert Wise's *Helen of Troy* (1956), while starting and ending at the same points in the Trojan War story as *TFOAC*, focuses on the romance between Helen and Paris to the exclusion of much of the Iliadic narrative, but does nonetheless briefly sketch a character for Torin Thatcher's Ulysses.[4] I shall conclude with some thoughts on the extent to which Season 1 prepares the ground for a Season 2.

Establishing Odysseus' Credentials

Louden argues that *Troy* (2004) "presents an Odysseus who remains largely Homeric," fulfilling much the same role as he does in the *Iliad*, but with additional reference to his characterization in the *Odyssey*, in keeping with the film's emphasis on survival.[5] Much the same can be said of *TFOAC*'s Odysseus, as we shall see, though with some important differences.

Odysseus does not appear in person until Episode 2, but his name is first mentioned in Episode 1, in a scene which, though brief, already has implications for his standing amongst the Greek leaders. During the embassy to Sparta, Paris is presented with gifts: "Odysseus of Ithaca sends his greatest tributes and affections, along with the finest alabaster from Syria, lapis lazuli from Bactria, and jasper from Minoa." Though clearly uninterested in the formal proceedings, Paris dutifully responds: "All of Troy is grateful and pays tribute to the great king Odysseus." Only two such presentations are made, the second being from Agamemnon. This scene thus identifies the two kings who, with Menelaus, will soon emerge as leaders of the Greeks.

We first actually see Odysseus in Episode 2, which strikingly invokes the relatively obscure myth of the Ithacan king feigning madness to avoid joining the Greek expedition. This story was related in the *Cypria*, the poem of the Epic Cycle which covered events leading up to the Trojan War, but it only survives in full in a handful of relatively late sources.[6] As Prince points out, the scene immediately establishes Odysseus as a family man, foreshadowing the concern with homecoming which motivates him throughout the series, providing some level of explanation for even his most questionable of actions.[7] The importance of family and home is likewise highlighted by the opening scene of *The Odyssey* (1997), in which Armand Assante's Odysseus runs to assist Penelope (Greta Scacchi), caught out in the Ithacan countryside by the onset of labor, arriving just in time to deliver the baby Telemachus in Eumaeus' hut. Throughout the mini-series, the action at Troy and on Odysseus' homeward journey is intercut with brief scenes on Ithaca, charting Telemachus' growing up, the grief of Anticlea (the magnificent Irene Pappas), and the arrival of the suitors—all leading up to Odysseus' homecoming. The original release of *Troy* (2004) does not cover Odysseus' recruitment, but the director's cut, released in 2007, includes a scene on Ithaca in which Odysseus tricks Agamemnon's ambassadors into thinking he is someone else. As Louden suggests, this "appears to glance at" the madness episode but has more in common with the *Odyssey*'s series of disguises and recognitions.⁸

In *Helen of Troy* (1956), the Greek leaders are already gathering at Sparta, rather than Aulis, before Helen's elopement, the original point of the expedition being economic gain. Ulysses' preference for plowing the fields of Ithaca is reported as a matter for mirth, as is Achilles' traditional attempt to avoid recruitment by dressing as a girl. Our first actual sight of Ulysses is in the aftermath of the discovery of the lovers' escape, when he is immediately characterized as devious by his backing up of Agamemnon's announcement that he will be the Greeks' leader: "Quite, quite, Agamemnon. And I will follow you. (*Aside*) And tell you what to do, as usual." *The Odyssey* (1997) omits the gathering of the Greek forces at Aulis altogether. The same is true of *Troy* (2004), in which the episode is effectively replaced by one depicting the recruitment of Achilles at Phtia (*sic*): Odysseus is sent by the triumvirate of Agamemnon, Menelaus, and Nestor as "the one man Achilles will listen to." This fits with the film's focus on Brad Pitt's Achilles, and apparent lack of concern with Agamemnon's backstory, while also establishing the character of Sean Bean's Odysseus as the persuasive facilitator of others' search for glory—a role hinted at in the questions of his opening voice-over, "will our actions echo across the centuries?" Playfully berated by Achilles for underhand techniques he responds: "You have your sword; I have my tricks." While *Troy* (2004)'s Odysseus has a significant part to play in the subsequent action, it is the relationship between Agamemnon and Achilles which drives the action.

In *TFOAC*, by contrast, events at Aulis are crucial to the subsequent action, and to the characterization of both Odysseus and Agamemnon. As Prince argues in detail, Odysseus' role in the sacrifice of Iphigenia establishes the complexity of his character in relation to the ethics of war.⁹ His relentless pragmatism in the face of Agamemnon's very human reluctance to kill his daughter makes him less sympathetic to a twenty-first-century audience than the earlier scene on Ithaca might have led us to expect, but an ancient audience would probably have applauded his understanding of the inevitability of the gods' will.¹⁰ The sequence at Aulis also immediately confirms Odysseus' preeminent position amongst the Greek leaders. On his arrival, Nestor (Peter Butler) declares him to be "the best strategist we have," and his influence over the vacillating Agamemnon is clear. It is at Aulis, too, that we first very briefly meet Odysseus' men Xanthius (David Avery) and Thersites (Waldemar Schulz). The former is signaled as trustworthy by Odysseus' reliance on him to keep Achilles out of the way, and by his friendly interaction with the dog which is to play a part later. The latter's insubordination—"Going behind the great fighter's back? He'll love that!"—labels him as a difficult character and presages later acts of disloyalty, although he will nonetheless play a significant part in Troy's fall. Ultimately, both men, and indeed the dog, will be on Odysseus' boat ready for the return journey to Ithaca.¹¹ To an extent this Thersites is inspired by his Iliadic namesake, who speaks out against Agamemnon and is put down by Odysseus, both verbally and physically (*Iliad* 2.211–77), but his role here is much extended.¹²

Odysseus' front-ranking position is again apparent as the Greek fleet arrives at Troy, the broad impression of the seascape being offset by close-ups on the faces of Odysseus,

Menelaus, and Achilles. The same faces are likewise picked out a little later as Agamemnon rouses the troops for battle, and it is the same three leaders, too, who make the initial embassy to Priam's court. Odysseus here is the voice of diplomacy, trying to hold Menelaus' explosive hostility in check; he smoothly shifts tactics when the Greeks' initial offer is rejected, and even exhorts Priam to "Make a counter-offer!" as they depart—at which Hecuba urges him to "Leave, and take your smooth tongue with you!" David Gyasi's Achilles is silent throughout the encounter, until he offers a parting "We *will* be back." The scene establishes this Odysseus as living up to the Homeric epithets "nimble-witted" (*polymētis*) and "wily" (*polytropos*), and his Iliadic role as the Greeks' foremost diplomat and persuasive speaker. While not directly narrated in the *Iliad*, such an embassy is referred back to as having taken place before the start of the war, in the scene where Priam and Helen are on the ramparts surveying the Greek heroes ahead of the duel between Menelaus and Paris (*Iliad* 3.191–224). Helen describes Odysseus as "knowing all kinds of tricks and cunning stratagems" (3.202), to which the Trojan Antenor adds his memories of the embassy, emphasizing Odysseus' extraordinary skill: Menelaus "spoke fluently" (3.213), but "when he projected his great voice from his chest, and words like snowflakes on a winter's day, then no other mortal man could rival Odysseus" (3.221–3).[13]

Odysseus is one of the heroes picked out for a blessing by the goddesses who walk amongst the troops as they prepare for their first major clash, hailed by his traditional patron Athena: "Odysseus, leader of the high-hearted men of Kephalonian Ithaca, I bless you." He comes into his own, however, only after the failure of Agamemnon's overly-optimistic initial tactics. The brief scene in which the humbled Agamemnon directly asks for Odysseus' help—"Tell me what to do!"—is framed by Odysseus' complaint to Nestor about the futility of the day's fighting: "We didn't make one inch of ground . . . I'll be an old man before I see home again," and his subsequent succinct report, "He's agreed."

Odysseus *Polytropos*: Real Leader of the Greeks?

The superiority of Odysseus' tactics over those of Agamemnon is seen at the beginning of Episode 3. Not only are the Trojans debating how best to manage rationing within the hard-pressed city, but Priam even exclaims: "Odysseus is strangling the life out of us to provoke a reaction"—apparently recognizing the architect of their suffering. Back in the Greek camp, Odysseus' pragmatism is again to the fore when he remonstrates with Menelaus for his precipitate killing of a Trojan captive: "Was that necessary? He could have been helpful." Menelaus' irate response, "You get my fucking wife back!," perhaps suggests that even his own brother has more faith in Odysseus than in Agamemnon to bring the expedition to a successful conclusion.

It is the next two scenes in the Greek camp, however, that reveal Odysseus' real cunning and long-term thinking. The dog, a German shepherd, which we have seen sent out from Troy via a secret tunnel by the "Thracian trader Telamon" finds his way to Odysseus, who greets it in a friendly fashion, explaining that it is from his own household.

The Curse of Troy: Odysseus' Story

Any viewer familiar with the *Odyssey* is immediately put in mind of the old dog Argos who is one of the first mortal beings to recognize Odysseus on his return to Ithaca, wagging his tail, and for whose state of neglect Odysseus sheds a tear (*Odyssey* 17.290–327). Argos is likewise conjured by the presence of a dog in the director's-cut scene from *Troy*, our attention drawn by a close-up on the pair accompanying Odysseus' remark, "Well ... I'm gonna miss my dog."[14] Here in *TFOAC* suspense is built by a cutaway to Hector and Paris' journey in search of help from Cilicia, and a brief scene in Troy, before we return to Odysseus explaining that he has set up Xanthius, his servant since childhood, as a mole: "I told him to get himself inside the city, in case negotiations failed, and send me the dog when the time is right. I wasn't sure he made it, until now." Achilles' amused response cements our impression that Odysseus' cleverness here is not a surprise to his companions: "Typical Odysseus ... Always a contingency plan." The plan, it transpires, is to get Achilles and Patroclus into Troy to extract Helen. Although the focus is on Achilles during the execution of this plan, we are reminded of its author at the start by Patroclus' line, "Odysseus says it's time," and again at the apparently unsuccessful conclusion by his question: "What will we tell Odysseus?" The episode ends with Achilles' portentous answer: "Besides, I have something Odysseus will love even more: information." Throughout this sequence, the relationship between Achilles and Odysseus is shown to be that of old friends, as they are in *Troy* (2004) and, arguably, the Homeric poems.[15]

Both Odysseus' respect for information and glimpses of his anomalous superiority to Agamemnon recur in later episodes. In Episode 4, for instance, he questions Litos, the exiled Trojan seer captured in the Greek raid on Cilicia, urging him to use his knowledge to help end the war. When Achilles withdraws from fighting, in response to Agamemnon's seizure of Briseis, Menelaus asks Odysseus, not Agamemnon, "What are you going to do now?" Likewise in Episode 5, after Menelaus' duel with Paris, it is Odysseus who has men out looking for the fugitive, and who counsels moderation in Menelaus' claims to victory: "I'm not sure you can claim the moral high ground." It is Odysseus, too, who does most of the talking when Hector makes a night-time visit to the Greek camp, letting him and Menelaus know that the Trojans are aware of Achilles' withdrawal: "Tell Agamemnon you have until morning to leave our soil." It is likewise Odysseus who bears the brunt of Agamemnon's consequent belligerence, his prudent suggestion that the Greeks should comply angrily refused. At the same point in the *Iliad*, at the start of Book 9, it is Agamemnon himself who proposes withdrawal, opposed by Diomedes (a character downplayed in *TFOAC*): the shift here fits with the series' emphasis on Agamemnon's greed and intransigence, as does his failure to admit to any mistake in having provoked Achilles' anger. Instead of the formal embassy to Achilles, with lengthy speeches and feasting (*Iliad* 9.182–668), Odysseus here visits Achilles on his own initiative, accompanied just by Nestor, and is fairly quickly rebuffed.

Nestor's response to Achilles' refusal to be swayed yet again calls attention to Odysseus' unconventional skills: "So in the absence of glory, you'll have to rely on your ways, Odysseus, the wiles of man. They've served you well up to now." An example of these wiles is provided almost immediately: as they leave Achilles' tent, Athena appears very briefly in order to alert Odysseus to the presence of a man hiding nearby. On taking this

"Trojan spy" to Agamemnon, Odysseus is quick to discover he is Briseis' brother Dolon, and to make use of him to carry out a rather underhand stratagem: returning to Troy, Dolon releases the city's horses onto the plain. Nestor's comment, "He's done it. City of horses no more," is perhaps an indirect reference to Hector's Homeric epithet "tamer of horses" (*hippodamos*). Despite their differences, even Achilles is impressed by the trick: "You see, they didn't need me. Never underestimate Odysseus!" The episode is of course a nod to the "Doloneia" of *Iliad* Book 10, in which Odysseus and Diomedes set out on a night-time reconnaissance but end up capturing the Trojan Dolon and raiding the camp of newly-arrived Thracians led by Rhesus, whose horses are among the booty they retrieve.

Odysseus is not quite so prominent in Episode 6. Menelaus suggests he may be able to "work his magic" on Achilles, but Odysseus' urging "You miss it, I know you do!" fails to persuade the warrior. This time his advice to move quickly to an attack on Troy is more to the liking of Agamemnon, who remarks, "You're in a hurry to get home, Odysseus." This brief reminder of the significance of homecoming to the broader Trojan War story is juxtaposed to a display of Odysseus' compassion in showing Briseis the body of her brother Dolon, who he claims has killed himself out of remorse for betraying Troy (his Homeric namesake is dispatched by Diomedes)—he will later give this compassion more concrete form when he helps Briseis escape (Episode 7).[16] Even Odysseus does not predict, however, and does not feature in, the subsequent devastating Trojan-Amazon attack on the Greek camp led by Hector, in which the focus is on Patroclus' ill-fated leadership of the Myrmidons. We next see Odysseus walking through the camp, then standing slightly apart from the other Greek leaders gathered around Patroclus' funeral pyre.

Trickery and Pragmatism

At the start of Episode 7, it is Odysseus who relays to Achilles the Trojans' request for the return of Hector's body, but to no avail. After Priam's nocturnal visit, however, Odysseus is for once in agreement with Agamemnon in remonstrating with Achilles for releasing the body without consultation; in particular, Odysseus comments, the twelve-day truce he has unilaterally agreed with the Trojans is too long. Achilles' response to his suggestion that they could have bargained with Hector's body in exchange for Helen again emphasizes the difference of Odysseus' approach from the conventional heroic concern with glory: "Strategy, trickery, guile—is that what war is?" This opening sequence sets up a story arc for the rest of the episode, which will conclude with Achilles' dying indictment of Odysseus' trickery. In the meantime, however, the pair's friendship is briefly reaffirmed in an exchange as Odysseus sits eating in front of his tent. The theme of homecoming is highlighted again, too:

Achilles When all this is over, you'll return to Penelope . . .

Odysseus If she remembers me!

Achilles Agamemnon will return to Clytemnestra... Menelaus will return with his prize. Where will I go?

Odysseus You'll find somewhere.

Directly after this Odysseus enters the tent of Agamemnon, who is making plans with Menelaus for an immediate assault, despite the truce. Odysseus' objection that Achilles will not be willing to break his promise is laden with foreboding for the viewer by the presence of Hera, traditionally a supporter of the Trojans. Soon afterwards, the other leaders' busy preparations are contrasted with Odysseus' stillness, the narrative focalized by close-ups on his thoughtful face as he catches sight of Menelaus talking to Thersites. This same perspective is maintained in the next scene in the Greek camp, where Thersites pretends to spot movement in the reeds and stages a fake attack, killing the hapless Myrmidon who accompanies him to investigate and cutting himself for bloody effect. His insistence that they were set upon by Trojans, including two of Priam's sons, supplies the excuse Agamemnon and Menelaus need: the truce has been broken. Achilles turns to Odysseus for confirmation—"Is this true?"–who responds after a pause, "True": he has clearly recognized the deceitful stratagem and decided to go along with it, despite the qualms which are betrayed to the viewer by the pause and his facial expression. Our doubts are confirmed by the scene's final shot of Odysseus, in which the words "the things that I do for my country" seem to be spoken in his head. Odysseus' willingness here to participate in *someone else's* trickery, at the same time betraying Achilles' trust and offending against the heroic code, is a truly extreme example of the pragmatism he displayed at Aulis.

This breaking of the truce for Hector's burial is of course a complete departure from the respectful observance indicated in *Iliad* Book 24—although *TFOAC*'s treatment of the twelve days as a period of mourning which continues after the funerary feast, rather than being a preparation for it, allows the actual cremation to have been carried out before the Greeks attack. Achilles leads the charge, cuts through the Amazons' line, dueling with Penthesileia, and is first to reach the city gates. In response to Priam's accusation, "You broke the truce: Greek trickery not ours," Achilles' assertion "Odysseus wouldn't do that!" is poignant. Shortly afterwards, stricken by Paris' arrow to his vulnerable heel, he finally understands that he has been betrayed by his friend, as he acknowledges in his bitter dying words: "Tell Odysseus, to him the glory. This was always a shabby war." Odysseus takes Achilles' death to heart, sitting shell-shocked in his place beside Patroclus' burnt-out pyre, and telling Nestor, "I loved him. Tell the king it's over. We're done here," before shunning company to walk alone on the beach.

Episode 8 opens with Odysseus still on the beach, where he seems to have slept overnight. The first thing that meets his eye is an untethered horse standing at the edge of the waves, an abbreviated reference to the conception of his most famous stratagem. In similar vein, *Troy* (2004)'s Odysseus is inspired by the sight of a soldier whittling a toy "for my son, back home," while *The Odyssey* (1997)'s hero's eye is caught by the horse standing next to Achilles' funeral pyre; *Helen of Troy* (1956)'s Ulysses is standing in a chariot just behind the Greeks' horse-shaped standard as he witnesses Achilles' death and declares, "So dies Greek courage—but not Greek cunning."[17] Only a few minutes later in *TFOAC* Episode 8, with no intervening explanation, we share with the Trojans our first sight of the Wooden Horse. It is Odysseus' man Thersites who is left tied up near the Horse to give the Trojans the false information that the Greeks have gone home. The Trojans find plausible his account that Odysseus said he had had enough, he wanted to go home to his wife, while the offering to Poseidon of a horse full of grain and wine was Agamemnon's idea. Later that night, amidst the Trojans' celebrations, Odysseus is first to climb down the ladder out of the Horse, working swiftly with Menelaus to dispatch various guards and to open the city gates for Agamemnon and the Greek army. While he plays his part in the sack of Troy, however, he is increasingly shown apart from the other Greek leaders, especially once they reach the palace, looking sickened and exclaiming, "There's no way out for them!" when Agamemnon bars its doors. His vain attempts to help Cassandra and Andromache suggest a resurgence of compassion in contrast to the uncompromising pragmatism he displayed at Aulis, and again in abetting the breaking of the truce, as does his reluctance to carry out Agamemnon's orders to kill the baby Astyanax. Prince discusses this last, shocking scene in detail in Chapter 12, exploring potential precedents for the action in Greek and Roman tragedy and pointing out the irony that Odysseus' hand is forced by Agamemnon's threat to his own wife and children—he is indeed a morally complex figure. Odysseus' final words in the whole series are his anachronistic plea for forgiveness, perhaps recalling Mawle's earlier role as Christ in the BBC/HBO series *The Passion* (2008).

Conclusion

"If they ever tell my story...." *Troy* (2004) ends with Sean Bean's Odysseus standing by Achilles' funeral pyre in the ruins of Troy, reflecting on the immortality won by the heroes of the war, on both sides: "Let them say I lived in the time of Hector, tamer of horses. Let them say I lived in the time of Achilles." Notoriously, however, Petersen's version of the Iliadic story creates difficulties for any sequel based on the *Odyssey* by having Menelaus killed by Hector to rescue Paris from their duel at the start of hostilities, and Agamemnon knifed in the neck by Briseis amidst the chaos of Troy's fall.[18] The homecomings of both Greek leaders would therefore have to be omitted, despite their importance in the Homeric epic as foils for Odysseus' experience. The makers of *Troy* (2004) may rather have envisaged a sequel based on Vergil's *Aeneid*, given the brief but loaded exchange in which Paris hands over the "sword of Troy" to Aeneas, exhorting him to lead the fugitives from the burning city, and "find them a new home." *TFOAC* gives Aeneas a larger role than *Troy* (2004)'s cameo—he features from Episode 2 onwards as the leader of one of the Trojans' allied forces, and is especially prominent in Episode 8 as the first to spot the departing Greek fleet and then the Wooden Horse—but his escape is eclipsed by the focus on Odysseus in that concluding shot.

The Curse of Troy: Odysseus' Story

TFOAC's closer adherence to ancient tradition in relation to the fates of Agamemnon and Menelaus leaves the way open for an *Odyssey*-based sequel.[19] Its brutal presentation of Iphigeneia's sacrifice would provide ample motivation for Clytemnestra's subsequent revenge, even before Aegisthus is brought into play. Its presentation of the dysfunctionality of the relationship between Bella Dayne's Helen and Jonas Armstrong's Menelaus even before Paris' intervention might make a reunion of the couple seem unlikely, but this aspect of the story is already surprising in Homer, and, as Safran demonstrates,[20] there are many continuities of characterization between *TFOAC*'s Helen and that of *Odyssey* Book 4. There would arguably be a slight difficulty with Telemachus' age: since he seems to be a child of six or seven in *TFOAC*, rather than a baby, when Odysseus leaves Ithaca, he would be twenty-six or twenty-seven by the time of his father's return, undercutting the Homeric poem's logic—Penelope must re-marry once Telemachus is no longer a child—and its narrative of Telemachus' journey from powerless youth to manhood. But Mawle's Odysseus would certainly be capable of the uncompromising, bloody slaughter of Penelope's suitors, as so shockingly described in the poem, an act which seems out of character for the milder hero portrayed by Assante in *The Odyssey* (2007).

Importantly, too, the role of the gods in *TFOAC* provides a precedent for the supernatural elements which are such a feature of the *Odyssey*.[21] As Llewellyn-Jones comments, lamenting Petersen's "astonishing lack of imagination" in their omission from *Troy* (2004), "the gods are central not only to the arc of Homer's glorious narrative, but to the symbolic heart of the *Iliad*."[22] While I would argue that their inclusion is desirable in any modern adaptation of Greek epic, the *Odyssey*'s story requires at the very least the representation of a number of monsters—the Cyclops, Scylla and Charybdis, the Sirens—and the two goddesses on whose islands Odysseus delays for so long.[23] Other fantastical elements such as the visit to the entrance to the Underworld are important, too, as well as the gods who help or hinder Odysseus along the way. *The Odyssey* (2007) features Athena as regular helper of both Odysseus and Telemachus, Hermes as the gods' messenger, and Poseidon as implacable enemy, as well as the non-Olympian deities encountered during Odysseus' wanderings, Aeolus, Circe, and Calypso.

As we have seen, then, while other modern tellings provide precedents for *TFOAC*'s presentation of some aspects of the tale, the series gives Odysseus a much more prominent role. Agamemnon quite openly relies on his advice, superior strategic thinking, and powers of persuasion from Aulis to the Wooden Horse, to the extent that Odysseus sometimes appears to be the real leader of the Greeks. His initiative and stratagems drive much of the action, both through his own actions and indirectly through the actions of his "man on the inside," Xanthius; the one vital plot development which does not depend on his ingenuity is the work of his man Thersites. Not only do we simply see more of Mawle's Odysseus than we do of his cinematic predecessors, but focalization techniques mean we often see the action from his point of view. Whether or not a sequel appears to relate the consequences of the fall of Troy, *TFOAC* is already very much Odysseus' story.

Notes

1. E.g., Dowell 2018, McEwan 2018, Gough 2018.
2. Verreth 2008; he remarks on "Odysseus' 'brand-name recognition' in our time" (66). Cf. Solomon 2015 for an overview of treatments of the *Iliad* in modern popular culture from the late nineteenth to the beginning of the twenty-first century. See, e.g., Stafford 2017: 152 and 158–9 on the role of the young Ulysses in the original *pepla* by Pietro Francisci *Hercules* (1959) and *Hercules Unchained* (1960).
3. Louden 2015. On the metatheatricality of these voice-overs, see Augoustakis and Raucci 2018: 1 and Cyrino 2007: 131.
4. *Helen of Troy* (1956) is briefly discussed alongside Mario Camerini's *Ulysses* (1954) in Elley 1984: 61–6 and Solomon 2001: 103–11 (p. 107: "1950s romantic fiddle-faddle").
5. Louden 2015: 180.
6. Hyginus' *Fables* 95; Apollodorus' *Epitome* 3.7; Servius' *On Vergil's Aeneid* 2.81. For discussion of these and possible earlier sources, see Gantz 1993: 576 and 580; see also Burns in this volume. On the *Cypria* passage, only preserved in brief paraphrase in Proclus' summary of the *Chrestomathia*, see Davies 2019: 129–30 and the chapters by Curley and Burton in this volume.
7. See Prince in this volume.
8. Louden 2015: 180–1; the scene is also discussed by Kofler and Schaffenrath 2015: 96–8, who comment on its programmatic significance.
9. See Prince in this volume.
10. See Maurice in this volume.
11. See Prince in this volume on Thersites' role in the death of the baby Astyanax in Episode 8.
12. Louden (2015: 183–4) discusses the scene in *Iliad* Book 2 as encapsulating Odysseus' Iliadic function as a check on Agamemnon's recklessness and restorer of order, as well as a persuasive speaker.
13. Translations of the *Iliad* adapted from that of Murray and Wyatt 1999. Louden 2015: 182 notes this Iliadic scene as illustrative of Odysseus' role as Agamemnon's ambassador, but there is no comparable early embassy in *Troy* (2004).
14. Louden 2015: 181, Kofler and Schaffenrath 2015: 97–8.
15. Louden 2015: 181–2 argues against some commentators' perception of conflict between the two in the *Iliad*. The conversation between Odysseus and the spirit of Achilles in *Odyssey* 11.471–540 certainly seems to be that of friendly comrades.
16. On Odysseus' sympathetic treatment of Briseis, see further Prince in this volume.
17. Verreth 2008: 68–9 humorously comments on film-makers' efforts to explain where the idea of the horse comes from: "Every science fiction buff, however, knows that the idea was originally suggested to Odysseus by Doctor Who, who landed with his Tardis time machine on the plains of Troy" (*Dr. Who* Season 3, Episode 9: *The Myth Makers: Horse of Destruction*, 1965).
18. On the cinematic justification for both deaths, in terms of *Troy*'s emphasis on Agamemnon's ambition as real cause of the war rather than Helen's abduction, see Cyrino 2007: 144–7.
19. For a discussion of the challenges involved in making a film based on the *Odyssey*, see Pomeroy 2008: 61–93
20. See Safran in this volume.

21. See Maurice in this volume.
22. Llewellyn-Jones 2013b: 17. Petersen's own justification for not showing the gods is quoted in Winkler 2007b: 457 and Winkler 2015b: 111. See especially Winkler 2015a for extensive discussion of the challenges the gods present to the film-maker, in terms both of how they might be represented and of modern audiences' expectations. He points out (pp. 113–16) that, like *Troy* (2004), both *Helen of Troy* (1956) and *Ulysses* (1954) almost entirely omit the gods, both films emphasizing human motivations for the story's action, rather than the kind of double motivation so common in Homeric epic.
23. Cf. Stafford (2022) on the need for gods in a hypothetical Hercules epic.

PART II
CAST AND CHARACTER

CHAPTER 6
RACIST REACTIONS TO BLACK ACHILLES
Rebecca Futo Kennedy

In 2001, the film *A Beautiful Mind* was released. Inspired by the life of Nobel Prize-winning mathematician John Nash, the film starred Russell Crowe as Nash and Jennifer Connelly as his wife, the inimitable Alicia Nash, a physicist and mental health care advocate. Connelly won an academy award for her performance. Most were unaware that Connelly's casting was what is called a "whitewashing," for Alicia Nash was Salvadoran/Latina, while Connelly is White.[1] Even had audiences recognized that Hollywood had cast a White woman to play a Latina, would they have cared? White actors being cast to play Asian, Latinx, MENA, Indian, Indigenous, and Black characters, even when the characters being played were historical (i.e., real) or even still alive, has a well-documented history.[2] Rarely has anyone batted an eyelash. Who raised a cry when Angelina Jolie donned what appeared to some to be a form of blackface to play Marianne Pearl, a French woman of Afro-Cuban descent, in *A Mighty Heart* (2007)?[3] There were some comments—enough that Marianne Pearl herself issued a statement defending the casting as her choice—but often it rarely makes headlines when a White actor is cast to play a non-White character (fictional or real). Attempts to diversify films and television by casting actors of color in what traditionally had been cast or written as "White" roles, however, has elicited much rancor—even when that character is unreal or mythical, even when that character is not "White" but only claimed as such by fans. Such has been the case with the casting of British-Ghanaian actor David Gyasi as Achilles in the series *Troy: Fall of a City*.

In March of 2017, it was announced that series creator David Farr, known primarily for his work in theater and for creating the BBC series *The Night Manager* (2016), had cast Black actors in the roles of Achilles, Zeus, Athena, Artemis, Nestor, Patroclus, Aeneas, and Pandaros (Fig. 6.1).[4] This initial announcement seems to have been generally ignored. As images from the filming and interviews with Black cast members began rolling out over the following year, however, comment sections online and in various social media exploded with what can only be described as racist reactions to the casting decisions. Commenters, often using Greek or Greek-sounding names, criticized the casting primarily of Zeus and Achilles, while ignoring most of the others. Achilles, however, seems to have been the most contested.

> **Kallikrates Leonidas**   Excuse me BBC Zeus and Achilles where not black. Get your history right. I don't care if it was filmed in South Africa. Thank you.[5]
>
> **Peter Priggen**   To have Achilles (Homer's blond super Greek hero) and the Greek god Zeus played by African actors is beyond belief. It's like having Brad Pitt play Shaka Zulu in a film about the founding of the Zulu people.[6]

Screening Love and War in *Troy: Fall of a City*

Figure 6.1 Achilles (David Gyasi) in Episode 6, "Battle on the Beach," and Athena (Shamilla Miller) in Episode 1, "Black Blood."

Ajax More PC blackwashing. When will this insanity end. It's simple, don't watch it and people will stop producing this junk.[7]

The focus on Achilles is striking, particularly in how the criticisms of the casting took form. The reactions were justified by commenters in three primary ways: (1) they assumed Achilles was a real, not mythological figure; (2) they were focused through the idea of "Greekness" and Greek descent; (3) the majority emphatically dismissed any African presence or contribution to the ancient story of Troy (and to ancient Greek history generally). All such commenters seem to agree with one another that Achilles should have been cast as a blond-haired man with blue eyes—anything else would seem to them to have been an insult.

This backlash has already been partially addressed by Tim Whitmarsh[8] and the scholars who have contributed to *Pharos*[9] (a website that documents racist and misogynist uses of the classical past on the internet), correcting errors of translation or misunderstandings of color terms in antiquity (was Achilles really "blond"?), or documenting the existence of black Africans in the Homeric world. Rather than "correct the record," I examine the problem from two different perspectives. First, I discuss the phenomenon of casting—whether we call it colorblind, color-conscious, diversity or integrated casting—using recent controversies surrounding the hit musical *Hamilton* (2015) as a comparison point.[10] As the producer of *TFOAC*, Derek Wax noted in an interview with Variety: "Diversity is at the heart of our casting and at the heart of what the BBC and Netflix wants. It's only a controversy if people try to manufacture a controversy out of it."[11] And yet, the casting was not diverse or colorblind.[12] Rather, the showrunners intentionally sought to cast Black actors for roles while not casting for any other races/ethnicities—despite, as some commenters pointed out, the Trojans and Greeks both being west Asian/Mediterranean people in our sources.

Second, I engage with the ideas that underlie the extreme forms of racist response over the casting. I emphasize the gap between myth and history and contextualize these responses within discourses of nationalism and heritage, historically racist claims over the Whiteness of classical antiquity that invests these characters with a specific racialized identity, and the issue of global anti-Blackness. Why are people so invested in the identity of an Achilles or Zeus and less so the other characters who were cast as Black? How is this backlash a response to diversity casting generally? How does the practice of diversity casting encourage this type of investment in identity when used in a color-conscious time?

In my exploration, I draw the sources for the controversy from the internet—that (sometimes) horrifying space where anonymous commenting, YouTube, and Reddit can bring out the worst in our collective ethnocentric, xenophobic, and White supremacist societies. I have focused on comments made directly on news reports and press releases about the casting, and I have refrained (for my own sanity) from quoting a number of YouTube videos with their comment sections. I also excluded Reddit forums as most became, to my mind, too extremist even for research purposes. I have also eliminated tweets and Facebook comments, as they can be even more ephemeral than other internet archives. That said, the material cited here is both representative and yet will doubtless appear to readers as extremist positions—whether extreme forms of Greek or Balkan nationalism, White supremacism, or anti-Blackness and colorism, a form of prejudice against those with darker skin tones within the same ethic group.[13]

It is important to remember also how this story is complicated by the long history of appropriation of ancient Greek cultural objects and pasts, by British, German, French, and other northern European colonialist treatment of Greece.[14] Greece has often been treated less as an independent nation than as an imaginary space for northern European, especially British and German, national identity formation, with ancient Greece being given preference and Greeks even today being excluded in many ways from access to their past.[15] The Parthenon and Bassai marbles in the British Museum are not the only contested objects. So too are the Homeric epics and the literary traditions of ancient Greece. This ongoing process has so alienated some Greeks from their past, that they are, as Hamilakis points out, the only people today who have to use the adjective "modern" in front of their name.[16]

In the building of the modern Greek nation, the ancient Greek past became national histories and figures, like Achilles, became national Founding Fathers. It is no surprise, then, when some Greeks object or express disgruntlement with how what they view as important cultural heritage and their own national histories are used and reproduced by others without Greek actors or participants. For Greeks, especially, there has been historically a close correlation between ethnic identity, culture, and the development of the modern nation-state.[17] This natural frustration at having their history appropriated while being excluded can lead to much uglier nationalism, especially when grafted onto racist currents of White supremacy and anti-immigration ideologies.

Further, within Greece itself, Whiteness is not a fully operative identity. When it does appear, it often appears among extreme groups like Golden Dawn, who have yoked themselves to narratives like the Dorian invasion in order to justify allying themselves with Nazi ideologies.[18] Within the Greek diasporas of the United States and the United Kingdom, where Whiteness is an important identity marker and set up in opposition to Blackness, access to Whiteness has come only within recent decades for Greeks. Not all embrace it as an identity.[19] Occasionally, we see people who identify as Greek commenting with some of the same irritation at the casting of the non-Greek Brad Pitt as they do at the casting of David Gyasi. But the majority of the responses engaged in this chapter are committed to Whiteness or at least see value in aligning with it. Or they position themselves as anti-Black, a position that reflects a global phenomenon that may have deep roots in the trans-Atlantic slave trade, but also in the colonial and imperial practices and propaganda of European powers in the nineteenth century and the development of scientific racism, especially in the United States and northern Europe.[20]

This controversy, then, over the casting of a Black actor as Achilles proves multivalent and complicated, though part of the controversy itself derives simply from the positionality and competing goals of producers and their audiences. We begin with consideration of the goals and positions of the producers. Then, we examine the very different expectations that the multifarious audience for a show like *TFOAC* has brought to bear and how this has shaped the worst of the responses to the show's casting.

Race and Diversity Casting in Theater, Television, and Film

The idea of diversity in casting has been part of the theater world since at least the 1950s in the US, but it has been more widely used and discussed since the 1990s.[21] Diversity in casting goes under different names: non-traditional casting, colorblind casting, color-conscious casting, or integrated casting. The different terms carry slightly different connotations, and the prevalence of their usage has changed over time based on the context. In the case of *TFOAC*, producer Derek Wax emphasized "diversity" as a core principle for his casting decisions for the show. What does that mean? It depends in part on which principal type of diversity casting the team followed and what sort of expectations and goals this implies.

Before considering the purposes and impacts of casting decisions, it is necessary, however, to clarify the terminology: what we mean by "race" and related terms and how do theater, film, and television intersect with it. In most public and academic discussions of casting, the term "race" refers to the commonplace idea of "biorace." Biorace relies upon specific physical features—predominantly skin color, but also hair texture and color, eye shape (and sometimes color), and nose shape—that signal individuals with specific combinations of these features belong to supposedly immutable biological or genetic group identities.[22] In "color" casting systems, skin color and even shade is emphasized. "Race," however, is better understood as a technology for organizing people in a society according to variously emphasized changeable markers. Race situates people into hierarchies according to those markers. These hierarchies position some peoples within it as superior and others as inferior according to these markers or signifiers of difference.[23] Thus, the "color" casting process relies upon the technology of race in that it focalizes casting around the signifier used in modern racial classification systems to craft and signal the existence of these hierarchies. Whiteness and Blackness can generally be understood as the artificial, oppositional categories constructed through our modern system of race that stand on the extreme ends of the hierarchy.

The system of race and the racialization of individuals into the categories is reproduced and maintained through what Fields and Fields have called "racecraft," a process through which prejudice and power are naturalized by everyday social, political, and legal practices.[24] We might consider film, television, and theater as participating in racecraft through casting and performance decisions, which impact the way a society views itself and others. This racecraft functions to reproduce or reify "race" as it functions in a specific culture, to maintain itself as natural or the norm. Within this framework, "racialism" is "accepting and acting according to a system of so-called racial difference," while "racism" is discrimination ostensibly based on the markers used within that system. Thus, when audiences react to the skin color of actors, they are responding to a system that has historically situated those people racialized as "White" as a norm against which those of "color"—a signifier or shorthand for the hierarchy—appear as assertions of difference from this norm. Racist reactions are those that reject the difference as a negative form of deviance or as implausible and inferior.

With this in mind, we should think of casting decisions for the show as a form of racecraft and the decision to cast Black actors in specific roles within the show as participating in a cultural dialogue about race within the contexts of the UK, the US, and more generally wherever the show reaches through the Netflix platform that have legacies of the trans-Atlantic slave trade or colonial or other color-based systems of racialization. The debates are over "biorace" and, at times, ethnicity, but the debate itself can help us understand race and racecraft. When Wax says that "diversity is at the heart of our casting," what form of racecraft is he enacting?

Colorblind casting refers to the idea that actors will be cast based on whether they are the most skilled person for that part and not with reference to skin color. The premise is that, unless a script explicitly states that a character should be racialized in a certain way, the visual aspects of biorace of the character are "the least consequential or least significant element when evaluated alongside age, physical ability, and gender . . . ."[25] Under this premise, casting for families would not take into account visual aspects of racialization and would result potentially in a family of four not being visually similar. The benefit of colorblind casting is that it can pretend to a sort of universalism. As discussed by Thompson and Young, productions of Shakespeare have been one of the primary vehicles for colorblind casting and, as Banks points out, the tradition of Black theaters performing Shakespeare is more than a century old, almost two.[26] In this sense, it is not even "non-traditional" to cast Black actors or even have an all-Black cast. But a commitment to colorblind casting would have meant that actors would not be racialized only as Black and White but would have represented a wider range of possible visually marked groups.

Because the casting of Black actors resulted in numerous lead characters being Black, contrary to more traditional ways in which Black actors are cast in antiquity as "Black slaves, Black prisoners, or Black savages,"[27] we might consider that *TFOAC* was employing what has been called color-conscious or "race-conscious" casting, i.e., they intentionally sought to cast specific actors based on visual identity for prominent characters. I say visual identity, because in a multiethnic world, it is often difficult to know a person's identity simply by looking at them—biorace does not equal actual identity. The choice of a Black and White cast eliminates this multiethnic ambiguity, but at the cost of reinforcing a false racialized dichotomy that assimilates all people "of color" as "Black," only because they are "not White."

Since the casting is clearly color-conscious, we should consider the expectations applied to such castings in performance arts. In a color-conscious casting, the casting typically aims to enhance or emphasize certain aspects of a performance through insisting on biorace as a recognizable theme or aspect of the story. A prime example of such a casting is *Hamilton*, which explicitly sought to cast non-White actors (and even caused quite the stir through its casting call) for the roles of America's Founders.[28] By means of the casting, show creator Lin-Manuel Miranda seems to have sought to reverse the norm of casting typically left unexpressed, the norm of Whiteness, from which deviation would enact a non-traditional, diverse, and inclusive position for any non-White actor cast. The purpose is similar to the recent film *The Private Life of David Copperfield* (2019); casting was done, according to screenwriter and director Armando Iannucci, to make the characters in the film reflect the members of the audience: "I didn't want people to feel, 'We're watching the past.' I want them to feel, 'You're in this story,' and therefore it's now."[29]

And yet, as critics of *Hamilton* like Lyra Monteiro note, in reversing the casting and placing Black and other non-White actors in the roles of the White Founders, the play erases the real Black men and women who lived that reality—that is, there are Black actors on the stage in *Hamilton*, but no Black characters.[30] Further, as Monteiro also notes (and this helps us return to *TFOAC*), responses to the casting that suggest "this is the story of America then, told by America now," serve to whitewash the past by suggesting it was, in fact, a White world that Black actors can temporarily inhabit but that Black people had no part in.[31] This is not true of colonial America, nor is it true of the ancient Mediterranean world.

We should expect, then, that both colorblind and color-conscious casting within a play/film/series, run the risk of either whitewashing the past it purports to represent by framing its casting as "diversity" while erasing the actual people of color who lived in that world, or of tokenizing those it casts who are non-White. A key critique of colorblind and color-conscious casting, as articulated most explicitly in a public lecture given by playwright August Wilson in 1996, is that while the actors may be non-White, the stories themselves remain White and ignore the Black histories and cultures that exist.[32] Wilson rejects the tokenism that casting an actor "of color" (a phrase he also rejects as assimilating all non-White peoples into a monolith) into a White story activates. Does the casting of these Black actors in *TFOAC* place Black actors into a White story? Or, is that, at least, one expectation? We must consider the way audience expectations of the past inform the responses to performance of it in the present and the place of the Trojan War myths within that past and present.

Contested Heritage, U(nu)sable Past?

Much of the racist backlash to the casting in *TFOAC* rests on the idea that Achilles and the Trojan myths reflect a specific historical past (or "heritage") that belongs to some people but not others.

> **Screwdriver** Hi, I don't have a problem with a bit of diversity in movies & TV, but isn't it a bit ridiculous to have a black guy playing a figure that is historically European? I mean, what would be the reaction if someone like Shaka Zulu was played by a White guy? I'm sure Black people's would be outraged, so I can't help but to feel outraged about this. Black Lancelot, Black Zeus, Black Achilles, I mean c'mon, let us keep our heroes. This is anti-White racism.[33]

> **Chris** Everything comes from Whites. From the clothes you wear to your education and the computer you use. Even the language you speak. Even the language you speak. You are a poor imitation of Whites. Nothing fragile about it. It is what it is. Whites are plain and simply superior in every aspect. White supremacy is a universal law and no amount of (((cultural ma[r]xism))) can change that.[34]

As the comments above demonstrate, there is a notion that certain pasts belong to certain people—Shaka Zulu "belongs" to Black people, while Achilles, Lancelot, and Zeus "belong" to White people. This belonging precludes artistic license to adapt or change representations of it, according to such thinking, to suit new audiences. They are only a usable past to specific groups. In this case, we should start by considering whether this past is real and then how this debate over ownership takes form.

There was definitely a city of Troy (Ilion) in the area surrounding what is now Hisarlik, the archaeological site of what we call Troy in modern Turkey, in the classical and hellenistic periods (c. fifth to second centuries BC). It has now been identified with the Anatolian kingdom of Wilusa, which experienced a series of wars with the Hittites and was at times allied with and at others against those we call Mycenaeans, who seem to have been the basis for the heroes of the *Iliad*.[35] The archaeology and the literary sources tell of numerous conflicts, none of which match up to the timeline or narrative of the Greek epics, but the existence of which could all have been inspirations for Homer's tale.[36] In other words, there was a real place called Troy, but probably not a real "Trojan War."

What about Achilles? The historical existence of any of the Homeric heroes is uncertain. What is certain, however, is that those peoples whom Homer variously calls Achaeans, Danaans, and Argives in Homer's *Iliad* did not think of themselves as Hellenes or Greeks, which are anachronistic terms in the time of Homer and certainly in the Bronze Age.[37] Further, we can never know if his hair was blond, brown, or shining (all valid translations of the word *xanthus* used to describe him), nor if he was "ethnically"' Greek. Who Achilles may have been—mythical or real—matters less than who he can be claimed to be in the name of modern identities.

There are three major buckets into which we can place claims over Achilles that have been made to explain why he should not be cast with a Black actor. These appear in the comments sections on articles about the show, on Twitter, and on YouTube videos devoted to the debate. These categories are: (1) Greek and other Balkan nationalisms, (2) White supremacism, and (3) anti-Blackness.

Nationalisms

More than an alleged ancient historical figure, Achilles and his Myrmidons serve as modern national heroes for various Balkan groups in modern debates over territorial control and ethnic identity. The following exchange highlights some of the intricacies:

> **Jean Plescha**   This is not an issue of racism, it is an issue of Historical accuracy towards a nation of people.
> 	... Hellenic (Greek) people, we take our history, modern and ancient, very seriously. We study it from 2nd year in elementary school, and it starts even earlier at home. if Achilles was African looking this would have been recorded, written, painted or told via oral tradition. It is not a historical fact to portray Achilles as African looking. Achilles was the son of Pelleus, King of the Myrmidons, fair skinned and blond, he was not a foreigner in Ancient Greece. It can constitute an insult to many too as evidenced by the whole controversy.
> 	Not because of skin color, or origins, simply because of the ignorance expressed about a people's history. Do you think it would be historically correct to make a series about Shaka the Zulu and have a European looking actor play him?
> 	It is misrepresentation of history and a shame that with 100 million dollar budget the producers, scripters researchers could not find the facts of history to represent these series heroes as accurate as possible in this expression of events and people of Ancient Greece.
>
> **adem**   Achileus, Is not greek hero but ilyrian-pellasgean Hero. Ancient History is fabricated. Has not been so called greeks in ancient times but Illyrian-pellasgean tribes in that times. All names of ancient times van be very easely understand in albanian language.
>
> **Dimitris Adam**   illyrians were not even in existence then. pelasgean was a greek tribe occupying modern Thessaly (were Achilles was born), they were talking Greek and they were not considered barbarians. if you understand the name

pelasgean, try to find a root in albanian language. ancient greeks knew exactly were barbarians were inhabitaing in all the balkans. also, then you talk about Achilles, spell it correctly at least. history is fabricated by mane people, especially from those that are questioning written history. PS at what time is the first albanian recorded manuscript is found?

SoCalGreek   You must be one of the those "descendants" of the Illyrians LOL You need to stop reading Enver Hoxha's text books bud!

θεοδωρος αργυροπουλος   NO NO NO NO BLACK Achilleas, MACEDONIA IS GREEK . Πρέπει στο NETFLIX και ο παραγωγός τις ταινίας να είναι βλάκας ηλίθιος και αγράμματος δεν εξηγείται διαφορετικά άκου ο ΑΧΙΛΛΕΑΣ ΜΑΥΡΟΣ ΧΑΧΑΧΑΧΑΧΑΧΑΧΑΧΑΧΑΧΑΧΑΧΑ. ΟΥΣΤ.[38]

Achilles is a political touchstone, contested over as part of modern political debates over ethnic and national boundaries. Is he Greek? Is he Illyrian/Albanian? Is he Macedonian? Are ancient Macedonians Greek? This exchange gives us insight into how the casting of Achilles intersects with the intense nationalist battles over history and heritage in the specific geographic regions where the ancient (mythical) Myrmidons are said to have lived. "Jean Plescha" roots their opinion in the importance of this heritage and history to Greek education. "SoCalGreek" disputes the claims of "adem" with the scathing "You need to stop reading Enver Hoxha's text books bud!" Nationalist education systems inform these claims. So too do political disputes over territory and naming rights. "θεοδωρος αργυροπουλος" chanting "MACEDONIA IS GREEK" has more to do with the United Nations-mediated dispute over the naming of the Republic of North Macedonia than it does with Achilles.[39] This is one layer of the controversy.

White Supremacism

Another layer assumes that ancient Greek history and heritage belong strictly to Europe, and therefore to Whiteness. Almost every quotation from the comment sections noted thus far points to Whiteness as a key identity marker for Achilles. Curiously, this assumption is repeatedly asserted by contrasting Achilles with Shaka Zulu, or Martin Luther King, Jr., suggesting some sort of racist playbook for disputing casting decisions that result in a Black actor playing a role assumed to be White: "[I]sn't it a bit ridiculous to have black guy playing a figure that is historically European?" "Screwdriver" asks. "Do you think it would be historically correct to make a series about Shaka the Zulu and have a European looking actor play him?" "Jean Plescha" asks. "This is anti-White racism," "Screwdriver" concludes, referring to any such casting. If Achilles is coded as "White," would August Wilson see David Gyasi's casting as tokenizing and suggest he play Shaka Zulu? Only if we grant that the Homeric world is an inherently White story.

Achilles shifts from "Greek" to "European" to "White," a shift that participates in a larger discourse of identity, reflecting over a century of movement toward "Whiteness" and then "Westernness" as the primary way of thinking about Europeanness in colonized landscapes. Importantly, ancient Greek literary works, and Homer in particular, have been central to this process as the ancient Greeks became understood as foundational to "Western civilization," a commonplace for much of the twentieth century that has only recently begun to be questioned. For example, in Oxford's *A Very Short Introduction to Classics*, Beard and Henderson write, speaking of the eighteenth-century scramble to loot archaeological treasures from Greece:

> The rediscovery of Greece was, in a way, the rediscovery of the origins of western culture as a whole. It offered a way of seeing the origin of all European civilization, that transcended local, nationalist squabbles ... the point was that Greece gave western culture common roots that all educated people at least could share ... [It] is in much the same spirit that, almost 200 years later, ancient Athens can still be seen as the ultimate ancestor of democracy world-wide, a unifying origin of a favored political system ... [40]

Beard and Henderson take for granted that any democracy throughout the world today had its ultimate source (even if indirect) in ancient Athens. They use "western culture" and "European civilization" as seemingly interchangeable terms.[41] This is such a commonplace that it graces the titles of popular books and textbooks on the ancient Greeks, such as Michael Grant's *The Founders of the Western World* (1991), one of the first books I ever read about the ancient Greeks and Romans, and Nigel Spivey's *The Classical World: The Foundations of the West and the Enduring Legacy of Antiquity* (2016), who begins his story of Europe and the "West" at Troy with Homer.

Such language is often mirrored in the responses to the casting of a Black actor as Achilles:

> **Yorgo** Whereas it has become acceptable to take liberties with Greek heritage (seeing that it is the roots of all Western civilization's heritage, artists feel entitled to riff on it) this [*TFOAC*] is one of those real missteps that takes "art" out of relevance.[42]

These types of books and stories of the Classical world draw a straight line from Homer to modern Europe to the idea of the West, containing the cultural identity of this "West" in what Appiah refers to as the "Golden Nugget."[43] There is an assumption, as Settis remarks, that

> ... the "classical" past contains an enduring contemporary relevance because it contains and distinguishes the common roots of Western civilization, provides the European Union with a shared identity and embodies important values that, together with the Judaeo-Christian tradition, unites European cultures with others who have a European background from America to Australia.[44]

Settis' conclusion, like Appiah's, is that such statements are "not convincing" even if they have become "acceptable."[45]

Racist Reactions to Black Achilles

The problem, however, is not just that many Europeans—or Americans and Australians—view the ancient Greeks as a sort of cultural ancestor. It is that we historians and students of the past know very well that the ancient Greeks and their culture had roots and branches and flowerings not just in Europe, but in Asia and Africa too. Their cultural orientation was not north to the northern Europe that most ardently claim, but to the south, east, and west. They borrowed and adapted from and intermarried and lived with non-Greeks from Asia and Africa for almost the entirety of antiquity. But these facts are contested or even erased because of a tiny and yet not insignificant slippage that occurred in the late nineteenth and early twentieth centuries with the idea of how the "West" as Europe came into being, where "ancient Greek" becomes "White" becomes "West."[46]

This slippage is what we see manifested in the comments sections fighting most fiercely over ownership of Achilles and the ancient Greek past. It is a slippage between "western" and "White":

> **Lincoln Spaur**   Please recast Achilles, I get it you want diversity in these new shows and movies. But the Trojan War shouldn't be subjected to this. Greeks were white and so were the Trojans. This isnt a debate.[47]

Such slippage is racecraft, the turning of racism into race that happens in everyday life. Ancient Greek culture has become situated as the root of a White, "Western civilization," the advocates of which consider it superior to other ancient global traditions.[48] Such views are encouraged in popular histories by authors such as Niall Ferguson and Victor Davis Hanson.[49] These ideas of "Western" ("White") superiority rooted in ancient Greece find expression also in interviews with US Congressmen, declarations from the Trump White House, and even rules about the architecture of US federal buildings.[50] It is not surprising to find them, therefore, in comment sections on television shows based on Homeric epic. The result, however, is that controversies over casting become battles not over favorite actors or quality of performance, but wars over history, heritage, and White supremacy.

Greeks themselves were excluded from Whiteness until well into the twentieth century and still now, as the debates surrounding the Greek debt crisis emphasize, sit uncomfortably on the edges of Europeanness.[51] The development of Whiteness as an identity category and the internal colonization and appropriation of ancient Greece as a foundation for the developing concept of "Western civilization" are the context for understanding the backlash to the *TFOAC* casting of Achilles. As complicated as these interactions of modern identities and claims to ancient Greek myths are, these modern identities are the vehicle for but not the force behind the backlash. The force behind of all of the claims made against these identities—Greek, European, White—is anti-Blackness.

Anti-Blackness

> **Cleverman**   A black Achilles and Zeus! So because the blacks don't have their own literature, historical epics, mythology, and legends, we have to let them usurp

and take over that of us white people? We allow them to play the race card and get what they want. That needs to stop. They can write their own stories and make their own films if they want to see more blacks on screen. What will be next? They will demand access to white wombs as well.[52]

While Greek and Balkan nationalism and White supremacism both underlie the attacks or dismissal of David Gyasi's Achilles, the root issue is not that someone of the "wrong" ethnicity was cast. Very few commenters in the various venues where the debates over the casting raged were upset at the idea of Brad Pitt having played Achilles before because he was able to *look* the part of the blond hero. Some were even nostalgic for him. Even those who expressed the most virulently Greek nationalist views, like Yorgo quoted below, were not opposed to another White person playing the role. The slippage between Greek–White–Western seems to have made such a casting palatable. But the fact that Gyasi was racialized Black? This was, in some cases, considered akin to genocide:

> **Yorgo** ... Given they chose to push it as a portrayal of the actual Homeric epic, their "art" has lost all credibility and is suspiciously akin to genocidl efforts of the past ... It's akin to watching a hostage getting beheaded with a switchblade. The terrorists are Derek Wax, David Farr, and Barney Reisz. Their funders are the BBC and Netflix. The hostage is Greek heritage.
>
> **Jeff Wright**[53]   Hi Yorgo ... Can I ask you to clarify that anger and outrage to help me understand your perspective? A few questions" 1) is your anger based exclusively on the "Black Achilles" casting decision? 2) if Netflix/BBC produced Troy: Fall of a City with a "White Achilles", would you be willing to watch it, prior to formulating your opinion on the merits of the series? 3) the 2004 Hollywood film "Troy", starring Brad Pitt as a "White Achilles", committed egregious errors and wholescale scene and character rewrites of Homer's Iliad ... So, I am curious. Are you (were you) willing to watch that version ...?
>
> **Yorgo** ... 1. I consider the "black" label to be a misdirection used to provide cover for the insult. The problem is not race (only), it's heritage, lineage, background and links to the culture of the hero. It would be equally insulting to have someone portray Achilles who in any other way looks nothing like the hero is described ... I am proud, work hard, try to do the right thing for the sake of my "clan" (the humans) because all of those people are part of my lineage. No short-sighted, myopic, self-enhancing "artist" may take that all away from us. Whether they are the "tools" or the instigators, they are committing a kind of cultural genocide ...
>
> **Crato**   i.e. it's because he is not white. Dress it anyway you like. It's still that.[54]

As the final commentator in this exchange, "Crato" surmises, the issue is David Gyasi's skin color.

Although "Yorgo" did take time to address the issue of Hollywood films generally (elided in the above quotation for length), he doesn't address the question of Brad Pitt or whether he would have watched a "White Achilles" version first before complaining. For him, Pitt seems to "look like" the Achilles supposedly described by Homer and that is good enough for him. But his desire to situate his outrage over the casting within the framework of his heritage is a red herring. And the fact that he refers to his "clan" as "the human" as he does functions to situate Gyasi outside of the category "human." This is a core principle of race and of the anti-Blackness found in many other comments outraged with the casting—the repeated use of the term "sub-Saharan" as if a technical term for "Black" emphatically operationalizes the "sub" and positions Gyasi and "sub-human."[55] Particularly in discussion on the article in the *Greek Reporter*, we see the comments diverge very quickly away from any discussion of Achilles directly to the issue of Blackness, Neanderthals, ("sub-Saharan") Africans, whether the Egyptians were Black and many other of the well-trod "hot spots" of Blackness in antiquity. We even see an appearance of the debate over Hannibal's skin color.[56] The anti-Blackness is only barely below the surface and even breaks through explicitly now and again:

> **queer boy** Clearly the BBC has been infiltrated by people who belong to the same cult of lunacy as you do. You blacks will do anything to overrun and desecrate the beautiful, white Europe with your unsightly blackness.[57]

It is important to contextualize these comments that link the casting of a Black actor as Achilles within the contemporary moment. Anti-Blackness in the United States is rooted in the trans-Atlantic slave trade and the history of White supremacism dating back to the Civil War. In Europe, however, the issue is more closely tied to the current immigration crisis, which has hit Greece and Italy particularly hard. Bettini sees the re-emergence of frameworks of heritage and tradition of the sort we see in the Black Achilles controversy as explicitly linked with the immigration crisis:

> It goes without saying that behind this retrograde movement towards the cultural past in Italy and in Europe, there is also a second impulse, in some ways complementary and inverse in respect to the first. What drives us towards tradition is not only our homogenization, but also, I would say, the *difference* of others. I refer to the presence of immigrants, whose numbers are always increasing in Europe and in Italy . . . It still happens that the simple fact of having a different skin color, of speaking a different language (or of speaking our language with an unusual accent) and of practicing a different religion raises immediately the image of different "customs" which inspire the lives of these people or seems to . . . The color of his skin, the accent with which he pronounces our language, his situation as an immigrant hawker of t-shirts, all this transforms him inevitably into the image of a tribal identity, or an Islamic identity, or inspired in some way by distant traditions.[58]

Anti-Blackness has a longer history than the current immigration crisis and is deeply connected to the imperialist and colonialist histories of Europeans, to the nineteenth-century developments of the nation-state, and to the legacies of the trans-Atlantic slave trade.[59] All of these historical precedents are also deeply implicated in the claims of Homer as heritage to a White, Western, and more than Greek identity. Because Achilles (and to a lesser extent, Zeus) is viewed as a historically nationalist hero (most akin to Alexander of Macedon), the only way to understand why the response to the casting of a Black actor evoked such virulent backlash is as a form of White supremacist anti-Blackness tied inextricably to the modern systems of race and racecraft.

Conclusions: Casting Against Expectations

> ...it's not enough if we have forward thinking actors, directors, and theater companies. If your audience doesn't understand what's going on, or your audience comes in with a different set of expectations, or your audience is highly resistant to whatever discourse you want to put forward onstage, then ultimately the production won't be as successful. I kept circling around non-traditional casting and realized, "Oh, more informed dialogues about race and performance can only be achieved if we alter the way we teach Shakespeare."[60]

The decisions of the producers of *TFOAC* to cast major roles in the show with actors racialized as Black engage with explicitly anti-Black histories of racism. They are also bound to the more subtle ways in which anti-Blackness and White supremacism have shaped the expectations of audiences—of television shows, in theaters, in our classrooms, and even as scholars. Part of this has to do with the ways in which race and racism have played a role in the history of the discipline of Classics and in the popularization of the ancient world by those who consume the ancient world in our classrooms and books. The expectation that Achilles is "White" is not truly a product of his hair being described as *xanthus*, it is in our assumption that the word *xanthus* when applied to Achilles should translate as "blond" and not "shining," just as we assume that Odysseus, when he is called *melanchroos*, translates as "tanned" and not "black."[61] We create an expectation of Whiteness.

Knox, perhaps, most famously represents this expectation in his *The Oldest Dead White European Males*:

> In spite of recent suggestions that they [Greeks] came originally from Ethiopia, it is clear, from their artistic representations of their own and other races, that they were undoubtedly white or, to be exact, a sort of Mediterranean olive color.[62]

He wrote this in response to the publication of *Black Athena* and subsequent debates it generated, but in doing so showed his own expectations of Whiteness of ancient Greeks.[63]

That assumption was paired with a postulation of homogeneity in the ancient Greek world and of direct links between those supposedly homogeneous ancient Greeks and himself.[64] The slippage between "white" and "Mediterranean olive" shows the literal translations used to construct such Whiteness. But we know from the study of antiquity that such homogeneity is not necessarily the way the ancient Greeks thought of themselves. It is the importation of modern assumptions that erase the realities of the multiethnic, multicultural, and multilingual ancient Mediterranean. This slippage is a claim made on the past and creates and reproduces an expectation of Whiteness for audiences who have been taught that this past is their present.

For this reason, then, it should come as no surprise that audiences reacted negatively to the casting of David Gyasi as a "Black Achilles." There is hardly an aspect of our teaching or popular representations of ancient Greeks that do not reinforce expectations of Whiteness. Thus, casting will always run the risk of generating controversy. For this reason alone, many proponents of such casting have rejected the name "non-traditional casting" as it rests on the premise that the White casting is the neutral or expected one. If we want audiences to embrace Black Achilles, we need to recognize and then work to dismantle the White supremacism and anti-Blackness that has infested the study of and assumptions about Greco-Roman antiquity.

Notes

1. Actor Jennifer Connelly is Jewish. Recent debates have flared up over whether Jews are included in Whiteness, but she is, at the very least White-presenting. See Roediger 2005: *passim* on both Jewish and Latinx relationships to Whiteness.
2. Simons 2016. MENA = Middle East and North African, i.e., non-Black, non-East Asian people from Asia and Africa.
3. Wiltz 2007.
4. www.bbc.co.uk/mediacentre/latestnews/2017/troy-fall-of-a-city.
5. Clarke 2017a. All comments from online forums are reproduced as posted, including spelling and punctuation; since writing this chapter, the comments sections have been removed or made inaccessible to those without a subscription on all *Variety* articles on *TFOAC*.
6. Clarke 2017a.
7. Clarke 2018.
8. Whitmarsh 2018.
9. Documentation can be found in two posts at: https://pharos.vassarspaces.net/: one from January 11, 2018 and another from April 6, 2018. The response of various scholars was compiled in three separate posts on May 11, May 18, and May 25, 2018.
10. *Hamilton* intentionally advertised for non-White actors in their casting call and has been criticized both on the right and left for the decision. See Monteiro 2016.
11. Clarke 2018.
12. See Eyring 2016 and Tran 2015.

13. It is worth noting that the actors cast as Pandarus, Athena, Artemis, and Aeneas are all light-skinned. Colorism most likely informed part of the backlash.
14. On this, see, e.g., Gourgouris 1996 and Hamilakis 2007. Berger and Conrad 2015: 187–8 address some of the specific motivations behind German appropriations of the ancient Greek past.
15. For a focused discussion, see Hamilakis 2007.
16. Hamilakis 2007: 19.
17. On the importance of national histories in the formation of European nation-states, see Berger and Conrad 2015. On the importance of racial and ethnic identity within the development of national history in Greece, see Berger and Conrad 2015: 200–4.
18. For a discussion of various ways such claims have been made, see Mac Sweeney *et al.* 2019. On Golden Dawn specifically, see Ellinas 2013.
19. On when and how different ethnic groups came to be "White," see Roediger 2005. Discussion of Greeks (and Italians) appear in almost every chapter.
20. See Hinsley 1981 and Conklin 2013. Mills 2015 offers a relevant discussion of what he calls "Global White ignorance."
21. See Syler and Banks 2019: 7–8 and Table 1.1. For an early discussion of diversity casting, see Harrison 1969.
22. Fields and Fields 2012: 4–5.
23. For this articulation of race, see Sheth 2009, especially 21–5.
24. Fields and Fields 2012: *passim*, but especially 25–74.
25. Young 2013: 57.
26. Thompson 2006, Young 2013, Banks 2019.
27. Murray (forthcoming).
28. Herrera 2017.
29. Stewart 2020.
30. Monteiro 2016. See also the responses to Monteiro's review, collected together at: www.ncph.org/history-at-work.
31. Monteiro 2016: 93.
32. August Wilson's lecture "The Ground on Which I Stand" was presented in 1996. All references or quotations come from Wilson 2016.
33. Clarke 2018.
34. Kokkinidis 2018. The use of the triple parentheses around "cultural marxism" is intended to signify its Jewishness and is a common anti-semitic signal in online fora and social media. See Yglesias 2016.
35. Evidence was uncovered in the 1990s connecting the site explicitly to the ancient city of Troy; see Mac Sweeney 2018: 30.
36. Mac Sweeney 2018: 32–5.
37. On the development of "Hellene" or "Greek" as an identity, see Hall 1997.
38. Kokkinidis 2018. My translation of the final comment: "NETFLIX and the producer of the film must be an idiot, a fool, and illiterate. There is no other explanation. Listen to this! Black Achilles. HAHAHAHAHAHAHAHAHAHAHAHAHAHAHAHA. Get lost!"
39. On the dispute over the naming of the Republic, see "Macedonia officially changes name to North Macedonia, drawing line under bitter dispute" (*CNN.com*, 13 February 2019) and releases at UN News on the dispute (www.news.un.org).

40. Beard and Henderson 1995: 15–16.
41. This trend goes back to only the latter half of the nineteenth century: "Western civilization" has a rather recent origin. See Bonnet 2004: 14–36 and Kennedy 2019.
42. Comment on Clarke 2018.
43. Appiah 2018: 187–212.
44. Settis 2006: 2.
45. See also Morley 2018 on the problematics of the "classical" as foundational.
46. Bonnet 2004 is the best discussion of the historical process by which "Western" came to stand in for "White." See Weller 2017 on current links to White nationalism and Eurocentrism.
47. Clarke 2018.
48. Discussed by Settis 2006, Morley 2018, Kennedy (forthcoming). For a powerful critique of the idea of cultural "roots," see Bettini 2016.
49. For example, Ferguson 2011 and most of Hanson's production dating back to 1989.
50. Former Rep. Steve King (Iowa) is the most notorious: see Lewis 2019. There have been numerous statements from the Trump White House, but see recently "Remarks by President Trump at the White House Conference on American History" (September 17, 2020, www.whitehouse.gov/briefings-statements). The "Executive Order on Promoting Beautiful Federal Civic Architecture" (December 21, 2020) fulfills then President Trump's promise to "Make Architecture Great Again" by mandating a return to neo-classical architectural styles (www.whitehouse.gov/presidential-actions).
51. Hanink 2017.
52. Clarke 2018.
53. Jeff Wright is the producer of the popular *Trojan War: The Podcast* (trojanwarpodcast.com).
54. Clarke 2018.
55. There has been a push since at least 2009 to move away from the use of the term "sub-Saharan," as a word for "Black Africa," as "disparaging and contemptuous" (Onyeani 2009) as it assumes no Black peoples, historically or currently, are indigenous to North Africa.
56. Kokkinidis 2018.
57. Kokkinidis 2018.
58. Bettini 2016: 12. Translation from the Italian by Max Goldman. For discussion of European racialization, see the essays in de Cesari and Kaya 2019.
59. Franz Fanon's body of work is still the best primer in global anti-Blackness. On links to immigration historically, see Bashi 2004.
60. Thompson 2019: 33.
61. This is a common translation of *Odyssey* 16.175, while the same word used of Eurybates at 19.246 is usually "black." See, for example, Wilson's 2017 recent translation, which follows this formulation. Murray (forthcoming) suggests it is because of an expectation of Blackness in enslaved or servile characters and of Whiteness for heroes.
62. Knox 1993: 26.
63. On the Black Athena debates, see Berlinerblau 1999, McCoskey 2012: 167–99, and Adler 2016: 113–71.
64. Knox 1993: 12.

CHAPTER 7
PUSSY POLITICS: WOMEN AND POWER IN THE HOMERIC PATRIARCHY
Kirsten Day

As someone who is interested in classical receptions, epic, and women in antiquity, I am always interested to see how modern film adaptations of the Trojan War story deal with the problem of women: when drawing on source material that seems to present women as marginalized, commodified, passive, and powerless, how do modern writers and directors navigate the line between staying true to the ancient sources and offering the sorts of complex, empowered female characters with robust storylines that appeal to modern audiences?[1]

Like many other epic depictions, such as Wolfgang Petersen's 2004 *Troy*, the makers of BBC One/Netflix's 2018 series *Troy: Fall of a City* tried to circumvent this difficulty by positioning the series as "inspired" by ancient material rather than "based on" it,[2] thus asserting the creative license to adapt these tales to their own purposes. And although much of the buzz about this series centered on its racially diverse cast, its treatment of women in the #MeToo era is also worthy of examination as the choices made in this regard, like casting decisions, have political implications that go beyond the reach of the small screen. While the series seems to aim at showing women as strong, multi-faceted, autonomous characters while staying within the parameters one would expect for a patriarchal culture of the distant past, a closer examination reveals that despite what seem to be their best intentions, the creators ultimately reflect the deeply ingrained misogynistic ideas whose roots stretch back to antiquity and whose presence is still felt everywhere from the bedroom to the boardroom.

Drawing from the Ancient Tradition

As a Trojan War narrative, *TFOAC* includes scenes featuring the objectification and abuse of women as parts of the ancient storyline that might be considered immutable. For instance, as we might expect, Agamemnon (Johnny Harris) sacrifices his own daughter Iphigenia (Lauren Coe) to further his ambitions without consulting his wife Clytemnestra (Emily Child) (Episode 2). As in Homer, Chryseis (Jamie-Lee Money)[3] is taken as a war-prize by Agamemnon, who in *TFOAC* sees her as a surrogate for the daughter he killed; when she will not play along, she is raped repeatedly and described by David Gyasi's Achilles as Agamemnon's "plaything" and "new toy" (Episode 4). Similarly, like her ancient counterpart, Briseis (Amy Louise Wilson) is first taken as Achilles' "[Spoil] of War" (as the episode is entitled) and then later appropriated by

Agamemnon and used as a pawn in the power struggle between the two men (Episode 4). And as in the stories from antiquity, the warnings issued by Cassandra (Aimee-Ffion Edwards) are repeatedly disregarded and when the city is taken, her rape is implied.[4]

Also consistent with the ancient tradition, when Troy falls, the women are treated as property to be distributed among the Greek kings, as Agamemnon puts it, "as compensation for injuries done by your husbands and sons" (Episode 8). Bella Dayne's Helen herself also functions largely as a pawn: she is described by the Greeks as "stolen treasure" (Episode 2), by Hector as a "trophy" (Episode 5), and by Achilles (Episode 7), Agamemnon, and Andromache (Chloe Pirrie) as a "prize" (Episode 8). In the final episode, Agamemnon characterizes Menelaus (Jonas Armstrong) as Helen's "rightful master" and locates her entire worth in her childbearing capabilities when he tells her, "You will go back with my brother now. Bear him more children if he wants them. And then you can die" (Episode 8), sentiments that, again, are not inconsistent with ancient attitudes.

The series also depicts women's cloistering, ostensibly for their own protection, but effectively as a means of controlling or suppressing them. Cassandra has been hidden away for years under the pretense of mental instability since her parents and the other Trojans do not want to hear her dire warnings (Episode 5). And when Louis Hunter's Paris is presumed dead, the problem of Helen's continued presence in Troy is solved by relegating her to the widows' quarters (Episode 5).[5] The series thus highlights the oppression of women in ways that their audience might expect to see in stories from antiquity, and indeed, most of these choices were either anchored in Homer or in other Trojan War narratives or could reasonably be seen as reflecting ancient ideas and practices.

At the same time, *TFOAC* also enthusiastically draws upon more powerful representations of women found in the Trojan War cycle; indeed, Bettany Hughes, the Classicist historian who advised the series, asserted, "it's very important that we show that the women in this story were protagonists, not just pawns."[6] As in depictions from antiquity, the Amazons appear as strong, independent warrior women, skilled in battle and courageous in the face of death: Sharleen Dziire's Ainia positions herself as Paris' equal on their first meeting when she aims an arrow directly between his eyes and asks: "Are you dangerous? … So am I" (Episode 6). Their queen, Penthesilea (Nina Milner), too, is all these things, as well as relentless in pursuing vengeance against Achilles for killing her daughters, her sisters, and her soldiers (Episode 6).

Although Erica Wessels' Penelope is a relatively minor character here, *TFOAC* consciously frames her as a more active player by giving her credit for the ruse of Odysseus' madness as a means of avoiding the war. When the Greeks arrive to fetch him, Penelope explains that a recent fever has gone to Odysseus' brain and he won't talk to anyone, only plows his field incessantly, so he would be of no use in war. To this, Carl Buekes' Diomedes responds skeptically: "Or maybe he's as cunning as he ever was. Maybe you both are." While Diomedes implicates both husband and wife, Garth Breytenbach's Ajax later attributes the ploy primarily to Penelope herself when he scoffs in amusement at the explanations Joseph Mawle's Odysseus offers for his tardiness: "Tricks of Hermes?

The tricks of Penelope, more like" (Episode 2). While no ancient source suggests that Penelope was behind the scheme, by making her the principal agent, the series seems here to draw upon the views of scholars like Felson and Winkler, who see the Penelope of Homer's *Odyssey* not as a woman whose fate is entirely at the mercy of the men in her life, but rather as a forceful character who works within the constraints of her position and her situation to manipulate her own destiny.[7]

TFOAC also opts to follow the lead of Euripides in his version of Iphigenia's sacrifice in his tragedy *Iphigenia at Aulis* (c. 405 BC) by depicting her as facing death heroically once she understands its inevitability.[8] While Michael Cacoyannis's 1977 *Iphigenia* likewise drew on this characterization, the more recent 2003 John Kent Harrison miniseries *Helen of Troy* made a very different choice, depicting a very young girl laughing in innocent obliviousness right up to the moment when her throat is slit. Rather than following Harrison's lead, in *TFOAC*, Iphigenia is of marriageable age and thus old enough to understand, and though she at first recoils in horror, she quickly puts on a brave face, offers her neck to her father, and says resolutely: "If it is to happen, let it be without struggle. Do it" (Episode 2).

In addition, the series taps into ancient traditions that bolster Helen's heroic stature by drawing a parallel between her and Achilles. In the *Cypria*, both Helen and Achilles were created because Zeus wanted to reduce the population of humans, who had grown numerous and impious, so he arranged for the birth of the two figures who would ensure that the Trojan War would take place.[9] According to Pausanias, after death Helen and Achilles were married to each other on the White Island, which was reserved for the souls of heroes. And Homer himself draws an implicit parallel between the two by having both concerned with and aware of their place in epic remembrance.[10]

In a seeming nod to these ancient strains that suggest a kinship between the two, *TFOAC* introduces a scene in Episode 3 where, having infiltrated the palace in a ruse worthy of Odysseus,[11] Achilles surprises Helen in her bedroom and announces his intention of taking her back to the Greek camp. In response, she reproaches him for doing Agamemnon's bidding while at the same time positioning him as her foil and her equal:

> The Achilles I knew obeyed no one. He answered only to himself. The Achilles I knew was a match for me ... This isn't war. This is you breaking into a defenseless woman's bedroom to appease a man I know you don't respect. It's beneath you, my warrior. And you know it.

In this scene, Helen presents a view of herself and Achilles as counterparts who are qualitatively above the general mass of mere mortals, much as Homer presents the two of them in the *Iliad*. In Homer, however, the equivalence is based on physical qualities: as Ruby Blondell puts it, "[Helen and Achilles] are the apogee of female beauty and male strength, respectively," while as the reason for the war and as the "principal agent of the slaughter ... her beauty is as deadly as his physical strength, her body as deadly as his body."[12] In *TFOAC*, the superiority Helen implies is framed in terms of character, a shift consonant with our modern view of ourselves as valuing moral qualities over physical ones.

Modern Modifications

In addition to including these nods to women's empowerment that have roots in antiquity, the series alters details of the ancient narrative or inserts entirely new elements in order to foreground women's strength and autonomy in service to the tastes and sensibilities of modern screen audiences. Unlike in the *Iliad*—but perhaps drawing on the *Odyssey*'s Phaeacian queen Arete as a model[13]—the Trojan queen Hecuba (Frances O'Connor) is said to be equal to her husband in position and authority. When Helen first presents herself to the royal pair to make a case for her actions in eloping with their son, she begins by addressing Hecuba herself: "I hear, my queen, that you rule Troy alongside your husband. That in this city, man and woman are equal in respect and power" (Episode 2). Trusty notes that this ostensible gender equality in Troy is visually reinforced by the fact that Hecuba's throne is the same size as that of Priam, a stark visual contrast to the unequal thrones occupied by Helen and Menelaus in Sparta.[14]

Alongside this attempt to bolster women's power, the series has Briseis becoming Achilles' spoil not via the normal means of loot distribution, but because he recognizes her worth by the courage she demonstrates in the face of death: when Achilles and his men make a surprise attack on the people of Cilicia, Briseis comes out swinging, and then, when her weapon is lost and she is confronted with the point of Achilles' sword, she lifts her chin silently in proud defiance rather than cowering or begging for mercy (Episode 4). *TFOAC* thus efficiently transforms Briseis from the *geras*—prize of honor— she is in Homer's *Iliad* into a proud and courageous individual who is valued for her own intrinsic qualities rather than as a commodity that merely serves to bolster Achilles' status.

In addition, the series takes pains in the early episodes to foreground the autonomy and resolve of Helen herself: in Sparta, it is Helen who in Episode 1 summons Paris to their initial tryst in her secret hideaway "She Shed," and although he suggests the elopement, Helen is the one who enacts it by stowing away in a "conveniently sized piece of antique furniture," as Sarah Hughes puts it, which she ostensibly sends as a gift for Hecuba.[15] Upon her arrival in Troy, Helen insists upon making her case to Priam (David Threlfall) and Hecuba with an assertive feminist speech that would find no place in the whole of the ancient canon: "Not for one moment have I been happy with Menelaus," she says. "I didn't choose him and never would have. I do choose to be with your son. I am not a possession. I am a woman" (Episode 2).[16] In the series finale, Helen again asserts her autonomy when she rejects Agamemnon's characterization of Menelaus as her master and tells the triumphant Menelaus: "You can take my body back; you can have it in your bed; but my heart stays here" (Episode 8).

These decisions seem designed to appeal to a modern audience with more liberated ideas about women and their place in society, and indeed, they seem to a certain extent to have succeeded: "I loved the idea that [Helen] choosing Paris was a statement of female will, not subjection."[17] Yet although these decisions create a veneer of female empowerment—helped along, for instance, by scenes in Episode 3 where a resolute Helen insists on giving her share of the palace grain stores to the common people despite pushback from the higher-ups—closer scrutiny reveals that the reality for women in *TFOAC* is far less progressive.

Undercutting Women's Empowerment

In looking at the ways in which the series gives women power with one hand and takes it away with the other, the Amazons provide a useful starting point.[18] In classical Greek society, this tribe of fierce warrior women who lived apart from men functioned as negative models for women, representing everything a virtuous woman should not be, and as cautionary tales, since despite their prowess in battle, they were always defeated by Greek men.[19] Nonetheless, as proud, capable, self-governing women who reject men almost entirely, today they are often seen as proto-feminist figures.

Accordingly, *TFOAC* emphasizes the strength and independence of the Amazons in order to appeal to today's more progressive audiences. Yet at the same time, the series undercuts this effort with a hackneyed depiction of the Amazons as wild, untamed, and hypersexualized, with clothing primarily constructed of torn animal hides and images of their camp (Episode 6) recalling a stage set for some "primitive" tribe in a South American jungle, complete with crude wood and bamboo huts with palm-thatched roofs—a setting enhanced by the twittering of exotic birds and the faint din of wild animals. And significantly, only here among mortal women do we find notable examples of racially varied casting.[20]

Their queen, moreover, in her quest for vengeance comes across not so much as a proto-feminist, but as an honorary male: Penthesilea is characterized as masculine both in her behavior, coming across as tough and hard rather than feminine, and in her appearance: attention is drawn to her flat chest, and she sports both a boyish haircut and a permanent scowl rivaling the most iconic vengeance-fixated male film heroes, from John Wayne to Clint Eastwood (Fig. 7.1). And like the ancient Amazons, who were received by the Greeks as a deviant "other" rather than as a model for women's empowerment, the creators carefully "otherize" Penthesilea by making clear her unwavering Lesbianism: "Men and me—it doesn't happen," she tells an infatuated Aeneas (Alfred Enoch) in Episode 7.

Next, while Hecuba is said to rule alongside her husband, this professed equality is undercut in several ways—much as was the case too with *The Odyssey*'s Queen Arete.[21] As rulers, even if Hecuba is consulted, Priam is the one who speaks in court on their behalf far more frequently, and he is the one who makes the final decisions. For instance, although Hecuba and Andromache had both argued vehemently that Helen should be sent back, Priam's instinct to keep her, helped along by Helen's "I am Woman" speech[22] (Episode 2), prevails, with the final decision seemingly resting with him. Then in response

Screening Love and War in *Troy: Fall of a City*

Figure 7.1 Clint Eastwood as Blondie in Sergio Leone's *The Good, the Bad, and the Ugly* (1966) and the Amazon queen Penthesilea (Nina Milner) in Episode 6, "Battle on the Beach."

to Odysseus and the other ambassadors, Priam first agrees to give Helen back to the Greeks ("She is yours"), and then rapidly rescinds that decision ("Your queen isn't going anywhere," he tells the objecting Paris), both without any verbal input from Hecuba (Episode 2). When Hector later suggests that he and Paris embark on a covert mission to Cilicia, Hecuba objects, but Hector continues to plead his case to Priam, who ultimately nods his approval despite disapproving looks from his wife (Episode 3); and when the Greeks suggest a duel between Menelaus and Alexander, Hecuba objects once more, again to no avail (Episode 4).

This public dynamic is replicated in matters that take place behind the scenes as well. Although Hecuba insists to Hector (Tom Weston-Jones) that Priam did not force her to give up Paris as a baby ("What we did, we did together," she says in Episode 5), when they are alone, a somewhat different version emerges: Priam admits "I did force you to give Alexander up," to which she responds in soothing reassurance, "You didn't force me. You persuaded me to sacrifice one life for all lives" (Episode 5). But even the framing of this as "persuasion" is undercut by flashbacks that show Hecuba sobbing and pleading as Alexander is taken from her: "Oh, please. Please. My baby! Please, no! No, please—my baby!" (Episode 1).

And in the end, Hecuba's suicide is contrasted with Priam's more noble death: while Priam takes up his sword to meet his fate at the hands of the conquering king, who characterizes him, albeit somewhat derisively, as "brave to the last," she retreats to the domestic space of the bedroom and opens her veins (Episode 8). Thus, in response to the fall of his city, Priam elects for a heroic warrior's death in battle, while Hecuba chooses a death that is a more typically "female" response usually found in the context of erotic disaster,[23] an association driven home when Agamemnon is alerted to her presence by orgasmic death-moans and enters the bedroom to find the dying Hecuba prostrate and bloody on her marriage bed.

Pussy Politics: Women and Power in the Homeric Patriarchy

With Helen, too, the suggestion of female empowerment is undermined in ways both subtle and blatant. The strength she attempts to convey to Achilles in the aforementioned scene where she positions herself as his "match" is undercut by her inability to control her reactions (Episode 3): she gasps when Achilles hits upon Cilicia when speculating on where Paris might have gone, thereby supplying him with the information he needs to cut off their supply lines, killing many of the Cilicians, including Andromache's father, in the process.

Furthermore, the moral high ground Helen attempts to claim in this scene is lost through her inability to own up to this blunder despite the deadly complications that ensue. In addition to the Cilician casualties, when the servant Harmon (Joe Vaz) spots Achilles leaving Helen's room in Episode 3 and is unsure of what to do, the Greek spy Xanthius (David Avery) perceives the threat (Episode 4) and kills Harmon in order to protect Helen by containing the information. Then, despite her insistence that she doesn't want his help and her demands that he abstain from violence, Helen stays quiet when Xanthius not only murders Priam's loyal chief advisor Pandarus (Alex Lanipekun), who is trying to ferret out who tipped off the Trojans, but makes it appear to be a suicide, complete with a note implicating Pandarus in treason (Episode 5). Indeed, she remains silent even while Pandarus' body is impaled and publicly displayed as "a lesson to us all," as Priam puts it, "that treachery wears a friendly face, and this is how it ends" (Episode 6).

Initially, in this reluctance to speak up Helen comes across as paralyzed with fear; but when Xanthius is captured and tortured but refuses to implicate her, she slips him a knife and actively helps him kill the guard so he can escape, asking the gods for forgiveness as she muffles the innocent guard's screams (Episode 7). As such, despite some early attempts to frame Helen as powerful and morally superior, the series soon shifts to depicting her as passive and cowardly, and then ultimately moves to the more traditional "blame" theme.[24]

Not dissimilar is Helen's role in Troy's fall: in what Sarah Hughes describes as "what may have been the first unselfish act of her life,"[25] Helen sends Menelaus a message, agreeing to come back to him provided that no one else gets hurt (Episode 7). But she sends it through Xanthius, who has already ignored her command not to hurt Pandarus, and she proposes the deal immediately after helping to kill Xanthius' guard. And even if we credit her with well-intentioned naiveté, her firm stance against anyone else getting hurt apparently does not include additional nameless guards, a handful of whom she distracts to facilitate the Greeks' exit of the horse and their opening of the gates, standing by in tacit acceptance while they are summarily dispatched (Episode 8). This characterization is in direct contrast with Homer's Helen, who, as Blondell has noted, is complicit in the action of the epic, but never simply passive,[26] whereas here, she is complicit largely *through* her passivity.

Less dramatic, but just as telling, are the many smaller ways in which Helen fails to exert strength and influence. In the first episode, she twice attempts to assert a point with Paris, but on both occasions, he quickly takes the upper hand. First, she offers the story of Acteon as a cautionary tale after Paris alludes to spying on her at a party the night before: "[Actaeon] spied on the bathing goddess, Diana [*sic*], and was turned into a stag for his pains. Dogs chased him through the forest and tore his flesh to pieces," she warns. Far from feeling threatened or even chastened, Paris responds with an amused smirk: "Maybe it was worth it."

Later in the "Chamber of Silks," Helen initiates another cautionary tidbit in an attempt to illustrate her immunity from the temptations of men: "These silks were given to my father by an Indian king ..."; but Paris interrupts her somewhat impatiently: "... by an Indian king. You turned him down. I know." In the ensuing conversation, Helen repeatedly attempts to reassert dominance by reminding him of his place and imposing boundaries ("Please don't look at me like that. I am your hostess and queen of this palace") in service to her marriage and the patriarchal *status quo* ("I'm a woman. We don't get to select our fate"; "You're royal now. Duty will be your master too"), but he responds by unmasking her true "wild" nature, now stifled, reassuring her that he knows what is what ("I know what freedom is, and this—this isn't it!"), and asserting his immunity from the social constraints of duty and position ("No one can master me"). Once again, he rejects Helen's attempts to steer their interaction and takes the upper hand, making clear that he knows both her true nature and what's best for her, thereby positioning himself as her hero and rescuer.

Once in Troy, we again see Helen's initial attempts to assert equality or dominance later undercut or rejected. She endears herself to the Trojan people by insisting on giving out her own palace share of grain during the siege (Episode 3), but when the prophecy that implicates her in Troy's doom through her relationship with Alexander is made public, she soon becomes a pariah, as is made clear by the pointed whispers and damning looks of servants (Episode 5). To ingratiate herself with Andromache who is struggling with infertility, Helen offers a fortified wine that she says helped her to conceive (Episode 3), but when she later tries to take credit for the ensuing pregnancy, Andromache cuts her off at the knees: "Some quack potion you brought with you from Sparta to keep your skin soft? This baby is mine. I thank the gods for its omens, not you" (Episode 5).

Eventually, even Paris rejects her impassioned pleas to flee the city together, explicitly placing his duty to Troy above his love for her (Episode 7). And in the end, as noted earlier, her ill-conceived attempt to bring a peaceful end to the war is used for precisely the opposite purpose. Overwhelmingly, then, in *TFOAC*, Helen's attempts at exerting agency or influence are at best ineffective, and at worst counterproductive.

In some ways, the creators of *TFOAC* may have been trying to tap into the complexity of the Homeric Helen: in both the *Iliad* and *Odyssey*, the question of Helen's culpability for the events that led to the war, for instance, is not an easy matter to decide, nor are her allegiances clear or consistent. But in Homer, despite positioning herself as a victim of the gods, Helen is constantly jockeying for position, actively working within the constraints of her situation to produce an outcome to her best advantage.[27] In *TFOAC*, in contrast, when Helen attempts to take the reins, she is cut down at every turn, and when push comes to shove, her ethical framework crumbles. Of course, in many ways, Helen is the most important character in the series, so the thematic weight that the undercutting of her moral integrity, her self-assurance, and her agency bears is hard to understate.[28]

But important too as a counterweight in *TFOAC* is the depiction of Andromache, who is set up by the series as a rival, and, as was the case in antiquity, as a contrast in the areas of marriage and motherhood.[29] As Vann has suggested, in the *Iliad*, not only is Helen's sexual betrayal of Menelaus juxtaposed with Andromache's devotion to her own husband Hector, Helen's failure to produce a son and her abandonment of her only daughter are contrasted with Andromache's close association with Astyanax, whose role as Hector's heir is made into an explicit point of pride.[30]

In most modern productions, sympathy is created for Helen by characterizing her marriage as loveless, oppressive, and sometimes even abusive, in order to absolve her from the "sin" of sexual infidelity, while the problem of her abandonment of her daughter is often solved by omitting Hermione entirely. In *TFOAC*, Menelaus is an overbearing husband who represses Helen, who was once free-spirited and wild, so that here, too, her infidelity is positioned as somewhat justified. But unlike most modern productions, in *TFOAC*, Helen's contrast with Andromache in the area of motherhood is on full display: not only does Helen abandon her daughter to elope with Paris, Hermione (Grace Hogg-Robinson) has even been betrothed to Paris, so that Helen's betrayal of her maternal role is amplified.

And while Andromache desperately strives to get pregnant, wanting nothing more than to give Hector a son, Helen more or less disavows the role of mother: "The truth is Hermione would be happier without me . . . Not all women are designed for motherhood," she tells Andromache. "I know it must seem ungrateful, but I never found it easy to be a mother." The contrast between the two is sharpened by Andromache's hostility toward Helen: she constantly frames Helen as a threat and questions her motives. If we are meant to see Helen as sympathetic, then Andromache might well be perceived as bitter and spiteful: after all, she is not only ungracious about Helen's attempts to help her conceive, but in Episode 3, she also unfairly blames her continued lack of success in this area on the midwife.

But on the other hand, Andromache is also "eminently sensible," as Sarah Hughes puts it,[31] and she is nearly always right about Helen, and about everything else. Yet, although she seems an A-lister in the royal family, no one ever really listens to her. In Episode 2, she argues along with Hecuba that Helen should be sent back, but as noted earlier, Priam's instinct to keep her prevails. When later informed that Greek forces are in fact mustering, Priam tells Hector, who had only objected after Priam's decision to keep her had been announced, "Well, you were right," ignoring entirely the women's earlier, more fully developed arguments (Episode 2).

It is notable, too, that Hector assumes authority in the city by telling Priam, "I'm taking over the running of the city now," and announces the transfer of power to Helen by again using the first person singular (Episode 5). There is no indication that Andromache will rule alongside her husband as had been said at least of Hecuba. Instead, that his decisions take precedence is made clear when Andromache argues that Helen should be sent back since Paris has left the city and Hector rejects the suggestion out of hand: "You mean give her back? . . . No. When Greek blood decorates our walls, we'll decide on Helen's fate" (Episode 5). Even after Hector's death, as the climax approaches and Andromache ramps up her warnings and accusations, she is dismissed: "I need someone to hear what I'm saying," she pleads with Priam, who dismisses her, advising that she leave finding "the truth" to the men and focus her own attention on her motherly duties (Episode 8).

Indeed, Andromache's warnings and advice are disregarded as insistently throughout the series as Cassandra's.[32] But, while the series at least pays lip service to empowering most of the women we've discussed, the series makes no attempt to make Cassandra into a feminist figure. In fact, as Ilkay has shown, whereas the more familiar ancient sources depict Cassandra as "a self-assured woman who is unapologetic and resists self-pity" despite Apollo's unjust curse, the series reduces her from a "divinely inspired seer" into an unstable, raving "Madwoman in the Attic Tradition," as Ilkay puts it in her title.[33] As such, in its depiction of Cassandra, *TFOAC* plays into misogynistic notions of women as mentally frail and prone to hysteria.

And it is not just that her prophecies are discounted: from the age of seven, she has been locked away under the pretense of madness. When Hector discovers that this has been a mere pretext so that word of her visions would not get out, he forces Cassandra against her will into their parents' chambers to confront them. "I don't want to be in here ... Please let me go," she urges, to which Hector insists, "Stay where you are, Cassandra" (Episode 5), so that, ironically, he reinforces her lack of agency even as he objects to her being stripped of it. Indeed, the completeness of the stifling of Cassandra's voice and the trauma she endures because of it are emphasized from the beginning: in Episode 1, Cassandra dreams of black blood seeping under the door, then looks into a mirror, and is horrified to see that in her reflected image, her mouth itself has been erased (Fig. 7.2).

The series finale draws attention to the pairing of Andromache and Cassandra as women whose (legitimate) voices are discounted when the two provide the lone objections to bringing the horse into the city. Andromache forcefully advises, "We should leave it. All things Greek are cursed. Let the sea take it," while Cassandra asks with fearful urgency, "Father, father, what if it's not a blessing?" Although he seems to weigh the decision carefully for a moment, Priam soon makes his pronouncement: "They have taken everything from us ... Let's steal their blessing from them ...!" In doing so, not only does he flout Andromache's clear misgivings, he seems to misread his own daughter's warning quite willfully.

Figure 7.2 Lalo Alcaraz's political cartoon depicting Christine Blasey Ford and Brett Kavanaugh (2018) and Cassandra (Aimee-Ffion Edwards) in Episode 1, "Black Blood."

Conclusion

Three months after the final episode of *TFOAC* aired, former President Trump nominated Brett Kavanaugh for Associate Justice of the US Supreme Court. Shortly following his four-day hearing by the Senate Judiciary Committee at the beginning of September, it came to light that Dr. Christine Blasey Ford had written in July to Senator Dianne Feinstein accusing Kavanaugh of sexually assaulting her in 1982 when they were both in high school. The vote on Kavanaugh's confirmation was postponed and a hearing ensued where Ford testified about the incident. Despite Ford's credible testimony and similar allegations of sexual misconduct in the 1980s brought forward by two other women, the Committee forwarded the nomination on to the full Senate, which confirmed Kavanaugh's nomination to the Supreme Court, where he sits today.

Ford's allegations were presented to the Senate, heard by the nation, and along with the accusations brought by her co-accusers, were the subject of a subsequent FBI investigation. But to many observers, the whole thing came off as pretense, with the hearings and investigations intended to give the impression of taking these women seriously. But with the President himself defending Kavanaugh as "one of the finest human beings you will ever have the privilege of knowing or meeting" and "a high-quality person,"[34] his confirmation was never really in serious jeopardy. Ford may have been given the opportunity to speak, but her voice was seemingly ignored as insistently as Cassandra's.

Not dissimilarly, *TFOAC* attempts to set up Hecuba as a ruler equal in power to her husband; Helen as a woman who asserts autonomy in choosing her fate; and Andromache as a respected wife who is forthright in expressing her opinions to both her husband and the powers that be. But any strength and influence the series attributes to them with one hand is taken away with the other.

In a sense, the series' creators have unwittingly turned the Homeric depiction of women's power inside out: in Homer, although they are technically disenfranchised, by managing information and working within the constraints they are given, women like Helen and Penelope are able to exert considerable influence and agency; but in *TFOAC*, the power and autonomy that are verbally attributed to women, or that they attribute to themselves, do not bear up to close scrutiny. While *TFOAC* might be commended for foregrounding women as complex individuals and for passing the Bechdel Test, if just barely,[35] the systematic silencing, discounting, and willful misuse of women's voices in this fictional series is a troubling replication of gender dynamics that remains all too familiar in the real world today.

Notes

1. Thanks to Monica Cyrino and Antony Augoustakis for their input on this chapter. I am also indebted to feedback from attendees at the November 2018 Film & History conference and the April 2019 Classical Association of the Middle West and South meeting.

2. As Trusty 2018 notes, *TFOAC* casts a wider net than most by acknowledging extra-Homeric mythological sources (the opening credits characterize the series as "inspired by Homer and the Greek myths") rather than reductively attributing everything to Homer (IMDb, however, credits five out of the eight episodes as "inspired by" Homer, while no other particular ancient source is acknowledged).
3. See Prince in this volume.
4. Amazon UK reviewer "Carole" (May 31, 2018) suggests that, among others, the scene depicting Cassandra's rape has been cut short on the DVD (only available in Region 2), suggesting that a different version may have aired in the UK.
5. For more on women's cloistering in classical period Greece, see Pomeroy 1975: 79–83 and Blundell 1995: 135–8.
6. Quoted in Sherwin 2018. As Emily Wilson 2014 points out, Bettany Hughes has also problematically framed Helen as "a real character from history."
7. Felson 1994: 15–42 and Winkler 1990: 129–61.
8. See especially lines 1368–1401.
9. Fragment 1 as noted by Blondell 2013a: 27.
10. Pausanias' *Description of Greece* 3.19.13; Homer's *Iliad* 6.357–8 and 9.185–94.
11. Achilles and Patroclus lure two Trojan soldiers out of the besieged citadel with a herd of seemingly unattended goats. When the Trojans approach, Achilles and Patroclus throw off the goatskins they'd been hiding under, kill the Trojans, and don their armor. So disguised and carrying two dead goats that will be a welcome (and distracting) sight to the hungry Trojans, the gates are opened to them and they walk in unchallenged. Compare stories of Odysseus' tricky entrances and exits at *Odyssey* 4.235–64 and 9.420–63.
12. Blondell 2013b: 51–2.
13. See *Odyssey* 6.303–15 and 7.64–77.
14. Trusty 2018.
15. Hughes 2018b (or as Larsen 2018 puts it, she "basically Fed Exs herself to Troy").
16. She emphasizes her autonomy again in Episode 3. See also Jenkins and Norgard in this volume.
17. Amazon UK reviewer "David" (April 10, 2018).
18. For more on the depiction of Amazons in popular culture, see Penrose in this volume.
19. See, e.g., Blundell 1995: 62 and Blondell 2005: 188–90.
20. This is one indication that the creators' attempts at post-racial casting have not succeeded entirely. My students were also quick to point out that in this series, paradigms of female beauty, both mortal (Helen) and divine (Aphrodite), are White. In addition, the casting of a Black man in the role of Achilles, a character known for his rage and murderous violence, is further problematized by the near-rape scene in Helen's bedroom.
21. When Odysseus pauses in his famous tale in Book 11 of the *Odyssey*, Arete first suggests that the Phaeacians offer him gifts, but although the elder Echeneus approves her words and suggests they be heeded, he stipulates that "deed and word depend on Alcinous" (11.346).
22. Hughes 2018b.
23. See Loraux 1987: 7–30.
24. See Safran in this volume.
25. Hughes 2018c.

26. Blondell 2013a, as noted in Wilson 2014.
27. See, for instance, Worman 2001.
28. In this series, as in antiquity and in many other cinematic versions of the Trojan War story, a clear parallel is drawn between Helen and the Trojan horse, an identification which amplifies her culpability and sharpens the negative traits associated with the female nature. For more on this, see Day (2022).
29. This juxtaposition is intensified by the fact that, as Amazon UK reviewer "Stephen Bishop" (April 21, 2019) puts it, Bella Dayne may be beautiful, but Chloe Pirrie as Andromache "acts her off the set."
30. Vann 2016. See *Iliad* 6.476–81.
31. Hughes 2018b.
32. Trusty 2018 has also pointed out that "it's not just Cassandra who is ignored, but all the women."
33. Ilkay 2018.
34. Holland 2018.
35. In a brief scene in Episode 2, for instance, Hecuba gives Helen a makeup lesson. Later in the same episode, Helen knocks on Cassandra's door, and a distressed Cassandra reproaches her repeatedly: "You should never have come! You should never have come!" In Episode 5, Hecuba tries to apologize to Cassandra for locking her away, but Cassandra quickly scurries away. Other rare conversations between women where men aren't explicitly mentioned revolve around or touch on motherhood.

CHAPTER 8
QUEERING TROY: FREEDOM AND SEXUALITY
Thomas E. Jenkins

Much ink has been spilled about the innovative presentation of race and ethnicity in *Troy: Fall of a City* (2018); comparatively less attention has been paid, however, to the portrayal of gender and sexuality. In this chapter, we argue that key and often anachronistic *political* terms—especially the concept of "freedom"—have been mapped onto the sexual constellations of characters throughout the series, particularly in the never-neverland of Troy itself.[1] Indeed, in some respects, *TFOAC* presents Orientalism in *reverse*: the West—exemplified by Sparta—is depicted as authoritarian, sexist, and benighted, while the East—exemplified by Troy—shines as politically enlightened and sexually progressive. (In other respects, however, *TFOAC* is as orientalizing as anything produced by Hollywood in recent years, and we will return to that fundamental tension shortly.) "Freedom"—in both its sexual and political senses—especially molds the narrative arcs of Helen and Achilles, each character idealizing and variously achieving a freedom in Troy hitherto unimagined. While the "freeing" romance of Helen and Paris eventually founders on the show's ideological tensions, the sexual freedom of Achilles actually leapfrogs over the usual (albeit controversial) reception of Achilles as gay, and into the uncharted waters of twenty-first-century queer polyamory. In this way, *TFOAC* pushes the envelope of using classical antiquity as a medium for interrogating *contemporary* sexual roles and stereotypes, though with generally more success (and fanfare) with the newly inaugurated threesome of Achilles, Patroclus, and Briseis.

From the very first episodes, the writers clearly signal the *ideological* stakes at play in the series: Paris seduces Helen not with desire *per se*, but with the possibility of an escape from male-dominated and hierarchical Greece to the fabled freedom of the East. Thus the first two episodes clearly establish Helen as a character trapped within the rigid sexual roles prescribed by the Greek patriarchy. In a crucial early exchange between Paris and Helen, Paris mocks the backward *mores* of Sparta and the city's treatment of Helen: "Your world here was wild: Your 'civilized' husband didn't want that—it scared him—so he tamed it and he tamed you too." Paris does not often employ irony so his sarcastic description of a "civilized" Menelaus here carries especial weight. He is disgusted not just by Menelaus the husband, but Menelaus as the figurehead of a so-called "civilization": Greece. Paris hints that the marriage to Menelaus took something (rather, someone) free and wild, and transformed her into a trapped *Hausfrau*. Helen explains such taming in the simplest and yet most political of terms: "I am a woman. We don't get to select our fate." In other words, Helen has yielded to the exigencies of the dominant political system: she is a sexual subject, not a sexual agent, one married to a man not of her choosing.[2] Paris next describes an unhappy married life straight out of Fitzgerald's *Great Gatsby*, a description that seems both ancient and modern at once: "[This is] a life of gritting your teeth through banquets, drugging yourself into oblivion." If true, this constitutes an ironic *inversion* of the Helen of Homer's *Odyssey*, who gleefully drugs *others* into oblivion; in *TFOAC*, Helen is so unhappy, she is compelled to self-medicate.[3]

Paris then woos Helen not just with sex appeal—but with *geography*. "I know what freedom is, and this isn't it," Paris offers in his typically artless way, a statement which maps the concept of (sexual) freedom onto *his* world, the world of the East.[4] Helen in return acknowledges the social pressures at work on them both: "You're royal now. Duty will be your master too" (Episode 1). It is a thought that Paris quickly rebuffs, as he interweaves the political and the erotic: "No-one can master me. Except maybe you." In other words, Paris is willing and eager to enter a liaison in which Helen is not just (sexually) equal, but *dominant*, even as he climbs the ladder of aristocracy in Troy. We may be suspicious of the legitimacy of Paris' claim, but it is striking that *power* is at the heart of his persuasive appeal: it is not just that he's a sexy slab of shepherd (a given, it seems) but that Troy will allow Helen to exert a political influence clearly denied to her, and *every* woman, in Sparta.

Visually, the series reinforces the idea of Helen as prisoner (of her sex, of her marriage) with numerous metaphors of cages and taming, of prisons and eventual freedom. A strange exchange between Helen, Paris, and Menelaus helps explain the recurring images of birds throughout the first few episodes: "Are those your birds, m'lady?" Paris queries, gesturing to the parakeets in the palace.[5] Helen explains: "Yes, my father always let them fly free in the house." Menelaus then interjects, in a mocking tone: "One of his little indulgences" (Episode 1). In other words, Menelaus considers it an indulgence to let a bird fly even a little bit free, even (or *especially*) within a house—and his wife Helen would seem to be such a bird. In fact, in Episode 1, we see Helen *costumed* like a bird: her head seems to be cannonballing from a truly epic assemblage of feathers (Fig. 8.1). So

Figure 8.1 Helen (Bella Dayne) costumed like a bird in Episode 1, "Black Blood."

Queering Troy: Freedom and Sexuality

while bird-like Helen tends to spend her evenings tamed within the women's quarters (*gynaikeion*)[6] of the house—in a homosocial gathering firmly set *within* the walls and social structures of Sparta—it is significant that her greatest act of sexual agency takes place *outside* the palace. Guided to an almost Spenserian bower by a wily handmaiden, the two lovers escape, for a spell, the cage of the palace, and create in effect a love-nest: one predicated on *actual* desire, and not social exigency or teen-age marriage.

Helen's escape from Sparta combines the series' political imagery with a novel narrative twist: instead of being snatched or kidnapped by Paris—or even simply eloping—Helen exerts agency over desire, as she surreptitiously arranges to be smuggled in a chest. She thus re-deploys the imagery of caging *against* the political structure that cages her in Sparta: she is fighting fire with fire. Paris is surprised by this clever inversion of the myth of Pandora's box: aboard ship, this man opens the chest to discover not a panoply of evils (Hesiod's *Works and Days* 95) but a woman successfully breaking "free" of the evils of Greece and its sexual rigidity. Helen is literally progressing.

We soon discover that Paris is at least partly right: there *is* a startlingly progressive freedom at play (and *of* play) in Troy, in a way that marks the series' departure from other versions of Homer. Helen introduces herself to Hecuba by noting the Trojan queen's extraordinary liberation: "I hear, my queen, that you rule Troy alongside your husband: that, in this city, man and woman are equal in respect and power" (Episode 2). This statement is impossible to reconcile with Homeric depictions of gender and power, but it is indicative of the series' targeted updating of power-relationships. Indeed, Troy's *political* progressiveness seems to warp the space-time continuum around it: not only will Helen and Paris attempt a "liberated" relationship modeled on the co-regents Hecuba and Priam (and heirs apparent Hector and Andromache), but, as we shall see, the fairytale world of Troy will allow an altogether different relationship to blossom. The *Iliad's other* famous wartime love affair—the oft-interpreted relationship of Patroclus and Achilles—will admit a *co-equal* third partner: the war-prize Briseis. In the single most striking scene of the entire series, Achilles, Patroclus, and Briseis engage in a startling *ménage à trois* that dissolves hierarchies of race, gender, and status: the characters are three equal points of a triangle. It's sexual freedom for 2018 (and beyond).

In other words, by mapping the concept of 'freedom' onto Troy (however anachronistically, however improbably), the series creators upend expectations of how sexual power is figured in the eastern Mediterranean and queue up the most surprising narrative swerve of the entire series. But there are stumbles along the way to this sexually liberated version of Homer. In some respects, *TFOAC* remains resolutely old-fashioned, particularly in its treatment of Helen's sexuality. As Cyrino and Nisbet have argued, Hollywood has long marinated in its own alt-version of antiquity, and has, over the course of over a century, built upon those fundamental signs:[7] in effect, Hollywood has innovated its own syntax of antiquity, with recurring symbols and motifs, like volcanos and gladiators, employed to sometimes striking effect.[8] An advantage of this new system is that, like all systems, it is semiotically rich from the get-go: a "new" viewer to *TFOAC* is still an old hand at Greece-on-film, and the series' brew of magic, religion, violence, and *realpolitik* will seem familiar to those who have imbibed such seemingly diverse influences as *Xena, Warrior Princess* (1995–2001), Oliver's Stone's *Alexander* (2004), and even the seminal 1981 *Clash of the Titans* (with its pantheon of ever-quarreling gods). *TFOAC* thus works *within the tradition* of Helen of Troy stories, including influences as diverse as *Helen of Troy* (1955), USA Network's mini-series *Helen of Troy* (2003), and the film *Troy* (2004). And from the beginning, *TFOAC* throws down the gauntlet with its striking additions to the abduction of Helen, here spun as an exercise of freedom and free will.

But this much-vaunted freedom of Helen—variously figured in her romance with Paris and in her surprising machinations within Troy itself—often founders on the shoals of the series' design and directing choices, which objectify Helen with surprising and sometimes disconcerting frequency. While the series attempts a reversal of the *political* orientalizing of Troy, it often doubles down on exuberant and over-the-top costuming, which is at times outrageous, and at other times merely sexy. While few characters in Troy escape unscathed from the show's visual Orientalism, Helen's prominence and her oversexualized garb demonstrate how difficult it is to shoehorn progressive sexual ideals into the Helen of Troy narrative.

A representative example of the show's overt orientalizing may be found in the portrayal of King Priam in Episode 3, where he could easily be mistaken for a character in *The 7th Voyage of Sinbad* (1958) or *The Golden Voyage of Sinbad* (1973). Plenty of orientalizing features are at play here: Priam wears a navy-blue turban, ostentatious gold jewelry, a barbarian torque, and clothing with a loud geometric print.[9] But the orientalizing is of a piece with the show's emphasis on gender and power: this is what *male* power looks like, Troy style. Unfortunately, these same orientalizing tendencies torpedo the *political* thrust of Helen's arc: having established Helen's wish to be seen as other than Menelaus' possession, the show *constantly* displays Helen both with possessions and *as* a possession. Most infamously, this collision occurs in Episode 2. It is a moment rightly ironized on Tumblr, and even converted into an animated .gif/meme for social media.[10] The *very* moment in which Helen declares her Troy-inspired political and sexual independence ("I'm not a possession!"), she is entirely *smothered* by possessions: from head to toe, she is shellacked with shells, jewelry, embroidered fabric, and precious metals, in what seems to be an homage to Heinrich Schliemann's real-life adornment of his wife, Sophia, in a much-celebrated picture with the "treasure of Priam."[11] Helen bears a strong resemblance to Sophia, here: her headdress is intricately beaded with several hanging tassel-like pieces on either side, as is Helen's. However, Sophia's piece is more fringe-like in its structure, whereas those in *TFOAC* are sort of intricate caps that rest upon the top of the head and come down slightly upon the forehead. Helen's archaeologically-inflected objectification is so complete that only a small smattering of flesh is allowed to break through the objects. This sort of cognitive dissonance informs much of the series: Helen is eternally metonymic to objects and luxury, to finery and show-pieces.

As Maguire notes, the depiction of Helen as an over-adorned prize has a long history in performance, and *TFOAC* is thus mainstream in how it portrays Helen sartorially. One notable example is the Royal Shakespeare Company's 1991 *Troilus and Cressida*,

Queering Troy: Freedom and Sexuality

with Sally Dexter's Helen described as "borne aloft on an enormous cushion, wrapped in shining gold fabric" and then "unwrapped" by Paris, quite aggressively figuring her as a possession, gift, or piece of jewelry. In the Royal Shakespeare Company's 1968 *Dr. Faustus*, Helen is quite notably nude; Maguire notes "if language is the dress of thought, a naked Helen ... cannot be described."[12] This presents the idea that Helen herself is enough to be the most beautiful woman; she needs no adornments. Perhaps they even distract or detract from her beauty, which seems the case in *TFOAC* – Helen is rendered *less* beautiful and more ideologically confusing by her outfits.

However, Maguire also notes that in the *Odyssey* Helen is described as making her own clothes, which is especially fascinating to consider in conjunction with her history of costume in various media.[13] If you were the most beautiful woman in the world, how would you choose to dress yourself? Helen seems to recognize that her power is in her sex appeal and thus she must intentionally enhance her natural gifts with her clothing.[14] In film, however, it is difficult to draw a distinction between the character's agency, and the designers'. The "Mummy" dress in Episode 2—an elaborately devised piece constructed of cords and accessories—could not be more orientalizing, like a fantasia from the Egyptomania of the 1830s. If Helen ever wanted to catch the eye of Tutankhamen, then here is the gown for it.

The rather more insidious aspect of objectification is the *visual* objectification: the 'male-gaze' of the camera that turns women (primarily) into objects.[15] This is sometimes subtle—as in Episode 5's sexy cleavage-flaunting gown—or explicit, when there is simply cleavage. The reunion of Paris and Helen in Episode 6 is particularly flesh-strewn and concludes with a startling and even prurient shot of a topless Helen (Fig. 8.2). To its credit, the series is not particularly shy with male nudity either. There are plenty of bare chests and backsides to go around, but something about the objectification of Helen

Figure 8.2 The reunion of Paris (Louis Hunter) and Helen (Bella Dayne) in Episode 6, "Battle on the Beach."

rankles: the show presents an *argument* about Helen (that she is *not* an object, that she *is* an agent) while preposterously cascading her *with* objects or stripping her naked *as* an object. And we cannot blame *TFOAC*, exactly, since it is working *within* the idiom of performed versions of Troy: is it even possible to put the "most beautiful woman in the world" onscreen without the full Hollywood treatment—including *haute couture* and frontal nudity?[16] But just because Helen is the most beautiful woman does not require her to be most *objectified*. Whether through her excessively gaudy outfits in Sparta, the lowest necklines in all of Troy, or her constant sex scenes with Paris, Helen's body often serves as little more than an object for the viewers' admiration, which undermines the series' otherwise progressive message. Only toward the end of Episode 8, when the world of *TFOAC* unravels and Helen seems destined to return home, do the costume choices again align with the politics (and even the poetics) of the series. Upon first seeing Helen, Menelaus notes, "You're more beautiful than ever," as he proceeds to stroke Helen's breasts through her clothes. She now wears longer sleeves and a less-revealing outfit, thus channeling (again) the appearances of a modest wife to appease her husband. Her costuming thus conforms to the expectations of a proper, submissive wife, and she aims to return home to Sparta, "tamed" once again.

In many ways, then, the political and sexual freedom that Paris promised Helen is a red herring, both within the narrative itself and on a meta-level. For the most part, Helen is as sexualized and objectified as other Hollywood Helens, even if she engages in more cloak-and-dagger intrigues than the norm. For all of their liberties with the Troy story, the creators have generally hitched their wagon to Homer's original epic: if they had *really* wanted to do something challenging with the 'co-regent'/women's liberation angle of Troy, they could have (but conspicuously *did not*) change the ransom scene. How powerful and provocative, how *genuinely* revolutionary would it have been for Hector's ransom to be accomplished by Hecuba instead of Priam? Otherwise, *TFOAC*'s rhetoric of female equality seems simply that: words, words, words—and the visual framing of female sexuality, particularly Helen's, displays quite another agenda. Surprisingly, it falls to a *different* relationship, and a different ideological argument concerning freedom, for *TFOAC* to come into its own as a truly novel reception of Homeric gender politics.

The Polyqueer Threesome

The series' startling take on a different sexual relationship, that of Achilles and Patroclus, demonstrates just how intertwined culture and reception can and must be. For instance, Barry Purves' short film *Achilles*, premiering in 1995, clearly reflects the *Zeitgeist* of its decade: it is a claymation version of the *Iliad* that promotes a clear gay-rights agenda (a *cri de coeur* well before *Lawrence v. Texas* in 2003 overturned sodomy laws in America), and which co-exists with a burst of coming out narratives in popular media, including Ellen DeGeneres' famous episode in her eponymous sitcom (in April 1997). As a version of the Homer story, *Achilles* makes explicit that there's a secret version of the *Iliad*, one never before told: "How can we forgive a love undeclared?" the narrator portentously intones, and the answer is clear: we cannot, *yet*. Indeed, it is surprising just how closet-y this cinematic *Achilles* is, as Achilles, in particular, struggles with newfound feelings for Patroclus. In order to make this version of the *Iliad* "read" as Western and gay(-ish), Purves swaps the Homeric ages of Achilles and Patroclus so that Achilles is now older, dominant, and stereotypically masculine, while Patroclus is younger, slender, and rather more submissive. In other words, they now map onto Athenian identities of *eromenoi* and *erasteis*, as well as the contemporary Western gay tribes of bears and twinks. The *Iliad's* famously heterosexual romance between Helen and Paris is focused through an entirely queer lens, as Achilles and Patroclus act out a flashback of that straight elopement—in drag. In other words, *Achilles* literally travesties the *Iliad*, a sort of fan fiction *avant la lettre*.

For all of its progressive flourishes, however, *Achilles* still labors under some contradictory impulses. The film's depiction of sexual assault—particularly Achilles' assault on Briseis—is employed primarily as an aspect of Achilles' character development. A subsequent homoerotic drinking scene proves that love, *especially* if undeclared, can still be demonstrated through dramatically lowered inhibitions, and Achilles again seems to fight against his natural impulses. Conquered at last by what comes naturally, Achilles and Patroclus engage in a surprisingly graphic sex scene, which, given the medium of clay, can only conclude in coitus or a perfectly thrown pot. Alas, the lovers cannot quite escape the plot of the *Iliad*: as in Homer's poem, Patroclus dons Achilles' armor and tragedy ensues. A surprising coda portrays the death of Achilles by the hand of Paris—the revenge of the epic tradition on this queering of Homer. A final, sentimental overhead shot depicts the two lovers as if on a bridal bed: but here it is a bier, a final resting place. Together, Achilles and Patroclus share one shield, one heart.

Achilles, the short gay film, didn't appear *ex nihilo*: Achilles and Patroclus—as 'friends'—had been code for homosexuality for eons. The ancient pedigree for such an interpretation is well-established: no less an authority than Aeschylus, in his now fragmentary *Myrmidons*, dramatizes an Achilles who recalls the holy offerings of Patroclus' thighs, the couple's swarm of kisses, and the intimacy (again) of his lover's thighs.[17] These images, thighs and kisses, are lovingly and graphically transferred to the film *Achilles*, whatever its other flights of fancy. Other twentieth-century receptions, however, are either more circumspect or outwardly hostile. Some receptions of their relationship lean into the couple's "friendship" without exploring the more physical (and perhaps off-putting) aspects.[18] This interpretative tactic is the 1990s descendant of the "friendship" movement exemplified by Carpenter's *Ioläus: An Anthology of Friendship* (1915), a tome that largely exalts male-male friendships such as Harmodius and Aristogeiton, Orestes and Pylades, and of course, Achilles and Patroclus.[19] But while *Achilles* attempted to push the West out of its comfort zone, and into a *very* erogenous zone, the headwinds were insurmountable. Hollywood's subsequent blockbuster *Troy* (2004), starring a buffed-up Brad Pitt and a baby-faced Garrett Hedlund as Patroclus, performed a virtual *damnatio memoriae* on gay versions of the *Iliad* by hilariously and offensively morphing the two of them into cousins. Indeed, the pair refer to each other as cousins *ad nauseam* in order to signal to the mainstream audience that this is *not* homosexuality; it is simply cousinage (and emphatically *not* "kissing cousins"). This crucial alteration thus neuters the relationship and nips in the bud any unwelcome ruminations about the exact (sexual) nature of their relationship.[20] In *Troy*, it is just blood.

However, receptions of the relationship between Achilles and Patroclus have tended to stay in lockstep with the wider cultural tug-of-war. Madeline Miller's novel *The Song of Achilles* (2012) presents a version of Achilles and Patroclus that seems to prefigure marriage equality in the United States—just four years before the Supreme Court decision. The two warriors are presented as being in a definitively monogamous gay relationship, and Briseis and Achilles are entirely separate from each other—united only by their love for Patroclus. While Briseis harbors romantic feelings for Patroclus, they are not reciprocated. In a tender moment, Patroclus notes Briseis is "one of us now ... a member of our circle, for life" (252), which demonstrates a reconfiguration of the notion of *family*, but not of romantic relationships, *per se*. The love triangle is unequal and thus tragic. Briseis and Patroclus share a friendly moment together on a hill—one that seems like it could blossom into something more—before Achilles interrupts and Briseis departs (268). This is the closest *The Song of Achilles* ever gets to the (future) world of *TFOAC*; it is an indication that the three of them, with the addition of Patroclus' and Briseis' (future) child, *could* live together as a family, but not as a romantic threesome.[21]

As we have seen in the arc of Helen and Paris, *TFOAC* proposes a Greece that is unequal and a Troy that *is not*—but that binary division is complicated by the show's *other* great love affair: Patroclus-Achilles-Briseis. In Episode 4, Achilles and Patroclus, having bucked the political imperatives of their generals, Agamemnon and Menelaus, retire to the beach for the most jaw-dropping sequence in the entire series. We see elsewhere how water functions as a liminal space for transitions and change.[22] For the Myrmidons Achilles and Patroclus, water provides the background for a new and enlightened spin on sexuality as the camera first films erotic moments from Aeschylus' fragments—the "classical" thighs and kisses of Achilles and Patroclus. But then, surprisingly, the camera swivels to *Briseis* and Patroclus, a move which seems to refigure (even to call into question) the sincerity, if not the mechanics, of the liaison between Achilles and Patroclus. But all such questions are answered by the revelation of a truly free and equal three-way sexual relationship between Achilles, Briseis, and Patroclus, one that (at least visually) eradicates their differences in power and status, and instead transports the scene into a sexual utopia, free from race, gender, and especially mononormativity.

The threesome beach scene is artfully constructed to surprise the audience by first reinforcing expectations of traditional Greco-Roman culture, and then exploding them, in ways that some viewers found frankly shocking.[23] It begins with Achilles and Patroclus engaged in the most stereotypical of "ancient" homosocial behavior: Greco-Roman wrestling. This beach-time wrestling is interspersed with thoughts of mortality: "You almost died," Achilles laments, while Patroclus shows he still has plenty of spirit within him. This sets up the beginning of the scene as a non-controversial, macho, and oh-so-Hollywood bromance. The scene then morphs into another aspect of the "traditional" (but perhaps unsettling) ancient world: homosexual kissing and tousling, into which Greco-Roman wrestling, already imbued with touches of the homosocial, ineluctably slides. But then the surprise: Briseis gazes on at Achilles and Patroclus, with longing or perhaps amusement, as Patroclus approaches. After a brief exchange with Patroclus—"I'm glad you didn't die," Briseis offers—the slave girl leans forward and, amazingly, initiates an erotic encounter with him, perhaps for the first time. Achilles takes notice, and instead of flaming into anger or jealousy (as one might expect), he *joins*, and initiates Netflix's most carefully constructed polyqueer threesome (to-date). Each character systematically, even mathematically, kisses the two others—meting out kisses equally—until they all kiss *simultaneously* in a close-knit triangle. The camera then swipes to the morning-after: this new scene is clearly post-coital.

Needless to say, the Internet melted down after this episode, but only a few voices placed the scene within the wider context of the series.[24] Binary divisions are rampant in the series (male vs. female, West vs. East, freedom vs. slavery, luxury vs. penury, humanity vs. barbarism) but this threesome explodes all of that. It is the most structurally and ideologically liberating moment in the entire show. And it was captured by graphic artist Elena Gogou in a Tumblr post that gets to the (literal) heart of the threesome's almost-sentimental take on human sexuality, with a realistic heart floating, disembodied, over the naked cuddling of the lead actors (Fig. 8.3). This artistic representation of the show's most famous moment makes some subtle reworkings to the original shot: there is a rotation of Achilles to align with the two other figures, and Patroclus' gentle stroking of Briseis is particularly romantic. Most obviously, there is a disembodied heart: one not iconic (like a Valentine's heart), but realistic and biological. These are *real* humans, *real* feelings, sundered from the mythopoetic world of Grand Epic and plopped into the liberating world of the 2018 Internet.[25] Indeed, in some senses, Gogou's Instagram art "one-ups" the show: it allows us to reflect on the moment *disrupted* from time and

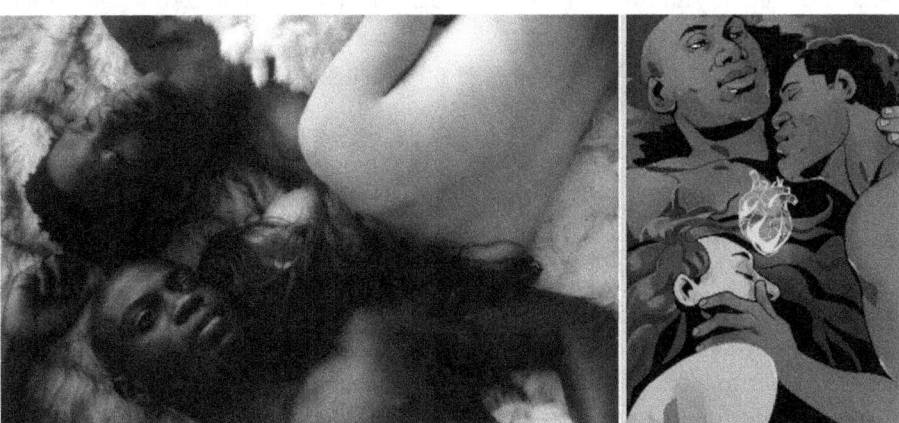

Figure 8.3 Achilles (David Gyasi), Patroclus (Lemogang Tsipa), and Briseis (Amy Louise Wilson) in Episode 6, "Battle on the Beach" (left), and Elena Gogou's Tumblr post of the scene reimagined (with permission from the creator).

disjointed from narrative. The series pans over the trio but then rushes back to the grim *mise en scène* of war. Even more jarringly, the camera returns to Agamemnon, whose shouting interrupts the slumber and the still life. Elena Gogou's Tumblr portrait, by contrast, captures the moment as in amber. The artist has indicated *why* this scene particularly seized her attention:

> [I am] interested in polyamorous relationships and how they might have worked in societies that are less strictly monogamous than ours. This interpretation of the relationship between the three characters seemed natural to me ... [The] addition of the heart was instinctive ... I believe my intention was to highlight the romantic aspect of the affair in contrast with the image of the physical aspect of it."[26]

For Gogou, then, the series provided the opportunity to highlight, and ruminate upon, contemporary polyamory, and particularly polyamory's romantic potential, not its mere physicality.[27]

Sociologist Mimi Schipper's recent scholarship on contemporary polyamory demonstrates how erotic threesomes are emphatically *not* created equal, and, indeed, may not register as transgressive, or liberating, at all. As the sociological data indicates, MFF (male-female-female) threesomes tend, in fact, to reinforce the (traditional) *heteronormativity* of the man: in fact, a male who fantasizes about such a threesome is considered as "normal as normal can be."[28] To the extent to which masculinity is symbolized/embodied by the penetrating phallus, MFF activity may be overdeterminedly heterosexual: for the man, it presents a redoubled opportunity for penetration, and thus confirms his identity as a dominating heterosexual. For this reason, contemporary FMM (female-male-male) threesomes are far more rare, both in reality and in fantasy, since such threesomes bring up the potentially unwelcome specter of (male) homosexuality as well as rivalry.[29] For some men, "acceptable" forms of FMM sexual activity might, then, be serial penetration by the two men or other sexual activities that minimize (or even obviate) the homosocial aspects.[30] In Schippers' view, FMM threesomes that *include* the homoerotic, penetrating activities are so rare they may be subsumed under the category of (imaginary) *polyqueer threesomes*, whose queerness inheres in their radical dissolution of masculine and feminine norms, and the attendant (socially-constructed) hierarchies of power.[31] Such polyqueer configurations dovetail with the emergent narrative structures of "slash fiction", in which heteronormative men, such as Capt. Kirk and Mr. Spock from *Star Trek*, are re-written as lovers. In this way, new social media-driven narratives, such as Gogou's Tumblr art, resist the inherited narratives of sexuality, and identify (in a positive way) how sexuality may be reconfigured now (and in the future).

Thus *TFOAC*'s polyqueer threesome of Achilles, Patroclus, and Briseis, a FMM trio, at last makes good on the show's promise of sexual freedom and the interrogation of social norms, a promise only fitfully fulfilled in the dyadic monogamy of Helen and Paris (and for that matter, Andromache and Hector, Priam and Hecuba). The filming of the FMM sex scenes avoids the unwelcome thought of a *heteronormative* FMM threesome by establishing the physical attraction of Achilles and Patroclus from the get-go before launching into the threesome itself. The evenhanded filming of the encounter establishes the equality of the relationship, and avoids any capitalist overtones of possession.[32] Menelaus even thunders in Episode 3 that he is the "rightful owner" of Helen; *TFOAC* thus draws a clear contrast between the tyrannical, capitalist treatment of Helen and the fair, democratic treatment of Briseis. The hot-potato notion of "freedom" is thus mapped, perhaps uncomfortably, onto a sexual freedom that possesses a true ideological and political charge.

Achilles and Helen: Tradition vs. Innovation

We have argued that the series attempts to map the concept of sexual freedom onto two main characters, Achilles and Helen, with various degrees of success. One of the surprises is that while Homer's *Iliad* never brings together the characters of Achilles and Helen, *TFOAC* includes one (awkward) scene in which the show's two great protagonists finally meet, and the results are extremely vexing for the show's argument concerning gender politics.[33] While Hector and Paris depart on a mission in Episode 3, Achilles surprises Helen with a surreptitious foray into the city. Achilles' actions there jibe very uneasily with the show's valorization of utopian polyamory elsewhere evinced.

Here, Achilles seems to exemplify old-school, stereotypical masculine Greek traits: sexual aggression and toxic masculinity. His exchange with Helen is laden with sexual import: Achilles remarks that it seems as though "one husband isn't enough for you" and that "you should have told me Menelaus wasn't satisfying you—I would have willingly obliged." (This is an explicit rejection of a polyamorous MMF threesome: Achilles wants Helen for himself.) He then segues to an admiring self-appraisal of his own masculinity, adding that "if you are going to sleep around, at least choose a real man." As Achilles puns, "no one wields a better sword" than he does, a turn of phrase that describes his military and sexual prowess in no uncertain terms. He (of *all* people) shames Helen for "sleeping around," an accusation which the series in fact disputes: in Episode 1, Helen explains that she was forced into marriage by her father and we learn later that she was given away as a prize to Menelaus. Helen defends herself by recourse to an anthropological analysis of the so-called "traffic in women": "How flattering it is to be passed among men," she bitterly complains.[34] Her statement focalizes the character of Achilles through the eyes of a woman who has been promised, but not quite given, the freedom of sexual choice.

The tensions in the scenes are not just verbal. Achilles' physical overtures further illuminate the literal position of a woman in Greece. Achilles throws Helen onto her bed and pins her down with his body. He is only a few inches away from her face and she is visibly startled as she wrestles and writhes in an attempt at escape. Her short gasps of breath also clearly convey her discomfort, as Achilles strokes her hair, and the situation worsens as Achilles attempts to kiss Helen non-consensually. This scene, in stark contrast to what will be seen later during the polyqueer threesome, depicts Achilles as an embodiment of Greece's misogynistic ideals.

This scene culminates with not only a further characterization of *all* Greek men, but with the appearance of a newfound characteristic of Helen. Helen leans into her skills as a wily manipulator of men, traits rather more akin to an Odyssean Helen than an Iliadic one. Helen manipulates Achilles by inflating his masculine ego and impressive self-regard, intimating that "the Achilles I knew obeyed no one. He answered only to himself." Addressing Achilles directly, Helen decries that he is "breaking into a defenceless woman's bedroom to appease a man I know you don't respect," an action that is beneath the great warrior. Lastly, Helen appeals to a combination of sentimentality and politics: "You, more than anyone, know that I do not love Menelaus, and never did." Here, Helen lays bare the contradiction at the heart of Western Greek marriage: that it is a union predicated on power, not love, whatever its pretexts and illusions. This argument surprisingly persuades Achilles—he recognizes that perhaps love *should* be an element of a female-male relationship—and he yields. For all of its oddities, the scene between Achilles and Helen demonstrates the show's enduring fascination with the intersection of gender and desire, and the fault lines that separate the worlds of staid Mycenae and chaotic Troy. Helen's bitter denunciation of Greek marriage may even have paved the way for Achilles' subsequent liberating threesome on the literal shores of Troy, as Achilles leaves traditional Greece—and traditional antiquity—far, far behind.

Conclusion

TFOAC presents itself with a challenge: the mapping of sexually progressive ideals onto a narrative that literally could not be more traditional. Indeed, that's the point. The series pins its ambitions on two characters from ancient epic who defy conventional morality—Achilles and Helen—and who thus seem naturals as stand-ins for *contemporary* (or even *future*) ideals concerning gender, sexual freedom, and power. This gambit achieves a generally greater pay-off with Achilles, because his reception-history has *always* veered into interesting and provocative re-figurations of his sexuality, an arc with particular traction at the end of the nineteenth century and well into the twentieth. Helen's reception-history, eternally scrambled with her monogamy and even loyalty to Menelaus,[35] presents greater problems, and the series' attempt to construct Troy-by-way-of-Seattle founders on some half-measures. Yes, Helen finally receives a degree of choice when it comes to romantic selection, and, yes, she does evince some autonomy in Troy; but the show's promise of political equality seems in scant supply. Hecuba's role as co-regent (and thus as a potential mentor to Helen) is weakly demonstrated, and the queen is largely relegated to the role of grieving mother and wife, and thus a traditional, "tragic" Hecuba, from both Euripides' *Trojan Women* and his *Hecuba*. And Helen herself seems trapped in a "Hollywood Helen" role: beautiful and duplicitous, but ultimately conventional.

It's the polyqueer threesome, anchored by Achilles, that will endure as the show's most innovative rewriting of the epic tradition, and the one that lands with the strongest explosion of contemporary ideological agitation: it's art with a point. By refiguring the (distressing) Homeric sexual relationship of Achilles and Briseis as a leg of a polyqueer threesome, *TFOAC* frees Briseis from the confines of Iliadic narrative and employs her as a catalyst for a decidedly modern configuration of sexuality. Thus the show's promise of sexual "freedom" and sexual autonomy is fulfilled not by Helen, who remains largely trapped in the heteronormative worlds of Sparta and Troy, but by the Myrmidons Achilles and Patroclus, whose incorporation of Briseis into a threesome opens up new vistas in Troy-reception. *TFOAC* is not, then, a mere doppelgänger of previous versions of Troy, or even previous versions of Greece: though aspects of its presentation are resolutely traditional, its redeployment of gender and sexuality (and their intersections with race, power, and hierarchy) is new and noteworthy. It is a twenty-first-century spin on an old formula that acknowledges the power of fan fiction, the liberalization of sexual categories in Western thought, and the diversity of both ancient and modern communities. For all of its missteps, it is worth saluting *TFOAC* for its chutzpah: when it comes to the presentation of sexuality, the series may occasionally stumble, but it never falls.

Notes

1. This project has greatly benefited from the undergraduate research of William Ramsey and Hope Walker-Tamboli, both Ancient Mediterranean Studies majors at Trinity University. In specific, Ramsey contributed primary research to the sections on the film *Achilles*, the dominant metaphors of Sparta in episodes one and two, and the scene between Helen and Achilles; Walker-Tamboli contributed primary research on Helen's reception-history, including her orientalism and costuming, and the novel *The Song of Achilles*.
2. On Helen, see also the chapters by Day, Norgard, Raucci, and Safran in this volume.
3. For an analysis of the gendering of Helen's *pharmaka* ("drugs"), see Bergren 2008: 111–30. On Bergren's reading, Helen (of the *Odyssey*) employs such drugs to achieve the impossible: the instantiation of a "painless painful memory," a way to remember the traumatizing past while still enjoying, or at least surviving, the present. *TFOAC*'s Helen seems to be employing those drugs on *herself*, which is a novel twist to the epic tradition. Christensen 2017 briefly analyzes the scholia on the "lotus eaters" scene from the *Odyssey* (9.82–97); the scholiasts sometimes characterize the men's addiction as an aspect of individual responsibility and not a biological or social one. Here, Paris unwittingly redeploys ancient literary criticism in a new and "modern" context.
4. This is, of course, a modern, post-industrial use of "freedom." Llewellyn-Jones 2013a: 103 cautions against indiscriminately applying the concept to ancient cultures, particularly those of the Near East. For Llewellyn-Jones, female public visibility (and mobility) should not be confused with "freedom," since it was the woman's *separation* from the male gaze that marked her as high-status and privileged. *TFOAC* paradoxically "frees" Helen in a modern sense as she travels East to a post-industrial, enlightened Troy.
5. The visuals are a little unclear, but parakeets seem likely as the species of bird. They are heard chirping through the scene (1:31:28).
6. Evidence for the materiality of the ancient *gynaikeion* is vexed, and the term may have signified a greater social demarcation than a physical one. See the discussion of Morris 2003: 265–7, which argues for the existence of a gendered 'spectrum' of spaces within an archaic house or complex.

7. Cyrino 2005a and Nisbet 2008.
8. Pomeroy 2008.
9. On Priam, see Cooke in this volume.
10. www.tumgir.com/helenoftroysdevotee.
11. www.commons.wikimedia.org/wiki/File:Sophia_Schliemann_wearing_Treasure_A,_Troy.jpg.
12. Maguire 2009: 45.
13. *Odyssey* 15.104–5.
14. See Cyrino in this volume.
15. The classic exposition of the camera's male-gaze remains Mulvey 1975.
16. It is telling that Homer's solution is the *opposite* of that evolved by film: the poet focalizes the beauty through the eyes of those around her, especially at *Iliad* 3.156–60; see Cook (forthcoming): "Homer leaves it to the listener's imagination to fill" in the blanks of Helen's unearthly beauty.
17. Fragments 135–6; see Leitao 2018: 65–6 for a detailed analysis. Leitao explains that the fragments are (likely) a response to a reproach hurled at Achilles: that he did not sufficiently reciprocate the erotic favors of Patroclus (an opportunity doomed to pass, since Patroclus is either dead or soon will be).
18. Drake 1998: 22: "We have neither confirmation nor denial that Achilles and Patroklos shared each other sexually. But what we certainly do have is a love story as passionate and powerful as anything ever created again in Western literature."
19. Carpenter 1915: 67: "[T]he romance of love among the Greeks was chiefly felt towards male friends."
20. For a withering review of *Troy* and its fetishization of cousinage, see especially Mendelsohn 2004.
21. Television series such as "Modern Family" (2009–2020) also explore the contested contemporary notions of "family," here widened to include gay marriage, adoption, and entire networks of caregiving and support.
22. Water is generally a happy element in the series: Paris' attempted suicide by water instead morphs into a virtual baptism into a new, reformed, man.
23. "[Really] uncalled for," www.twitter.com/Relentlizz/status/1251420353022197760.
24. For example, www.athenianinspector.wordpress.com (October 14, 2018); www.can---i--slytherin.tumblr.com/post/171738503380/troy-fall-of-a-city; www.aelarsen.wordpress.com/category/troy-fall-of-a-city (June 14, 2018).
25. www.elenagarts.tumblr.com and www.twitter.com/ElenGog.
26. Email from Elena Gogou (November 2, 2020).
27. Gogou is also a contributor to the volume *Greek Love* (2019). For Gogou and her fellow artists, Greek Love, typically glossed as homoerotic customs, practices, and attitudes, is too limiting and freighted a term: instead, the artists chose to "just. be. queer." (Gogou *et al.* 2019: back cover).
28. Schippers 2016: 149.
29. Schippers 2016: 140, citing the research of Karlen 1988.
30. Schippers 2016: 149.
31. Schippers 2016: 159

32. Schippers 2016: 175.
33. Schiller's play *Mary Stuart* (1800) innovated the same solution: though Queen Elizabeth and Mary Stuart never met in real life, the playwright felt compelled to include a scene in which they meet.
34. For the classic analysis of the traffic in women in Greek tragedy, see Rabinowitz 1993.
35. For a monograph-length overview of the multiform versions of Helen's story, see Austin 1994.

CHAPTER 9
HEROIC HAIRSTYLES AND MANLESS AMAZONS AT TROY

Walter Duvall Penrose, Jr.

Where were the Amazons in Petersen's *Troy* (2004)?[1] Imagine if Angelina Jolie had played Penthesilea and taken Brad Pitt's Achilles by storm. That moment has surely passed, but nevertheless the Amazons have finally descended upon the Greeks in BBC/Netflix's *Troy: Fall of a City* (2018) mini-series, led by their queen Penthesilea. Nina Milner portrays an androgynous Penthesilea who seeks revenge against Achilles (Fig. 9.1). The contest between Penthesilea and Achilles is not found in Homer's *Iliad*, but it was part of

Figure 9.1 Penthesilea (Nina Milner) in Episode 7, "Twelve Days."

the Trojan Epic Cycle poem the *Aithiopis* by Arctinus, which is known to us from the brief summary of Proclus.[2] In the *Aithiopis*, Achilles defeats Penthesilea, stabbing her with his spear, then kills Thersites who mocks him for his "alleged" *eros* for his victim. In Quintus of Smyrna's later epic poem (third century AD), *Fall of Troy* or *Posthomerica* (1.655–74), as Penthesilea lay dead from his spear, Achilles pulled back her helmet and, smitten, fell madly in love with her. While Quintus relates a story that seems to have been hopelessly heteronormative, *TFOAC* has queered the scene. A bisexual Achilles shows no desire for Penthesilea but rather turns his grief for his slain male lover Patroclus into rage.[3] Likewise, Penthesilea, though she flirts with Aeneas briefly, avows that she does not sleep with men. Thus, like Amazons portrayed in some versions of the myth, she is "manless."[4] Penthesilea's short haircut and refusal to wear a helmet seem to be symbolic of her overconfidence in battle, although they may also serve to demonstrate her uncivilized, wild, and barbaric Amazon nature, in addition to her unavailability to men as a sex object. When dueling Achilles, she appears to be woefully under-equipped, at least at first, until she pulls out her dual blades, but even they are of no avail: Achilles quickly kills her. While the series is novel in that it incorporates the Amazons at all, its depiction of them is carefully styled both to exoticize them and, at the same time, like some other recent depictions of Amazons, to present them in a somewhat feminine fashion that will be palatable to a general audience.

I will begin this chapter by comparing and contrasting the representations of the Amazons in *TFOAC* with the ancient Greek sources that detail their involvement at Troy. Next, I will discuss the implied homoeroticism of the Amazons in contrast to the explicit homoeroticism and polyamory in the representations of Achilles, Patroclus, and Briseis. I will then discuss the costumes of Penthesilea and her Amazons, noting their lack of armor and sculpted hairstyles. Finally, I will focus on the multiracial composition of the Amazons in the series, noting similarities to the recent depiction of the Amazons in *Wonder Woman* (2017).

The Amazons Come to Troy to Assist, Seek Revenge, and Die

TFOAC, as noted elsewhere in this volume, loosely follows the story of the Trojan War as known from the existing fragments of the Epic Cycle as well as Homer's *Iliad*, while taking some liberties with the plot. The Amazons enter the story in order to rescue a wounded, disgraced Paris who has lost a duel with Menelaus, fled from Troy, brought death and destruction to his adoptive father, and finally attempted (or, according to Aphrodite, committed) suicide. Paris' disgrace from the duel is a well-known theme from Homer's *Iliad* Book 3, but in the *Iliad*, Aphrodite sweeps the defeated Paris up from the battlefield just before Menelaus delivers the death blow and redeposits him inside the city walls (3.373–82). It is not surprising that the screenwriter refashioned this scene in *TFOAC* since Paris fleeing on his own two feet would be more realistic to a contemporary audience. That said, Aphrodite does still save him. After leaping off an enormous cliff to kill himself, Paris is found by the Amazons and revived by Aphrodite, who tells him that he did actually die but came back to life. In Episode 6, he bubbles up from the depths of a shallow stream in a scene that is reminiscent of Steve Trevor in *Wonder Woman* plunging into the depths in his airplane. His rescue and return to the "world of men" with the assistance of the Amazons is reminiscent of *Wonder Woman* as well. He is taken to the Amazon camp, where, like on Paradise Island, Amazons spar with one another and train for war, all while leering at a creature who is foreign to them: a man.

As he awakens from being unconscious, Paris is greeted by an Amazon aiming an arrow at his skull. "How come you're alive? Are you dangerous?" Paris nods yes (after all, he carries a curse on his head even if he is not out to kill Amazons directly), to which she retorts, "So am I." Like several of the other actors, this unnamed Amazon is Black, but she remains nameless throughout the two episodes (6 and 7) that feature the Amazons. The only named Amazon, in fact, is the very White Penthesilea, played by actress Nina Milner. Of course, it is Penthesilea to whom Paris is brought by the fierce, unnamed Amazon. After much interrogation, Paris finally states that he is Alexander, Prince of Troy, son of Priam, to which Penthesilea retorts: "So it was nobility that made you to jump?" "It was a prophecy," Paris retorts. "It always is with boys like you," a rather jaded, makeup-wearing Penthesilea wryly comments. With both her look and her comment, Penthesilea is reminiscent of a club diva perhaps more so than a regal Amazon queen.

One immediately wonders how familiar Penthesilea, the queen of the women-only Amazons, might even be with "boys like" the Trojan prince. Quickly we learn that she harbors a grudge against Achilles. As the plot unfolds, Penthesilea reveals her allegiance to Troy and her enmity for the Greeks, saying "I wish to fight for whoever wants to kill Greeks." "What did the Greeks do to you?" Paris responds. "Most of them, nothing. I'll kill them anyway. I'll kill any man who fights under the banner of the Myrmidons," Penthesilea replies. "So you wish to kill Achilles?" Paris asks. "I wish to try" Penthesilea responds. "We ride for the city tomorrow. Come with us and fight for your people. If it makes you feel any better, you'll almost certainly die in the process." With these final words, Penthesilea acts more like a seer than an Amazon queen, fully predicting the prince's death and foreshadowing her own.

Instead of just one Amazon returning the injured man to his "world of men," as in *Wonder Woman*, in *TFOAC* Paris is returned by a whole army of Amazons. This, of course, is necessary to return to the plot of the Epic Cycle, where the Amazons do show up at Troy to fight on behalf of the Trojans. While Penthesilea remains a tragic figure in both ancient epic and on the modern screen, her story has been dutifully adapted. Arctinus' *Aithiopis* is no longer extant, but we learn from the later epic *Fall of Troy* that Penthesilea had actually come to Troy on a suicide mission of sorts, after feeling guilty for having accidentally killed her sister, Hippolyta, with an errant spear (1.18–26).[5] Penthesilea is followed by the Furies who seek to avenge Hippolyta's death while her own Amazons continually reproach her for the murder (1.27–31).

Thus, the Amazons are made to serve a new function in *TFOAC* when they return Paris to Troy. Furthermore, Penthesilea's desire to "try" to kill Achilles out of revenge is novel. When Alexander enquires into the source of Penthesilea's hatred for Achilles, his Amazon patron explains: "He killed her daughters, sisters, soldiers. There's a price to pay.

He hasn't paid it yet." Penthesilea is thus placed squarely into the role of the hero seeking revenge against the bad guys. This plot mechanism seeks to give Penthesilea a motive that she is not given in the ancient sources—one which will be all too familiar to those who have seen *Gladiator* and other action hero stories. Although revenge is not a part of the legend of Penthesilea (at least what is still extant of it), the Amazons do desire revenge upon the Greeks in other versions of the Amazon legends. After the capture of Antiope (and the Greek slaying of other Amazons) by Theseus at Themiscyra, the Amazon homeland, the Amazons attack Athens in revenge.[6] The revenge motif would surely have more appeal for modern screen audiences than Quintus' suicide mission; and the screenwriter has here admirably conflated Amazon legends.

In any event, the Amazons assist Paris in returning to Troy. The precision aim of the Amazons archers allows Paris to reenter the city, as they kill each and every Greek who seeks to prevent his entrance into Troy from outside. The fierceness of the Amazons is further illustrated as they assist the Trojans in making a raid on the Greeks to destroy their supplies. As she meets Hector for the first time, Penthesilea responds to his greeting of "Good evening your majesty," with a question: "Has Greek blood been spilt?" When Hector responds in the negative, she retorts: "It's not a good evening yet, is it?" Penthesilea does bravely spill Greek blood that very night, beheading one of the enemy in a rather graphic scene. Furthermore, she and her Amazons do not wear helmets, unlike their Trojan counterparts and their Greek enemies. This could be compared to boxing without the gloves, always dangerous for a fighter, although here the stakes are much higher: life or death. The lack of helmets seems to emphasize the Amazons' wild, uncivilized state, although, at least in Penthesilea's case, this emphasis is somewhat undercut by her thickly applied makeup. As Sherry Inness notes, "the popular media are still deeply ambivalent about how to depict tough women so that they do not challenge gender conventions too dramatically."[7] Inness further observes that "[t]he threat posed by the killer woman is mitigated in part because she is commonly portrayed as sexually appealing to men."[8] Penthesilea's haircut is definitely butch in *TFOAC*, but her makeup tones down the butchness.

Furthermore, despite their female masculinity, the Amazons in *TFOAC* are largely put in their place, so to speak. This happens first of all with the unnamed Amazon with whom Paris had his first encounter back in Themiscyra. For it is she who is captured by an enraged Achilles, and brutally slaughtered by him as he calls for Hector outside the city walls. As Achilles prepares to slit her throat in Episode 7, the Amazon taunts him: "My queen will open your heart and drink your blood you son of a whore." Achilles' reply, "son of a goddess, actually," puts the Amazon in her place as he coldly slits her throat. As in the Greek legends, patriarchy ultimately reigns supreme.

Of course, we already know that Penthesilea cannot slit Achilles' heart open, even if she would like to, as her death at his hands is prescribed by thousands of years of consistency in the legends, starting with Arctinus' *Aithiopis* and culminating in this most recent retelling.[9] In *TFOAC*, Penthesilea bravely takes on Achilles in a duel similar to that which was once reported in the now lost Epic Cycle. Penthesilea fights not with one but rather with two swords, while, true to the Greek original, she is overpowered by

Achilles, despite having fought bravely. As he thrusts his weapon into her for the final death blow, Penthesilea again speaks presciently: "You'll soon follow me."[10] Upon Penthesilea's death, the rest of the Amazons now rise up to defeat the lone Achilles, but, despite being completely outnumbered, he kills all of them. Despite being confronted with the Amazons, Achilles remains the tragic hero until he is finally brought down by Paris' arrow in his heel.

Homoeroticism, Achilles, and Penthesilea

In the extant summary of Arctinus' *Aithiopis*, we learn that immediately after the death of Penthesilea, Achilles also killed Thersites, because the latter mocked him over his alleged *eros* for Penthesilea. According to Quintus, after he killed Penthesilea, Achilles pulled back her helmet and was smitten by her as she lay dying in his arms: "The son of Peleus was grieving greatly when he saw the lovely strength of the maiden [lying] in the dust; on account of this his heart was devoured with a deadly grief as great as that which he had formerly experienced when his companion Patroclus was killed" (*Fall of Troy* 1.718–21). Quintus also elaborates on the role of Thersites, who, mocking Achilles for his *eros* toward Penthesilea accuses him of being *gunaimanes*, or "woman-crazy" (1.726). True to form, Achilles flew into a rage and killed Thersites. This entire incident has been omitted from the plotline of *TFOAC*, in part, because it would have detracted from Achilles' grief-stricken fury over the death of Patroclus, whom he seems to realize, all too late, that he really did love.

That said, Achilles' love for Patroclus, and the subsequent grief that he feels when Hector slays him, is an important theme in the *Iliad*. Although Homer does not tell us that Achilles and Patroclus were erotically involved, he does have Achilles say that Patroclus meant as much to him as his own life (18.78–82). Dover notes that

> the peculiar features of Achilles' devotion to Patroklos, as portrayed in the *Iliad*, were not only insane extravagance of this grief at Patroklos' death but his decision to stay on at Troy and avenge Patroklos even though he knew that by doing so he doomed himself to an early death when he could have gone home and lived to a peaceful old age.[11]

Aeschines (*Against Timarchus* 142) suggests that although Homer did not discuss the *eros* between Achilles and Patroclus, the astute reader would nonetheless infer, from the intensity of their bond, that *eros* had been present. He further notes, in the same speech, that it is said that the love (*philia*) of Achilles for Patroclus extended from *eros* (133).[12] Aeschylus is the first extant author to have interpreted the myth of Achilles and Patroclus in an explicitly erotic fashion. In his trilogy *Myrmidons*, *Nereids*, and *Phrygians* (fragments 135–7), Aeschylus presents the Homeric relationship between Achilles and Patroclus as an amorous one. He portrays a bereaved Achilles speaking to the ghost of Patroclus: "You felt no shame at my adoration of your thighs."[13] Plato's Phaedrus in the

Symposium (180A) takes issue with Aeschylus' depiction of Achilles as the lover (as opposed to being the beloved) of Patroclus, noting that Achilles, according to Homer (*Iliad* 11.787), was the younger of the two (180A).[14] Plato's Phaedrus asserts in the *Symposium* (179E–180A) that Achilles chose to die for Patroclus' sake in order that he could join him.

While the age difference between the two was a decidedly Greek concern, *TFOAC* presents the erotic relationship (without reference to the age of either partner) in a way designed to appeal to a contemporary twenty-first-century audience. First of all, Patroclus and Achilles are both fully grown men. The first (and only) love scene between the two men is actually a three-way that also features Briseis, Achilles' war prize who is subsequently commandeered by Agamemnon.[15] As Achilles sulks in his tent over the loss of Briseis, refusing to fight, Patroclus waits patiently for him to come around. But when the Trojans make a surprise attack on the Greek camp (accompanied by the Amazons, of course), Patroclus finally loses his patience. In the ensuing dialogue, we learn more about the dynamics of the men's relationship. Patroclus encourages Achilles to fight:

Patroclus You've lost a prize and you've been sitting around like sour milk ever since.

Achilles Are you done?

Patroclus I'm done sitting around waiting for you to remember that you have a pair of balls and a sword. I would like to go home, now. And I cannot until this war is finished.

Achilles Then perhaps you should leave before I forget that I once had affection for you.

Patroclus It's not affection. It's love. I'm not afraid of it.

After explaining that his mother loved him so much that she failed to completely dip him into the River Styx for fear that she would drown him (thus leaving his ankle vulnerable to the fatal wound that would later kill him), Achilles exclaims: "Love is weakness." "It doesn't have to be," Patroclus responds passionately. "Fight with me. If not then, fight for me," are his final words to Achilles. Achilles refuses, and Patroclus, wearing Achilles' armor, is killed by Hector. Achilles then rages on to kill Hector and Penthesilea in his grief.

The context of the homoerotic love story is decidedly modern. Patroclus' exclamation that what he feels for Achilles is not affection but is rather a love of which he is not afraid, appeals to a twenty-first-century audience that has known the deep stigma of homosexual orientation that we have inherited and with which, unfortunately, we as the audience still grapple. Achilles, on the other hand, seemingly realizes all too late that what he felt for Patroclus was more than simple affection. Achilles' bisexuality is presented in the early three-way scene with the two lovers and Briseis. In his sulking over the loss of Briseis, Achilles has failed to love the one he was still with: Patroclus. While he has refused to fight up to this point, the loss of Patroclus stems the tide and Achilles comes out in full force. If he had subsequently fallen in love with Penthesilea, Achilles' realization that he had truly loved Patroclus (or at least the implication of that realization, as it is not explicitly stated), would have been far less poignant.

Moreover, Penthesilea expressly states that she is not interested in men, and to have had Achilles fall in love with his dead conquest, a woman of man-spurning Amazon orientation, would perhaps not have been palatable to an audience steeped in the #MeToo movement.[16] Before her final duel with Achilles, Penthesilea has an exchange with Aeneas that is telling of her sexuality. As she and her fellow Amazons mourn the unnamed Amazon killed by Achilles, Aeneas turns up to ask Penthesilea for reinforcements from among her Amazon troops. She complies with his request, but he doesn't leave immediately. "I saw you at her grave. You were close," Aeneas says to Penthesilea. "I lost my love, my home city," he adds. As he starts to leave, Aeneas hesitates. Sensing his attraction to her, Penthesilea responds "Men and me—it doesn't happen. It's a shame. You're quite a picture."

This dialogue tells the story of the Amazons in much the same way it has been handed down to us, with vague references to man-spurning that suggest the Amazons were lesbians but give us little firm proof. The earliest references to the Amazons are found in Homer's *Iliad* (3.189, 6.186), where the Amazons are described as *antianeirai*, "the equals of men." Although their Greek name *Amazones* could imply the inclusion of men among their ranks, the use of *antianeirai*, a plural feminine adjective, leaves no doubt that Homer's Amazons were a group of women warriors only.[17] Homer's references to the Amazons are otherwise brief and vague—we learn only that they fight and they are women. In tandem, Aeschylus describes the Amazon corps as both "man-hating" [*stuganor*] and "manless" [*anandros*]. Hellanicus does tell us that the Amazons were "man-loving" [*philandros*], but he also notes that they were "male-infant-killing" [*arsenobrephoktonos*], thus suggesting that they had sex with men to procreate, although they raised only the daughters from such unions.[18]

When we first meet the Amazons in *TFOAC*, they are a tribe of women only living in a rudimentary village with no men present other than Paris, who has literally fallen off a cliff into their "world," landing in a stream. As noted above, *TFOAC* seemingly borrows from *Wonder Woman* where Steve Trevor's plane crashes into another "world" of Amazons, this time the waters off of Paradise Island. Although Penthesilea in *TFOAC* swears that she does not sleep with men, we learn that she hates Achilles because he killed not only her sisters and soldiers but also her daughters. While no further context is given, the suggestion that Penthesilea had procreated (and thus would have had to have had some sexual contact with a man, or at least with male semen), is offered up when we hear of her daughters. As for the Amazon village in *TFOAC*, it is not named. It looks more like the primitive Amazon dwellings presented in the 1994 *Hercules and the Amazon Women* than it does the fabled Amazon city of Themiscyra as shown in the recent film *Wonder Woman* (2017).[19]

Penthesilea's "Helmet" and Costuming

Stylistically, Penthesilea's short-cropped haircut also presents the Amazon queen in the guise of a boyish lesbian. At the same time, it differentiates her from her subordinate

Amazons, all of whom have longer hairstyles. Further and to the point, Penthesilea and her Amazons do not wear helmets or utilize armor. In fact, Penthesilea's hairstyle is her helmet, so to speak, in that it is shaped more like a helmet than anything else. If it does not protect her in battle, perhaps it might protect her from the advances of men. As we have already discovered, in Quintus of Smyrna's *Fall of Troy*, Penthesilea did wear a helmet, and Amazons on Greek vases are often depicted wearing helmets and other armor, although sometimes they are depicted wearing Scythian caps as well.[20]

The question which immediately arises is why the producers of the show decided to feature the Amazons without helmets, and how we viewers should "read" this choice. The lack of Amazon armor seemingly indicates the "wildness" of the Amazons. As Tyrrell notes, the Amazons "are figments of the outdoors, and, like Greek men, they are on the move."[21] Although she does don a helmet on a celebrated vase by Exekias (c. 540–530 BCE), Penthesilea is otherwise dressed in a leopard skin, which seems to denote her barbaric wildness.[22] The creators of *TFOAC* may have borrowed from more recent representations, however; the 1995–2001 TV Amazon-like Xena, played by Lucy Lawless, and her sidekick Gabrielle don their long hair rather than wear a helmet. Additionally, the Amazons in *TFOAC* are presented as "badass" women who have little concern for danger when we first meet them in their home village.[23] As the Amazon women engage in target practice, young Amazon girls run back and forth among the arrows but do not get hit.

In terms of costume, *Troy: Fall of a City* seems to veer further from Greek iconography[24] than *Wonder Woman*, although the series' costumes have been less scrutinized for scantiness than those of the latter.[25] Milner's boyish haircut, her most masculine attribute save perhaps for her swords, marks her status as queen, whereas her subordinates sport a longer style. The Amazons of *Wonder Woman*, in contrast, wear their hair long and/or in fish-tail braids, in a fashion that is similar to the Caryatids of Greek art.[26] Of course, archaic and classical Greek art does not necessarily tell us what the Amazons of the Trojan era would have actually looked like (if, indeed, they had existed then), but more so how the Greeks of the classical era thought they should be dressed.[27] Additionally, while *Wonder Woman* seemingly inverts the myth of the Amazons by making them the sworn enemies of Ares, rather than his daughters as in Arctinus, *TFOAC* follows Greek legend more closely while still adapting it for a contemporary audience.

Multiracial Amazons

Despite these differences, representations of Amazons in these recent depictions do have something in common: the Amazons are multiracial. In this sense, they are perhaps meant to represent a twenty-first-century vision of all women united in feminist sisterhood, not unlike the Amazons of *Wonder Woman*.[28] Indeed, the decision to represent the Amazons as a multiracial group seemingly stems from the idea of "colorblind" casting[29] that is present among the ranks of the Greeks and the Trojans as well. In *TFOAC*, race is not an issue among the Trojans, the Greeks, or, most importantly for my purposes, the Amazons. As with the depictions of the Amazons in *Wonder Woman*, the producers of *TFOAC* seemingly sought to depict post-racial societies where race is not at issue.[30] Derek Wax, one of the producers, provided the following explanation: "Diversity is at the heart of our casting and at the heart of what the BBC and Netflix wants. It's only a controversy if people try to manufacture a controversy out of it."[31]

The controversy stemmed, in part, from the decision to deviate from Homer's depiction of Achilles as blond (*Iliad* 1.197).[32] And while purists may balk at such choices, they have less ground to stand on when it comes to the casting of the Amazons, as African Amazons are described by Diodorus Siculus (*Historical Library* 3.52–5).[33] Diodorus (3.53.4–5) explains that the Amazons originated in Libya on an island called Hespera in Lake Tritonis (a location that may actually be in modern-day Tunisia—the Greeks called Africa either Libya or Ethiopia).[34] After having been defeated by Heracles, the Amazons, led by the queen Myrina, migrated to Asia Minor (3.55.4–9). A tomb of Myrina in the Troad is mentioned by Homer in the *Iliad* (2.814). Although Homer does not state that this Myrina was an Amazon, other Greek authors suggest that the tomb mentioned by Homer was of Myrina the Amazon queen described by Diodorus.[35] Thus, the presence of Black women among the Amazons of Asia Minor is not problematic from a source perspective.

Furthermore, in Arctinus' *Aithiopis*, Amazons arrive just before the Ethiopians to fight on behalf of Troy. After Achilles kills Penthesilea, the Ethiopians arrive to assist the Trojans, but they suffer the same fate as the Amazons: defeat. Like Penthesilea, Memnon, the leader of the Ethiopians, is killed in a duel with Achilles. In *TFOAC*, the Ethiopians do not make an appearance. On ancient Greek vases, Amazons are depicted with Black male warriors, interchanged with them, and perhaps depicted as Black women. On a black-figure neck amphora, a bearded, black-skinned warrior is depicted with two white-skinned Amazons.[36] In a group of white-ground alabastra, the motif of a solitary warrior is presented along with a palm tree, an altar, and sometimes a helmet. On some of these vases, the warrior depicted appears to be a white-skinned Amazon.[37] On others, the Amazon is replaced with a Black warrior (or vice versa), who has been understood as either a male Ethiopian warrior or as an "Ethiopian Amazon."[38]

The white-skinned Amazon and the black-skinned warrior were seemingly interchangeable in the scene, as both appear in the same setting, and both wear the same types of distinctive, often Thracian or Scythian clothing and generally have the same attributes. There are numerous examples of each of these two main variations.[39] On the one hand, the black-skinned figures present as African, as they have woolly hair and stereotyped Afrocentric facial features; thus a consensus has arisen among most scholars surveying these vases that the individuals depicted are probably Ethiopian. On the other hand, some scholars have argued that, at least in the Greek mindset, the Ethiopians came from Asia.[40] Moreover, the individuals depicted are wearing what has been described as "Asiatic garb."[41] It should be here noted that the term Ethiopian derives from the Greek *Aithiops*, meaning "burnt-faced."[42] Thus, the ethnic distinction *Aithiops* would have been more vague to a Greek than the term Ethiopian is to us today, and could refer to persons from Asia.[43]

The most significant point, however, is whether or not the black-skinned warriors should be designated as Amazons (or not). A number of considerations here arise. First of all, the fact that the black-skinned warriors are used interchangeably with the white-skinned Amazons is suggestive of at least a relationship between the two types. I am not aware of any scholars who doubt that the white-skinned individuals are Amazons. Fröhner identified them as Amazons due to their white skin and long hair.[44] They also wear trousers and Scythian caps. The black-skinned type is also usually dressed in trousers, although some wear chitons in more of a Greek fashion.[45] On the one hand, none of the black-skinned warriors have beards, although they do wear their hair short. In contrast, as mentioned above, on an amphora dated to *c.* 550–525 BC and attributed to the so-called Swing Painter, a black-skinned, bearded warrior is depicted with two Amazons.[46] On the other hand, the masculine adjective *kalos* ("beautiful") is found on several examples in the Group of the Ethiopian alabastra.[47] On an alabastron attributed to the Syriskos painter, the word *kalos* appears four times: above the handle zone, on the altar, and on either side of the black-skinned warrior. Webster asserts that the inscription does not refer to the warrior pictured (and the only person on the vase) but rather to some other "youth who was a beauty at the time."[48] Webster's assertion is incorrect and prejudiced: if the term is on either side of the African warrior, it seems apparent that it *does* refer to him. Given the masculine ending of the adjective *kalos*, it would appear that the warrior is *not* an Amazon because he is male.

At the same time, the relationship of the Amazons to the African warriors is of interest, even if the African warriors may not be Amazons. Von Bothmer followed Beazley and Webster in interpreting the white-skinned Amazon as a soldier of Penthesilea, and the black-skinned figure as an attendant of Memnon.[49] Von Bothmer draws his assessment from the *Aithiopis*, in which the Amazons turn up to aid the Trojans and are defeated. Afterwards, the Ethiopians, led by Memnon, arrive on the scene as Trojan allies, only to suffer the same fate as their Amazon counterparts.

Several scholars attribute the association between the Amazons and the Ethiopians on vases to the fact that both arrived from Africa.[50] If this is correct, then there may have been a Greek source going back to at least the sixth century BC that Diodorus utilized to write his first-century-BC account of the Amazons migrating from Libya to Asia Minor, but we cannot be sure.[51] Thus the tantalizing hypothesis arises that the idea of African Amazons goes back to the Epic Cycle. Furthermore, the vase painters may have stuck to standards of iconography that did not allow them to depict black-skinned Amazons. Memnon, for example, was "always represented at this time as a white man," despite being the leader of the Ethiopians. This is why Webster endorses Beazley's identification of the Amazon and Ethiopian warriors on the white-ground alabastra as attendants of Penthesilea and Memnon rather than as Penthesilea or Memnon themselves.[52] Vase painters tended to depict either mythological scenes or activities of daily life, but not current or recent historical events. Neils asserts that on an unpublished, privately-owned vase dating to the sixth century, Psiax depicts a black-skinned archer "in what seems to be an indisputable Trojan setting."[53]

Conclusion

Amazons are often portrayed in modern receptions with a feminist and/or other agenda. The Amazons of *Wonder Woman*, for example, were portrayed in a feminist fashion that sought to empower women first in the comic books and later in the television series and 2017 film.[54] By allowing the Amazons to escape from the world of men rather than allowing them to be defeated by patriarchy, William Moulton Marston, the creator of *Wonder Woman*, inverted the Greek myths in which the Amazons are ultimately defeated by men. To the contrary, the 1963 film *Le Gladiatrici* does the opposite by portraying the Amazons as barbaric savages who have risen up and enslaved their menfolk. In this dystopian "sword and sandal" genre film, marketed as *Thor and the Amazon Women* in the United States, the Amazons are also gladiators who fight one another in matches until one of them dies, and they keep the men of their societies enslaved in their quarries, where the conditions are of squalor.[55] The Amazon queen is Black and never named. The matriarchal society of the Amazons in *Le Gladiatrici* is barbaric, and the choice of a Black actor to play the queen "signals an engagement with social issues, such as racial equality and civil rights."[56] As the queen is presented as an evil dictator who is ultimately overthrown by the men (with the help of some of the women), the film seemingly seeks to decry the advance of the feminist and civil rights movements.

At first sight, the representation of the Amazons in *TFOAC* appears less ideological than in the above-mentioned depictions. The appearances of Black Amazons seem to point toward the feminist goal of a sisterhood of all women. Yet, as in *Wonder Woman*, the Amazon queen is White while Black Amazons are subordinate to her. This may simply have been a casting choice, but nonetheless seems to reinforce (even if unintentionally) a racial hierarchy among the Amazons. While Black male actors do take important and powerful roles in *TFOAC*, most notably as Zeus, Achilles, Patroclus, and Nestor, the main protagonist is Paris, played by White actor Louis Hunter.

TFOAC largely follows the plot of the Epic Cycle and Homer's *Iliad*, with a few twists and turns. With respect to the Amazons, the mini-series is mostly in sync with the brief summary of the now lost *Aithiopis* of Arctinus, save for the business of Thersites mocking Achilles over his alleged *eros* for Penthesilea. Of course, the brevity of the summary necessitates interpolation. Instead of turning to the later texts (such as Quintus of Smyrna) to fill in the blanks, however, *TFOAC* charts its own course. The Amazons rescue Paris and bring him back to Troy in a plot reminiscent of Diana rescuing Steve Trevor and returning him to the "world of men" in *Wonder Woman*. Most significantly, Achilles does not fall in love with Penthesilea after mortally wounding her, as in Quintus' account. Achilles falling in love with a dying or dead woman might just be too close to necrophilia to suit modern screen audiences; in addition, such a love interest on the part of Achilles would have detracted from his seeking of revenge for his lost love Patroclus. Penthesilea, for her part, rejects Aeneas and keeps the Amazons to their original script of man-spurning man-lessness.

Notes

1. I am grateful to Monica S. Cyrino and Antony Augoustakis for their generous assistance with this essay. All translations are mine.
2. Proclus' *Chrestomathia* 2. On Arctinus (and the Epic Cycle more generally), see further Blok 1995: 147–8, 195–8, Burgess 2001: 1–46, Cyrino 2007, Penrose 2016: 127–33.
3. On Achilles' queer polyamory, see Jenkins in this volume.
4. See Aeschylus' *Suppliant Women* 287.
5. On the date of Quintus of Smyrna's *Fall of Troy* (*Posthomerica*), see James 2004: xviii–xxi.
6. Pausanias' *Description of Greece* 1.2.1; Plutarch's *Life of Theseus* 26–8.
7. Inness 1999: 5.
8. Inness 1999: 69.
9. On the legend of Penthesilea, see further Penrose 2016: 127–9, 133–4, Mayor 2014: 287–304.
10. In Quintus' poem (1.592–629), once injured, Penthesilea is tempted to offer Achilles "gold and bronze" in exchange for her life rather than continue fighting, but is killed before she has the chance to do so. In the Latin translation of Dictys of Crete's *Journal of the Trojan War* (4.3), after having been wounded by Achilles "because she had risen above the nature of her sex," Penthesilea was maimed, dragged, and finally drowned, a clearly misogynistic version of the story.
11. Dover 1989: 41.
12. See further Dover 1989: 197.
13. Dover 1989: 197. See also Leitao (2018), Jenkins in this volume.
14. See also Jenkins in this volume.
15. According to Homer (*Iliad* 11.786), Patroclus was the elder of the two. See Dover 1989: 197.
16. A variant of the story in which Achilles has intercourse with Penthesilea's corpse is reported by the scholiast on Sophocles' *Philoctetes* 436–50. See further Blok 1995: 200–1.
17. The fact that *antianeirai* is a compound adjective, which would normally not even have a feminine ending, furthers this reading. Homer *deliberately* casts his Amazons as a group of women only. See Blok 1995: 160, who suggests that *antianeirai* may have originally been a substantive, and hence defies the rules of epic grammar because "the rule on terminations does not apply to composite nouns." See also Penrose 2016: 126.
18. Hellanicus *FGrHist* 4 F 167; Penrose 2016.
19. On *Hercules and the Amazons*, see Blondell 2005.
20. Veness 2002; Penrose 2016: 95–100.
21. Tyrrell 1984: 48.
22. See further von Bothmer 1957: 101, Veness 2002: 96, 105, Cohen 2012: 462. On the historical reality of the Amazons, see further Mayor 2014 and Penrose 2016.
23. Voller 2018.
24. On costumes, see Raucci in this volume.
25. Chason 2017, Penrose 2019: 178, 216–17.
26. Schwab and Rose 2015, Penrose 2019: 217.
27. Veness 2002. Fitton 2007: 101 notes that vase painters and other artists usually showed "clothes, armor, physical settings, and other accoutrements ... based on contemporary classical reality" and did not "strive toward the recreation of times past."

28. Cocca 2014: 98, Penrose 2019: 183, 200–1, 217.
29. See Kennedy in this volume.
30. Trusty 2018.
31. Famurewa 2018.
32. Famurewa 2018. See Kennedy in this volume.
33. While *TFOAC* takes the "women-only" approach to the Amazons found in other sources besides Diodorus, Diodorus' Amazons live in a matriarchal setting that seemingly inverts Greek patriarchy: the women plow and go to war while the men remain indoors to care for children and perform domestic labor (3.53.1–3).
34. See further Siraj 1997, Penrose 2019: 139–42.
35. Strabo's *Geography* 12.8.6, Tzetzes on Lycophron's *Alexandra* 243.
36. Brussels Musees Royaux A130; Beazley Archive Pottery Database record no. 301561 (www.beazley.ox.ac.uk/pottery/default.htm). See Neils 1980, Fröhner 1871: 14–18.
37. Richmond, VA Museum of Fine Arts, 78.145; Beazley Archive Pottery Database record no. 30308.
38. Ethiopian Warrior on Attic alabastron from the early fifth century BC, Cambridge, MA Fogg Art Museum, Harvard University 1960.327.
39. These were first catalogued by Beazley 1963: 267–9 and later by Neils 1980, both of whom referred to most or at least a significant portion of them as the "Group of the Negro Alabastra." I use "Ethiopian" or "black-skinned" instead of "Negro."
40. Graindor 1908: 25–33, Beardsley 1929: 48–54, Neils 1980: 14.
41. Neils 1980: 14.
42. *LSJ* s.v. *Aithiops*.
43. See further Beardsley 1929: ix–xii, 1–9, Snowden 1970: 151.
44. Fröhner 1871: 14–18, Neils 1980: 13.
45. Those wearing chitons include Neils 1980: pl. 3,9; 3,11. One of the black-skinned warriors wears a chiton over striped trousers: Neils 1980: pl. 6,7.
46. See n36 above.
47. Webster 1947: 7.
48. Webster 1947: 7.
49. Beazley 1931–1932: 16 no. 52, Webster 1947: 9, von Bothmer 1957: 157–9, Neils 1980: 14.
50. Snowden 1970: 292–3 n15, Thimme 1970: 12, 25 n3. See also Hanson 1974.
51. Hanson 1974 argues that this tradition may have gone further back than the Hellenistic period.
52. Webster 1947: 9, Beazley 1931–1932: 16 no. 59.
53. Neils 1980: 22.
54. Penrose 2019.
55. Augoustakis 2015: 63.
56. Augoustakis 2015: 65.

CHAPTER 10
COSTUME CHANGES: DRESSING HELEN OF SPARTA AND TROY
Stacie Raucci

In recent years, costumes have taken center stage in a number of hit television shows. For instance, in AMC's *Killing Eve* (2018–), one of the central characters, an assassin named Villanelle (Jodie Comer), displays her eccentric personality through her ever-changing and always trendy wardrobe.[1] One writer, Neha Prakash, described Villanelle's constant costume changes in the series as "the ultimate manifestation of dressing for the job you want: If you're going to commit murder, you might as well be dressed to kill."[2] A viewer might expect sartorial style in *Sex and the City* (1998–2004), but in a show centered around an assassin, such fashionable costume design may be a bit more surprising and therefore stands out in a significant way. In another recent example, an audience could watch the TV show *Schitt's Creek* (2015–2020) just for the costumes, from the flowy dresses and golden hair ornaments of Alexis Rose (Annie Murphy) to the fashionable t-shirts and sweaters of David Rose (Dan Levy) to the impressive wig collection of Moira Rose (Catherine O'Hara). Some costumes have become symbols of a show itself, such as the white bonnets and red dresses of *The Handmaid's Tale* (2017–) or Midge's (Rachel Brosnahan) array of dresses in *The Marvelous Mrs. Maisel* (2017–).[3]

In discussing costumes in film, renowned costume designer Deborah Nadoolman Landis noted that "the best costume design may be invisible when the audience is truly invested in the story and its outcome. Filmmakers want the audience to believe and the costume's role is to disappear."[4] Yet given the outsized role of the costumes on TV series like the ones mentioned above, disappearing into the background or even into the characters themselves no longer seems to be always the primary goal. While still serving as potential markers of their characters' personalities and virtual time machines to transport audiences, these TV wardrobes stand out, making their visual narratives more important than ever to audiences.

Although not having drawn the same critical attention as the shows named above, the costumes in *Troy: Fall of a City* (2018) are likewise visual standouts. The wardrobe of the character Helen (Bella Dayne), of Sparta or Troy depending on the episode, is a spectacle all on its own and provides a complementary narrative to the obvious action of any scene. In every episode, and sometimes multiple times in a single episode, she appears adorned in a new dress, regularly enhanced with elaborate jewelry and hair ornaments. While the series is not in contemporary dress, her low-cut dresses and avian adornments often look like they would be at home on the fashion runway as part of the collection of the latest season.

In line with recent increased critical and popular attention to costume design, this chapter will trace the costumes of Helen over the course of the eight-episode arc of *TFOAC* and map out patterns.[5] It will consider how Helen's self-dressing on screen essentially mirrors the work of a costume designer. Helen's costume changes enable a type of meta-performance, a self-aware action of dressing in which she turns herself into both designer and actress for each new audience she encounters. As she moves from Sparta to Troy, she crafts the appearance that is expected of her, simultaneously standing out from other women in small visual ways and yet blending in enough to assimilate into a group. The internal Helen remains stable while her morphing outward appearance blends with her shifting circumstances. In addition, this Helen uses her clothes and other adornments to become an internal narrator of her own well-known mythology, making possible for viewers an extra-textual reading of the series. In order to outline Helen's costume changes, I will consider the work of costume designer Diana Cilliers for *TFOAC*, but I will also include the work of other on-set artisans, such as the designers of hair, makeup, and jewelry. These additional considerations will provide a more holistic view of Helen's appearance on screen.

The Art of Costume Design

Film scholar Richard Barsam points out what we would expect: "Beautiful clothes worn by beautiful people attract audiences."[6] Well-designed costumes can be a significant draw, but costume design is more than eye candy, more than aesthetically pleasing fabrics draped on actors. It is a complex art, one that needs to work in tandem with the narrative. Costumes are "one of the director's most effective tools for telling a story,"[7] essentially creating visual intratexts to be read by the audience. As fashion historian Kimberly Chrisman-Campbell reminds us, clothes in general are not just "ornament or protection, but communication."[8] Because of this communicative role, the costume designer is a critical member of the filmmaking team. Despite the central role of costumes in any production, costume designers and scholars alike have noted that costumes in cinema, and by extension television, too often get overlooked.[9]

The costume designer should, as Piers D. G. Britton notes, "be understood as occupying an important position in the complex 'authorship' process of a television series."[10] While Britton's point of focus is the long-running series *Dr. Who*, the same idea could be applied to *TFOAC*. Diana Cilliers and the other on-set artisans should be seen as having central roles in the "authorship" of this series. Along with them, the character of Helen also becomes an authorial presence within the series, writing her own visual text that speaks to the many representations of Helen that viewers may have come to know from other works and media. Her clothes are more than mere representation of the obvious character on screen here; they become vehicles for participating in the complex reception of the famous Helen of Troy.

The goal of the rest of this chapter is to look closely at this particular construction of Helen. The episodic nature of the series allows the audience to read the sartorial arc of

Costume Changes: Dressing Helen of Sparta and Troy

Helen differently than the earlier cinematic Helens. Rather than watch the transformation of a character over a two-hour period, the audience gets to know this Helen as she takes a central role in the action over an extended amount of screen time. As such, she is unlike the Helen of Wolfgang Petersen's 2004 feature film *Troy*, who as Blondell notes, takes a backseat to the star power of Brad Pitt's Achilles.[11] Just as we read *Sex and the City*'s clothes (and Carrie's shoes in particular) not only over many episodes, but throughout the six seasons of the show, the audience of *TFOAC* can read the visual fabric of the fashioned mosaic of Helen, strategically dressed and undressed repeatedly on screen in front of their eyes.

Dressing and Reading Helen

Konstantinos Nikoloutsos notes how in ancient texts there is a lack of corporeal detail about Helen and instead a focus on her general beauty, allowing for her body to be turned into a "sign and a locus for the inscriptions of signs."[12] In *TFOAC*, Helen uses her own body and her clothes as a canvas for such an inscription. Paris introduces the audience to the notion of reading Helen as work of art prior to her first appearance on screen. When Paris (Louis Hunter) arrives at the palace of Menelaus (Jonas Armstrong), he rubs dust from a wall to reveal the famous fresco of the Ladies in Blue from Knossos. He marvels at the beauty of the women on the wall, with elaborately coiffed hair and jewelry. The camera angle is a close-up of the back of Paris' head with the fresco fully in the frame, enabling the audience to participate in his viewing. It is the scene that directly precedes the fateful meeting of Helen and Paris and therefore it is an excellent signal to the audience of the iconic beauty they are about to witness, in a sense even a roadmap of sorts for reading Helen's adorned body. Her clothes and accessories will hereafter quickly become spectacles in this series and the audience is prepared early on to read them as a painted text within the televisual text.

In the first episode alone, Helen has five different costume changes, with only one repeated (a nightgown). Even with this many costume changes, her first appearance is thirty minutes into the first episode, during a feasting scene in which Paris has been sent as an envoy to Menelaus by Priam (David Threlfall). Helen's initial entrance sets her up as a spectacle for not only Paris, but for the audience as well. After an establishing shot of the room and some casual conversation, the camera captures a direct view of Helen walking into the banquet hall. As she enters, the camera cuts to a side view and we see her through the transparent curtains, from the viewpoint of those in the room watching her. The audience becomes implicated right away in the watching of Helen. Once she is seated and Paris is speaking, there is a close-up shot of Helen's face and it is in this shot that the distinctive feathered top of her costume stands out most clearly. Helen continues to change outfits multiple times in each episode. For example, in Episode 2, Helen changes from her elaborate traveling outfit to a white dress back to the original outfit and then another white dress with a windowpane veil.

After the distinctive clothing of her entrance (to be discussed in more detail later), Helen's costumes come to have patterns over the course of the series: she is often clothed in V-neck dresses, sometimes with sashes placed low on the dress. Even at the funeral of Hector in Episode 7, Helen's mourning clothing retains this low neckline. Her dresses, more so than those of other women in the Trojan family, are often tightly fitted, in particular in the bodice area, revealing more skin. By contrast, the outfits of the other women (such as Andromache, Hecuba, and Cassandra, the other women in the palace household) most often cover the body up to the line of the shoulder. While the other women may sport the occasional V-neck (especially Hecuba), they are not ones plunging as low as the lowest of Helen's outfits. The characters wearing the most revealing outfits (at least when clothed) are the three goddesses: Aphrodite, Athena, and Hera. It is visually and thematically appropriate that Helen, the supposed beauty of mythology and closely connected to Aphrodite, would stand out in such a manner.

Jewelry, Makeup, and Hair Ornaments

Helen tends to wear what we would likely refer to now as the "natural look" or the "no make-up makeup" look. On a few special occasions, she is more adorned with shimmery eye shadow and eyeliner. Her lips occasionally have the slightly reddened appearance of a wine-kissed color, but generally appear quite natural.

In addition to the two rings on her right hand, she also frequently has wrist cuffs and necklaces. Her bird necklace, although frequently worn, is far from the only one she wears. In fact, it is one of the least showy ones of the series. Her other necklaces are quite large, sometimes covering a significant space, if not all of the space on her upper-chest area. The necklace that she wears to the second dinner with Paris in the first episode is one of the largest, consisting of four attached circles surrounded by white stones (or shells). The same shells are mirrored hanging from each side of her headdress. The other large necklace Helen wears in Episode 2 when she enters the city of Troy and also for her meeting with Hecuba and Priam. The middle piece hangs down as far as her feet and the largest part of it consists of rows of small white shells.

Although there are scenes in which we see Helen's seemingly naturally wavy hair hanging, many scenes show a more coiffed approach. Her hairstyles extend from braids to loose curls and her waves often frame her face. She frequently has small pieces of gold woven into the curls or braids of her hair. Her headdresses are highly ornamented and stand out in a scene. They range from ones with shells and gems to her final one that appears to be a rustic looking crown that sits atop her head. Others are circle headbands with beads. One has a pearl that hangs down the middle of her forehead and another has three on the forehead. The style and color of Helen's veils change throughout the series, like her dresses. Some cover her head and others provide ornamentation, hanging from her wrists.[13]

Helen's daughter Hermione appears to be a mini-Helen. Whereas the 2004 *Troy* left Hermione out completely, this series utilizes her as a visual point of comparison. Both

Costume Changes: Dressing Helen of Sparta and Troy

characters are dressed often in white or cream, with white veils, and with curls or waves in the hair. Instead of a bird theme, Hermione wears a snake bracelet around her arm and her hair is adorned with small shells, similar to the gold pieces in Helen's waves.

Penelope, wife of Odysseus, and in mythology supposed relative of Helen, in Episode 2, in the one scene we see her, wears a dress that might remind us of Helen's dress in the opening scene. Instead of a feathered collar, she wears one with a blue fringe that matches the rest of the highly embroidered blue outfit.[14]

Feathered Fashions

Although Helen's dress changes throughout the series, a few visual elements remain constant throughout, reflecting the very foundations of her character and her mythological background. Most notably there is an avian theme to her dress, occasionally along with other natural elements such as seashells. Even as her costumes transition from the bright whites and creams of Sparta to the more colorful dress of the royal Trojan family, she continues to wear bird-themed items, including and most significantly a golden bird ring on the ring finger of her right hand. In the first scenes in which Helen appears, she is already wearing this ring and it is a mainstay that reappears throughout the series.

The bird on the ring is positioned upright and is three-dimensional with discernible beak and a long tail (Fig. 10.1). She wears it turned away from herself and it is therefore directed toward any person to whom she speaks, and, depending on the camera angle, the audience itself. Thanks to the number of close-ups of Helen, and even of her hands at times, the ring is often visible to the eyes of the audience.[15] She also frequently sports a bird necklace and unlike the other elaborate jewelry she wears, it has a simple rope-like

Figure 10.1 Helen (Bella Dayne) and Paris (Louis Hunter) join hands in marriage in Episode 3, "Siege." Helen's signature bird ring and wrist cuff are visible.

appearance, more in keeping with the theme of nature than luxury. From the rope hangs a series of golden birds, two on each side and in the middle dangle another two. Finally, in addition to those two pieces, she wears a set of studded wrist cuffs that have two large golden birds on each, facing in opposite directions. Sometimes she wears these accessories as a set and at other times, only the ring.

This theme of birds extends beyond her jewelry to her full costume and is further reflected in the set design at various points in the series. The first significant moment in this theme is Helen's very first entrance in the series in Episode 1. Helen enters wearing a sleeveless dress that has a distinct white collar with long feathers that reach all the way up to her chin.[16] The collar, thanks to the feathers, has the appearance of a turtleneck neckline. There are additional feathers on the breast area of the dress that are spotted brown. The feathered collar and feathers that adorn the top of the dress seem to be from different types of birds. In that same episode, when she is outdoors with Paris and Hermione, Helen wears a plunging V-neck dress augmented with a collar that has white thin material sprouting from it. Although a different look than her collar of feathers the evening before, she still retains the appearance of a delicate bird. The dialogue in this episode also notes the connection of birds to Helen when Paris asks her if the birds in the house belong to her and she replies that, "Yes, father always let them fly free in the house."

This line demonstrates one of the reasons for the presence of Helen's bird costumes in the series. As many have noted, the birds show her connection to the themes of being trapped and freedom. Bella Dayne remarked on the effect of birds on her portrayal of Helen: "what I loved is I worked very closely with the costume designer that we had and would really discuss small details from like a necklace with feathers in it. Recurring themes of the character of Helen and the theme of birds and wanting to break out of the golden jail that she was in."[17] Helen's words to Paris, combined with her costume, reflect that she is the bird, trapped in this marriage with Menelaus. It is therefore not surprising that when Helen leaves Sparta, so do her birds and we see Menelaus walk past multiple empty bird cages in Episode 2.

In addition to the idea of trapped/free, birds can also function as a mythological entryway for the audience into the complicated narrative of Helen's life. By wearing bird adornments, Helen speaks to her own mythological story and her overt bird theme may be explained by her connection to the goddess Aphrodite. As Cyrino explains, Aphrodite was associated with many birds (the dove in particular) and birds had an erotic connection.[18] Helen, with the wearing of feathers in this series, overtly identifies as one of Aphrodite's flock. In *Westworld* (Season 3, Episode 4), host Dolores tells her new ally Caleb that humans wear expensive suits because "It's tribal. They use plumage to identify themselves." In *TFOAC*, Helen indeed wears plumage to identify herself.

Scenes in which love and passion are center stage are prime moments (but not the only ones) for the wearing of these accessories. For example, in Episode 3, during the wedding scene in Troy, there is a very clear view of the bird ring, as there is a close-up shot of the joined hands of Helen and Paris. This is a particularly fitting moment for the ring, in that it subtly ties together the circle of the mythological story: it was Aphrodite who gave Helen to Paris and here we have one of her symbols as they join in marriage.

Costume Changes: Dressing Helen of Sparta and Troy

In Episode 4, the camera again provides a clear shot of Helen's hand with the bird ring while she is in bed with Paris. Finally, at the duel in which Helen's marital fate should be decided, she wears her bird necklace. Given that in the Iliadic version of this story, Aphrodite plays a crucial role in the ending of this duel and leads Helen back to her bedchamber to wait for Paris, the necklace could be considered a mythological substitute for the famous version of this part of the Trojan War narrative.

Birds appear in other settings besides costumes, enhancing the theme. Although the appearance of one particular bird was deemed by some viewers to be rather amusing, the presence of an ostrich in the palace of Menelaus following directly behind Paris can be read as yet another example of Aphrodite's ubiquitous presence.[19] The ostrich walks Paris right to the chambers of Helen, where he finds her surrounded by her scantily-clad female companions. Helen is smoking a pipe, with her long hair falling down her back, loose and wavy with gold and silver threads mixed in and wearing a white gauzy dress. In this same scene, the feathers even bring Helen sensual pleasure, as one of the women brushes her left ear and side of her neck with one. In the background, we can also see other women stroking each other with feathers.

The sets complement the costumes and extend the reception of Helen. For instance, in her room with Paris in the Trojan palace, there are birds on the yellow walls. Birds as backdrop become particularly appropriate during love scenes. In Episode 2, when Paris and Helen first have sex, the act takes place outside in nature, in a tent that is decorated with many feathers. In Episode 6, when Helen reunites with Paris and birds are pictured prominently, the topic of conversation is Aphrodite's earlier visit to Paris. With the birds as background, the lovers exchange "I love you's" and undress each other passionately. In any episode in which Helen's makeup table is visible, birds can also be seen on the wall behind it, emphasizing the connection between Helen, beauty, and Aphrodite.

The bird theme may also figure into Helen's mythological narrative by hinting at her divine lineage as the daughter of Zeus, hatched from an egg after he united with her mother in the guise of a swan.[20] Helen's costumes are also tied to Aphrodite through connections to nature. Helen often adorns herself in seashell necklaces, as we see in Episode 2 when she arrives in Troy.

Beauty Practices

As an extension of Helen's costumes, her beauty accoutrements link her continually to the goddess Aphrodite and her known mythological connections to beauty and love.[21] Importantly, Helen's beauty is not merely given to the viewers, it is also in part actively created by Helen herself and a few others. Helen is depicted as participating in traditional feminine beauty practices, from the applying of makeup to the combing and adorning of her long hair, and the wearing of luxurious clothes and jewelry. When she is in her chambers, there is a makeup table set up for her with small pots of products and a large mirror. In her room upon arrival, we find her with a golden comb in her hands, mindlessly running it through the ends of her hair.

Screening Love and War in *Troy: Fall of a City*

Mirrors, as well as other beauty tools, are the domain of the goddess Aphrodite, so Helen's connection to them here provides a further visual connection to the goddess.[22] In the final episode, Helen's mirror again makes an appearance, right before the fall of Troy. Helen stares at herself in the mirror and sees her distorted image.

Helen allows others to help transform her from Helen of Sparta to Helen of Troy. In Episode 2, Hecuba sits at her own makeup table together with Helen and the two women bond as mother and daughter-in-law. Hecuba shows Helen how to use mulberries as blush, even teasing after Helen puts too much on her face. She shows her how to dab her lips with gold and after this scene, even her nails are painted with the same shimmering gold. In addition, in Episode 2, there is an extended showing of Helen's bath, including a close-up of a female attendant's hand wringing water out of a sponge over a basin of water and washing her back.

Transition from Helen of Sparta to Helen of Troy

Helen's external appearance changes as her societal associations shift from Sparta to Troy. Diana Cilliers, in the DVD extras ("Inside Troy"), says that she purposely had changes in the colors of costumes in mind. She notes how she "tried to establish the different regions or a different feel for the regions ... concentrating on cream for Sparta. It was slightly colorless ... and Troy was rich, warm." Thanks to Helen's move, this goal was made evident in her costumes and Cilliers says that, "when she [Helen] is accepted as a Trojan woman, she starts dressing in color." At times, Helen's unclothed body acts as a good transition between the costumes, as she moves from the creams of Sparta to the rich colors of Troy.[23] Before points of transition, Helen often appears unclothed, a type of unpainted canvas, such as in the bath at Sparta before she leaves for Troy and in bed with Paris in Troy before their marriage. The appearance of unclothed Helen can also make the audience more aware of the clothing worn at later points.[24]

The transition from Helen of Sparta to Helen of Troy is seen right away once she departs. In Sparta, Helen is in white and feathery outfits (with the exception of a very light blue veil in Episode 1 when she is outside). In Episode 2, upon arrival in Troy, Helen's bit of color that appears in her clothing is her rosy pink veil that is light at the top and darker as it goes lower. Andromache and Hecuba wear deeper and richer colors right away. When Helen appears before Priam and Hecuba, she still has the appearance of her homeland, wearing a headdress as she did the first evening at dinner in Sparta and with elaborate accessories. While there are no birds here beyond her ring, there is still a nature theme with long flowing strands of seashells. Likewise, when she is first meeting with the Trojans, Helen appears in white whereas the Trojan women wear blue (Andromache, matched with a burgundy veil) and olive green (Hecuba). Other women in the crowd also wear colorful garments, some red, some yellow, and others terracotta.

After the official wedding of Paris and Helen in Episode 3, Helen starts to look more Trojan in her appearance, assimilating to the looks of her in-laws Hecuba and Andromache. Despite the fact that Andromache insists Helen does not belong, her dress continues to

Costume Changes: Dressing Helen of Sparta and Troy

Figure 10.2 Helen (Bella Dayne) distributes food to the people of Troy in a stunning red dress in Episode 3, "Siege."

adapt to her new home. Episode 3 verbalizes the transition when a Trojan woman in the crowd addresses Helen. Helen stands before a crowd of people, about to share her grain stores with them, wearing a red dress and a red, yellow, and orange veil that is reminiscent of the silks hanging in her former palace in Sparta (Fig. 10.2). The woman in the crowd tells her, "You are not Helen of Sparta, you are Helen of Troy." In the 2004 *Troy*, it is Paris who speaks similar words, noting to Priam early in the film that Helen is no longer Helen of Sparta, but Helen of Troy. As Cyrino notes, it is this moment in the film that "signals the destruction of her adopted city."[25] In this series, it takes until the third episode out of eight for the moment to arrive, but it has much the same effect. As her external appearance transforms from Helen of Sparta to Helen of Troy, the fate of the city is sealed. Later in the same episode, Achilles (David Gyasi) visits Helen and tells her she is "even dressing like them now." When she marries Paris at the start of Episode 3, she is covered with a light-colored veil that is then burned, symbolizing the completion of her transition.

Helen most acutely blends in with the Trojans at the funeral of Hector in Episode 7. The Trojans are all clothed in blue and even the curtains in the room of Priam and Hecuba match the mourning garments. An aerial shot of the funeral shows the sartorial harmony, with even baby Astyanax wrapped in a blue cloth. Helen's blue outfit looks very fashionable by both ancient and modern standards with a plunging V-neck, cinched waist, and blue scarf hanging from the waist.

In the last episode, at the festivities celebrating the supposed end of the war and the arrival of the Trojan Horse, Helen is clothed in a red gown with embroidered blue birds and a red veil. She dons a flowery headdress that looks like a bird's nest, combining the looks of her two lands. The colors also seem to mimic that of the Trojan Horse with its red, blue, and gold. Like the Trojan Horse, Helen is depicted visually as the destruction of Troy.

Fashion Trends

Many scholars have noted that there is a difference between fashion and costume design and that a conflation of the two does a disservice to both artistic fields.[26] Sometimes there are indeed fashion films (such as *Coco Before Chanel* (2009) or *The Devil Wears Prada* (2006)), but historical costume design typically does not fit into that category. At the same time, some overlap in the discussion of costumes and fashion is necessary when we study film. As fashion historian Butchart notes, fashion and costume are not the same thing, but "there is no doubt that film reflects the fashions of its age."[27] Llewellyn-Jones says that "films are products of their time" and that "[c]urrent issues in taste, perception, and reception are always and unavoidably present whenever history is narrated."[28] Cilliers herself (in the DVD extras) describes how she adapted the costumes to a modern audience, saying that she

> ... wanted something unique, something original, something new, so we did use creative license. We tried to deal with everything that would have historically been correct (you know, hand sewing, natural fibers, natural dyes, colors, that sort of thing). But of course we did want to doctor to the modern eye, so that contemporary people could actually relate to it.

It is in this light that we can connect the clothes of Helen with trends in the fashion seasons at the time of *TFOAC*. For example, in 2018–2019 there was a clear trend to include feathers in the collections of a number of designers. Feathers were included in the dresses, headpieces, and shoes at the designer shows from Dolce and Gabbana to Valentino, and as fashion writers quickly noted, they were near ubiquitous on the runway that year. As Hannelly said, "2018 is the year of the bird, at least where designers are concerned."[29]

Although it is not clear that Cilliers was in any way influenced by these trends (or was the origin of them), the viewing audience will likely have made connections between what they were seeing in the pages of *Vogue* and other magazines and what they were seeing on Helen. Of course, Helen's obsession with feathers, as I have noted above, is well placed in terms of her personal mythology. But for viewers without a sense of that mythology and its trajectory in the reception of Helen, it need not matter. There is always the well-established multidirectional relationship between cinema/TV and fashion.[30] Runway styles may affect the dress of characters, and styles seen on characters make their way not only to the runway, but also to everyday wardrobes, with fans wearing the fashions they see on their television screens. One clear example on another recent show is the Bergdorf Goodman collection connected to *The Alienist: Angel of Darkness* (2018–2020) with an ad that says the clothes have a "surprisingly modern appeal."[31] Audience members can become consumers of the fashions seen on their screens.

Conclusion

After working at the fashion magazine *Runway* (a *Vogue*-like magazine), Andy (Anne Hathaway) in *The Devil Wears Prada* declares to her boyfriend Nate (Adrian Grenier): "I'm still the same person I was. I still want the same things. I promise. Same Andy, better clothes." But Nate seems to understand that this statement is not accurate. As Andy changes her wardrobe, her attitude toward those around her and her life goals change. At the end of the film, Andy changes back to a fashion style closer to her old self and her attitude to life changes too. While *The Devil Wears Prada* is a true fashion film (focusing on the world of modern fashion design), Andy's attitude to clothes reminds us of the performative aspect of dress. Clothes can be, as Andy sees it, a means to an end, the costume we use to play a role. But unlike Andy whose change in dress additionally reflects an ongoing internal change in personality, Helen's dress in *TFOAC* serves a purely external and performative function. Helen is a designer and artist for her respective audiences, whether one reads her actions as a matter of choice or survival.

Furthermore, the Homeric Helen, in both the *Iliad* and the *Odyssey*, is depicted as a weaver, the narrator of stories through her creations.[32] Mueller argues for "woven objects as coded acts of communication between women and as sources for the production of female *kleos* (lasting fame) in the *Odyssey*."[33] In *TFOAC*, with the expert intervention of costume designers, makeup artists, and set decorators, Helen can be read as doing something similar through her changing costumes with their subtle messages. The costume designer, too, weaves stories for the audience and Helen in this same vein creates her wardrobe and therefore a visual text for the audience, inside the screen and outside of it.

Although we never see Helen actually weave in this series, she still weaves a narrative for us. She controls the placement of her bird adornments that follow her from Sparta to Troy. These are the very base of her persona that never changes. Her costumes reflect a self-aware approach to mythology and she almost winks at the audience. Given that many have reduced Helen to her legendary beauty, it is logical that the Helen in *TFOAC* tells her story through clothes and takes control of her own mythology once and for all.

Notes

1. Thanks to Natasha Wright for her help in compiling bibliography on Helen and to Mitchell Toolan for compiling bibliography on costumes and dress.
2. Prakash 2020.
3. On this idea, see Britton 1999: 345. See also Lenker 2017 in which costume designer Donna Zakowska acknowledges that she carefully considered the changing colors to reflect Midge's state of mind and when to insert the color pink into the wardrobe.

4. Nadoolman Landis 2018: 95.
5. This chapter will not refer to the various Greek terms for dress, such as the *peplos* and *chiton*. Instead, the chapter will think about how a modern audience might see the clothing. It will also not consider the dressing of the many cinematic Helens. On her many iterations, see Nikoloutsos 2015, Winkler 2009: 210–50, and Winkler 2016. Nikoloutsos 2015 analyzes costumes, hair, and makeup of Helens of the 1950s, connecting the stardom of the actresses to Helen's beauty and "iconicity."
6. Barsam 2010: 172.
7. Nadoolman Landis 2007: xvii.
8. Chrisman-Campbell 2017.
9. See Warner 2009: 181–2 on the study of "fashion-forward" television shows. There are now significant scholarly works on costume and cinema, e.g., Bruzzi 1997, Street 2001, Munich 2011. In the field of Classics, there have been recent excellent works on costumes: Llewellyn-Jones 2018, Nikoloutsos 2015, Toscano 2008, Valverde 2017.
10. Britton 1999: 345.
11. Blondell 2013b. See also Roisman 2008: 128.
12. Nikoloutsos 2016: 195.
13. On veils in Homer, see Llewellyn-Jones 2003.
14. On this outfit and its relation to Helen's, see Burns in this volume.
15. She also wears a simple golden ring on her index finger of the same hand, but that one does not appear to be bird-related.
16. See also Jenkins in this volume.
17. Carter 2018. On Helen as a caged bird, see also Trusty 2018.
18. See Cyrino 2010: 120–2.
19. Doran 2018.
20. On the various versions of this story, see Blondell 2013a: 27–52.
21. On the connection of the comb to Aphrodite, see Cyrino 2010: 67.
22. On Aphrodite's connection to mirrors, see Cyrino 2010: 61–2, and on mirrors as associated with women in particular, see Lee 2015: 165–7.
23. See Bonfante 1989 on nudity as costume. See also Lee 2015: 172–97 on the "body as dress."
24. See Blundell 2002: 143–4 on how depictions of clothing can "heighten the effect of this interplay between concealment and display."
25. Cyrino 2007: 137.
26. On clothes vs. fashion vs. costume design, see Stutesman 2011: 20–1.
27. Butchart 2016: 7–8.
28. Llewellyn-Jones 2005: 18.
29. Eckardt 2017; Hannelly 2018.
30. See Meltzer 2013 on the impact of TV costume design on the fashion world.
31. www.bergdorfgoodman.com/c/bg-the-alienist-cat630204.
32. On this idea, see Kennedy 1986.
33. Mueller 2010: 1.

PART III
TRAGIC RESONANCES

CHAPTER 11
FALLEN HEROES: RECASTING AJAX AND THE GREEKS ON SCREEN
Anastasia Bakogianni

In the BBC/Netflix co-production *Troy: Fall of a City*, the Greek warriors are recast as the villains of the piece, but this is neither a new nor a surprising development when we contextualize the 2018 series within the wider framework of the reception of the Trojan War in popular culture in the twentieth and twenty-first centuries.[1] The antiwar interpretation of ancient Greek texts, especially the *Iliad* and the Athenian tragic corpus, has become one of the dominant trends in the history of their reception in this period.[2] Over the course of the twentieth century, these classical texts were gradually appropriated in the service of a liberal, feminist, and antiwar agenda that would condemn the behavior exemplified by the Greeks in *TFOAC*. On screen, Agamemnon, leader of the Greeks, becomes a man obsessed with power and status, and largely indifferent to the human cost of his political and military decisions. Achilles, the Greeks' greatest warrior, is equally obsessed with his honor and position. Menelaus' reception is more mixed, but his desire to get his wife Helen back leads him down a dark path. Odysseus is generally, although not always, presented as a more complex character (as in *TFOAC*), and is the Greek hero who most often escapes the confines of the narrative of the ten-year war at Troy thanks to his adventures in the *Odyssey*, a popular subject in both cinema and television.[3] The receptions of these famous Iliadic heroes have their roots in the Homeric epic, but on screen they are painted in shadier tones.

Their portrayal in *TFOAC* is covered in other chapters in this collection, so my analysis focuses on two minor players in the series, Ajax and Thersites, who nonetheless serve to reaffirm the overwhelmingly negative interpretation of the Greek side's motives and actions in the Trojan War, an ancient conflict that has in the modern imagination become paradigmatic of all wars. In the Homeric epic, Ajax the Great, leader of the contingent from Salamis, is labelled the "bulwark of the Achaeans" (*Iliad* 3.229). Thersites appears only once in Book 2, but is memorable as perhaps the only common soldier in the Greek army referred to by name. Odysseus brutally chastises him for daring to criticize Agamemnon (2.211–77). In *TFOAC*, Thersites has a slightly expanded, but deeply sinister role to play, in line with what audiences have come to expect of the Greeks in popular narratives of the war at Troy. The overall effect of Ajax and Thersites' portrayal in the series, brief as it is, is to reinforce the negative interpretation of the Greeks at Troy. These minor characters are symbolic of the whole of the Greek army, its brutality, greed, and callousness. An in-depth comparison of Ajax and Thersites in both the series and in relevant classical texts allows us to revisit the complex nexus that the Trojan War has come to occupy in the popular imagination, a place where multiple classical and reception strands collide and recombine to create a steady stream of new adaptations that shows no immediate sign of drying up.[4] An essential step in this process is the detailed examination of the appeal of this portrayal of the Greeks at Troy to modern filmmakers and audiences, both transhistorically and within their specific political, sociocultural, and economic contexts.

In this chapter, I build on my previous work on the reception of Ajax on screen, transhistorically connecting his story of loyal service in the Trojan War depicted in the *Iliad*, and his descent into madness and suicide as dramatized in Sophocles' *Ajax*, with the portrayal of the impact of war trauma on soldiers in post-9/11 war movies.[5] Unlike my previous work, however, in this chapter I focus on a "direct" reception, the screen adaptation of the Greek warrior in *TFOAC*, rather than a series of avatars in twenty-first-century war movies. My analysis is filtered through a "tragic" lens, one that both reflects and refracts the tragic arc that the series superimposes on the story of the war at Troy. To fully appreciate the complexity of the series' reception of the Greek army at Troy, requires an examination of the repurposing of the tragic narratives centered on the Trojan War to promote a liberal, antiwar agenda on stage, screen, and in the public imagination in the first two decades of the twenty-first century.

Enter Ajax and Thersites

Ajax's most iconic moment in the series takes place in the opening battle between the Greeks and the Trojans. This visually striking sequence weaves together slow-motion with regular-speed edits to depict the first engagement between the two armies. The momentousness of the occasion is further underscored by a soundtrack that builds a sense of tension. The scenes of Hera, Athena, and Aphrodite drifting unseen among the warriors on both sides, inspiring them to great feats of valor, constructs a cinematic version of the ancient concept of *aristeia* ("excellence in battle"). Compared with the big battles scenes in Hollywood's blockbuster epics set in the ancient world, this is neither a large-scale nor a particularly long sequence, but what renders it so effective is its adoption of a powerful visual and aural aesthetic that conveys a mounting sense of excitement. The scene earns the right to be described as "cinematic," a label generally applied to depictions of battles in the Hollywood "sword and sandal" epic genre. During this memorable sequence, it is Ajax (Garth Breytenbach) who is the very first warrior on either side to be blessed, in his case by Hera who names him as "Ajax of Telamon, unbeatable in brawl." But even in this scene the audience only catches a glimpse of Ajax running into battle in slow motion, carrying a formidable-looking war hammer (Fig. 11.1), but not his famous leather shield. Ajax's legendary prowess in battle in the ancient epic is reduced in *TFOAC* to the lesser accomplishment of being a champion brawler. His moment to be the best of the best is all too brief, as is this short catalog of the great warriors on both sides, a distant echo of the famous Catalogue of Ships in Book 3 of the epic poem, when Helen names the Greek leaders arraigned against Troy.

Fallen Heroes: Recasting Ajax and the Greeks on Screen

Figure 11.1 Ajax (Garth Breytenbach) goes into battle in Episode 2, "Conditions."

This is one of the few scenes in the series that offers spectators a sense of the excitement of battle and the pursuit of *arete* ("excellence") that pervades the *Iliad*. In the series, the emphasis is on the cost of war, which is signaled by the screen turning red, as blood splashes onto the eye of the camera, when the warriors engage with each other and viewers witness the killing begin. In *TFOAC*, the mood quickly shifts, and the narrative fast-forwards to the battle's aftermath. Against a soundtrack of the agonized cries and groans of the wounded warriors, we witness one last exchange of javelins between Achilles and a Trojan, as the Greeks retreat back to the beachhead. Achilles' spear penetrates the back of the Trojan soldier's skull and protrudes out of his mouth. The camera lingers on his last gasping breaths, blood dripping out of his mouth, as he collapses onto his knees, his corpse gruesomely propped up by the javelin embedded in his back. This graphic scene is reminiscent of the explicit nature of the series' ancient source text. The *Iliad*'s descriptions of wounded and dying warriors is often shocking for modern readers. The sense of tragedy is compounded in the series by Odysseus' pronouncement that they have not gained "one inch of ground." All this pain, suffering, and death has gained them no real advantage. The Greek warrior's palpable frustration powerfully echoes the famous narratives of fighting in the trenches in World War One (1914–1918), whose one-hundred-year anniversary was being commemorated in the year the series was released. This scene exemplifies *TFOAC*'s antiwar stance, aligning the series with the dominant interpretation of the Homeric epic in public debates.[6]

The antiwar interpretation of classical texts gained new momentum in the late 1960s, with the rise of protest movements against contemporary conflicts like the Vietnam War. The popular perception of World War One generals as deluded and incompetent also dates back to this period, and is exemplified in *TFOAC*'s version of Agamemnon, who arrogantly believes that the Greeks can capture Troy in an outright assault. After the failure of their opening diplomatic overtures, the expedition's leader decides to attack. Agamemnon's strategy is a textbook example of the theory of the "western way of war" in practice. Agamemnon's "desire for open, decisive battle, which aims at the annihilation of the enemy,"[7] as Sidebottom describes the style of fighting this theory ascribes to the "West," is unquestionably the wrong approach. According to this debunked theory, this philosophy of war supposedly differentiated Greeks from non-Greeks (and later Romans from their opponents), but in classical literature and history, as indeed in the series itself, the theory is repeatedly disproved. The Greeks are more than prepared to use *dolos* (deceit/trickery) when it suits them. The famous motto, "Beware of Greeks bearing gifts," turns the Trojan Horse into the ultimate example that disproves the existence of a "western way of war" that dates back to the ancient Greeks. Agamemnon's deluded belief that the gods have guaranteed him a quick and decisive victory because he sacrificed his daughter, Iphigenia, at Aulis is an early sign of his bad leadership both on and off the battlefield, his descent into madness, and the destruction of the last shreds of his humanity.

The dehumanizing effects of Agamemnon's leadership, and the protracted war on his army, are thus prefigured in this first engagement. The marked downwards trajectory of the Greek characters, including minor players like Ajax and Thersites, is designed to disquiet and disturb audiences. As a result of the war, the Greeks become ever more brutal and deceitful as the story unfolds, but *TFOAC* makes it clear from the beginning that they possess few, if any, redeeming qualities. The viewers' introduction to the character of Ajax is a case in point. Ajax is depicted as a burly warrior, eating and drinking in the army camp at Aulis, sitting next to Odysseus who jokingly remarks to his fellow soldier: "Ajax, what do you know about women? Stick to fighting and spitting." Viewers might at first be inclined to ascribe this unprepossessing first encounter with the character to the banter of soldiers, but everything we see of Ajax in the series reaffirms this negative first impression, which aligns with the dominant trend in Ajax's reception on screen as a man who relies on his brawn rather than his intellect (more on that below).[8]

Ajax appears throughout the series, but he serves as a glorified extra, added to scenes featuring other Greek leaders, who are codified as his intellectual superiors. He is portrayed as a man who is used to following orders rather than thinking for himself, a foil to the series' angst-ridden Achilles and his existential questioning. Ajax tends to blend into the background in *TFOAC*, he is present in the two war councils in Episode 5 for example, but leaves the talking and strategizing to the other characters. His complicity is underscored, however, in Episode 7, when he silently endorses the plan to deceive Achilles into believing that the Trojans broke the truce, which leads directly to Achilles' death. When Menelaus faces Paris in single combat in Episode 4, Ajax bangs his warclub as a show of support for the Greek champion, and his fellow-soldiers pick up the beat. Even without using words, Ajax endorses the decisions and actions of his leaders and helps put them into effect. In the last episode, the final touches are added to his characterization in the series as the Greeks' brutish henchman. He manhandles Helen, forcing her back into the city, so she can witness Troy's destruction first-hand, and after Menelaus kills Paris in front of her, he lifts her up bodily and carries her away. Ajax sets up Menelaus' kill by first headbutting and then disarming Paris. In a later scene, he physically prevents Andromache from stopping Odysseus when he takes baby Astyanax to the top of the walls and drops him to his death. The Iliadic Ajax's loyalty is thus cast in a dark light in the series, transformed into unthinking obedience and a willing participation in war crimes.

Audiences first encounter Thersites (Waldemar Schultz) in Episode 2, when he eavesdrops on a conversation between Odysseus and Xanthus, who are discussing the necessity of maintaining the deception used to lure Iphigenia to Aulis. The false story of her supposed marriage to Achilles had to be kept a secret from Greece's greatest warrior. Thersites' low status is signaled by the fact that he has been assigned the mundane task of stirring a cooking pot, but his thirst for obtaining information in whatever way possible is telling. His belligerent nature, defiance of authority, and callousness is demonstrated more clearly in Episode 4, when he needles Patroclus, arguing that it was the Myrmidons who won the fight against the Cilicians, not Agamemnon's troops. His statement is punctuated by Chryseis' screams as she is being raped by the Greek expedition's leader, who has claimed her as his war prize. In a later scene, Thersites suggests to Achilles that they should "gut" the captured Cilicians, who are staging a silent protest against the Greek king's actions.

Thersites' role is expanded across several episodes in *TFOAC*, and he embodies all the worst Greek traits, rampant self-interest, cruelty, and greed. War brings out his worst instincts and sanctions his brutality, mirroring Agamemnon, but on the lowest rung of the social ladder. In the series, he is a vital cog that sets the Trojan Horse deception in motion. When the Trojans come across him staked out on the beach, he professes that this was his punishment for his loose tongue. The Greeks abandoned him because of his ongoing criticism of the Greek leadership, on this particular occasion making a crude joke about Menelaus's inability to keep his wife in line. Thersites joins the Trojans in their celebrations, but in truth he is lying in wait to aid his fellow Greeks hiding in the wooden horse. He is immune to Helen's charms because his focus is on conquest and on securing what he can grab for himself. His narrative arc concludes on one of the Greek ships eating an apple and ogling the dead Astyanax's maid.

Ajax and Thersites interact in two key scenes that cast a spotlight on their negative characterization. In Episode 4, Ajax brutally attacks Thersites for his outburst, a short expletive that succinctly captures the Greeks' fear of the impact of Achilles' withdrawal from battle. This scene both echoes and reinforces the Iliadic episode where Odysseus brutally silences Thersites for criticizing Agamemnon. The rigidity of the Greek social hierarchy is thus played out in front of the series' audience. Greece is codified as a place where the strong abuse the weak and high-status individuals can brutally chastise those below them in rank. But by the end of Episode 8, Ajax and Thersites are working in concert to crush the final embers of the survivors' hopes for the future (or so they believe). It is Thersites who reveals the presence of Troy's last surviving male heir,

Figure 11.2 Thersites (Waldemar Schultz) reveals Astyanax and his nurse in Episode 8, "Offering."

Astyanax, the son of Hector and Andromache. He thus undoes Odysseus' act of mercy during the previous night's orgy of killing. Odysseus had planned to leave the baby alive behind with his nurse. Thersites drags them into the light (Fig. 11.2), while Ajax restrains his mother, desperate to stop Odysseus from carrying out Agamemnon's command that he kill Troy's last male prince. The Greeks are thus re-envisioned in *TFOAC* as archetypes of toxic masculinity, treating their women, and their subordinates appallingly and quarreling amongst themselves over status and the spoils of war. Their greed and ambition are what unites them, but it is a fragile, unstable alliance. In the BBC/Netflix version of the story, the war ends up destroying both sides, death and enslavement for the Trojans (as in the Epic Cycle and in Greek tragedy) and moral debasement for the victorious Greeks, although if Ajax and Thersites are anything to go by, there was not much to admire about the Greeks in the first place. *TFOAC*'s negative portrait of the Greeks is not the exception, however, but rather the norm, a new addition in a long cinematic tradition that was in turn inherited by television.

The Screen Context

Stories about the Trojan War, its prequel and the aftermath, have been retold countless times in movies, television series, and documentary formats. The Trojan War is not only inextricably linked to the origins of cinema, it also found fertile ground in the newer medium of television, which broadly defined now includes streaming platforms like Netflix.[9] As far back as 1895, Thomas Edison included a scene featuring the famous duel between Achilles and Hector in his *The Kinetoscope of Time* peep-show, a forerunner of cinema. The scene ends in a fadeout signaling the Trojan prince's death,[10] but unlike this proto-cinematic version of Hector, the story of Troy did not fade away, it flourished. This is in large part due to the power and appeal of cinema and television and their ability to reach large audiences. Both mediums have, however, also helped to popularize a particular interpretation of the story that favors the Trojans. In what follows, I briefly outline the history of this trend in the mediums of cinema and television, with particular reference, wherever possible, to Ajax. Thersites is largely consigned to obscurity, becoming part of the anonymous mass of Greek soldiers, the unsung extras that help populate the screen. Thus we can locate *TFOAC* within the wider framework of the ancient myth's long and illustrious screen reception history, and reflect upon its impact on the popular imagination, now aided by the ever-widening dissemination made possible by streaming platforms like Netflix.

The destruction of Troy was captured again and again on film, showcasing the perennial appeal of violent spectacles.[11] One of cinema's earliest epics, *The Fall of Troy* (*La caduta di Troia*, 1911), an Italian film directed by Luigi Romano Borgnetto and Giovanni Pastrone, focuses on the destruction of Troy. Early cinema audiences could finally "witness" the Greeks pouring into the city and setting it on fire. The film ends with an atmospheric scene of columns crashing to the ground, wreathed in smoke, symbolizing the utter destruction of Troy. The film also features a scene in which Paris and Helen perform an extended pantomime of grief for the city of Troy, the dark foil to their earlier scenes of falling in love and finding happiness with each other, their doomed romance, being the other popular strand of the reception of the ancient story on screen. The majority of this short film is devoted to the fall of the city, as its title indicates, with the early scenes in Sparta laying the ground for Troy's destruction, a visual and narrative pattern that *TFOAC* examines in more detail over its eight episodes. One of the Greek leaders who supports the distraught Menelaus when he receives the news of Helen's abduction, and later embarks on the ships for the final assault on Troy might have been intended to be Ajax, but he is not identified as such in the film or its title cards. The brothers Menelaus and Agamemnon are the only clearly recognizable Greeks. They wear royal crowns, while the rest of the Greeks wear horse-hair helmets that visually transform them into the Atreids' supporting cast. In today's "ocular"-centric society, so focused on visual spectacle, the manner in which *TFOAC* visually reimagined the story of the destruction of Troy, and the orgy of violence and death that it depicted, are arguably more important than dialogue in conveying a sense of both the epic scale of the story and its doom-laden narrative.

On screen, as on stage, greed is often cited as the true motive for the Greeks' war against Troy. An early example of this motif can be found in *The Private Life of Helen of Troy* (1927), directed by Alexander Korda. The silent film survives only in fragments (both reel and textual evidence), but we know it featured an early cinematic version of

Ajax (Mario Carillo).[12] The character plays a key role in pressurizing a reluctant Menelaus to go to war against Troy. In this burlesque version of the story, Menelaus is tired of his wife, whose demands and extravagances he resents. He is relieved when she leaves him for Paris. His fellow Greeks, however, are eager to make Helen the pretext for a war. Together with Achilles and Ulysses, Ajax explains to Menelaus that Greece must make the most of this opportunity by attacking the Trojans and destroying their clothing industry. The true motivation for the war is devastatingly simple, it boils down to the fact that Greek women, like Helen, prefer Trojan luxury goods over plainer, Greek products. Ajax's character is instrumental in making audiences understand that the economic reasons for starting the Trojan War far outweigh the empty rhetoric of Greek honor. When Helen tries to return to her husband, Ajax and Achilles send her back, so that the war can continue unabated. Ajax's character is designed to embody the film's ideological critique of consumerism.

TFOAC revisits the question of the Greeks' financial motives for attacking Troy. Menelaus might be criticized for being a "lovesick jackass" in *TFOAC*, but it is Troy's strategic position at the nexus of several trade routes that is the true prize the Greeks seek, as demonstrated in the early negotiations between the two sides in Episode 2. The King of Troy and his heir angrily reject the Greeks' heavy economic demands that will plunge their city into an economic crisis. Helen again serves as an excuse, it is Troy's riches that are the main attraction for the Greeks, although Menelaus' jealousy and insulted pride are very much on display in this scene and throughout the series. The transactional nature of Menelaus and Helen's marriage is emphasized, as he views her as nothing more than his property. One of the distinctive aspects of *TFOAC* is that it dwells on the economic impact of the siege on Troy's inhabitants. In Episode 3, a year after the Greeks' arrival, agricultural activities and trade have stopped, resulting in rationing and hunger for the entire population. The Trojans' increasing desperation is directly linked to the effects of this deprivation.

Many of the early established cinematic tropes and ways of interpreting the story of Troy resurface in *Helen of Troy* (1956), together with another "bad" version of Ajax. Achilles (Stanley Baker) jeeringly calls Ajax (Maxwell Reed) his "imitator" and a "disgusting glory hunter." This Ajax is a thoroughly unpleasant character, an arrogant loudmouth who overestimates his fighting skills. The other Greek leaders are just as unpleasant, but unfortunately for the Trojans more effective. Before Helen even leaves Sparta, the Greeks convene a council to discuss how to engineer a war with Troy. Once again, the Greeks' true motive is their greed for Troy's wealth. As in the 1927 film, however, the Greek leaders are less interested in reacquiring Helen and more in economic reparations, a cinematic theme that is echoed in *TFOAC*. In the 1956 film directed by Robert Wise, Ajax gets his chance to be the Greeks' champion, and a short sequence from this scene was even included in the trailer for the movie. But it is neither an Iliadic-style example of excellence, nor does it take place on the plains of Troy. Ajax and Paris engage in a boxing match in Sparta, as a means of confirming the Trojan prince's identity before the assembled Greeks. Only, Ajax loses the match, revealing that his supposed prowess is nothing more than empty boasting. This cinematic version of Ajax spends the rest of the film as a subordinate player relegated to the background, while his fellow Greeks make war on Troy and eventually destroy it. In this aspect, his portrayal anticipates that of *TFOAC*'s Ajax. In the 1956 movie, the Paris-Helen romance becomes the moral center of the story, while the Greeks are cast in the role of greedy, ambitious, and treacherous villains.

In the 2004 Hollywood blockbuster *Troy* (2004), Ajax (Tyler Mane) is again peripheral to the action, but his prowess as a warrior is restored to him. He features in the scene of the arrival of the Greek fleet at Troy during which he is granted a short *aristeia*. Envious that Achilles was the first Greek to engage the enemy on the beach, he forcibly removes a rower and takes his place. He is eager to fight and does so with great gusto in the film, his battle scenes marked by graphic violence. Even an arrow in the thigh does not stop his momentum in battle, he simply snaps the end off in irritation and carries on fighting. He is pictured wielding a huge war hammer and large shield, visual symbols of his superhuman strength. But in *Troy* he is killed by Hector, rather than their duel ending in a draw, as depicted in the *Iliad* (Book 7), where the two warriors are evenly matched, so neither can prevail. In the Hollywood blockbuster, Hector manages to overcome Ajax despite his brute strength, by outthinking him. Like in *TFOAC*, this Ajax is encoded as "brawn", but at least he was granted a few more scenes to make his mark. The portrayal of the Greeks is more balanced in *Troy*, but once again they are led by a bad king (the British actor Brian Cox playing the villainous Agamemnon with great gusto).

Like in the 1956 film, the Paris-Helen love-affair is turned into a romantic story of doomed lovers in *TFOAC*. But before the 2018 version, there was also the television mini-series, *Helen of Troy* (2003), produced by the USA Network. It retold the story from the perspective of Helen (Sienna Guillory), while Ajax is barely mentioned. The lovers' main antagonist is Agamemnon (played by Rufus Sewell, a British actor specializing in playing villains), whose ambition, greed, and jealousy is taken to new heights. This small screen version of Agamemnon desires Helen and goes so far as to rape her at the end, while his soldiers bodily restrain an anguished Menelaus. As in *TFOAC*, Sewell's Agamemnon wields the sacrificial knife himself, rather than letting Calchas kill Iphigenia (who is a little girl rather than a young adult in this incarnation). In a later conversation with Helen, he reveals his anguish at having to kill his daughter and claims that she is the true reason he refuses to accept the compromise she offers him by surrendering herself in return for a promise to stop the war. Once again, we witness the leader of the Greek expedition send Helen back to Troy, this time because nothing less than the annihilation of the city can satisfy him, another connection with *TFOAC*'s portrayal of Agamemnon.

As these highlights from the long history of casting the Greeks in the role of screen villains demonstrate, filmmakers and audiences tend to be on the side of the Trojans. The relegation of Ajax to a minor character (if he appears at all) is a small but telling piece of this narrative strategy. In the *Iliad*, Ajax is the second-best warrior that the Greeks put in the field. But in his reception on screen, Ajax's strength, courage, and steadfastness are, as we have seen, either downplayed or turned into a negative characteristic. If included at all, Ajax is cast as a lesser Greek warrior, who is a cog in the Greek machinery of war. *TFOAC* has inherited these tropes, as its version of Ajax testifies, elaborating on them by emphasizing his unquestioning obedience, and his brutish nature. A telling example is an interaction he has with Menelaus, who enraged by Achilles' refusal to fight, vents his frustration by saying that he plans to commission a thousand songs to immortalize the Myrmidons' cowardice. Ajax replies, "as long as you aren't expecting me to sing any of them" (Episode 6). This metatheatrical touch both alludes to the orality of *The Iliad*, and has one of the epic's protagonists reject it. *TFOAC*'s Ajax is dismissive of the value of storytelling and its role in the construction of the past. The series thus positions him on the wrong side of history.

Ajax's dismissal of the power of stories is particularly ironic, given that this incarnation of the ancient Greek hero is a character in a series distributed via a streaming platform with global reach (at the time of writing, Netflix is available in over 190 countries).[13] Netflix does not disclose its ratings, or reveal which series its subscribers in different countries choose to watch, but the company's inclusion of this version of the story of Troy as a "Netflix Original" in its catalogs increases the potential for multinational dissemination.[14] At the same time, it further undermines the long-held view that the Classics are elitist rather than, as in their original contexts, popular entertainment. In 1986, the Peacock Report on the financing of the BBC advocated *not* giving the public what it wanted because it did not trust viewers (and listeners) to know what was good for them.[15] In a time when the BBC had few broadcast competitors such a patronizing attitude was possible to maintain, but in the new landscape of the second decade of the twenty-first century this model is no longer sustainable. The Classics have in the past benefited from such discourses about the type of stories audiences *should* be watching, not only because of the cultural capital they enjoy, but also because of their close links with the origins of cinema, and the new medium's emphasis on the educational benefits it could confer on audiences.

In today's culture wars, the conversation has shifted with the reemergence of long-held anxieties over national borders, and the competition that streaming giants like Netflix represent for local broadcasters like the BBC.[16] Discussing the creation of *TFOAC*, Sarandos, Chief Content Officer for Netflix (and Co-CEO since 2020), explained that Netflix wanted to work on the project with the BBC because "we can put more effort, more money, more resources into making it a big global show."[17] As in the story of the Trojan War, finances and budgets remain central, as does the marketability and appeal of spectacle and romance on screen, which dates back to the origins of cinema. But in the two years since the series was broadcast, other factors eclipsed this emphasis on monetary incentives. For example, the new deal with the EU necessitating investment in local productions,[18] and the cultural imperative to produce more diverse programmes,[19] have helped reinforce Netflix's public commitment to "bring culturally diverse stories to a wide national and international audience."[20] Returning to the metaphor of Menelaus' desire to commission a thousand songs, classical stories available on streaming platforms are part of a large catalog of offerings. *TFOAC*'s creator, David Farr, wanted to retell the story from "the Trojan point of view,"[21] in the belief that this would appeal to contemporary audiences disillusioned by ongoing conflicts around the globe and their impact on civilian populations. In order to explore the impact of this

Fallen Heroes: Recasting Ajax and the Greeks on Screen

creative decision on the portrayal of Ajax in the series, we need to add one final element into the mix, Greek tragedy and its reception on stage, screen, and in public debates.

A Tragic Lens?

In *TFOAC*, the epic narrative of the Trojan War is recast as an ancient example of tragic fate, but this is the modern understanding of the concept of "tragedy," as ending in catastrophe and death. In fifth-century BCE Athenian theatre, a play did not necessarily have to end in total destruction and the annihilation of its protagonists, although many of the famous ancient tragedies that survive to this day, do in fact showcase such devastation in memorable and striking ways, for example, Euripides' *Trojan Women*, which dramatizes the terrible fate that befalls the civilian population of Troy in the aftermath of the war. This particular conceptualization of tragedy has proven markedly enduring, especially in the tragedies' performance reception in the twentieth and twenty-first centuries, which has in turn helped shape not only their screen reception, but our very understanding of history. The series maps this tragic arc onto the story of Troy, but in order to complete this transformation, it becomes necessary to eliminate the majority of Greek tragedy's plotlines. One example relating to the above-mentioned drama is sufficient to illustrate this key point. Hecuba dies alongside her husband Priam in *TFOAC*, so cannot deliver her moving lament over her fallen city in *The Trojan Women*. This creative decision gives the series a powerful, cohesive narrative, bookended by Paris' birth and the destruction of Troy that was foretold in the beginning. Applying a tragic prism can re-open some of these avenues and explore further the interlinked questions of how, and more crucially why, the antiwar interpretation of the Trojan War has gained such currency in the public imagination but has bifurcated the reception of Ajax into an Iliadic and a tragic strand.

TFOAC offers its audiences a powerful "us vs. them" narrative positioning Greece as an imperialist power bent on conquest and subjugation and motivated largely by greed rather than honor. Nestor's claim in Episode 2 that the assembled army is comprised of "Lovers and defenders of Greece" rings hollow and by the end of the series has been proven to be blatantly untrue. Ajax and Thersites' portrayal in *TFOAC* is emblematic of the view that the Greeks are "mad, bad and dangerous to know," and this is as much representative of the lower end of the social hierarchy as it is at the top. The series predominantly showcases the Trojan point of view, thus encouraging viewers to form what in Media Studies is known as "a positive affective disposition" toward the Trojan royal family and its people and a correspondingly negative one toward their attackers.[22] Giving the Greeks less screen time solidifies this impression. *TFOAC* further undercuts the Greek position by its brutal portrayal of Greek society. An enraged Menelaus threatens the Trojans with dire consequences in Episode 2, because they refuse to return Helen to him. His construction of them as a foreign "other" owes more to Herodotus' pro-Greek narrative of the Persian Wars (490 and 480–479 BC), and fifth-century Athenian prejudices against the foreign invaders who burned their city and its sanctuaries

165

in 480 BC, than it does to *The Iliad*. Then, as in modern times, crisis and war push older stories into new molds that better fit contemporary needs and agendas.

In the twentieth century, classical literature once more became a way to conceptualize soldiers' experience in war, as well as a modern therapeutic tool for veterans. In his ground-breaking study, *Achilles in Vietnam: Combat Trauma and the Undoing of Character* (1994), Shay argued that he saw strong parallels between the *Iliad* and the stories of the Vietnam veterans he was treating. In the wake of the Afghanistan and Iraq wars, Sophocles' *Ajax* enjoyed a new lease of life on American and British stages, as a topical classical example of the impact of war trauma and PTSD on soldiers.[23] We can turn Ajax into another flawed antihero for the twenty-first century,[24] but only if we interweave his Iliadic and tragic traits, which *TFOAC* deliberately eschewed, because such a portrayal would have run counter to the series' anti-Greek stance.

But even if we side-line Ajax's tragic incarnations and focus on the Homeric epic alone, Ajax is not the simple-minded muscleman we encounter on the screen. If Achilles is the Greeks' fiercest attacker in the *Iliad*, Ajax is their best defender, famous for protecting the Greek ships when the Trojans attempt to set them on fire in Books 13–15, and rescuing the body of Patroclus in Book 17, a scene that is radically altered in *TFOAC*, where it is Achilles who retrieves the corpse of his friend, without encountering any opposition from the Trojans, who, unlike the Greeks, show respect toward the dead. In modern Film Studies parlance, we can therefore apply to the Iliadic Ajax the label of "protector-killer," a term used by Lawrence and Jewett to describe Chris Kyle (Bradley Cooper) in *American Sniper* (2015).[25] In Clint Eastwood's war movie retelling the story of the "most lethal sniper in U.S. military history," as the subtitle of Chris Kyle's autobiography (2012) proudly proclaims, the protagonist's worldview is established early and valorized as that of a natural born warrior like Ajax. When a young Chris gets into a fight in the schoolyard, his father does not reprimand him, but tells him that his instinct to protect others is one that he should cultivate. This is a formative moment for the protagonist who states that he is fighting to protect his fellow soldiers from harm. Building a meaningful connection between *American Sniper*'s ideological narrative and Ajax's modern performance reception puts his story into dialogue with modern war movies and allows us to problematize the modern protagonist's heroism.[26] But it also serves as a reminder that such a reading goes against the grain of Ajax's direct receptions on both the large and small screens.

In the *Iliad* and in Sophocles' tragedy that bears his name, Ajax, son of Telamon, deserves the sobriquet "the Great," not only because it distinguishes him from Ajax the Lesser, but because he is a hero capable both of great and terrible actions. But on screen, as well as in popular culture, the Greeks' second-best warrior is reduced to one essential quality, his exceptional strength, while on stage and in public debates he is being used as a therapeutic tool, a connection that veterans can forge with ancient warriors and the famous war at Troy. Greek tragedy problematizes any easy judgment of the Trojan War. In Sophocles' *Ajax*, the Iliadic warrior is transformed from a great protector into a suicidal man, desperately trying to regain his lost honor. At the beginning of the play, Ajax wants to exact revenge against his former comrades, who dishonored him by awarding Achilles' armor to Odysseus. He fails even in this endeavor, blinded by Athena's clouding of his mind. The goddess makes him believe that he is torturing and killing the other Greek leaders, when in fact he is abusing the camp animals. The Athenian tragedian uncovers the dark side of the stalwart hero of the *Iliad* and of the warrior code. An Iliadic hero's identity was predicated on how others perceived him, so dishonor meant a loss of self and of identity. The tragic version of Ajax does lend itself to the antiwar interpretation of the nexus of stories surrounding the war at Troy in the twenty-first century, but has so far not been translated into a similar approach in cinematic and television portrayals, because it clashes with another potent screen narrative that casts the Greeks in the role of irredeemable villains.

Ajax does not make an appearance in any of the screen receptions of Greek tragedy created thus far. This small, but distinctive number of independent films, informed by a desire to create "quality" cinema or television that claims to askew commercial concerns, tend to adopt liberal, feminist, and antiwar interpretations of the tragic corpus, inspired by the plays' reception on stage.[27] A notable representative is Michael Cacoyannis' Euripidean trilogy: *Elektra* (1962), *The Trojan Women* (1971), and *Iphigenia* (1977). The final film, modeled on *Iphigenia at Aulis*, features a portrayal of the Atreidae, in the process of becoming the villains we encounter in *TFOAC*, and its many screen predecessors. Greed and ambition do motivate Cacoyannis' Agamemnon (Kostas Kazakos) and Menelaus (Kostas Karras), but the brothers, especially Agamemnon, are more conflicted than they are generally portrayed on screen, rendering them more rather than less culpable, because we witness them making the choice to sacrifice Iphigenia.[28] Slotting in an additional tragic lens alongside the others that refract the story of the Trojan War enriches our understanding of *TFOAC*, and allows us to interrogate the current state of our relationship with this famous ancient story.

The palimpsestic Homeric text stands in not only for the *Iliad*, but also the lost epic cycle, and at times even of the Athenian dramas whose plots are connected to the Trojan War. The long history of the story's transmission in a variety of media both literary and visual adds further layers,[29] and each character has their own reception trajectory. Ajax's dominant trait is his extraordinary physical strength that makes him such an asset to the Greeks in the *Iliad* and in the mythical tradition. But his "tragic" descent into madness and suicide split his reception into two competing strands in the twenty-first century. We encounter the more familiar version on screen, the ancient Greek warrior becomes the muscles from ancient Greece. But another version of the Greek warrior is gaining ground on stage and in public debates about ancient and modern conflicts. He is also the product of an antiwar interpretation of the Trojan War, but one that traces its roots back to Sophocles' tragedy and draws attention to the Greek soldiers' war trauma. Whether the two strands of Ajax's reception will ever recombine, or Thersites will make more appearances, remains to be seen. I, for one, cannot wait until my next encounter with Ajax.

Notes

1. Many thanks to the editors of this volume for all their hard work. I would also like to thank my dedicated group of undergraduate students who discussed their impressions of the series as an extracurricular activity during New Zealand's first lockdown.

2. Hall 2004: 1 and Bakogianni 2015: 305.
3. See Stafford in this volume.
4. Augoustakis and Raucci 2018: 1–3.
5. Bakogianni 2018 and 2020.
6. Torgovnick 2009: 1840–1.
7. Sidebottom 2004: ii.
8. Bakogianni 2020: 60.
9. Jenner 2018: 6–7.
10. Michelakis 2013: 164.
11. Berti 2020: 5–6.
12. Malamud 2013: 339–40 and 343–4.
13. www.help.netflix.com/en/node/14164.
14. Lobato 2019: 70.
15. Collins 2004: 38–41.
16. Savage 2020.
17. Gill 2017.
18. Fioretti 2018.
19. Conlan 2020.
20. Buck and Plothe 2019: 6.
21. Hughes 2018d.
22. Lee and Shapiro 2014: 147–8.
23. Cole 2019: 151–60.
24. For a discussion of antiheroes in post-9/11 movies set in the ancient world, see Tomasso 2018: 209–11.
25. Lawrence and Jewett 2016: 33–4.
26. Bakogianni 2018: 156–9.
27. Bakogianni 2017.
28. Bakogianni 2013a, 2013b, and 2015: 301–5.
29. Haywood and Mac Sweeney 2019; Fitton, Villing, and Donnellan 2019: 184–271.

CHAPTER 12
FAMILY VS. COMPASSION: ODYSSEUS AND THE ETHICS OF WAR
Meredith Prince

War raises ethical questions concerning its justification or cause, means of warfare, extent of civilian losses, whether morality or humanity can coexist with it. The BBC/Netflix limited series *Troy: Fall of a City* tackles the dilemma of maintaining one's humanity or honor under the duress of war through the character of Odysseus and his involvement in two of the most agonizing dilemmas, and horrific acts, of the series, the sacrifice of Agamemnon's teenage daughter Iphigenia (Episode 2) and murder of Hector and Andromache's newborn son Astyanax (Episode 8).[1] Odysseus' repeated displays of compassion toward women and children throughout the series may derive from love of his own family. Yet his overwhelming desire to return to and protect his family collides with and overrides his moral code, leading to an ethical power struggle with Agamemnon and his pivotal role in the deaths of Iphigenia and Astyanax. These two events are well-known from Greek tragedy and define Odysseus as a behind-the-scenes villain, yet they rarely are represented in screen texts of the Trojan War. This chapter considers Odysseus' conflicting aims of preserving both his moral code in war and his family, which ultimately condemn him to the events of the *Odyssey*, against the backdrop of the ancient tragic sources, as the series reinvents the detestable, conniving, hated man of tragedy to create a new tragedy and tragic Odysseus.[2]

Introducing the Family Man

Episode 2 introduces Odysseus and his family on Ithaca, when Diomedes arrives, telling Odysseus' servant Xanthius that Agamemnon "demands" Odysseus' "support." Xanthius insists that Odysseus is "distracted" and "not fit to see anyone." Meanwhile, Penelope tries to shush their crying baby, but Diomedes finds them, telling her that Odysseus "and his army are required to join the war effort against Troy." She responds that she has read the letters but that Odysseus for the past week has suffered from a brain fever and will not talk to anyone, even her. Diomedes insists on seeing Odysseus, and as they come upon him plowing his fields with two oxen, Penelope explains, "He plows it day and night." "There's no point taking him to war. What use would he be?", she further tells Diomedes, who answers, "Maybe. Or maybe he's as cunning as he ever was. Maybe you both are." He grabs and places the baby in the path of the plow. Penelope yells at Odysseus to stop, which he does, as she runs to the baby. Odysseus rushes at Diomedes, only refraining from pummeling him when Penelope again tells him to stop.

The scene draws on the ancient tradition of Odysseus feigning madness while plowing (Hyginus' *Fables* 95). Odysseus, having received an oracle he would not return home from Troy for twenty years and having lost everything, put on a felt hat and plowed his fields with an ox and horse. Palamedes called out Odysseus' deception by placing Penelope and Odysseus' infant son Telemachus in the way and ordered him to join the others who also had sworn the oath to attack Troy.[3]

The scene, unusual for its inclusion,[4] also establishes Odysseus as a family man. He tries to evade military service, supported by Xanthius' and Penelope's attempts to keep Diomedes away, and stops his plow to save the baby. Diomedes, who replaces Palamedes of the ancient sources, notes when Odysseus refrains from hitting him, "You're not so mad after all." He knows them well enough to see through Odysseus' ruse and how to force him to betray himself, by playing on his familial love. The series further expands the role of Penelope in the deception, as Diomedes himself recognizes, as she gives him evidence of her husband's madness. But the series also reveals the sway she has over Odysseus, as he readily responds to her orders to stop, both plowing and hitting Diomedes. And Diomedes simply reports that Agamemnon "demands" Odysseus join him in going to war, omitting any reference to an oath, setting up a potential power struggle between them.

When Odysseus tearfully says goodbye to his son Telemachus and tells him to take care of his mother and sister for him, the audience discovers the baby is a daughter! The invention of, and inclusion of, a daughter whom Odysseus chooses to save, but commits him to war, will echo, and be reversed by, Agamemnon's decision to choose war over his

Figure 12.1 Odysseus (Joseph Mawle) remembers leaving Penelope (Erica Wessels) in Episode 2, "Conditions."

own daughter's life, a decision in which Odysseus himself will play a major role and contribute to another decision about letting a baby live or not.[5]

A flashback later in the episode shows Odysseus and Penelope's emotional and private farewell, where he repeats "Remember," while she says, "You come back to me" (Fig. 12.1). Achilles, after the ransom of Hector (Episode 7), tells Odysseus that after the war he will go back to Penelope, to which Odysseus responds, "Yeah. If she remembers me." Odysseus' concern over how long it will be before he can do so and whether Penelope will remember him motivates him and references his well-known desire to return home to his wife and Penelope's memory of and longing for her husband in Homer's *Odyssey*.[6] His desire to go home, even his impatience, is mentioned often. Agamemnon accuses Odysseus of wanting to leave (Episode 5), even telling him to do so, but that he is not leaving without Helen. Odysseus quickly defends himself, "No one is recommending leaving." When Agamemnon argues that they can still capture Troy without Achilles (Episode 6), Odysseus counters that it would be faster with Achilles, as Agamemnon accuses him, "You're in a hurry to get home?" Odysseus admits it, but Agamemnon warns him, "Don't start rushing." And, as part of the ruse of the Greeks' departure and offering of the horse (Episode 8), Thersites uses Odysseus as an example, perhaps assuming this was well-known of him: "Odysseus said he'd had enough. Wanted to go home, see his wife." As the only one reluctant to join Agamemnon and shown being summoned and at home, Odysseus furthermore stands in contrast with the other Greeks, whose families are never mentioned or appear or whose marital relationships are strained, especially those of Agamemnon and Menelaus, emphasizing how important Odysseus' home and family are to him.

The Sacrifice of Iphigenia

Odysseus' desire to return home trumps his morality if something advances or guarantees it; as Achilles accuses him, "You like to win regardless of the cause" (Episode 5). The role Odysseus plays in convincing Agamemnon to sacrifice his teenage daughter Iphigenia so that they can go to war reveals a complicated side to Odysseus as he begins to navigate the balance between morality or humanity and war. While Odysseus may be testing Agamemnon, even getting back at him by forcing him to commit to war and to choose a daughter over war as he had to do, his forcefulness speeds up the timeline of returning home after fulfilling Agamemnon's "demands" and sets up Odysseus' own tragic dilemma at the end of the series.

Once Odysseus has arrived at Aulis, the last to arrive, Menelaus and Agamemnon find themselves consulting this unwilling participant about not being able to sail (Episode 2). Although Menelaus and Agamemnon believe the "cruel" wind will improve, Odysseus questions if it does not, they will be unable to sail, which for him means delaying the war and thus his homecoming. Odysseus asks if they offered anything to the goddess, but, as Agamemnon answers, "In the haste of anger, rituals may have been neglected." Odysseus simply states, "She's offended."

When offerings requested by Agamemnon fail, and Calchas reveals Artemis wants his daughter as sacrifice, Agamemnon insists, "This will be prevented. Try again." Odysseus, however, emphasizes, "The goddess was clear."

Agamemnon   Why? Why demand that? To kill my own blood, why?

Odysseus   So you can look a Trojan in the eye as you break their city, and know that nothing they suffer can compare to what you suffered here.

Agamemnon   What kind of justice is that?

Odysseus   The justice of war.

Agamemnon refuses to go to Troy. When Menelaus objects to this, and that he sacrifice his daughter Hermione, Agamemnon offers himself, the father prevailing over brother or leader. Odysseus argues, "Then we lose a leader and gain nothing. There is no negotiation, sir. You know that." He continues, "We must find the best way (pause) to expedite." Agamemnon slaps him, yelling, "Expedite? Expedite? Do you have a heart?" As he grabs him by the throat, Odysseus gasps, "Yes, my lord. But we are here, now. The winds will not change unless you do. Your men will not follow a king the gods have abandoned." Odysseus plays on Agamemnon's kingly role and perception of public opinion, much as Diomedes had played on his own familial feelings but makes sure the divine aspect is intertwined with it. After subsequent sacrifices fail to convince Artemis, and Odysseus tells Agamemnon that his daughter will arrive soon, believing she is going to be married, Agamemnon pleads with him, "Help me. Get me out of this." Odysseus responds, "I'm sorry. I don't know how."

In the ancient sources, Odysseus' role in the sacrifice of Iphigenia primarily was one of escort or ambassador, the one who brought her to Aulis under the pretense of her marrying Achilles, referenced by Iphigenia herself in Euripides' *Iphigenia among the Taurians* (24–5). In Euripides' play *Iphigenia at Aulis* (405 BC), although Odysseus remains behind the scenes and never appears onstage,[7] he has the greatest sway in determining whether or not Iphigenia will be sacrificed. While Menelaus initially plays a role in convincing Agamemnon to sacrifice Iphigenia (lines 97–8), he then agrees with his brother's change of heart not to follow through with it (481–503). Although Odysseus is one of a few who knows about the sacrifice (107, 524) Agamemnon's fear that a politically ambitious, self-serving, unscrupulous Odysseus will reveal all to the entire Greek army ends his wavering to kill his daughter and reverses his decision not to go through with it; Agamemnon acts to save his family, as he fears the army would kill Iphigenia, even his own family, and destroy his city if he does not kill her himself (511–35, 1267–8).

Here, however, Odysseus moves center-stage as he unhesitatingly and mostly single-handedly—as Menelaus proves rather ineffectual—convinces a distraught and reluctant Agamemnon that Iphigenia must be sacrificed for war to proceed. Euripides' Odysseus acts out of political ambition, and other characters hint that "he is exploiting the situation in his own interests."[8] He also has been described as "an opportunistic politician and conspirator with no consideration for morality or justice," and a man who "is ambitious and unreliable, and uses the support of the army to promote his own plans."[9] The series' Odysseus still looks toward his self-interest but politics and power are replaced by homecoming and family. Odysseus' implied motivations are privatized and personalized, while Agamemnon's are more public and political, for saving face. But Odysseus' concern for his family in the final episode will bring full circle the tragic threat of which Euripides' Agamemnon was so concerned.

Once Agamemnon's wife Clytemnestra and their daughter Iphigenia arrive at the Greek camp, it is Odysseus, not Agamemnon, who explains that the king himself will take their daughter to the altar while he will bring her to Achilles. While Odysseus handles the situation diplomatically and better than Agamemnon, Clytemnestra suspects something is not right with her husband and questions Odysseus about it, afraid Achilles no longer wants the marriage. He reassures her, that Achilles is getting ready by himself. When she persists, questioning the hurry, Odysseus answers, "You know Menelaus has been humiliated." Her suspicions increase, however, when they enter a tent and no Achilles is present. While Agamemnon repeatedly lies to his wife and daughter, Odysseus reveals the truth to her, emphasizing, "The gods, they didn't demand Iphigenia's marriage." Clytemnestra questions the implications of this, but the look he gives her reveals all as she repeatedly screams "No!" Odysseus restrains a horrified and distraught Clytemnestra.

Agamemnon, meanwhile, tells his equally suspicious daughter, "The wind blows hard against us. The goddess gave me no choice," emphasizing the divine as Odysseus had. Iphigenia pleads with him, "But I'm your daughter." Yet she accepts her fate, telling him, "No. If it is to happen, let it be without struggle." "Do it!," she yells several times at her father. Agamemnon quickly slits her throat, and we hear and see Clytemnestra's anguish and Agamemnon's, whose repeated plaintive "Why?" carries over the Greek camp.

Once more, Odysseus has moved to the forefront, instrumental at every stage of the sacrifice, from convincing Agamemnon of its divine necessity, and playing on his public reputation and persona, to handling Clytemnestra. While Achilles in Euripides' play reveals to Clytemnestra that Odysseus would, if necessary, drag Iphigenia to the altar (and that he was willing and chosen to do so, 1362–4), the series further shifts Odysseus' involvement to Clytemnestra herself. Similarly, the play allowed Clytemnestra, having discovered the truth from the old servant, to confront her husband about the real reason he summoned Iphigenia there (1129–43, 1208), while here Odysseus steps in to handle what Agamemnon should have done, further contrasting the two men's marital relationships.

Once at Troy, Agamemnon presumptuously assumes the war will be over quickly, in just one day, because, as he tells a doubtful Odysseus, "The gods have guaranteed it. With my daughter's blood." While the play offers the conditional guarantee of sailing and sacking Troy with Iphigenia's sacrifice (92–3, 1261–3), and here Helen tells Paris, "Agamemnon killed his own daughter to guarantee success" (Episode 2), only the winds and Artemis' offense were of issue, nothing of winning the war. And while no full explanation is offered aside from Artemis being upset for being neglected, Agamemnon manipulates the divine element to justify his daughter's death to himself and others.

Grief-stricken and guilt-ridden after their unexpected, to him at least, opening setback (Episode 2), Agamemnon exclaims to Odysseus, "I know she's dead. So why do I keep seeing her? Why did I do it? What was the point?"

Odysseus   It was demanded.

Agamemnon   And what's my reward? More death. More blood. Is that justice?

Odysseus   War is like a grief, sir. You can't force it to be over in one day. We will prevail, but not like this.

Agamemnon   Tell me what to do.

Odysseus returns to camp, telling the men, "He's agreed. Surround the city." He uses Agamemnon's emotional state to implement his war strategies, such as building ditches and digging themselves in, initially rejected by Agamemnon as unnecessary, thus making winning the war and returning home more likely.[10]

Strikingly, the flashback of Odysseus and Penelope's farewell occurs right after Agamemnon's assurance of success and further emphasizes Odysseus' drive to return to her. After the opening battle (and before his conversation with Agamemnon), Odysseus, complaining about what they should have done, tells Nestor, "This isn't warfare. This is a madness." He continues, "When Hector refused our demands, I saw the years open up before me. I'll be an old man before I see home again," prompting him to do what he can to prevent that.

Odysseus also manipulates the sacrifice earlier in the episode to emphasize to the Trojans during the embassy the seriousness of their presence there and encourage them to accept their terms, thus avoiding war. When Hecuba explains that Helen wants to stay and "I'm sure Agamemnon does not desire the shedding of blood," Odysseus replies: "My lady, blood has already been shed. The king sacrificed his own daughter to appease the gods in coming here." Priam asks, "His own child? Killed?" Menelaus responds, "By his own hand." Odysseus emphasizes to the Trojans, "So I hope you will understand how our conditions for peace are non-negotiable."

Viewers reacted negatively to the scene here and were shocked by the violence done; while the episode adheres faithfully at times to the source material, strikingly (to those who are familiar with the tradition) Iphigenia is not saved by being replaced with a deer as she is at the end of the play.[11] Furthermore, of mainstream Trojan War films, only the 2003 mini-series *Helen of Troy* includes the sacrifice of Iphigenia, who appears as a young child, with no role for Odysseus.[12] The sacrifice, lasting only a few minutes, appears at the end of part one of two of the mini-series. After two months without winds, Calchas explains that Artemis asks for Agamemnon's daughter and that Agamemnon must do it himself. He, without hesitation, agrees to do "a terrible thing" as "the gods demand it." Her death haunts Agamemnon and he refuses to accept Helen returning herself because of Iphigenia, emphasizing "no trade." More importantly, it sets up his own murder at the hands of Clytemnestra to avenge her daughter at the end of the movie.

Family vs. Compassion: Odysseus and the Ethics of War

The series' deviations from Euripides' tragedy, and novelty of its inclusion, build up the tension between the two men, associate both with choosing between a daughter's life and war, and contrast their interactions and relationships with their wives. The sacrifice further emphasizes the reversal and swapping of the tragic Agamemnon and Odysseus in terms of private and personal versus public and political motives and sets the stage for Agamemnon to hold this over Odysseus.

Odysseus' Treatment of Women and Children

Yet Odysseus' love for his family positively affects his treatment of women and children, including the enemy, as he respects, protects, or saves them. He serves as a foil to the brutish Agamemnon and Menelaus, who either verbally or physically abuse women, including their wives. While Agamemnon hides the truth of Iphigenia from Clytemnestra, Odysseus handles her as compassionately as he can, given the circumstances. When Menelaus rudely demands, during the embassy, to know where his wife is and then orders Helen to call him husband, Odysseus asks her, "My lady, you've been treated well?" (Episode 2). When Helen, during the taking of the city, realizes that Menelaus has betrayed her and has no intention of letting the Trojans live, she turns to Odysseus as her last resort, suggesting his compassion is well-known (Episode 8).

Odysseus also treats Hecuba respectfully during the embassy. Although Hecuba counters Odysseus with a reference to his tragic persona when she orders him to "leave and take your smooth tongue with you" (Episode 2),[13] after negotiations have broken down and the Greeks have revealed they want the Dardanelles, he does not exhibit any angry outbursts as Menelaus does.

After Agamemnon has taken the captive Briseis from Achilles, Odysseus not only protects her when her brother Dolon, a spy, is captured (Episode 5) and later leads her to his body (he apologizes to her, Episode 6), he also ensures she escapes from the Greeks. When Agamemnon threatens what he will do to Briseis when he returns (Episode 7), she grabs a knife, as Odysseus walks in. Once Agamemnon leaves, Odysseus tells her, "That was foolish." She tells him, dropping the knife, to kill her, so she can be with her brother. Odysseus returns the knife, advising Briseis, "Flee tonight, when the battle begins. My men won't stop you." While Achilles treated her with respect (he did not desire a slave, but believed she "deserved to live," Episode 4), Odysseus' compassion and actions ensure that she does live.

Odysseus also feigns ignorance of a baby's cries as he escorts Andromache out of the palace after the fall (they stop when they hear the cries and exchange a look in Episode 8). And it is not just women and children, but the enemy in general. When Menelaus beats a Trojan captive for information, then kills him after the revelation that Helen and Paris are married, Odysseus questions whether Menelaus needed to do that, noting he "could have been helpful" (Episode 3). His compassion for the enemy also extends to his man Xanthius, who spares from detection two Trojan youths (infiltrating the city as a spy, he had lived with but was betrayed by them); they, along with Briseis, are among the few Trojan survivors.

Odysseus is best known for his compassion in Sophocles' *Ajax* (440s BC), when he refuses to partake in Athena's mockery of a raving Ajax, pities his former friend turned enemy, and notes that what has happened to Ajax could just as likely happen to him (lines 121–6). He further convinces Agamemnon that Ajax is worthy of burial (1332–68).[14] But it his compassion toward the actual enemy Andromache and her infant son here that leads to further conflict with Agamemnon and places Odysseus in a difficult moral dilemma.

Killing a Baby

Odysseus' earlier handling of Agamemnon, his "justice of war"/Iphigenia's death demanded, backfires in Episode 8 when Agamemnon discovers Astyanax's survival and Odysseus' deceit after they have taken the city. Although the other Greeks repeatedly question a noise (crying baby), Odysseus, hustling Andromache away and advising her, "my lady, it's best if we leave quickly," responds to Menelaus that it is "nothing, our business is done here." After Agamemnon's "What the hell is that", Thersites, who, although one of Odysseus' men, acts against him and stands as a foil to Xanthius, brings out the baby and his nurse. When Agamemnon asks whose baby that is, Thersites, nodding toward Andromache, reveals it is hers, and explains, "found them hiding in the family tomb, by her husband's body."[15] Odysseus takes the baby, while Menelaus whispers to Agamemnon that Odysseus claimed "he found her alone."

Agamemnon asks Andromache, "An heir to Troy? We can't have that." Andromache, running toward Agamemnon, yells, "No! No! No! Give him to me! Give him to me!" Falling to her knees, she continues her plea, "Take me. Have me. Spare him. Do what you want with me. Kill me. Have me." Agamemnon, turning to look at Odysseus holding the baby, points and orders, "You throw it off the walls." Andromache resumes her plaintive yells of "No" and "Please" as a guard grabs her, struggling and screaming, while Thersites holds back the nurse. Odysseus walks toward Agamemnon, while Andromache still sobs, screaming please.

While Odysseus begs Agamemnon, "Please, no," Agamemnon states, "There must be no future king of Troy. You know that." He continues his orders to Odysseus, "You do it. And then we can all go home to our wives and our children," adding, "If you want yours to live." Agamemnon steps away from a shell-shocked Odysseus. Andromache is still screaming as Odysseus walks toward the walls, and she is thrown to the ground. The camera shows Menelaus, a crying Helen, and follows Odysseus' slow path, all the while Andromache still sobs, yelling "please!" The camera follows him to the top of the walls, accompanied by dramatic music and a long pause. Various camera angles emphasize his dilemma, with close-ups of his face, then the camera pulls back. Odysseus whispers, "Forgive me," as he holds out the baby from the walls (Fig. 12.2) The viewer sees the baby drop from below, from inside the gates, followed by the sound of a thud and Andromache's screams.

Family vs. Compassion: Odysseus and the Ethics of War

Figure 12.2 Odysseus (Joseph Mawle) holds Astyanax at Troy's walls in Episode 8, "Offering."

The off-stage villain who is responsible for deciding Astyanax must die in Euripides' *Trojan Women* (415 BC) here in *TFOAC* becomes a conflicted man center-stage and the actual murderer.[16] The earliest epic sources were split, whether Achilles' son Neoptolemus or Odysseus was responsible for the death of Hector and Andromache's son, but eventually the blame shifted exclusively to Odysseus.[17] The Greek messenger Talthybius announces to Andromache that the Greeks will kill her son (by throwing him from the walls), as Odysseus prevailed over them, that they cannot have the son of a noble father grow up (lines 713–25). Euripides' play emphasizes the public threat of future Trojan vengeance against all Greeks' families; Hecuba also suggests this, in her lament over the dead boy's body, that the Greeks feared he would raise up a fallen Troy (1160–1). Astyanax's death is justifiable, and, regarding Odysseus' role, it has been noted that "in every case Odysseus' actions are *pro bono publico*: the success of the expedition is at stake. Odysseus' killing of ... Astyanax ... was cruel; but ... it was necessary as a means of preventing a war of revenge."[18]

Agamemnon here, although he ostensibly uses the issue of an heir, further personalizes the risk of allowing the survival of the Trojan heir, threatening Odysseus with the deaths of his children if he does not kill Astyanax. He reverses both the threat Agamemnon sees in Euripides' *Iphigenia at Aulis* to his entire family if he does not kill his daughter and the arguments that Odysseus used here. Agamemnon's threat to Odysseus' family also recalls Andromache praying the same fate for Odysseus' children in Euripides' tragedy (line 724) in response to Talthybius' remark about not letting her son grow up. While in Seneca's *Trojan Women* (mid-first century AD)[19] Calchas makes the decision that both

Astyanax and Polyxena be killed if they wish to sail (lines 361–70, 533), Ulysses (the Roman name for Odysseus) himself again brings up the issue of a Trojan heir (529–55) and the threat it poses to his son Telemachus (589–93) in his effort to convince Andromache to tell him where she has hidden her son. Ulysses notes that, while Andromache's grief moves him, it does not as much as that of Greek mothers (736–8), and he claims that he cannot pity her (762–5), that the best he can do is provide her with time to mourn her son. As much as Seneca's Ulysses may exhibit a glimmer of compassion for Andromache's situation, the public good is of utmost importance.

Odysseus' attempts to protect the child here further contrasts with a scene from Seneca's play, where Ulysses interrogates Andromache about the boy's location, hidden in Hector's tomb as here (503–12), but she is the one that tries to keep his whereabouts a secret. There, she also supplicates Ulysses to save her son, asking him to pity a mother and offering well-wishes for his return home (691–704), unlike in Euripides, where Andromache does not plead for her son but rather laments his impending death and fate (740–79).

As Andromache here supplicates Agamemnon in place of Seneca's Ulysses, she evokes both Andromache in Euripides' *Andromache* (mid-420s BC), when she pleads with Menelaus for the life of her son by Neoptolemus and is willing to die in his place (lines 406–20), and especially Hecuba in Euripides' *Hecuba* (424 BC). There the anguished mother Hecuba pleads with Odysseus for her daughter Polyxena's life (lines 251–94) and offers herself as a substitute as the sacrifice demanded to the ghost of Achilles (383–8).[20] Hecuba fails to convince Odysseus, who becomes instrumental in another innocent's death, and accuses him in her plea of not repaying her previous kindness to him, prioritizing Achilles' honor over her daughter's life, and valuing his public interests above all else. Like the tragic Hecuba, the grieving mother Andromache here, in her effort to save her child, is unable to sway Agamemnon, whose motives are not politically motivated, but have shifted to gaining the upper hand over Odysseus and avenging a personal wrong against his family. Furthermore, the Odysseus of the *Hecuba*, no longer just acting behind the scenes, shows how "it is his sheer inhumanity that repels us, and his ability to believe that political loyalty can justify murder."[21] Similarly, the series' Odysseus, although under compulsion to save his family, chooses to do Agamemnon's bidding rather than spare Andromache's son.

Unlike her counterpart in Euripides, who already has departed from Troy before her son's death (*Trojan Women* 1130), this Andromache must witness her son's murder. To add to the heartbreak, Andromache and Hector had issues conceiving, otherwise unattested, and she was obsessed with having a child, causing conflict with Helen because she abandoned her own child to come to Troy. Furthermore, Astyanax has been made much younger than in the ancient sources, at most only several days old. Astyanax is old enough to talk, according to Hecuba, in Euripides' *Trojan Women* (1180–4), while even older in Seneca's play, as the messenger describes the boy as walking, climbing, and even jumping to his own death (1088–103). Although he is also an infant in 2004's *Troy*, mother and baby escape slavery and death.

A baby's crying, as with Penelope and Odysseus' daughter, gives the child away and again forces Odysseus to obey Agamemnon's demands; although Odysseus saved his

Family vs. Compassion: Odysseus and the Ethics of War

child, he cannot save Andromache's now. Odysseus' "Please, no" recalls Agamemnon's "get me out of this" concerning Iphigenia as both men are forced to kill a child, one to go to war, the other to go home. Andromache is Agamemnon, offering herself up to him in her child's place but also Clytemnestra with her anguished negations. The episode's title, "Offering," could refer to Astyanax, another parallel with Iphigenia, as Odysseus again is instrumental in the killing of a child, this time guaranteeing his return home. Andromache's pleas and sobs further echo Hecuba's own, in a flashback in Episode 1, where Hecuba cries out, "No, please! My baby!", as the newborn Paris is taken away from her.

The decision whether or not to kill a baby, and its associated request or need for forgiveness for such a cruel act, brings the series full circle to Episode 1, which opened with the birth of Paris, whom later a devastating prediction reveals would bring destruction to Troy. Later in the episode, as Priam and Hecuba discuss Paris, who was abandoned and not killed, Priam reassures Hecuba worrying about Paris in Sparta, "The gods have forgiven us, Hecuba. Why can't you?" When Paris is on the run in his effort to protect his family and city (Episode 5), Hecuba tells Hector, who condemns them for not saving their baby, that Priam did not "force" her to abandon the baby. As she reiterates that to Priam himself later in the episode, she reassures him that instead he "persuaded" her, "to sacrifice one life for all lives," and emphasizes that they need to "face what we did." Priam ruefully notes, regarding Paris' return to them, "I honestly thought that the gods had forgiven us." The gods, obviously, have not forgiven them for even indirectly sparing Paris. When Aphrodite, who blames Zeus for setting up Paris, asks Zeus for forgiveness regarding Paris, "Forgive him—for me", Zeus, believing Priam himself should have killed Paris as a baby, tells her, "Thing is, forgiveness isn't our way, is it?" (Episode 5). While Hecuba and Priam do not go through with killing Paris and are not forgiven for it, Odysseus does abide by the mantra of killing one to save others, in his case his family, and asks for forgiveness in following through.

Odysseus' "forgive me" further evokes Agamemnon's words to his prize Chryseis regarding Iphigenia (Episode 4), as he explains to her, "The gods gave me no choice", and emphasizes, "She knew I had to do it. She forgave her father for doing what had to be done. To forgiveness?" Chryseis responds, "You do not deserve forgiveness." Agamemnon presumptuously equates his daughter's encouragement to kill her with forgiveness. It is unclear to whom Odysseus utters his request; is it Astyanax, Andromache, the gods? Other characters throughout the series ask for forgiveness from the gods for themselves or someone else, but also from other people.[22] Odysseus does respect the gods the most and is more deserving of forgiveness than Agamemnon. Yet forgiveness, as Zeus explains, is not the purview of the gods. Odysseus' request also Christianizes and modernizes him, as forgiveness, in our sense of it, was not familiar to the ancient Greeks and did not start developing until the early Christian era.[23]

The scene is startling for its stark horror, from camera angles, sound effects and music, to the emotional intensity surrounding nearly every character in it. Viewers were described as being "left pretty heartbroken" by the death of Astyanax.[24] His death deviates significantly from the sources, as Odysseus does all he can to save the baby but is ordered by Agamemnon to kill him, Andromache is present, and Astyanax's age makes him a most innocent victim. Furthermore, the death of Astyanax usually is omitted from screen. While Michael Cacoyannis's *Trojan Women* (1971), staying faithful to Euripides' play, includes a brief mention of Odysseus and offers the young boy's perspective as he is pushed off a cliff by a Greek soldier, Andromache and her son survive the fall of Troy in *Helen of Troy* (1955) and *Troy* (2004).[25]

A grieving Andromache's curses, echoing Cassandra's predicting Odysseus' well-known sufferings from the *Odyssey* in Euripides' play (*Trojan Women* 424–43), reveal the deterioration of Odysseus' humanity as they prepare to leave Troy: "Odysseus, may your crimes haunt you like ghosts. May the gods plague you, and may your heart be shattered as mine is now. May Troy be the curse that follows you all your life." Season 1 ends with a lingering close-up of Odysseus' troubled face, hinting that a possible Season 2 will include the *Odyssey*.[26] While Odysseus proves distasteful in Euripides' tragedies due to his "inhumanity in his treatment of the weak, no matter how much the doctrine of the greater good of the greater number seemed to justify it,"[27] the series' Odysseus becomes a much more complicated, and conflicted, figure. As has been argued about compassion in Greek tragedy, "the requirement of harsh duty compels an individual to shunt aside the compassion that restrains him from carrying out a merciless act";[28] the choice of saving or sparing a child is not always possible in Greek tragedy, "since it often arises in conflict with a duty or requirement to do harm, this impulse to spare will sometimes be overpowered or suppressed by that contrary compulsion, often to the regret of the agent or agents involved."[29] Suppressing one's compassion to an enemy, in wartime, is understandable, but Odysseus' is directly overridden, not by duty, authority, political loyalty (or the gods), but by his family. His anguish emphasizes the difficulty in compromising his morals to carry out a cruel but necessary act.

Conclusion

The series' most psychologically and morally complex character, Odysseus surpasses the other Greeks in honor, compassion, and accountability. The series rehabilitates the tragic, behind-the-scenes, detestable, heartless villain and instigator of killing children or innocents, who acted out of political ambition and currying mob favor, and merges those acts with his well-known desire for home. Yet Odysseus' compassion and family love put him into these moral dilemmas, forcing him to make difficult ethical choices at great personal cost and creating a new tragedy for himself. The finale suggests that Agamemnon and Andromache set into motion the trials of his homecoming, self-inflicted sufferings caused by incompatible attempts to keep both his humanity intact and family safe during war.

Notes

1. This chapter began as a conference paper, "Odysseus and the Ethics of War: Family versus Compassion in *Troy: Fall of a City* (2018)," presented in Winston-Salem, NC at the Classical Association of the Middle West and South Southern Section meeting in October 2018.

2. On the general nature of Odysseus/Ulysses, from antiquity and beyond, see Stanford 1976; on the range of attitudes to "the moral worth of Ulysses," see Stanford 1976: 5 and in connection with his intelligence, on his "inherent ethical ambiguity," see Stanford 1976: 7. On Odysseus in Greek tragedy, see Stanford 1976: 102–17 and Montiglio 2011: 3–12. Also see Esposito 2010: xi–xiii on the fifth-century political and social background for Odysseus' appearances in tragedy, namely that of the demagogue, sophist connection, and the mastery of persuasion. On other aspects of Odyssey in *TFOAC*, see the chapters by Burns and Stafford in this volume.
3. Apollodorus' *Epitome* 3.7, omitting the animals, notes that Odysseus faked his madness and that Palamedes took Telemachus from Penelope to put in front of the plow; Servius' commentary on Vergil's *Aeneid* 2 adds that Odysseus had placed salt in the fields. On his madness, see Stanford 1976: 82–3.
4. In the 2003 mini-series *Helen of Troy*, Odysseus remarks, before they draw lots for Helen: "I have a family. I'd rather plow a field with salt than go to war."
5. See Burns in this volume on parallels between the two men and their daughters.
6. Even though Penelope is not as beautiful as Calypso and is mortal, Odysseus tells Calypso how much he wants to return home (*Odyssey* 5.215–25). Penelope, in her distress over Phemius' song about the Trojan War, states that she remembers and longs for her husband (1.343), while Agamemnon's ghost remarks that Penelope well remembered Odysseus (was faithful), thus earning her glory (24.195–6).
7. On this play, see Stanford 1976: 114–15, Michelakis 2006, Johnson 2016: 124–6, Collard and Morwood 2017. Stanford 1976: 111 describes Odysseus, in this play and Euripides' *Trojan Women*, "as a sinister, malign influence." On Euripides' *Iphigenia at Aulis* and *TFOAC*, see also Norgard in this volume.
8. Stanford 1976: 115.
9. Michelakis 2006: 44.
10. Compare Homer's *Iliad* 14.82–102, where Odysseus does not agree with Agamemnon's strategy and convinces him to abandon his plan for retreat.
11. Daly 2018 notes in her review of the episode that "viewers were in complete horror" and the fact that all the characters but Iphigenia and Clytemnestra were aware of the impending sacrifice "made it difficult viewing." See also the chapters by Burns and Norgard in this volume on the sacrifice.
12. The sacrifice is the focus of Michael Cacoyannis's 1977 movie *Iphigenia*, faithfully based on the play. Odysseus has greater visibility there, as he appears early on in the film, speaks to the army, and knows about the situation. He comes to retrieve Iphigenia for the sacrifice, then addresses the army after being rebuffed, again intervenes against Achilles, who claims Odysseus lies, and again riles up the army. As Achilles notes he could drag her away, Odysseus does come for her once more.
13. Hecuba mentions his two-fold tongue in Euripides' *Trojan Women* 285–7.
14. See Stanford 1976: 104–8 and Johnson 2016: 32, 213 on Odysseus and his compassion in the play. On Ajax, see Bakogianni in this volume.
15. Earlier in the episode Andromache was shown directing the nurse with the baby down a hall, presumably toward the tomb and likely the source of the crying when Andromache and Odysseus hesitated on their way out of the palace.
16. On the *Trojan Women*, see Stanford 1976: 114, Lee 1976, Goff 2009, Johnson 2016: 118–20.
17. Although the burden is on Odysseus as decision-maker in Euripides' play, the Chorus says that the Greeks killed the boy (lines 1120–2). In Seneca's *Trojan Women*, while Ulysses leads

181

Astyanax to his death, the boy decides to sacrifice himself, jumping from the walls on his own, as reported by the Messenger (1088–103). Ulysses also shifts the blames to all the Greeks and fate (524–8), while Andromache, in denouncing Ulysses and his deceit, blames him for the decision to kill her son (750–6).

18. Stanford 1976: 85.
19. On this play, see Fantham 1982 and Boyle 1994.
20. On this play, see Stanford 1976: 111–14, Gregory 1999, Foley 2015, Johnson 2016: 113–18.
21. Stanford 1976: 114.
22. When Achilles thinks that the Trojans have broken the truce after Hector's ransom, he tells Priam as he intends to kill him (before being hit by Paris' arrow), "May the gods forgive you" (Episode 7). As Helen is about to kill Xanthius' Trojan guard, she says, "May the gods forgive me" (Episode 7). Hecuba tells Cassandra that she won't forgive herself for living with all this, having lied about Paris' disappearance as a baby and Cassandra's mental state all this time (Episode 5). After Paris has burst into the Greek embassy and they have been committed to war by refusing to return Helen, Paris asks his father to forgive him (Episode 2). During the celebrations under the presumption the war is over, Andromache says to Helen, "If I misjudged you, forgive me" (Episode 8), referring to her constant suspicions of Helen and accusations of treachery against her, partly due to Andromache's inability to believe that a mother could leave behind her child. And Menelaus, after Agamemnon has blamed Helen for everything, tells her, "I forgive you, wife" (Episode 8).
23. As Konstan 2010: 21 notes, there was an "absence" in ancient Greek thought of forgiveness as "a bilateral process involving a confession of wrongdoing, evidence of sincere repentance, and a change of heart or moral perspective . . . on the part of the offender," combined "with a comparable alteration in the forgiver, by which she or he consents to forego vengeance on the basis precisely of the change in the offender." On forgiveness in antiquity, and the development of the modern concept of it, see Konstan 2010 and Griswold and Konstan 2012.
24. Warner's 2018 review of the finale includes comments from viewers, ranging from them pleading with Odysseus not to follow through with killing the baby to disbelief that he did so.
25. Andromache and son are both omitted from the 2003 mini-series *Helen of Troy*.
26. At the time of the series airing in spring of 2018, there was talk of a Season 2, possibly with this focus, but at the time of writing this in the spring of 2020 there is no indication one is moving forward. See also Stafford in this volume.
27. Stanford 1976: 116.
28. Johnson 2016: 127.
29. Johnson 2016: 16.

CHAPTER 13
BLOODY BRIDES: IPHIGENIA, HELEN, AND RITUAL EXCHANGE
Amy L. Norgard

"What do I have to do with the marriage of Helen and Paris? Why must I die because he came to Sparta?" These are Iphigenia's words when she learns she is to become a human sacrificial offering in Euripides' tragedy *Iphigenia at Aulis*.[1] As the Greek fleet is stalled at the port city of Aulis due to unfavorable winds, only a human sacrifice—that of King Agamemnon's eldest daughter—will appease the goddess Artemis and send the Greeks to Troy to retrieve Helen. Iphigenia, in questioning the logic of how her death serves this outcome, sheds light on a recurring motif within Greek tragedy: women are treated as objects of exchange.

This motif of exchange—that one woman's life could be exchanged or substituted for something (or someone) else—is explored extensively in the mini-series *Troy: Fall of a City* (2018). This chapter provides a close analysis of the parallel editing sequence featuring Iphigenia and Helen at climactic moments in their respective stories, which highlights their intertwined fates. Drawing upon the scholarship of Helene Foley on the blending of marriage and sacrificial rituals in *Iphigenia at Aulis*, and Victoria Wohl's treatment of the commodification and exchange of women in Greek tragedy, this chapter will demonstrate how the connection between Iphigenia and Helen in *TFOAC* is innovatively represented.[2] By not adopting the (albeit spurious) ending in *Iphigenia at Aulis* where a sacrificial deer is substituted and dies in place of Iphigenia, *TFOAC* offers Iphigenia herself as a perverted ritual substitution, whose life is exchanged to further the interests of (and others' interest in) Helen. Through this substitution, the women exchange roles: the matron Helen takes on the role of a maiden once again by pursuing an illicit second marriage, and the maiden Iphigenia becomes a "bride of Hades" in a sacrificial ritual highly evocative of a marriage ceremony.

The long format of the *TFOAC* series allows the audience to relive the dramatic experience of Iphigenia's death as the writers explore resonances of Iphigenia at later key moments. They employ the Iphigenia-Helen exchange model as a blueprint for the treatment of other women in the series, especially Chryseis, Briseis, and Hermione. Through the interplay between Iphigenia and Helen, *TFOAC* underscores just how vulnerable a woman's life could be—not just vulnerable to the demands of powerful men, but also vulnerable at times of transition in her own life. In treating women as commodities—interchangeable with monetary wealth, objects, and even the lives of other women—an individual woman has no inherent value on her own.

Screening Love and War in *Troy: Fall of a City*

Iphigenia and Helen: Blushing Brides or "Bloody" Brides?

TFOAC portrays the events of Euripides' *Iphigenia at Aulis* in a brief but impactful sequence in Episode 2. This section analyzes the seven-minute sequence that begins with Iphigenia arriving at Aulis anticipating marriage to her death, in order to demonstrate the ritual parallelism and exchange that takes place between Iphigenia and Helen. *Iphigenia at Aulis* is one of the definitive literary sources that survives from antiquity detailing the sacrifice of Iphigenia. Composed at the end of Euripides' life, it was performed posthumously in 405 BC.[3] In Euripides' telling of the myth, Agamemnon, the *de facto* leader of the Greeks, must appease Artemis for favorable winds to sail to Troy to retrieve the errant wife of his brother, Menelaus. Upon learning that a steep human price must be paid in the form of his maiden daughter, Iphigenia, he summons her to Aulis under false pretenses of marrying the Greek hero Achilles. She arrives with Clytemnestra, her mother and Agamemnon's wife, both anticipating the upcoming nuptials, only to learn of Agamemnon's true, deceptive intentions. Although the women are supported by a sympathetic yet self-serving Achilles, Iphigenia comes to accept her fate willingly to uphold the ideals of preserving Greek marriage—an institution in which she will never take part, ironically, due to her untimely death. At the last moment, however, Artemis takes pity on Iphigenia and substitutes a deer to die in her place. Iphigenia is saved and whisked away to safety.

TFOAC follows this basic narrative through a unique expression of visual storytelling. The editing of the Iphigenia sequence is a quick succession of cross-cutting that intermingles scenes of the sacrifice at Aulis with that of Helen's actions in Troy. Although the scenes are seemingly unrelated, cross-cutting implies their simultaneous action and also suggests a deeper symbolic relationship. The cross-cutting of these two parallel scenes initially stresses where the stories of Iphigenia and Helen converge—namely, through weddings. Both scenes portray a mother-figure seated with a daughter-figure partaking in pre-wedding social rituals that a contemporary audience would understand. Helen and Iphigenia adopt the roles of young brides who exhibit concern with how they will fit into the families of their husbands-to-be. The first scene opens with Iphigenia and Clytemnestra, daughter and mother, traveling to Aulis after being summoned by Agamemnon under the ruse of a false wedding. As she sits across her mother in the carriage, Iphigenia (Lauren Coe) nervously expresses concerns typical of an inexperienced young bride. What exactly will marriage mean for her future? Will she reside with Achilles? Will she leave her family? As a mother giving her daughter advice on her wedding day, Clytemnestra reassures Iphigenia that marriage focuses on joining houses, not leaving anyone behind.

The scene then cuts away to Troy where a parallel event is taking place: Helen (Bella Dayne), in the posture of a bride-to-be, applies cosmetics in an intimate bedroom setting with Hecuba, her future mother-in-law. The mood is one of carefree levity as the women are seated close together at the mirror. Hecuba (Frances O'Connor) applies gold to Helen's lips and rouge to her cheeks, rendering her a literal "blushing bride," as the adage goes. In an earlier scene, Helen and Paris arrived in Troy like a recently married couple.

Hecuba had criticized her son Paris for parading Helen "right up the street like his bloody bride" in the manner of a wedding procession (Episode 2). But here, in an apparent change of heart, the Trojan matriarch conveys a tacit sign of approval of Helen in her new role as Paris' partner through a beautification ritual.

Initially, Iphigenia and Helen's scenes express parallel circumstances through marriage rituals. Quickly, however, it becomes apparent that both weddings are a sham and the marriage rituals take on a perverted meaning. As it is revealed that Iphigenia's wedding to Achilles is a deceit to secure her presence at Aulis, her fictional wedding morphs into a different ritual—that of sacrifice—bitterly underscoring that she will never experience her own wedding. But Helen's marriage is also fraught because she is already married to Menelaus, making her union with Paris a perversion of a socially acceptable marriage. Despite this, Helen's scenes remain heavily marriage-focused as they lead up to the consummation of her union with Paris. For Helen, the marriage rituals are perverted and reveal her obliviousness about the ramifications of her illicit marriage.

The conflicting interests of Iphigenia and Helen in *TFOAC* have their roots in Greek tragedy, particularly Euripides' *Iphigenia at Aulis*. *TFOAC* writer-producer David Farr's engagement with ancient tragedy is apparent in his retelling in this serialized drama. As noted elsewhere, Farr has a background in theater, including the Shakespeare Company and a contemporary production of the *Odyssey* at the Old Vic in 2004;[4] and Farr conducted extensive research on ancient sources within the Trojan War *mythos*, including reading Homer, Euripides, and Vergil, and visiting the alleged ruins of Troy in Hisarlik, Turkey. Like *TFOAC*, Euripides' telling of Iphigenia's sacrifice also contains resonances of marriage, emphasizing the dramatic irony that no wedding is to take place. For example, when Achilles learns that his name has been used to lure Iphigenia to Aulis, he assumes the role of a husband to protect Iphigenia (lines 919–1036). He refers to Iphigenia as his "future wife" (1354), even though it means incurring the ire of his own war-hungry Myrmidons (1352–3). Iphigenia reminisces about conversations she and Agamemnon used to have about marriage in order to gain her father's pathos: Agamemnon had wanted a good match for her, and she looked forward to welcoming her father into her new home (1222–30). While speaking these powerful lines Iphigenia holds her baby brother, Orestes, in a visual reminder that she will never bear her own children. In the starkest mention of marriage in the play, Iphigenia ultimately changes her mind and decides to die willingly in order to preserve the integrity of marriage for all of Greece by ensuring that barbarians "pay for the ruin of Helen whom Paris snatched away" (1381–3).[5] She goes on to say that Helen has "stirred up strife," but with her death she hopes to bring salvation to Greece (1418–20). After her speech, Achilles eroticizes Iphigenia's marital values, saying, "If I could only win you as a wife" (1404), and "Now that I have seen your character, I long still more to marry you" (1409–10). And finally, as Iphigenia is led out to the sacrificial altar, she offers her heartbroken mother marital advice: "Do not hate your husband" (1454) for his part in her sacrifice—another dramatic irony, seeing that this heinous murder is the impetus for Clytemnestra plotting Agamemnon's murder.[6]

For a play in which no wedding takes place, there is a great deal of emphasis on weddings and marriage rituals, to the point that Helene Foley argues marriage "shares almost equal weight with the sacrifice itself."[7] In her book, *Ritual Irony: Poetry and Sacrifice in Euripides,* Foley discusses how the ritual of sacrifice disguised as a fictitious marriage rite showcases the analogies between the two seemingly opposed rituals. On the surface marriage represents the beginning of a new life and symbolizes procreation, whereas with sacrifice comes death. However, Foley argues that Iphigenia unites these two disparate rituals: she is sacrificed to Artemis, but also becomes a bride to all of Greece in her decision to self-sacrifice.[8] Another possible interpretation is that Iphigenia becomes what was known in antiquity as a "bride of Hades." As Agamemnon says, "Hades, it seems, will soon marry her" (lines 460–1). A young woman who died early was effectively considered married to death rather than a living person, which underscores the similarities between marriage and death through their associated myths and rituals.[9]

In an interview about his version of the Trojan War, David Farr affirmed his commitment to innovation: "What we do know is what Homer and Euripides and Virgil handed down to us. It's all layers of myth and story. It liberated me a little. They invented. They completely re-imagined. It allowed me to do a little bit of the same."[10] Although David Farr outright names Euripides as one of his sources, likely for the Iphigenia content, his interpretation of the ancient material also exhibits innovation. The blending of marriage and sacrificial rituals adopted from Greek tragedy is also established in *TFOAC,* but the cross-cutting sequence between Iphigenia and Helen fosters a direct comparison of their respective "marriages" that the ancient play does not provide. In recreating Helen's marriage to Paris and incorporating it into Iphigenia's sacrifice scene, *TFOAC* can further explore the nature of the relationship between these two characters, especially as their circumstances begin to diverge from one another.

In *TFOAC,* as the sequence continues to cut back and forth between Aulis and Troy, Iphigenia's marriage rituals turn deadly when she learns that her wedding is a fiction. The anticipation Clytemnestra and Iphigenia initially felt gradually dissipates as they begin to suspect deception. The groom, Achilles, does not make an appearance—in stark contrast to his role in Euripides. Clytemnestra grows suspicious of everyone's apparent gloomy moods: "My husband is not himself," she observes warily. At the same time, Iphigenia approaches the sacrificial altar on a small cliff by the sea and innocently remarks, "This doesn't look like a marriage altar. Where are the flowers? What is it father? You look afraid" (Episode 2). Rather than her father leading her to a marriage altar, which a contemporary audience would understand as part of a traditional marriage ritual, Agamemnon leads Iphigenia to a sacrificial altar. This is no sea-side wedding ceremony; rather, the diegetic sounds of the crashing waves, constant throughout the scenes in Aulis, are an auditory reminder of the unfavorable weather conditions that demand Iphigenia's life. The sound continues to fill the screen but abates at the conclusion of the sacrifice, indicating the god's appeasement. As Iphigenia's wedding takes a morbid turn, the scene cuts away to Helen in the bedchamber with Paris. The two lovers consummate their relationship for the first time in Troy as though it were part of a wedding ritual that began earlier in the episode when Paris paraded Helen through the streets of Troy and followed by Helen's boudoir beautification.[11] Helen's wordless scenes are an intimate portrait of the couple kissing, laughing, and having sex.

Bloody Brides: Iphigenia, Helen, and Ritual Exchange

The cross-cutting sequence between Aulis and Troy gains speed and intensity as the events rush toward their climax: for Iphigenia, the climactic moment is her death, whereas for Helen it is the climax of an orgasm. As the sequence escalates, the shots of Iphigenia's sacrifice and Helen's passionate sex alternate quickly and nearly blur together. In fact, throughout this entire sequence the scenes jump back and forth between Aulis and Troy twenty-eight times since Coe's Iphigenia makes her first appearance. Despite the apparent dissonance between sex and death, the eroticism of Helen's scenes infiltrates Iphigenia's sacrifice. Her death, then, shares features with a young virgin's wedding night. Iphigenia's tender throat is slit on the sacrificial altar by a blade that pierces her neck and draws blood, standing in for the penetration of a woman's body during sex. In addition to the blade as metaphor for a penetrating phallus, the presence of blood can be associated with cultural traditions about a virgin's first sexual encounter, thus also suggesting an erotic element to the sacrifice.[12] However, when Iphigenia articulates a conditional willingness ("if it is to happen, let it be without struggle"), the sexualization of violence committed against her begins to look more like rape—perversely committed by her father who leads the sacrifice, in contrast to ancient sources.[13] Additionally, at the close of their respective rituals, Iphigenia and Helen are portrayed in a similar recumbent position, but with vastly different implications. Helen lies satisfied in bed with Paris, which is visually comparable to, but tonally dissonant with, Iphigenia's violated bloody body laid on the offering table (Figs. 13.1 and 13.2). Their wedding rituals are complete: Helen has consummated her marriage, while Iphigenia has become a bride of Hades through death. A thunderclap completes the sequence of parallel editing, indicating appeasement of the gods and perhaps even their tacit approval of the events.

Figure 13.1 Helen (Bella Dayne) and Paris (Louis Hunter) consummate their union at Troy in Episode 2, "Conditions."

Screening Love and War in *Troy: Fall of a City*

Figure 13.2 Agamemnon (Johnny Harris) mourns a deceased, bloody Iphigenia (Lauren Coe) on the offering table in Episode 2, "Conditions."

Manipulation of cinematography in *TFOAC* shot-by-shot makes visually explicit the perverted trade-off that occurs between the two women's fates. The visual interruptions between scenes from Troy and Aulis allow the viewers to understand the cost of Helen and Paris being together. As the post-coital couple lie together in bed, a tone-deaf Helen is overcome with emotions and whispers, "I'm happy" (Episode 2). It is as though Helen and Paris exist in their own world; they are completely focused on one another and value being together over all reason. Ignoring the ramifications of her illicit new union, Helen's happiness comes at the price of Iphigenia's death: the iniquitous exchange is implied through parallel editing. More to the point, Iphigenia's unrealized future as a living bride is traded for Helen's second marriage to Paris—a detail that is new to film and television portraits of these characters,[14] and which expands upon the ancient sources.

The cross-cutting between Iphigenia's and Helen's scenes further emphasizes the dubiousness of Iphigenia's self-sacrifice. By comparing Helen's scenes with Iphigenia's, the viewers witness the wedding rituals on which Iphigenia is missing out: bonding with her mother-in-law, consummating her union with her husband, and engaging in post-coital pillow talk. Through death, Iphigenia is denied passageway into the next natural phase of her life as a young Greek woman: marriage. Portraying Iphigenia as a bride of Hades is no substitution for a marriage with the living. In an exchange of roles traditionally assigned to women in antiquity, it is not the maiden who gets married, but rather the matron gets married—again.

Maidens for Matrons: Exchange and Substitution of Women

This section treats the trade-off that occurs between Iphigenia and Helen in their roles as maiden and matron, respectively. The trade-off suggests one manifestation of how women in antiquity were treated as objects to be exchanged. Iphigenia and Helen are rendered objects of exchange by men, but they also undergo an exchange in their roles as maiden and matron, thus disrupting the natural order that women were to follow in ancient Greek society. I first observe Helen and Iphigenia as exchanged objects within their own right, and then analyze how they are exchanged relative to one another.

In her book *Intimate Commerce: Exchange, Gender, and Subjectivity in Greek Tragedy*, Victoria Wohl explores the many ways that women are commodified as objects of exchange in Greek tragedy: "imported as brides, captured as war-booty, given as gifts, won in competitions, stolen through rape, hoarded as treasures, bequeathed as inheritances, even offered as sacrifices to the gods."[15] Helen, whom Wohl calls the "quintessential fetishized commodity,"[16] exhibits the qualifications of a stolen woman because she is viewed by the Greeks as a precious, desired object that must be retrieved. A "fatal accountancy" takes place around Helen, whose worth is determined to be more precious than the lives of soldiers and innocents who die to recover her.[17] By contrast, Iphigenia becomes an object of exchange through her sacrifice: the gods are thought to provide divine favor and goodwill in exchange for a gift—in this extreme case, the gift is Iphigenia herself.[18] With men initiating these exchanges, Wohl identifies the system of exchange as reinforcing a man' role as subject and a woman's as transacted object, thus reflecting social hierarchies in ancient Greece.

Ancient portrayals of Iphigenia and Helen in tragedy also highlight the connection between the two women as one of exchange or substitution. Aeschylus' *Agamemnon* (performed 458 BC)[19] opens with a summary of the events in Aulis occurring ten years prior, when Agamemnon sacrificed his daughter as a "first offering" in order "to stay the strength of war waged for a woman" (lines 225–6). The "woman" refers to Helen, thus establishing a trade-off has occurred between the two women: one is offered for the chance to retrieve the other. Euripides' *Iphigenia at Aulis* is also filled with examples of exchange and substitution between Iphigenia and Helen, and even outright questions this connection. Cited in the introduction to this chapter, Iphigenia questions the logic of her connection to Helen. Clytemnestra, too, criticizes the apparent exchange that she is told is necessary: "Is it then destined that Helen can only return if Iphigenia is killed?" (883–4). Clytemnestra goes on to give a valuation of the exchange and determines that it is not a fair one: "It would be a fine thing to pay for a bad woman with the life of a child! We are buying what we hate the most with what we love the best" (lines 1168–71). In Euripides' play, the women are often discussed in language of buying, selling, returning, and exchanging. Even Menelaus, initially in support of sacrificing his niece, abruptly changes course when he considers the problematic economy of exchange involved in the sacrifice: "Am I to win Helen by losing a brother ... exchanging good for evil?" (386–7). He sees that the requested trade-off—the death of his young niece for the chance to regain his wayward wife—is an unequal one because Helen's duplicity is being paid for with Iphigenia's innocence. This point is underscored when Menelaus calls his niece a "wretched girl ... who is about to be sacrificed for the sake of my marriage. What has your daughter to do with Helen? Disband the expedition!" (491–4).

There is little salvation in the male characters in *TFOAC* involved in Iphigenia's death, like Odysseus (Joseph Mawle), Menelaus (Jonas Armstrong), and Agamemnon

(Johnny Harris). They make it clear how little a woman's life is valued, both in their orchestration to kill a young girl, and in their myopic quest to seek a wayward wife because she is deemed another's property.[20] Armstrong's cold and calculating Menelaus helps expedite Iphigenia's murder which he sees as a necessity to right the outrage and embarrassment of Helen abandoning their marriage. For him, there is no question that the trade-off is a fair one because his pride is at stake. Agamemnon is hesitant at first, uttering such lines as, "Help me. Get me out of this" and "What if I offer myself? I'll slit my own throat." But as Odysseus reminds him, "Your men will not follow a king the gods have abandoned" (Episode 2). Agamemnon stays the course and brutally performs the sacrifice himself, in a divergence with ancient portrayals of the myth. Trading Iphigenia's life establishes Agamemnon's worthiness and authority to lead the expedition in the eyes of the Greek soldiers.[21] These male characters comply with the death of Iphigenia to fulfill what they believe to be a larger purpose, whether it be to retrieve Helen or for the opportunity to gain more wealth—more objects, more commodities (including women as war prizes)—through sacking Troy.

The politics of exchange are apparent elsewhere in *TFOAC* in how Helen and Iphigenia are treated as objects to be procured or exchanged. Iphigenia's opening conversation with Clytemnestra is solely focused on the logistics of her marriage, itself a transaction in which brides are given to husbands, along with a monetary settlement in the form of a dowry, as a symbol for joining two families together. Helen as a matron has already lived the experience of a woman exchanged in marriage and expresses her criticisms of the institution. When she arrives at Troy, Helen observes that there is an apparent equality between men and women, unlike in Greece—including between the king and queen. Helen adroitly appeals directly to Hecuba invoking the equality she shares with her husband Priam in ruling, refusing her role as a commodity (Episode 2):

> I hear, my queen, that you rule Troy alongside your husband. That, in this city, man and woman are equal in respect and power. I humbly claim that respect now. I was married at 14 against my will, to a man I had not met and would never love. Not for one moment have I been happy with Menelaus. I didn't choose him, and never would have. I do choose to be with your son. I am not a possession. I'm a woman. I think. I feel. And I'm here because I want to be.

Helen asserts her agency, for what she claims is the first time in her life, by choosing Paris as her mate and refusing to be an object: "I am not a possession." To this point, Bella Dayne intentionally plays her character Helen beyond the trope of the "unfaithful woman" to evoke sympathy for her situation as a woman in antiquity "just producing a child and then having no role in society anymore. Thinking about what that would make you as a person, it made me truly understand why she would do what she does."[22] Troy is the perfect place, it seems, for unhappy women to go when they leave their overbearing husbands. But, as Debra Trusty observes in her review of the series, the "egalitarian oasis" that Troy presents is a myth, which Helen slowly realizes over time and erodes her sense of agency.[23]

Bloody Brides: Iphigenia, Helen, and Ritual Exchange

While ancient literature is not consistent on Helen's role in her departure to Troy (whether she was raped, stolen, or willing), in *TFOAC* she is a deliberate agent in her choice. In *TFOAC*, Helen gets to share her story in her own voice. But asserting one's authority where there previously was none can have consequences. Sometimes, Wohl notes, the distinction between male subject and female object breaks down when the woman attempts to shed her role as object, such as if "the woman refuses to go from one man to another, or goes with vociferous complaint, or tries to exchange others rather than be exchanged herself."[24] Helen refuses to be "a possession," but does not fathom the consequences of her actions on others. She seems unaware that the freedoms she seizes for herself will in fact limit the freedoms for others who will be exchanged in pursuit of her—the soldiers who fight and Iphigenia. While Helen asserts her subjectivity by leaving her husband, Iphigenia accepts her role as object when she agrees to die as a sacrifice "without struggle" and bids Agamemnon to execute the sacrifice (Episode 2). Iphigenia's death undercuts Helen's expression of autonomy within a social structure where women are not granted that authority. So, in a very twisted way, *TFOAC* encourages viewing the punishment of Iphigenia by the men around her as payment for the sins of another woman stepping out of place. The viewer is given mixed signals to place the blame on Helen for Iphigenia's death, although she is not its direct agent; rather, the guilt should fall on the men who orchestrate the sacrifice as a justifiable end for waging war.

Iphigenia and Helen are treated as objects in their own right, but also objects that can be exchanged for one another. When the Greeks arrive at Troy and enter negotiations with the Trojan leaders, the primary discussion concerns whether Helen should be returned. As her own agent, Helen speaks for herself and refuses to go, which Priam and Hecuba support. However, when they learn that Agamemnon sacrificed his own daughter to appease the gods to wage this war, Priam falters: "His own child? Killed?" (Episode 2). Here the death of Iphigenia is used as an indication of the gravity of Agamemnon's intentions and, by extension, the Greeks'. Priam sees power, and likely madness, in trading one's child for a successful war effort—especially seeing that Agamemnon performed the slaughter himself. Priam initially accedes to returning Helen, but he rescinds the offer only after the Greeks demand further monetary reparations from Troy. This scene highlights how women were used as bargaining chips in the war as they are freely discussed as prizes to be gained alongside monetary wealth; Helen's worth, even to Priam, is directly weighed against what it will cost the Trojans to exchange her.

This scene also suggests that women could be seen as commodities to be exchanged for one another—even in death—as the fact of Iphigenia's death translates to a claim on Helen's life by the Greeks. In fact, the key theme of Iphigenia's story is one of exchange and substitution: the focus on marriage in her story, her sacrifice to the gods, and the ritual substitution that occurs in some versions of the story. At the end of Euripides' *Iphigenia at Aulis*, in a narrative describing the sacrifice scene, Iphigenia is reportedly saved by a deer who is substituted and dies in her place, called a ritual substitution. Some characters doubt the truth of this account—namely Clytemnestra, leading the audience to also doubt the miracle;[25] and scholars tend to think it is a spurious addition to the text.[26] Yet, the salvation of a faultless Iphigenia represents a canonical variant of the myth.

TFOAC's Iphigenia, however, is not so lucky. She is killed on the altar with no mitigating circumstances, no substitution, and no *deus ex machina*. In establishing the trade-off between Iphigenia and Helen so strongly through the parallel editing sequence discussed in the previous section, it can be argued that *TFOAC* mutates the concept of the ritual substitute: rather than Iphigenia being substituted and saved, she herself becomes the ritual substitute through her own sacrifice for Helen's chance at a second marriage. So, the idea of the ritual substitute is alive and well in *TFOAC*—but Helen is the one who comes away with a second chance at life, and Iphigenia is the object of exchange.

Additionally, there is more at play here than simply a transaction of exchange happening between Helen and Iphigenia. On a deeper level, the women are also exchanging roles: a matron, in pursuing another marriage, is reverting back to maidenhood to relive the experience of marriage. This would have been perceived as an unnatural path for a woman in antiquity, who would go through established stages that marked important events in her life: marriage shortly after reaching puberty, and having children. By her own account, Helen was married as a young girl to Menelaus and had a child, thus fulfilling her purpose as a woman in Greek society. The maiden Iphigenia is prevented from becoming a wife because of her untimely death, which was committed as a direct result of Helen pursuing another marriage. As another way to think about it, Helen gets to participate in a second marriage, while Iphigenia participates in none, despite her age and status as a virgin making her an appropriate bride. Even the association of Iphigenia with the goddess Artemis—she demands the sacrifice, and then becomes the agent of the ritual substitution—signals Iphigenia's perpetual affiliation with maidenhood. In being sacrificed at the demand of the virginal goddess Artemis, Iphigenia's status as a maiden is confirmed; and, according to some ancient accounts, Iphigenia, saved by the deer, becomes a priestess to Artemis at her cult at Brauron which oversees the initiation rites of young women into adulthood.[27]

Surprisingly, Helen is also associated with Artemis in *TFOAC*, albeit briefly, suggesting her reversion to maidenhood. In Episode 1, Paris spies on Helen getting high and engaging in polyamory with the palace women in Sparta. Commenting on Paris' voyeurism the next day, Helen recounts the myth of Actaeon, in which he is turned into a stag and torn to pieces by hunting dogs for seeing Diana bathing naked (using Artemis' Roman name, perhaps to signal reliance on the Roman Ovid's *Metamorphoses* as source material). And so, Helen too seems to align herself with maidenhood through the goddess Diana/Artemis, albeit through a scandalous episode whose eroticism is only highlighted by Paris' playful remark about Actaeon's vicious death: "Maybe it was worth it." This episode prefigures Helen's intention to act as a young girl again and embark on a path to pursue a (second) marriage with her maidenhood metaphorically restored.

In fact, Helen has a track record of acting like an available maiden who interferes with other young women. Helen assumes the role of lover and wife to Paris although the match was intended for her own daughter, Hermione, to forge an alliance between Sparta and Troy (Episode 1). In scenes with Paris, Hermione (Grace Hogg-Robinson) confesses deep-seated anxiety about not measuring up to her mother, especially when it comes to romance: "I'm not sure what to say or do. I'm not like my mother. I'm not skilled in these things." Hermione is of marriageable age, but Helen intervenes and asserts that she is just a girl and "not ready for courtship" in an attempt to block her marriage to Paris. Paris does not show romantic interest in Hermione, although she easily intuits the primary cause of his disinterest is a growing attraction to her mother. In fact, it seems as though it is a common theme in her life to witness other men—perhaps even potential suitors for herself—falling for her mother instead. Helen causes a distraction to Hermione's marriage prospect, and she even intervenes in the potential union to serve her own interests. Ultimately, Helen will abandon her role as wife and mother, take up with Paris as though she were never married, which disrupts marriage opportunities for other maidens: Iphigenia through her death, and Hermione by stealing her intended.

Eventually, Helen comes to realize that Troy treats its women no better than anywhere else. She decides to willingly return to Menelaus (whom she again calls her "husband") and her daughter Hermione, and even helps the Greeks infiltrate Troy (Episode 8). In doing so, Helen reverts back to her role as an object, and reverts back to a matron. She willingly becomes the dehumanized prize for the Greeks to win. This leaves the viewers wondering for what purpose was Iphigenia sacrificed and Hermione abandoned by her mother. It also sheds light on other instances in the war where young women become subject to exchange and substitution, following the model established by Iphigenia and Helen.

Conclusion: Resonances of Iphigenia

Head writer David Farr embraced the format of the mini-series which allowed him "to explore longer and more complex psychological narratives, bring in new characters, and hopefully move the story away from the more comic-strip elements to something that delivers on an emotional level."[28] The long-form facilitates exploration of characters whose stories resonate throughout the mythos, although they may only spend a brief time on screen. One such character is Lauren Coe's Iphigenia. Although actress Coe only spends several minutes on screen in Episode 2, the shocking death of her character by the hand of her father is unforgettable. Farr and his fellow writers, cognizant of the impact of this scene, resurrect the specter of Iphigenia at key moments later in the series to great dramatic effect. This grants Iphigenia a staying power throughout the series beyond her minutes of screen time, and also works to foster a thematic connection between the individual episodes to forge a cohesive whole. We see these themes related to Iphigenia played out through other narratives, specifically, the rape and return of Chryseis and the sack of Troy.

Resonances of Iphigenia are felt through Agamemnon's heinous rape of Chryseis (Jamie-Lee Money), a prisoner of war and daughter of a priest of Apollo. Struck by Chryseis' resemblance to Iphigenia—and certainly Money and Coe share similar physical traits to make this believable—Agamemnon says, "You're not her," as though to convince himself that he is not seeing a ghost of his deceased daughter. Back at his tent, Agamemnon has a one-sided conversation with Chryseis as though she were Iphigenia and asks for forgiveness, saying "I had no choice, you know," and "She knew. She knew I had to do it." Although initially Chryseis wordlessly does not meet Agamemnon's gaze, she comes to rebuke him for his monstrous actions: "You do not deserve forgiveness. And I thank the gods you are no father of mine." At this, Agamemnon's initial affection is perverted into rage and he rapes her repeatedly, as her screams are heard outside the tent (Episode 4). The implications of Agamemnon viciously raping a young girl who resembles his daughter is undeniably disturbing. The sexualization of Iphigenia's sacrifice discussed earlier, represented metaphorically by the penetrating blade and the presence of blood, becomes literal when revisited through the rape of a look-a-like maiden. Later Chryseis is released to appease Apollo who has brought a plague to the Greeks as punishment, and Agamemnon watches as she is returned to the open, loving arms of her father. Not only does Agamemnon relive the conditions of Iphigenia's sacrifice by giving up Chryseis at a god's behest, but the tenderness of the reunion of father and daughter is a reminder of his ultimate failure to protect his own daughter. Agamemnon's bitterness about Chryseis is magnified because it recapitulates his role in the sacrifice of Iphigenia, which sheds new light on infamous resentment between Agamemnon and Achilles over Briseis that is the setting of Homer's *Iliad*.

Iphigenia's brutal death is also used to represent Agamemnon's own resolve in sacking Troy. It has already been discussed above how the mention of Iphigenia at the negotiations table between the Greeks and Trojans shakes King Priam to his core and he nearly hands over Helen (Episode 2). Agamemnon's role in killing his daughter is invoked again at the end of the series during a pivotal moment in the sack of Troy: the death of King Priam. As the Greeks infiltrate the city, Agamemnon faces Priam, fully dressed in armor, in his bedroom. Priam addresses Agamemnon, saying, "You rape my city. You defile my daughter," upon hearing the cries of Cassandra from another room. Agamemnon's quippy response to this is, "Don't talk to me about daughters," a reference to the pain of killing his daughter to bless the war effort, and he easily cuts down the Trojan king (Episode 8). The suffering he experienced from Iphigenia's death, in his mind, justifies the suffering of others. Invoking Iphigenia's sacrifice, a prewar offering made to facilitate the Greeks' voyage, at the conclusion of the war creates a sense of narrative closure. For Agamemnon, the war is not about procuring Helen for his brother, but about asserting dominion in the Mediterranean. The sacrifice of his own daughter, then, demonstrates his claim to lead the Greeks—and the price he was willing to pay to achieve absolute domination.

The violence committed against Iphigenia only breeds more violence against young women who are viewed as sexualized objects to be passed and exchanged. The cycle of exchange and substitution of women, prefigured by the complex exchange that occurs between Iphigenia and Helen, continues throughout the series. Just as Iphigenia's death left a void within her father, Agamemnon replaces Iphigenia's memory with a look-a-like war bride. Just as Iphigenia life was exchanged to retrieve Helen, Agamemnon exchanges Chryseis with another war bride, Briseis. Just as Iphigenia's life was traded for a successful war effort by her father, the women in a fallen Troy are treated as prizes: killed, raped, or imprisoned. In the end, even Helen reverts back to the status of an exchanged woman when she returns to Menelaus. Although she only spends a few minutes on screen in

Bloody Brides: Iphigenia, Helen, and Ritual Exchange

TFOAC, Iphigenia represents the many ways women could be exchanged in antiquity, thus serving as a constant reminder of women's vulnerability, dehumanized treatment, and devaluation.

Notes

1. Euripides' *Iphigenia at Aulis* 1236–8. Translated by Morwood 2008.
2. On Helen, see Safran, Day, Raucci, and Burns in this volume; on Iphigenia and the sacrifice scene, see also the chapters by Burns and Prince in this volume
3. Foley 1985: 66.
4. White 2018 writes that "Farr had previously written a 'weird' adaptation of *The Odyssey*, set in a modern-day detention center, for the stage." In Preece 2018, Farr says this about the production: "Telling the story from the Trojan point of view was my way in. I'd done the same with a theatre adaptation of *The Odyssey*."
5. Compare Iphigenia's willing declaration in *Iphigenia at Aulis*: "I have made the decision to die. I want to do this gloriously, to reject all meanness of spirit" (1375–6), and "I shall offer my neck with a brave heart in silence" (1560–1), to her conditional willingness in *TFOAC*: "If it is to happen, let it be without struggle" (Episode 2). It is also notable that in Aeschylus' *Agamemnon*, Iphigenia never conveys willingness: "Her supplications and her cries of father / were nothing" (227–8, translated by Lattimore 1953).
6. The choral odes are also full of references to weddings and treated extensively in Foley 1985: 78–84.
7. Foley 1985: 69.
8. See Foley 1985: 68–78.
9. Foley 1985: 86–7.
10. https://www.bbc.co.uk/mediacentre (February 14, 2018).
11. It should be noted that Helen and Paris will have a real wedding ceremony that takes place at the start of Episode 3, with similar parallel editing between scenes of the ceremony and Trojan allies dying at the hands of the Greeks.
12. The sexualization of Iphigenia in this moment of violence echoes a tone-deaf Achilles confessing his passion for the maiden at her declaration of self-sacrifice in *Iphigenia at Aulis* (1403–14), discussed above.
13. Consistently across sources, the priest Calchas performs the sacrifice ("the crafts of Calchas fail not of outcome"; Aeschylus' *Agamemnon* 249), or he is prepared to commit the sacrifice ("the priest took the knife, uttered his prayer and looked at her throat to see where he should strike"; Euripides' *Iphigenia at Aulis*, 1579–80). It seems a deliberate choice by *TFOAC* to have Agamemnon in the role here.
14. Cf. the films *Iphigenia* (1977) and *Helen of Troy* (2003).
15. Wohl 1998: xiv.
16. Wohl 1998: 67.
17. Wohl 1998: 59. See also the choral ode in Aeschylus' *Agamemnon* that dubiously portrays Greek soldiers dying in pursuit of "some strange woman" (lines 437–55). For more on Helen as a commodity, see Wohl 1998: 83–99.
18. Wohl 1998: 68.

19. Lattimore 1953: 2.
20. See also Burns in this volume.
21. Agamemnon is pressured by the Greek troops in *Iphigenia at Aulis*, saying that "in the army of the Greeks there rages some mad desire to sail with all speed to the land of the barbarians" and that the army is so incensed they will kill him "if I frustrate the oracle of the goddess" (lines 1263–8); elsewhere the Greeks form a mob to demand Iphigenia's death (1345–53). Wohl 1998 interprets Iphigenia's death in sociological terms as an "exchange for symbolic capital": "sacrifices can be seen as a gambit in aristocratic competitive gift exchange, acting both to solidify the group and to establish hierarchy within it" (69).
22. Preece 2018.
23. Trusty 2018.
24. Wohl 1998: xiv.
25. "How can I be sure that this story has not been made up to console me?" (Euripides' *Iphigenia at Aulis*, lines 1615–16).
26. In her introduction to Morwood's 2008 translation of *Iphigenia at Aulis*, Edith Hall notes, "This comforting alternative ending . . . radically affects both its theological meaning and its emotional impact." Hall also speculates that the ending could have been added to set up the plot of the already-known *Iphigenia in Tauris*, in which an older Iphigenia is very much alive and well (2008: xxv).
27. Foley 1985: 86; Wohl 1998: 72; Dowden 1989: 9–47.
28. https://www.bbc.co.uk/mediacentre (February 14, 2018).

CHAPTER 14
KINGS OF MEN AND SACRIFICIAL DAUGHTERS
Krishni Burns

There is a moment seventeen minutes into Episode 2 of *Troy: Fall of a City*, in which Odysseus, Agamemnon, and Menelaus stand confronting each other in Agamemnon's command tent (Fig. 14.1). They have just received the news that the goddess Artemis has demanded Agamemnon's daughter Iphigenia as a sacrifice. Agamemnon is centered, looking toward the camera, and Odysseus stands on his left, facing him. The two men are arranged so that they are the same height. Menelaus stands to Agamemnon's right, turned toward him and slightly foregrounded. The subsequent scene is staged like an ancient Greek tragedy. There are three actors present, and the action is comparatively static. The characters trade short, choppy sentences back and forth, statement and counterstatement, just like the *stichomythia* exchanges that are an essential part of Greek drama.

These three men are the most prominent characters on the Greek side of *TFOAC*. In this moment, they are positioned as the three leaders of the Greek army. Each, in his own way, is essential to the Greek campaign. Odysseus supplies the strategy, Menelaus the drive, and Agamemnon the authority to win one of history's most famous victories. They have all been introduced individually, but now viewers are asked to compare them. The point of comparison offered, though, is neither martial nor political; it is deeply personal. Each man has been asked in some way to sacrifice a daughter for Troy's sake, and how

Figure 14.1 Menelaus (Jonas Armstrong), Agamemnon (Johnny Harris), and Odysseus (Joseph Mawle) contemplate the sacrifice of Iphigenia in Episode 2, "Conditions."

they respond to the challenge establishes their characters and their leadership capabilities for the rest of the series.

These sacrifices draw on the ancient mythic tradition for their narratives, but they also engage with and subvert one of the most malignant of modern narrative tropes: the disposable woman. This plot device of the disposable woman is one where a female character is harmed or killed solely to motivate a male protagonist.[1] *TFOAC* takes the filial sacrifices of the ancient tradition and uses them to flip the modern script, so that the characters' own choices to sacrifice or save their daughters drive their narrative arches. This chapter will begin with an analysis of each sacrifice individually, then consider them in contrast to each other.

Odysseus and His Infant Daughter

Thematically, the comparison starts with Odysseus. Earlier in the episode, the series introduces him by way of a fairly obscure yet poignant event near the beginning of his mythical biography. The story holds that Odysseus pretended to have gone insane in order to avoid joining the Greek expedition. The events in *TFOAC* follow the narrative preserved in Hyginus' *Fables*.[2] The Greeks' messenger arrives to recruit Odysseus—Diomedes in *TFOAC*, rather than Palamedes or the sons of Atreus, Agamemnon, and Menelaus, themselves as in the ancient sources—and is met with the report that Odysseus has gone mad. As proof, he is shown Odysseus compulsively plowing a field with a donkey and an ox hitched to the plow. Knowing Odysseus to be wily, the messenger sets Odysseus' infant son, Telemachus, in front of the plow. Odysseus stops to save his child, proving that he is sane after all.

In Episode 2, Penelope delivers the news while carrying an infant whom knowledgeable viewers immediately assume to be Telemachus. After all, canonically Odysseus only has one child at the time, and the baby is carefully presented without any gender signifiers. Penelope keeps it wrapped up in an enveloping blanket, although the viewers are given a flash of yellow baby garment underneath. Diomedes is confronted with the plowing Odysseus, forces him to abandon the ploy by dropping the snatched-up baby in his path, and gloats smugly when Odysseus stops the plow and punches him for reckless child endangerment.[3]

It is a surprise when Odysseus later says goodbye to Telemachus, who looks to be about eight years old. Odysseus tells Telemachus that he must take care of his mother and sister. A nurse stands behind the boy holding the infant seen earlier, who is presumably the sister in question.

In most retellings of the myth, the story serves to establish Odysseus as a man with a talent for clever strategies based on deceit, even though this particular trick fails. It first appeared in a lost seventh-century BC epic called the *Cypria*, which recounted the early events of the Trojan War mythic cycle. A summary of the epic attributed to Proclus survives from the late Roman period, which has allowed modern classicists to reconstruct it.[4] The plow trick is relatively infrequent in surviving ancient texts, although it seems to have been very popular in fifth-century Athens.⁵ Sophocles produced an *Odysseus Mainomenos (The Madness of Odysseus)* based on the story.⁶

Besides the version in Hyginus' *Fables*, the most complete account to survive is found in Servius' commentary on Vergil's *Aeneid*. Servius recounts the story to explain why Odysseus might have wanted to kill Palamedes. In the second book of the *Aeneid*, Sinon, the Greek left on the beach to convince the Trojans to bring the Trojan Horse into the city, claims that Odysseus had treacherously abandoned him because he had sworn to avenge Odysseus' equally treacherous murder of Palamedes.⁷ Vergil glosses over the murder and its motivation with a simple sentence ("I speak about things hardly unfamiliar"), which suggests that he expected his well-read audience to recognize the reference without his help.⁸ Evidently by Servius' day (c. AD 400), the story was not so well known.

While Vergil's audience might have been familiar with this particular myth, the same cannot be said of *TFOAC*'s audience. Modern screen versions of the Trojan cycle seldom include Odysseus' attempt to stay home. The 2004 movie *Troy* paints Odysseus as a reluctant participant, but he only references his wife, not his child. The 1997 television mini-series *The Odyssey* puts a great deal of emphasis on Telemachus' birth, but the series glosses over Odysseus' recruitment with a voice-over reference to his oath set against a visual of Odysseus and the two sons of Atreus staring grimly at each other across a Mycenean hall.

The story does appear occasionally in novelizations of the Trojan cycle that are particularly well researched. Madeline Miller recounts the tale in chapter 16 of her novel *Circe*, Marion Zimmer Bradley has Odysseus himself divulge the failed trick in her novel *The Firebrand*, and Clemence McLaren tells the story in *Waiting for Odysseus*. In each case, the episode reveals some particular character trait that will be important later in Odysseus' narrative. In *Circe*, it demonstrates the devotion of Odysseus to his family, and the paradox that he is forced to abandon them to keep them safe.⁹ In *The Firebrand*, Odysseus tells the story to his friend King Priam to prove both his own cleverness and his reluctance to join the campaign.¹⁰ In *Waiting for Odysseus*, Penelope plans the trick, which demonstrates that she is as wily as her husband.¹¹

All these elements are also present in *TFOAC*'s version of the incident in Episode 2. Odysseus' rage at Diomedes for endangering his daughter, his solemn admonition to Telemachus to take care of his family, and the long hug that he gives his son, indicate both his reluctance to leave and his familial devotion. Penelope's active role is indicated when she explains Odysseus' supposed mental breakdown to Diomedes, and Diomedes responds: "Maybe, or maybe he's as clever as he ever was. Maybe you both are." When Odysseus later blames his delayed arrival on "The tricks of Hermes," Ajax responds: "The tricks of Hermes? The tricks of Penelope, more like." By putting the assessment in the mouth of a character typically known for his lack of imagination, the series demonstrates that Penelope has a reputation for subterfuge that matches that of her husband.

In terms of her characterization, Penelope's costume is interesting. She is dressed in a multi-tiered skirt and tailored bodice that evokes the Minoan statuette known as "the Snake Goddess." A Minoan wall painting was used earlier in the episode "Black Blood" to suggest that Sparta had a very different culture that gave greater freedom to women before Menelaus became king, so Penelope's costume indicates a more egalitarian culture in Odysseus' Ithaca.[12]

The short sequence does a great deal of narrative work. It establishes the character of Odysseus as a tricksy strategist, a reluctant fighter, and a devoted family man. It also proves the excellence of the classical background of the series, since the myth is not widely known today. Finally, it introduces Penelope and Telemachus, thus providing for a possible second season based on the *Odyssey*. The resonances of Odysseus' failed deceit continue throughout the rest of the series.[13]

That said, there is a precedent for all of these qualities in the retellings of the story mentioned above. The one truly innovative element is replacing baby Telemachus with an unnamed daughter. It is a small enough change that it does not affect the narrative or its semiotics, but it is jarring to any viewers familiar with the Greek original. Since the story was included in part to prove *TFOAC*'s mythological chops, the divergence is marked. However, the significance of the change only becomes clear when Odysseus' choice to save his daughter to his own personal cost is contrasted with Agamemnon's choice to sacrifice his daughter, Iphigenia.

Agamemnon and Iphigenia

Iphigenia's sacrifice is one of the most impactful set pieces in *TFOAC*'s eight episodes. It establishes the character of Agamemnon and evokes real tragedy in less than ten minutes. Had there been additional seasons of the show, the mythological vengeance that her mother Clytemnestra wreaks for her daughter's death would have certainly been awaiting Johnny Harris's Agamemnon. During the existing season, Agamemnon's leadership is deeply affected by the price that he has already paid for the privilege of sacking Troy. It resonates in every choice that he makes, turning him from a loving family man and competent leader of men into a temperamental monomaniac.

Amy Norgard offers an in-depth study in the present volume of *TFOAC*'s sacrifice of Iphigenia *vis-à-vis* its ancient source, Euripides' *Iphigenia at Aulis*, so there is no need to retread that material here. However, it is worth noting that none of the extant Greek sources for the sacrifice of Iphigenia actually end with her death.[14] In each case, as in the Euripides play, the goddess Artemis substitutes a deer for the human girl on the altar.[15] Agamemnon's guilt is in no way expiated; according to the ethical code of Greek Tragedy he is still morally responsible for killing his daughter. He was willing to commit the act, even if he was prevented from completing it.[16] The fact that the sacrifice was imposed on him by a goddess does not free him from the responsibility.[17]

Today's concept of guilt is different. A modern audience typically does take extenuating circumstances—that is, divine will—into account and differentiates between the will and the act. By modern standards of interpretation of intention and culpability, in order for Agamemnon to be guilty of Iphigenia's murder, he must both make the choice to kill her and physically carry it out. Agamemnon's character arc in *TFOAC* is dependent on his

Kings of Men and Sacrificial Daughters

feelings of extreme guilt over his daughter's death, so the audience needs to see him actually slit her throat, no substitutions allowed. The great irony of the sacrifice of Iphigenia is that the real cause of her death is the modern audience watching.

Unlike Odysseus' bout of feigned madness, the sacrifice of Iphigenia is interwoven into every genre of modern storytelling and is recognizable across the world. It might be adapted directly, such as in Robert Icke's 2015 stage adaptation of the *Oresteia,* or indirectly, such as in Yorgos Lanthimos' 2017 movie *The Killing of a Sacred Deer.* Adaptations appear in both "high" and popular culture, from Albanian author Ismail Kadare's anti-fascist novella *Agamemnon's Daughter* (2006) to the 2018 mega blockbuster *Avengers: Infinity War.*[18] Even so, the event was shocking when the episode "Conditions" debuted.[19]

At the point in Episode 2 when Agamemnon kills Iphigenia, the audience knows very little about him. He has only had about eight and a half minutes of screen time, only five and a half minutes before he tacitly agrees to her sacrifice. Still, in that brief time he had shown signs that he was a loving family man and a capable leader.

Agamemnon is first introduced in a nearly wordless scene in *TFOAC*'s first episode. He is presented in shadow, half reclining on a draped throne with his wife and daughter at his feet, watching his father's funeral. At first, he seems enigmatic. His boneless sprawl could be read as arrogant disinterest. When Menelaus approaches him and calls him "brother," he hugs Menelaus with a desperation that betokens great sorrow and comfort found in familial grieving. The interaction changes Agamemnon's earlier posture from disdain to depression. Menelaus had previously informed Paris—and the viewers—that his father's death was expected, but still Agamemnon displays signs of deep mourning. Agamemnon's manifest grief at his father's timely death, the presence of his wife and daughter, and the way he clings to his brother indicate that he is deeply devoted to his family.

Agamemnon next appears on screen in Episode 2 as the leader of the Greek army. The various kings are mustering at the port of Aulis in preparation for sailing against Troy. Agamemnon meets the newly arrived Odysseus and his column of soldiers. It is the viewers' first introduction to Agamemnon as a leader, and it has the potential to go poorly. Everyone involved, audience included, knows that Odysseus made an ignominious attempt to avoid joining the expedition. The two independently powerful kings are meeting in front of their troops, so their interaction will have public ramifications for their future power dynamics. At risk are Agamemnon's authority as supreme leader and the audience's initial impressions.

As before, Agamemnon's first actions are ambiguous. He responds promptly to Odysseus' arrival, rather than keeping him waiting, and chooses to come out of his tent to meet Odysseus, rather than making Odysseus come to him. As a result, their first interaction happens in public as equals. The camera follows Agamemnon as he leaves his tent, encouraging the audience to focus on his point of view, and, by extension, his choices. However, his face is blank, so that the viewers cannot be sure how he will greet his delinquent ally.

Agamemnon is not conciliatory. However, he does adopt a diplomatic approach, which allows Odysseus to be diplomatic in turn. Agamemnon offers no greeting and says simply, "You're late." His blunt word choice and his lack of cordiality could be read as confrontational, but they do still leave space for a neutral explanation. Odysseus takes the opportunity to blame a third party, claiming that he did not receive Agamemnon's summons, and then he bows to demonstrate that he will submit to Agamemnon's commands in the future. In return, Agamemnon hugs him, the same gesture that he used to greet his brother in the previous episode.

The exchange demonstrates that Agamemnon is not the power-hungry tyrant of *Troy* (2004), or *Helen of Troy* (2003), the most recent TV adaptation of the Troy tale. Instead, he is a competent leader that balances his powerful position with respect for his allies. He needs to establish his right to command the expedition, so he confronts Odysseus publicly. Nevertheless, he realizes that a good working relationship with his fellow kings is equally important, so he acknowledges Odysseus as a friend and equal by embracing him after Odysseus acknowledges his authority.

Finally, Agamemnon turns to the crowd and announces, "Now we are complete! No more delays!" The choice to engage with the crowd further demonstrates that Agamemnon is a competent leader. His use of the pronoun "we" completes the process of integrating the kings' various forces into one unified whole. Furthermore, it shows that Agamemnon is an active general who engages directly with his troops and considers himself to be one of them, in contrast to the *Troy* Agamemnon's hands-off approach. His statement also flatters his reluctant ally. It implies that Odysseus is an indispensable part of the collective, since the expedition could not leave without him. All signs point to *TFOAC*'s Agamemnon diverging from past iterations of the character to be the leader of men necessary for so great a venture.

However, the potential for a positive interpretation of Agamemnon is shattered by his choice to sacrifice his daughter. *TFOAC* structures the decision explicitly as a choice between his kingship and Iphigenia. When Agamemnon is first confronted with the idea, he violently rejects it, both verbally and physically. The arguments that Odysseus and Menelaus make drive Agamemnon to first try to find an alternative with increasing urgency, then bodily assault Odysseus. He is gripping Odysseus' throat, half strangling him, when Odysseus says: "Your men will not follow a king the gods have abandoned." Agamemnon then loosens his grip, signifying an end to his active opposition. When the choice is framed as a choice between his dependent child and his position of power, he surrenders.

TFOAC's Iphigenia is introduced solely to be sacrificed, yet she has too much character to fit the trope of the disposable woman. The series makes the viewers care about her as a person, not just as Agamemnon's daughter. She is young and sweet, but neither foolish nor weak. She is first introduced in a traveling vehicle with her mother, Clytemnestra, on her way to her supposed wedding at Aulis. Her youth is shown by her giggling admission that she thinks that Achilles is handsome, and her sweetness comes out in her sorrow at leaving her family home. However, this Iphigenia is intelligent enough to question the discrepancies in her hasty wedding. Her confusion also suggests that her parents have not been previously considering any marital alliances for her, which points again to her youth.

That said, her only objection to the wedding is that she does not want to leave her childhood home. Her comfortable banter with her mother shows that she feels safe to express her opinions. Both she and Clytemnestra trust Agamemnon, in spite of the red flags surrounding the current situation. All in all, this Iphigenia is happy as her parents' daughter to the point she has not thought seriously about her adult life yet. She is totally unprepared for her father's betrayal.

When her father greets her, the scene is staged to establish their close parent-child relationship. He holds her head between his hands, a gesture that mirrors Odysseus' farewell to his son Telemachus and brings the two men's opposing choices into contrast. They are equally loving fathers, but do not have equal strength of character. Agamemnon kisses Iphigenia's forehead and then holds her tight. As a visual cue in the culture of modern cinema, a father might kiss his daughter's cheek at a wedding, but a kiss on the forehead is more appropriate for a shorter, younger child. Agamemnon clearly loves his daughter and thinks of her as still a child, not an adult.

Between her father's stricken expression and the blazing sacrificial altar, Iphigenia's initial disbelief seems naïve. However, a sudden marriage would be much more plausible. The Greeks did not practice human sacrifice.[20] There are a handful of Greek myths that can be interpreted as human sacrifice, such as Tantalus' serving his son Pelops to the gods for dinner.[21] However, as in the case of Tantalus and Pelops, the gods find these sacrifices deeply offensive and the perpetrator is punished. Still, when Agamemnon explains the situation to Iphigenia, she does not ask why Artemis would want her, or what proofs there are for such an unpredicted act. She says simply, "But I'm your daughter." At this point in the series, the audience shares her belief that her father's love is a greater safeguard than the gods' benevolence, so his betrayal is all the more shocking.

The great irony of Agamemnon's decision is that it is a false choice. In *TFOAC*'s world, a man cannot be a good leader and still betray the person most dependent on him. When he chooses pure power over its benevolent exercise, he loses the judgment necessary to be an effective leader.

Agamemnon loses his ability to lead as soon as he stops opposing the sacrifice. He does not even actively make the decision. The closest the series comes to permitting him to verbally agree to the sacrifice happens fourteen minutes into the episode. He and the priest, Calchas, stand on opposite sides of the screen with the shoreline as backdrop, so that the sea is framed between them. When Calchas tells Agamemnon that Artemis is unmovable, he looks out toward the waves, signifying that he has chosen his sea passage over Iphigenia. It is a beautiful piece of nonverbal storytelling but shows that Agamemnon is no longer in control. He is totally passive. Even in the moment of sacrifice, Iphigenia has to order him, twice, to slit her throat.

Agamemnon clearly loves his daughter, but he still chooses his leadership over her life. His initial refusal and paralyzing shock give the act the appropriate shattering weight of horror and grief. That said, the sacrifice of Iphigenia is explicitly casted as a choice, and Agamemnon makes the choice to kill her. Afterward, he keeps his position as leader, but loses his ability to lead. Every bad decision that Agamemnon makes for the rest of the series, and there are many, has its roots in this one traumatic event.[22]

Screening Love and War in *Troy: Fall of a City*

Menelaus and Hermione

Iphigenia is also explicitly compared to her cousin Hermione, who appeared in the previous episode. The girls look to be the same age, and they are both presented as prospective brides. Greek tragedy frequently used weddings as a metaphor for the death of a young, female character.[23] As a result, Iphigenia's fate causes the viewers to reevaluate Menelaus' treatment of Hermione in Episode 1. She, too, is offered by her father as a sacrifice to win Troy's wealth.

The association between the two girls begins even before Iphigenia comes on screen. Back in the command tent, when Agamemnon, Menelaus, and Odysseus first grapple with the necessity of sacrificing Iphigenia, Menelaus and Agamemnon have a telling exchange. When Menelaus argues the necessity of the sacrifice, Agamemnon shouts, "Then you give up your child!," to which Menelaus responds, "Hermione wasn't asked for!" The interchange reframes Menelaus' past attempt to arrange a marriage for Hermione as another kind of sacrifice for Troy.

Hermione is *TFOAC*'s first real innovation to the screen tradition of the Trojan cycle. She first appears about thirty-seven minutes into the first episode, when Menelaus introduces her to Paris as a possible wife. Her very existence may be as much of a surprise to some of the viewers as it is to Paris. Until that point, there had been no indication that Menelaus and Helen have any children. Paris had already attended a formal dinner in Sparta, where Helen's absence is both conspicuous and discussed. Hermione attends every other meal moving forward, so her original absence should have been equally marked.

When the scene shifts to Troy, it is clear that Paris' parents knew about Hermione and deliberately kept the possibility of a marriage alliance from him. These obfuscations are out of character for Menelaus, Priam, and Hecuba, but they allow Hermione to be a surprise to both the viewers and Paris. The choice differentiates the series from past screen versions of the Troy tale and sharpens Paris' disorientation. Consequently, Paris is further centered as the audience's point-of-view character. With Hermione in play, neither the audience nor he knows what to expect.

Hermione is so surprising because she upsets the previous pattern of the Trojan cycle adaptations on screen. Her very existence makes for a much more complicated scenario. Screen versions of the Troy tale tend to present the story of Helen and Paris as a straightforward romance. *Helen of Troy* (2003) and (1956) depict them as tragic lovers, and the most recent major cinematic player, *Troy* (2004), skips the tragedy and sends them off to a new life together after the city's fall. The choice slots Menelaus neatly into the role of "brutish husband" to make Helen's infidelity excusable.[24] Adding a daughter into the mix complicates that simple narrative. Today, a mother has a responsibility to her child that cannot be negated by bad treatment or superseded by True Love. However, *TFOAC* was already planning a more complicated Helen, and the choice to include Hermione instantly gives new scope to her character.[25]

Hermione has never previously appeared on screen, nor is the character well known today. However, she is a stable feature of the Trojan cycle, albeit a minor one. Her narrative has remarkably little variation for a myth. She is the only daughter of Menelaus and Helen, and Helen leaves for Troy when she is a young child. When her parents return, Menelaus marries her to Pyrrhus, the son of Achilles.[26] Hermione's marriage is actually the main focus of her story. Her grandfather, Tyndareus, had previously promised her to Agamemnon's son, Orestes, whom she much prefers. Orestes has some family business to take care of first, but once his father is avenged, his matricide expiated, and his sister, Iphigenia, rescued from the temple where Artemis stashed her after her deflected sacrifice, Orestes reclaims his promised bride.

The principal ancient sources for Hermione are set during her unhappy first marriage. She initially appears in Book 4 of the *Odyssey*, when Odysseus' son Telemachus arrives in Sparta for a visit during her wedding. Hermione is a substantive character in Euripides' play *Andromache* and Ovid's poetic letter from Hermione to Orestes in the *Heroides*. Neither is among the best known of their respective authors' works.[27]

Euripides' Hermione is not a sympathetic character. While her husband is away, she spends her time tormenting Hector's widow Andromache, who is now Pyrrhus' unhappy slave/concubine. Hermione first enters dripping in gold and bragging that her father's high position gives her the right tyrannize her household, both negative stereotypes in the play's original performance context.[28] She makes a failed attempt to kill Andromache—whom she considers a rival—and Andromache's infant son by Pyrrhus, then runs off with Orestes to escape the consequences of her actions. Her defection allows the cast to comment on the hereditary disloyalty of Spartan women and the treachery of Spartans generally, appropriate themes for a play written during the Peloponnesian War.[29] Euripides' Hermione is a spoiled, spiteful daddy's girl, and the clear villain of the drama.

Ovid's portrayal of Hermione is more sympathetic, but she is still neither sweet nor submissive. His Hermione writes to Orestes to demand that he come and rescue her from Pyrrhus.[30] She claims that she refused to marry him, and he had to drag her home by her hair, kicking and screaming Orestes' name. She cleverly recasts herself as a victimized version of her mother and orders her erstwhile betrothed to follow her father's example in rescuing his stolen wife. In the meantime, Ovid's angry heroine is making her kidnapper's life miserable. She neglects her appearance, spends all of her time wailing and lamenting, treats Pyrrhus as if he has some kind of corrupting disease, and calls him by Orestes' name in intimate moments. Ovid's Hermione is strong, angry, and pugnacious.

Without any prior film conventions to prejudice the audience, and with only a couple of obscure ancient texts as source material, *TFOAC* is free to construct an entirely unique character from available screen tropes. She is younger than either of her main literary precursors, but it is easy to see how the series' youthful princess could grow into the ancient texts' manipulative spitfire. She wears an unusual amount of gold jewelry while the other Spartan women, particularly Helen, wear shells and pearls. *TFOAC*'s Hermione is also clearly her father's partisan. After Helen leaves, Hermione is the one who tells him where she has gone. Finally, she is undeniably acerbic, although that is not necessarily a negative trait. One review called her "entertainingly stroppy."[31]

TFOAC's Hermione is smart and observant. That makes her a welcome change from the rest of the cast thus far, who range from sadly shortsighted to dangerously ignorant.

She is the only person to notice Paris' attraction to her mother. However, this Hermione is also deeply insecure. The adolescent anxiety that naturally accompanies being the daughter of the most beautiful woman in the world is the main inspiration for this iteration of the character.[32]

From her first introduction, the audience is asked to compare Hermione with Helen. The two actresses do look sufficiently alike to be related, and their costumes echo one another enough to heighten their similarity. However, they are styled to encourage the audience to see Hermione as an immature, less desirable version of Helen.[33] Both are in long dresses of the same fabric, but while Helen's costume is low cut and cinched around the waist and breasts, Hermione's is high cut and loosely belted, and she has extra layers of fabric around her hips and draped across her torso. Helen wears full makeup, whereas Hermione's freckles are visible. The impression is one of glamour verses adolescence, and a comparison between the two would make any young woman feel insecure.

As Hermione comes to stand next to Helen, Menelaus immediately draws Paris' attention to Hermione's physical appearance. His first words are "Beautiful, isn't she?" Since the audience knows that Paris has already identified Helen as "the most beautiful woman in the world" and his divinely promised bride, Menelaus' rhetorical question is dripping with dramatic irony. Hermione is beautiful, but she cannot possibly compete with her mother. Menelaus' proposal of a marital alliance heightens the sense of comparison between the two. Both are now potential wives for Paris, although the contest is unequal. Helen is offered as divine prize; Hermione as a civic duty. Still, Menelaus is genuinely proud of his daughter. His *TFOAC* profile page says, "Menelaus admires his daughter Hermione, greatly."[34] He does not realize that Helen overshadows her, and he claims proudly that her intelligence is equal to her appearance.

The rest of the episode proves Menelaus' assertion that Hermione is clever. She notices that Paris only talks about her mother, and watches her chair when Helen is absent. Menelaus, on the other hand, blithely leaves his wife and her potential lover alone for five days, and even tells Paris to get to know Hermione better while he is away. Hermione correctly deduces that Paris leaves Sparta early because Helen has rejected him, although she does not realize what form the rejection took. Her last words to Paris before he leaves, "Don't come back," are exactly what every other character should have said to him the whole episode. Had the Trojans said that to Paris when he first arrived, Troy would never have fallen.

At first, Menelaus' apparent affection for his daughter pushes against his established cinematic character. He is possessive of Helen, but does not threaten or abuse her, nor does he womanize as prior iterations of his character have. Consequently, it is difficult to know how to interpret his behavior. In the face of that ambiguity, his fatherly relationship with Hermione becomes the crux of how to read his actions. At the end of the episode, it is entirely possible to interpret Menelaus as a sympathetic character.

Menelaus' proposed marital alliance is surprising, but not unreasonable. He makes it clear that he values Hermione and implies that her happiness is an important consideration in the negotiations. At face value, it is a good match. Paris is a good-looking prince who is close to Hermione's age, and Menelaus spends some time assessing him before suggesting the alliance. He is also not willing to commit immediately. Instead, he introduces the marriage as a potential future event, which mitigates the distasteful picture of Hermione as a child bride. Paris tells Menelaus, "I'm honored to be considered worthy of her," and Menelaus responds, "I didn't say you were. Not yet," like a doting father should. All in all, Menelaus' caring dynamic with his daughter and his interest in marrying her to Paris presents him as an obstacle, but not a villain.

That impression changes in the command tent scene in Episode 2. Menelaus' statement, "Hermione wasn't asked for," is a factual conditional clause. He is saying, "Hermione wasn't asked for, so I will not sacrifice her." The corresponding contrafactual condition is "If Hermione were asked for, I *would* sacrifice her." That circumstance recasts all of his past interactions with his daughter. He values her because he can use her to get what he wants and does not want to sell her cheaply. His fatherly pride was actually a bargaining tactic. In Episode 1, he wants a lucrative trade deal with Troy, so Hermione's value as a marriageable daughter is high. In Episode 2, he wants to sack Troy instead of trade with it, so Hermione is no longer valuable. Menelaus is revealed to be a villain after all. He is fundamentally selfish and deeply vindictive, two of the hallmarks of a petty tyrant.

Fathers to Leaders

When Odysseus, Agamemnon, and Menelaus confront the necessity of killing Iphigenia, they each have been asked to sacrifice a daughter. How each meets the challenge defines who he is as a father. When placed in contrast with one another, their responses demonstrate what kind of leaders they will be.

Odysseus is a good enough person to put his daughter's life above his own desires. His choice shows an intrinsic decency that the sons of Atreus lack. As a leader, the audience can expect that he will make the best decision for his people, even when it comes at a high price. Odysseus fulfills that promise in Episode 7, when he tricks Achilles into rejoining the fight and comes up with the ultimate strategy to win the war. Both plans are dishonorable, but they protect his men's lives.

In a sense, Agamemnon, in the person of Diomedes, has already forced Odysseus to make his morally compromised choices by using his infant daughter's life as leverage. Therefore, the audience forgives him for the crimes that he commits during the war. For example, the audience does not blame Odysseus for arguing in favor of sacrificing Iphigenia because his stake in the fight is his family, which is at least of equal worth to Agamemnon's daughter. In addition, Odysseus' words can be measured against his actions. When he was put to the test, he did not kill a daughter for Troy. It is impossible to believe that if Agamemnon refused to slit his daughter's throat, Odysseus would pick up the knife himself.

Agamemnon, on the other hand, does kill his daughter. Still, it is not an easy choice. He tries desperately to find an alternative and demonstrates that the decision is emotionally devastating. His first response is that they "won't go to Troy" and his second is that he should kill himself instead. In the end, though, he falls short of the moral strength to be a good leader. He values the life of his daughter before the war and his own life, but not before his position of power.

Ultimately, Agamemnon's need for power is the fatal flaw, hubris in the modern sense, that causes his downfall. Agamemnon in the *Iliad* is a bad leader. He alienates his most valuable ally, his strategy in Book 2 is rash and ill-conceived, and he almost gets his entire army killed through his stubborn refusal to give up his war prize. In *TFOAC*, the psychological damage caused by the experience of killing his daughter motivates those bad choices. Sacrificing his daughter both defines and creates his failure as a leader.

Although Agamemnon murders his own daughter for the sake of power, at least it is a hard decision. Menelaus does not have the emotional depth to even struggle with the concept. Agamemnon easily describes killing himself graphically. He says, "What if I offered myself? I'll slit my own throat." However, he cannot even use a verb for killing in relation to the girls, nor can he bring himself to use the name of his daughter or his niece in the context. He says to Menelaus, "Then you *give up* your *child*." He never directly puts the idea that they should kill either girl into words, never names any names. Menelaus, on the other hand, easily agrees to the concrete picture of killing his daughter, rather than a hypothetical "child," as he demonstrates through the use of her name.

Menelaus cannot be a leader at all because he is too selfish to care deeply about other people, even those closest to him. His selfishness prevents him seeing the campaign's stakes and complexities. He argues that if they do not sacrifice Iphigenia, they will look like cowards, even though slitting an adolescent girl's throat is not a test of bravery, nor is starting war over a single errant wife.

As a result of their trial by child sacrifice, Odysseus and Agamemnon are aware, viscerally, of the human costs of the war. They have literal skin in the game. Odysseus must redeem his daughter's life by winning the war, and Agamemnon must validate his daughter's murder. Menelaus has no emotional investment in anything but his own image. Correspondingly, the war itself is beyond his understanding. That is why he is incapable of leading the Greek expedition in *TFOAC*. Odysseus cannot sacrifice his daughter, and he becomes a successful leader. Agamemnon does sacrifice his daughter, albeit unwillingly, and he fails as a leader. Menelaus would have willingly sacrificed his daughter, and he is no leader at all.

Notes

1. Åström 2011, Cuklanz 2000: 6. See also Norgard in this volume.
2. Hyginus' *Fables* 95. Also see Servius on Vergil's *Aeneid* 2.81, Tzetzes on Lycophron's *Alexandra* 384, and Aelian's *Historical Miscellany* 13.12. Apollodorus provides the earliest surviving version of the story, in which Palamedes threatens the baby with a sword (*Epitome* 3.7).
3. The creative team kindly hitched two oxen to the plow instead of the equine/bovine pair cited by Hyginus, Tzetzes, and, obliquely, Servius. See n2 above.

4. Only about fifty lines survived in quotation. See Hansen 2002: 414, Scaife 1995.
5. Jebb, Headlam, and Pearson 2010: 115. Hansen 2002: 414–15.
6. Jebb *et al.* 2010: 115–20.
7. Vergil's *Aeneid* 2.77–104.
8. Vergil's *Aeneid* 2.91.
9. Miller 2018: 215.
10. Bradley 2003: 251.
11. McLaren 2004: 27–30.
12. On clothing, see Raucci in this volume.
13. See Prince and Stafford in this volume.
14. The final scene of the Euripides' *Iphigenia at Aulis*, in which a messenger tells Clytemnestra that her daughter was miraculously saved, is generally held be to a later addition (West 1981: 74–6). If so, the play would have ended with a choral ode predicting Iphigenia's divine rescue (West 1981: 73–4). In either case, *Iphigenia at Aulis* ends with Iphigenia alive.
15. Some scholars have argued that there was an early variation where Iphigenia did actually die on the alter. See Kovacs 2010: 59–60 for a review of the debate, and Chapters 2–4 for an overview of the extensive surviving ancient sources for the myth.
16. Nussbaum 2001: 41–4. The evidence for Agamemnon's guilt is present in the prologue to Aeschylus' *Agamemnon* (217–48), a major influence on Euripides' *Iphigenia at Aulis*.
17. Lloyd-Jones 1962, Nussbaum 2001: 31–9.
18. These examples are all recent, but the story never went out of fashion. There is no exhaustive list, but Kovacs 2010: 220–6 offers an analysis of some notable stage adaptations from the last 500 years.
19. Daly 2018.
20. Hughes 1991: 71–138.
21. Pindar's *Olympian Ode* 1.
22. See Norgard in this volume, who also demonstrates that Iphigenia's arrival and murder are paralleled with Helen's happiness in Troy.
23. See Rabinowitz 1993: 31–99, Rehm 1994, and Ormand 1999. On Hermione, see also Safran in this volume.
24. The mini-series *Helen of Troy*'s Menelaus is more sympathetic than either movie version of the character. He objectifies his wife, but his poor treatment of her stems from his brother's tyranny, which allows the mini-series to reunite husband and wife at the end in a bittersweet resolution.
25. See Safran in this volume.
26. Homer's *Odyssey* 4.1–15. Pyrrhus is also known as Neoptolemus.
27. Storey 2017: 158–9 finds the transitions in Euripides' *Andromache* good and the themes interesting, if confusing. Ovid's *Heroides* are generally well received, but the text is overshadowed by the *Metamorphoses*.
28. Skouroumouni Stavrinou 2016.
29. This war between Athens and Sparta lasted nearly forty years, on and off. For an interpretation of the play as an invective against Sparta, see Kitto 2002: 363–73.
30. Ovid's *Heroides* 8.

31. Hughes 2018a. My thanks to Sarah Hughes for adding to my vocabulary. As a note, "stroppy" means "bad-tempered and argumentative."
32. www.bbc.co.uk/programmes/profiles/2MsmmH4bKJgl5YQtNpz5qjB/hermione. Interestingly, Hermione has a character profile page, while more prominent characters, like Patroclus, do not.
33. See Raucci in this volume.
34. www.bbc.co.uk/programmes/profiles/N7qDw58f36rKhCB1VW4Gvv/menelaus-king-of-sparta.

CHAPTER 15
LESSONS FOR LEADERS: DESTINY, DEVOTION, AND SELF-DECEPTION
Brian Cooke

Although I am not a professional scholar, my life and career have been influenced by extraordinary teachers whose mastery and love for the classics guides my own understanding and interest in crafting lessons for leaders based on history and literature.

From the perspective of reception studies, viewing *Troy: Fall of a City* rekindled my interest in the Homeric texts, inspired me to revisit Bill Moyers' interviews with Joseph Campbell and George Lucas,[1] and ignited my search for myth-related lessons to help us make better leadership decisions.

Reminded by the artifice of the Trojan Horse that sealed Priam's fate, I deepened my study of ways leaders select, shape, and distort facts to suit their conscious and unconscious biases and self-interest. More specifically, I focused on four themes and associated questions for leaders I coach:

1. *Destiny*: To what extent is our experience, success, and performance determined by forces beyond our control?
2. *Decision-making*: How do our choices shape our experiences, opportunities, hardships, and greatest achievements?
3. *Devotion*: To whom and for what reasons are we obliged and motivated to live, work, and fight as may be required?
4. *Self-deception*: How and why do we tend to see the world the way we would like it to be rather than the way it is?

Although each of these themes deserves leadership consideration, recognizing our human tendency toward self-deception is especially urgent today when many people seek, select, and trust information that rationalizes and confirms their own beliefs and preferences.

Strengthening leadership awareness of self-deception may also help answer the question that confounds me most throughout *TFOAC*: how could Priam—one of the most powerful, experienced, wise, and successful leaders of the ancient world—be so easily deceived and defeated?

The Judgment of Paris: Destiny and Decision-making

Rarely cited in Homer and Greek myths,[2] and groundbreaking for its dramatization onscreen, *TFOAC* presents in Episode 1 the Judgment of Paris and introduces Greek gods as characters who actively influence but do not dictate mortal decisions.[3]

In his leadership role as ruler of the cosmos, Zeus is a king who both preserves order and is himself subject to it. Although he has prophetic authority and maintains broad command of human destiny with help from the Fates,[4] Zeus delegates power to other gods who choose, guide, and protect their favorite mortals. In this classical world order, our fate and fortune are determined both by divine destiny and by our own choices—mortal decisions that Homer tells us sometimes frustrate and anger Zeus.[5]

As the story of the Judgment of Paris goes, Zeus did not invite Eris, goddess of discord, to a marriage banquet for Peleus and Thetis. Although uninvited, Eris arrives with a gift—a golden apple to be given to the most beautiful goddess. When Hera, Athena, and Aphrodite claim the prize, Zeus—ever politic—directs Paris to judge the beauty contest.

Paris' reputation for fairness notwithstanding, each goddess offers him a bribe in exchange for his favor. Hera, Zeus's wife, promises to make Paris the king of Europe and Asia, "the most powerful man alive." Athena, who later became protector of triumphant Odysseus, offers to make Paris famous, wise, and skilled in war, "the most admired man on earth." Aphrodite, well-known for her own deceptive and seductive charm, promises Paris the world's most beautiful woman.

Power. Fame. Beauty. What would you choose? Paris chooses beauty. And the rest, of course, is Trojan history! But why, may we ask, did Paris choose Aphrodite? And, what might have happened if Paris had chosen Hera or Athena? Is it not true that all three goddesses are beautiful and powerful albeit in different ways? These are important questions for a leader whose decision determines the fate of two great civilizations.

Although for Homer, Paris's choice was no choice at all since Helen's breathtaking beauty was quite simply irresistible,[6] the answers to our questions may be explained both by modern science and our own natural inclination toward beauty. Thousands of years after the Judgment of Paris, we know from direct experience and research in evolutionary psychology that our hunter-gatherer brains are deeply conditioned to recognize and favor beauty.[7] That's why we tend to make choices that preserve, protect, and perpetuate our genes. And, as Paris perhaps discovered, this genetic bias toward beauty may not always serve our best interests!

Priam's Folly: Devotion and Self-deception

While Homer and the Greek myths tell us the Trojan War was fought to resolve a dispute over a beautiful woman,[8] we know from history and archaeology that the Greeks and Trojans battled for control of a prosperous city that commanded trade between Asia Minor and the Mediterranean. This ancient competition for wealth and power becomes clear when Paris first meets Helen (Episode 1).

> **Paris** Is Troy that important?
>
> **Helen** Troy controls the Straits of Asia. Everything passes through your city. Tin from the east to make bronze. Spices from India. So, everyone wants a piece. Welcome to the world, Prince.

Lessons for Leaders: Destiny, Devotion, and Self-Deception

As King of Troy, Priam had the duty, honor, and responsibility to lead one of the most prosperous city-states of the ancient world. Earlier in his life and career, Priam was distinguished for his leadership in war and his skill negotiating and managing regional alliances.[9] As an elder, Priam was respected for his integrity, piety, and counsel.[10] Today, Priam is portrayed in *TFOAC* as a brave, honorable, stubborn, old patriarch whose unwavering devotion to family hastened the destruction of a powerful, wealthy city-state.

As king and father, Priam consistently puts family first. This leadership commitment is both personal and practical. Priam was father of fifty sons, including Hector and Paris. This large family was an unusual blessing and an extraordinary asset for securing alliances that assured peace, political stability, and commercial success. Soon after welcoming his new-found son to the royal family, Priam directs Paris to do his duty and begin work on behalf of his city-state (Episode 1):

Priam   The party's over. No more visits to the lower city. No more late nights. It's time for work.

Paris   I thought princes didn't work.

Priam   [chuckling]

Paris   I thought that was the point.

Priam   Well, they don't herd cows if that's what you mean. [calls for Pandarus]

Paris   What's this?

Priam   Your first official engagement. I have a friend across the waters. King Menelaus of Sparta.

Paris   Father?

Priam   I want you to represent me. Pandarus will go with you. Introduce yourself. Pay tribute. The rediscovered son. Strengthen the ties between our two lands.

Paris   How exactly do I do that?

Priam   Well, you'll learn. Prove yourself a prince, son!

When Helen first meets Paris in Sparta in Episode 1, she continues his orientation to dynastic and domestic politics. She says: "Dynastic marriages strengthen all parties involved. They are like hands held fast across the water. That's the reason your father sent you here, Paris."

Paris' tutorial advances when he asks Hector about his marriage (Episode 3:

Paris   How did you meet Andromache?

Hector   It was arranged by our fathers. Cilicia is an important ally. So—my father wanted that connection.

Paris   A political marriage.

Hector   A political alliance. But a marriage of love. Love doesn't need to involve stealing someone away. It can be a formal exchange of vows. Two cities and two families joined.

Paris   Sure.

Hector   Alexander, your love got us into this trouble. Mine might just get us out of it!

No doubt, Priam's devotion to family was a great strength and political asset. And, like many successful leaders whose strength becomes a weakness, his unwavering faith in family and dynastic diplomacy is also a fatal flaw.

Priam's tendency toward illusion or self-deception is not uncommon among successful leaders whose power, authority, wealth, and career success seem to confirm the wisdom and merit of their own beliefs and decision-making talent (Fig. 15.1).

Little by little, decision-by-decision, Priam filters facts and interprets information to confirm his view of the world or distort it to suit his greatest hopes and ambitions. This self-deception begins when Priam defies sensible counsel from his wife and daughter-in-law and refuses to return Helen in Episode 2.

Figure 15.1   Priam (David Threlfall) during the festivities at Troy in Episode 8, "Offering."

Lessons for Leaders: Destiny, Devotion, and Self-Deception

Andromache Agamemnon needs no excuse to fight. She must be sent back, before they do something foolish.

Hecuba Andromache is right. Agamemnon will have rallied all the kings of Greece. We can't waste any time. We'll send a message that we regret the discourtesy, return Helen, and send gifts of our own.

Priam Why should I bow to him? We made this city prosperous through sweat and blood. This city bows to no one.

Hecuba And will continue to do so. Our pride can afford to take one hit if it's to save the city from future harm. She must go back, Priam.

As one hopeful rationalization leads to another, Priam's self-deception grows when he considers making an offer to compensate the Greeks for their humiliation by Paris and Helen in Episode 2:

You are our son (Paris), and whatever we may feel on the matter, we love and defend you. We will therefore seek an agreement with our Greek friends. We will keep the queen but send ambassadors with gifts of Troy that will more than match those you have brought from Sparta. Hopefully, our embassy will arrive before the Greeks' anger turns into action. Who knows? This may even strengthen bonds, not break them.

Despite Hector's logical protest, Priam is stubborn and resolute.

Hector This won't work. You must know that the Greeks—they won't accept gold as a substitute for a queen. She is flesh and a symbol. They'll just throw it back in your face.

Priam This is the decision of myself and the queen.

Although King Priam knows better, Priam—the father—ignores his better civic judgment.

Priam Alexander is our son. My instinct is to defend him—even though he is wrong.

Hecuba Mine, too.

Dismissing a flicker of awareness that he has become dangerously sentimental, Priam remains steadfast in devotion.

Priam You remember the first time I saw you? The spring games at Hatusha. I was spellbound by you in seconds. Wouldn't you like to be young again? To have what Alexander's got in his eyes? That self-belief? Age mellows.

Hecuba   But it's supposed to make us wise.

Priam   [grunts]

This is poor leadership posture for a king preparing to engage an enemy led by an angry general who had sacrificed his own daughter to guarantee divine favor! In Episode 2, near blind now to the root cause of Greek belligerence, Priam stumbles into a negotiation where his once formidable bargaining skills fail him.

Odysseus   King Agamemnon wishes you to understand he has a large military force in support of his claim.

Hecuba   It is clear Queen Helen desires to stay here as a guest. I'm sure Agamemnon does not desire the shedding of blood.

Odysseus   My lady, blood has already been shed. The king sacrificed his own daughter to appease the gods in coming here.

Hecuba   [gasps]

Priam   His own child—Killed?—By his own hand?

Odysseus   So, I hope you will understand how our conditions for peace are non-negotiable.

Hecuba   Name them.

Odysseus   The immediate return of the Queen of Sparta to her husband.

Priam   She doesn't want to go back.

Odysseus   With all due respect, King Priam, what she wants is of little interest to us.

Priam   [concedes Helen] She is yours.

Like many leaders who learn how the cost of self-deception multiplies as the depth and duration of that lie increases, Priam is shocked when the Greeks make bigger, bolder demands.

Odysseus   These are King Agamemnon's demands. The Straits of the Dardanelles—you control them. You tax every cargo, every ship.

Priam   Is this a joke?

Odysseus   I assure you not.

Priam   This'll break us.

Odysseus   A few years' hardship. Nothing more. A lesson learned.

Priam   Oh, I see. This is why you are here? To destroy the economy?

Lessons for Leaders: Destiny, Devotion, and Self-Deception

At this point, the negotiation escalates to violent words backed by drawn swords, "a breach of protocol" that surprises Odysseus who expects to bargain fairly with a more sensible and reasonable leader: "Don't be hasty, King Priam, consider the best option for your city ... Think again. No one wants this war. Make a counter-offer."

But Odysseus' counsel falls on deaf ears. Priam and Menelaus make this conflict personal and the negotiating positions harden with devastating consequences—ten years of stalemate in battle and thousands of lives lost for lack of more prudent leadership.

Blind Men, an Elephant, and the Trojan Horse

There is a familiar parable told in many cultures about blind men and an elephant.[11] I like to discuss this parable with leaders because it highlights the hazards of misperception and the challenge of decision-making based on incomplete, biased, or inaccurate information. This parable and its lessons are not unlike those that leaders can learn from Priam's self-deception and the brilliant deceit of the Trojan Horse.

As the parable goes, when several blind men encounter a large, strange object, they try to identify it by feel. While one blind man touches the elephant's tail, another man touches its tusks, yet another man touches its leg, and a fourth man touches its side. Each man is certain they can identify the large object based on their own observation. Of course, it is a snake, a spear, a stump, or a wall! But the men cannot determine the elephant's identity because each man is touching a different part and none of them connect their own observations to reveal the big picture. Since the most powerful man says it is a snake, they all agree it is a snake. And they are all wrong!

Like the blind men touching the elephant, the Trojan leaders debate the intent, risk, and utility of the wooden horse left behind presumably as a peacemaking gift and votive offering for the Greeks' safe passage home (Fig. 15.2). While each Trojan leader interprets the horse in ways that justify their inclination to move it inside the city walls, the Trojan women see more clearly (Episode 8).

Cassandra, as always, offers fearful warning: "Father, father, what if it is not a blessing?" Paris insists the grain in the horse's belly is sorely needed to feed starving Trojans: "We should take it in the City." Andromache urges caution: "Don't be hasty. I don't trust them. We should leave it. All things Greek are cursed. Let the sea take it." And Priam, more blind and unduly optimistic than ever, makes the final choice that seals Troy's fate:

> They have taken everything from us. They've killed our men, our children. They've wrecked our city. Let's take something of theirs for a change. [Forgetting that they had already taken the greatest prize—Helen!] We saw their boats on the ocean. We've checked the hills. They've gone. Let's steal their blessing from them and make the gods curse them and drown them in their boats.

In my profession, coaching executives, we direct great attention to leaders' motivation and responsibility for communicating a vision that engages and mobilizes followers. In this regard, Priam's vision to rebuild Troy is clear and compelling.

Screening Love and War in *Troy: Fall of a City*

Figure 15.2 The Trojan Horse in Episode 8, "Offering."

> These years have cost us. Every family here has lost someone. My son, Hector, rests in the tomb just through there. He won't be forgotten. No one will. They stay in here. [places hand over heart] [sighs] But remembering's not enough. It's our duty to honor the dead by rebuilding this city. And it starts tomorrow. [people cheering] We will do it for every man, woman, and child that died. So that we could live. This is our home. It's in our hearts. No one can take that from us [people cheering] Victory and freedom!"

But, as we discover quite often too late, following the persuasive vision of a leader with narrow or distorted perception can be fatal. Hence the expression, "in the land of the blind, the one-eyed man is king."

The Fall of Troy

In the end, the Greeks won a war by guile that they could not win by force. As dramatized onscreen in *TFOAC*, this victory was enabled by a Trojan king who ignored significant warnings, disregarded reasonable objections, and insisted on seeing the world the way he wanted it to be, no matter whether that view was true or not. After all, "it's good to be the King!"[12]

Lessons for Leaders: Destiny, Devotion, and Self-Deception

King Priam's representation by Homer, however, is more heroic, especially when the king mourns his loss and appeals to Achilles for the return of Hector's body for proper burial. This difference between onscreen and textual representation of Priam highlights the limitation and potential hazard of studying the classics solely through modern media.

> But what is left for me? I had the finest sons
> In all wide Troy, and not one of them is left.
> Fifty I had when the Greeks came over,
> Nineteen out of one belly, and the rest
> The women in my house bore to me
>
> It doesn't matter how many they were,
> The god of war has cut them down at the knees.
> And the only one who could save the city
> You've just killed as he fought for his country,
> My Hector.[13]

Likewise, the apocalyptic result of Priam's decision to trust the semblance of Greek piety by moving the horse within Troy's walls is described by Vergil in the *Aeneid*.[14]

> Fifty bedrooms (for a rich supply of grandsons),
> Pillars that flaunted gold barbican spoil—
> Everything fell. Where flames failed, Greeks laid hold,
> Perhaps you want to know how Priam died.
> He saw his city fallen, taken, gates
> Torn open, and the enemy deep inside.
> On shaking shoulders, he set armor, last worn
> Decades ago, strapped on a useless sword
> And rushed to die in crowds of hostile soldiers.

Thus falls King Priam and his mighty city, doomed by self-deception and the fading leadership, as told by Homer, of "an old man lost in reverie and wonder."[15]

Lessons for Leaders

As Priam's folly and the fall of Troy illustrate, the clarity of vision required for effective leadership decision-making can be difficult because several factors tend to distort leaders' judgment. Learning from Priam's demise and my own coaching experience, here are five common causes of self-deception that diminish leadership objectivity needed to make better decisions.

1. *Confirmation bias*: Because we have been right thus far, we are confident we will continue to succeed if we keep on doing what we believe is working.

2. *Underestimating others*: Since we are successful, we tend to discount or dismiss the opinions and capabilities of others with whom we interact, collaborate, or compete.
3. *Unfounded optimism*: Because we know self-confidence is essential for survival and advancement, we tend to exaggerate our strength, talent, strategic position, and likelihood of success.
4. *Arrogance*: As our power grows with each achievement, we become more likely to believe we are right and less likely to consider information or opinions that diverge from our beliefs and prejudices.
5. *The illusion of control*: Because we want and need assurance that our lives and careers are safe, successful, and predictable, we tend to exaggerate our ability to dictate or influence outcomes that protect or advance our self-interest.

Dinner with Richard Feynman

Sooner or later, I like to ask executives: "What leader, past or present, would you most like to have dinner with?" This question always initiates lively discussion about leaders we respect and admire. As for me, I would enjoy dining with Richard Feynman, Nobel Laureate physicist, extraordinary teacher, and mischievous prankster who explained the cause of the Space Shuttle *Challenger* disaster by dipping a rubber washer in a glass of ice water.[16]

In 1974, Feynman offered "some remarks" at the Caltech commencement "on science, pseudoscience, and learning how not to fool yourself." Although Feynman directed his talk to the next generation of scientists, King Priam would have been wise to heed his advice. "The first principle," said Feynman, "is that you must not fool yourself."[17] And as Priam discovered too late and Feynman reminds us, "You are the easiest person to fool." This wise counsel is especially urgent today for many leaders who seek, select, and trust information that confirms what they already believe—a tendency that, in turn, sharpens and deepens division among groups who might otherwise find constructive common ground for better collaborative decision-making!

Notes

1. The conversations between Campbell and Moyers took place between 1985 and 1986 at George Lucas' Skywalker Ranch and the Museum of Natural History in New York City and became a PBS series; Flowers 1988 edited the book. The discussion with George Lucas can be found in Moyers 1999.
2. Homer's *Iliad* 24.31–4 as translated by Lombardo 1997; the story can be found in the lost *Cypria* (see Curley in this volume), Ovid's *Heroides* 16, Lucian's *Dialogues of the Gods* 20, Apollodorus' *Epitome* 3.2, and Hyginus' *Fables* 92. See also Burton in this volume.
3. See Cyrino in this volume.

Lessons for Leaders: Destiny, Devotion, and Self-Deception

4. The Three Fates (*Moirai*) spin, measure, and cut the threads of life: Clotho spins the thread; Lachesis draws and measures the thread; Atropos cuts the thread.
5. Homer's *Odyssey* 1.37–9 as translated by Lombardo 2000.
6. *Iliad* 3.160–5: "Such were the voices of these Trojan elders / Sitting on the tower by the Western Gate. / When they saw Helen coming / Their rasping whispers flew along the wall: / Who could blame either the Trojans or the Greeks / For suffering so long for a woman like this."
7. See, most notably, Trivers 2011; see also, Wright 1995, one of three books Keanu Reeves read to prepare for *The Matrix* (1999).
8. See Boitani 2020: 23.
9. *Iliad* 3.151–7 (Achilles speaks to Priam): "We hear you were prosperous once . . . No one could match you in wealth or in sons."
10. *Iliad* 3.151–7: "Priam, Panthus, Thymmetes, Lampes, Clytius, Hicetaon . . . Ocalegion and Antenor / These veterans sat on the wall by the western gate / Too old to fight now, but excellent counsellors."
11. Variations on this parable are told in ancient Hindu, Buddhist, Sufi traditions as well as in modern Asia Pacific, Indo European, and Western tales. My brief narrative about the Blind Men and the Elephant is influenced by the Buddhist *Udana* 6.4 as translated by Strong 1902.
12. Quoted from the film *History of the World: Part I* (1981).
13. *Iliad* 24.528–37.
14. Vergil's *Aeneid* 2.503–11 as translated by Ruden 2008.
15. *Iliad* 3.191.
16. See Feltman (2016) and the Rogers Commission Report (1986) ("Report of the Presidential Commission on the Space Shuttle *Challenger* Accident"), where Richard Feynman wrote Appendix F.
17. See Feynman 1974.

EPILOGUE
TROY: FALL OF A CITY AND ITS ANCIENT SOURCES
Diana Burton

Troy: Fall of a City (2018) presents itself as: "Inspired by Homer and the Greek myths."[1] As with most modern takes on the story, the *Iliad* plays a large part—and is at the forefront of critics' and audiences' responses, even if they are a little shaky about what the *Iliad* actually includes. But David Farr's script also draws on a series of less familiar tales, and many of the characters take their cue from sources other than the myths and sources more familiar to modern audiences. In saying this, I need hardly add that I am not implying there existed any kind of canonical version of the myths in antiquity; as has been repeatedly noted, the ancients constantly invented new variations of their own myths, from small shifts in tone through to complete and drastic plot changes. Even so, we can talk in terms of more and less well-known versions, and it is also possible to see some points at which *TFOAC* completely diverges from the ancient sources: Priam's death, Briseis' role, Paris' character, elements of the sack itself. These are not mistakes or misreadings or invalid interpretations. Rather, they are interesting variations. As David Farr notes, "These are mythic stories, not history. They're created through telling, not reliant on fact, but organic, growing layer by layer, story by story."[2]

I will begin, as the series does, with Paris. The story of Paris' exposure and fostering by a herdsman is first seen in Pindar's *Paian* 8a, and the Judgment of Paris is even earlier, depicted in art from the seventh century BC.[3] While literary sources do not comment on Paris' reaction to the request to judge between three goddesses, Paris' initial dismay in *TFOAC* ("I herd cattle. How can I decide something like that?") finds an equally tongue-in-cheek echo in several vase paintings in which Paris runs away from the approaching deities.[4] Compared with Helen, Paris is of less interest to the ancient sources, and the character development he undergoes in *TFOAC* is unparalleled in Greek myth. That may partly be the result of a dearth of surviving sources; very few detailed depictions of him survive, and those that do (e.g., *Iliad* 3.30–75, 426–54; Ovid's *Heroides* 16) present him as a shallow and rather selfish character, with something of the brashness that characterizes him in the early episodes of *TFOAC*. But the fish-out-of-water motif as Paris struggles to adapt to his transformation from herdsman to prince is also uncharacteristic of Greek myth in general, in which long-lost princes tend to fit seamlessly into their new responsibilities (although, as in *TFOAC*, they do not always fit into their new families so easily). Both Sophocles and Euripides wrote plays named *Alexandros* which dealt with Paris' return to Troy. We know more about Euripides' version, though the two tragedies seem to have been similar: ignorant of his true parentage, Paris enters the games Hecuba has established in his memory and defeats all contenders (Euripides' *Alexander* fr. 61a–d), including his brothers, with the result that Deiphobus plots to kill him despite Hector's disagreement with the plan (fr. 62a–b). In the Euripidean version, Hecuba is the one who attempts to kill Paris because she is insulted that a slave should defeat her sons (fr. 62d). Paris is subsequently recognized, and in spite of Cassandra's warning (fr. 62g), is welcomed into the family. The reversal in *TFOAC*'s version in which Hector comprehensively defeats and nearly kills Paris in the games serves to illustrate both Paris' immaturity and Hector's dislike of him, laying a foundation for a development of maturity on the part of Paris, and a slow building of loyalty to Troy, that is not evident in the surviving ancient sources. Similarly, Aphrodite's interest in him contrasts with the ancient sources, in which she is primarily focused on Helen. The delineation of Paris' two roles through the contrast between his two names—Paris focused on his desire for Helen and Alexander focused on the safety and defense of Troy—does find echoes in mythical sources, in which his parents name him Alexander and the herdsman names him Paris (e.g. Hyginus' *Fables* 91).

The motif of parents and children is used to shed light on the characters of those involved. Priam and Hecuba are strongly motivated by their desire to have Alexander back, blind to the risks involved, and Paris, in turn, wavers between being the irresponsible Paris and the Alexander who is loyal to his city and family. Andromache's desperation to have a child sets her against Helen, who deliberately chose to abandon Hermione. The sacrifice of Iphigenia (Episode 2) is a turning point for the plot, as it marks Agamemnon's irrevocable commitment to the war and his abandonment of whatever slight moral compass he had to start with. The episode echoes Euripides' *Iphigenia at Aulis*—the excuse of a marriage with Achilles, Clytemnestra's fury, Menelaus' willingness to sacrifice Iphigenia for Helen, Iphigenia's desperation and final shift to a courageous acceptance of her fate. Agamemnon's anguish over his sacrifice of his daughter is part of every ancient depiction of the sacrifice, as is his eventual choice of the army over her. Agamemnon himself, rather than Calchas, wields the knife, and there is no last-minute substitution of a deer for Iphigenia's life.[5]

Agamemnon is haunted by the sacrifice of Iphigenia, referring to it at intervals throughout the series. But it does not move him to compassion for other children and their parents. He asks Chryseis for forgiveness one moment, and then, when she denies him ("I thank the gods you are no father of mine"), rapes her (Episode 4). He forces Odysseus to drop Astyanax from the wall by threatening Odysseus' family: "There must be no future king of Troy, you know that. You can do it, then we all go home to our wives and children—if you want yours to live" (Episode 8). The scene is based on the scene in Euripides' *Trojan Women* in which it is Odysseus who suggests that "they should not raise to manhood the son of a noble father" (723). Instead, his failed attempt to protect Astyanax counterbalances Diomedes' threat to Odysseus' baby daughter in the first episode and brings the plot full circle. Andromache's chilling curse on him at the end, after he has been forced to kill Astyanax, evokes Hecuba's fury at him at *Trojan Women* 282–92. Odysseus himself asks the gods for forgiveness before he drops Astyanax from the wall, but he does not expect it to be forthcoming.

Compared with the *Iliad*, the presence of the gods in *TFOAC* seems slight: the scenes in which they appear are few and short. Yet despite this they are pervasive throughout the

Epilogue: *Troy: Fall of a City* and Its Ancient Sources

series, owing to the constant awareness of them on the part of the mortal characters, who talk about them, call on them, pray to them, invoke them in retribution and—in Agamemnon's case—slight them, with predictably bad consequences. The beginning of the first battle (Episode 2), in which Hera, Athena, and Aphrodite single out particular heroes for blessing and urge them into battle, epitomizes the favoritism shown by the gods in the *Iliad*. The short scenes with the gods go a long way: the brief but evocative scene of Apollo threading his way through the Greek camp and stooping to confer plague upon a sleeping soldier (Episode 4) is not as dramatic as the god striding down from Olympus in *Iliad* 1.43–52, but it is unsettlingly effective in evoking the power of the gods against helpless mortals. As in Greek myth, even the gods cannot overcome fate, and they will push if necessary to see it fulfilled—as Zeus does, causing the storm that keeps Paris in Mycenae for long enough for Helen's resistance to crumble (Episode 1, a quick glimpse of him in the dark). *TFOAC* draws both on the *Iliad*'s concentration on Zeus' plan and on fate, and on the prodigies and oracles characteristic of the Epic Cycle (Cassandra's visions, for example).[6] In both the epic and the series, Zeus does not take sides. All this is neatly encapsulated in Episode 5, where Aphrodite accuses Zeus of setting the whole thing up to satisfy the omens, and Zeus replies that he simply gave Paris a chance to seize his own destiny.

The degree of Helen's responsibility for the war was a topic of fascination to the Greeks early on, and our ancient sources offer a wide range of views regarding her character and culpability.[7] She was a stronger and more interesting figure in antiquity than she often is in modern films. *TFOAC*, like the *Iliad*, offers us a Helen who bitterly regrets the consequences of her actions, although she lacks the self-recrimination and the consequent dislike of Paris which characterize the Iliadic Helen (e.g., 6.342–58). The love between her and Paris is a more prominent and sustained motivating factor than is usual in the ancient sources. Conversely, she is less certain of her place in Troy, and, unlike Paris, she is not convinced of Aphrodite's involvement. Ultimately, too, the Iliadic Helen is powerless to act, whereas the *TFOAC* Helen can and does take matters into her own hands, albeit with unanticipated and usually unfortunate results: the conversation with Achilles in Episode 3 which leads the Greeks to sack Cilicia, the death of Pandarus in Episode 5, the entry of the Greeks into the city in Episode 8. Tragedies in particular make much of Helen's destructiveness, often linking it with a willful selfishness which is also a component of *TFOAC*'s Helen, particularly in the earlier episodes (e.g., Aeschylus' *Agamemnon* 681–781). However, she is not intentionally destructive. She does make the decision to sacrifice herself by turning herself over to the Greeks (Episodes 2 and 7)—another motif drawn from tragedy (Euripides' *Trojan Women* 951–65, although it is not clear that we should actually believe her in this version). The kind of enmity expressed to her by the Trojans and particularly Andromache is suggested in the *Iliad* (24.766–75) but is more characteristic of tragedy, for example Euripides' *Trojan Women* in which both Andromache and Hecuba speak of her in bitter terms (766–73, 969–1032; compare Andromache's accusation in Episode 2 that Helen has tricked Paris). Furthermore, she is committed to Paris, but never entirely to Troy. As late as Episode 7, she frees the Greek spy Xanthius, and urges Paris to desert Troy and flee with her. It is only at the end of that episode that, addressing Paris as Alexander for the first time, she acknowledges his duty to Troy, and at that point she is planning to leave him and return to the Greeks in exchange for Troy's safety. Her help is not needed, since Menelaus and Odysseus are already inside the city in the Trojan Horse, which the Trojans have brought into the city, since it is full of much-needed grain as an offering to Poseidon—which is a better reason than ancient myth usually gives us. But Helen is thus made to be complicit in letting the Greeks into the city: the moment at which she looks up at the Trojan Horse inside the walls, knowing who is inside of it (Episode 8), evokes the contradictory tales she and Menelaus tell in *Odyssey* 4.235–89, of Helen helping Odysseus before the sack and of Helen attempting to get the Greeks to betray themselves by walking around the Horse and calling out in the voices of their wives. There are traces of a tradition in which Helen aids the Greeks in some way in the sack: for example, the ghost of Deiphobus tells Aeneas that she signaled the Greeks and removed Deiphobus' sword so that Menelaus could mutilate and kill him (Vergil's *Aeneid* 6.511–27). In *TFOAC*, her complicity is unwilling but nonetheless disastrous.

The scene in Episode 3 in which Achilles is smuggled into Troy to meet Helen is mentioned only in the *Cypria*, where "Achilles has a desire to look upon Helen, and Aphrodite and Thetis bring the two of them together." That would seem to imply that they had never met before (Achilles is not always one of her suitors), but in *TFOAC* they clearly know each other and have some degree of mutual respect. Achilles' initial sexual approach to her perhaps reflects Lycophron's statement that he would be her fifth husband (139–74), likely derived from the link between Helen and Achilles in Achilles' cult in the Black Sea.[8] But the meeting serves primarily to bring together these two strong and in many ways like-minded figures; it is Helen's reminder of his honor that finally serves to make Achilles leave without her (Fig. E.1). Critics have noted that Achilles in the *Iliad* has a breadth of vision, and a richness of vocabulary with which to express it,

Figure E.1 Helen (Bella Dayne) and Achilles (David Gyasi) meet in Troy in Episode 3, "Siege."

Epilogue: *Troy: Fall of a City* and Its Ancient Sources

that other characters lack.[9] Something similar is at work in *TFOAC*: Achilles, more than any other character, is concerned with the honor of war, and with its place in the wider world. He defends his honor at all costs: just as in the *Iliad* he stays out of the fight while the Trojans reach the Greek ships, so in *TFOAC* Episode 6 the Trojans ride straight past the watching Myrmidons on their way to sack the rest of the Greek camp while the other Greeks are off near Troy, with Hector noting that the Myrmidons will not attack unless Achilles gives the order, "so don't kill any of them." That makes the vindictive and bloodthirsty brutality Achilles exhibits at Hector's death, while Andromache looks on in desperation, all the more horrifying (Episode 6)—as is also true of Hector's death in the *Iliad*, with Achilles' refusal to grant any honor to the dying man (22.344–54). An even closer parallel is Aeneas' killing of Turnus in the *Aeneid* (12.938–52), which shows the same unexpected and shocking turn toward savagery. Hector's dying warning to Achilles about Achilles' death at *Iliad* 22.358–60 is postponed until Episode 7, and put into the mouth of the dying Penthesileia when she predicts to Achilles that he will follow her. Achilles instead tells the dying Hector, "When you get to the riverman, pause a while. Your wife and your son will be there shortly."

As in the *Iliad*, the struggle for honor and glory and the question of what that means for an individual are central. If Achilles is the most concerned with the honor of war, Odysseus is the character most aware of the practical implications of that struggle.[10] He is reluctant to leave Ithaca in the first place; as in the *Cypria*, he feigns insanity, and as in Hyginus' *Fables* 95, he is caught out when his infant is placed in front of the plough— though in *TFOAC* it is a baby daughter rather than the slightly older Telemachus, whom Odysseus appoints as the man of the house as he departs. Once involved, he accepts that there will be no return to his family, until the war is won, and puts all his mind to that end: his level-headed approach and skill in strategy fit the *mētis* (cunning intelligence) which is the most essential characteristic of the Homeric Odysseus. So does the flexible moral code he employs in order to get the job done. Achilles' denunciation of him in *Iliad* 9.307–47 is picked up in Episode 5 when Agamemnon refuses to return Briseis: "I'm not like you, Odysseus. You like to win no matter what the cause ... In the absence of glory, you'll have to rely on your ways, Odysseus: the wiles of man." The difference from the epic Odysseus is the cost of that flexibility, as he is forced into more and more dubious actions, until the end of the series presents an Odysseus who can no longer live with the decisions he has made.

Agamemnon and Hector act as counterweights to this struggle. Hector is much like his Iliadic self, even down to his occasionally exasperated affection for his younger brother. As in the *Iliad*, his sense of honor encompasses not only his own glory but also his duty to his city and his affection for Andromache and his son, and it is the first of these which ultimately drives him to his death. His words to Andromache before he goes out to fight Achilles—"The city's watching. I can't refuse"—are the same reasoning as lies behind his decision in *Iliad* 22.105–10. Agamemnon, by contrast, has many of the same character defects familiar from Greek myth: the blind entitled arrogance that leads him to decisions that are not in the army's best interests, the cruelty to those who are not in any position to fight back, the lust and sacrilege (compare his treatment of Chryseis with that of Cassandra, Euripides' *Trojan Women* 247–58). The scene in Episode 6 in which he asks Briseis to picture the market in Troy and then promises to destroy it has no direct parallel in the ancient sources, but this is very much the Agamemnon of the *Iliad* and of Aeschylus' *Agamemnon*.

Briseis in the *Iliad* is little more than a cipher, with very little personality of her own, save for the point at which she mourns Patroklos (19.286–300). The key difference in *TFOAC* is that she is never returned to Achilles—who does not, in the end, make her return a condition for his return to battle—and finally escapes to the ruined Troy with the connivance of Odysseus. The women in *TFOAC*, including Helen, serve more than any other characters to illustrate the costs of the war. One of the areas in which *TFOAC* is faithful to the *Iliad* and to tragedies such as Euripides' *Hecuba* and *Trojan Women* is in the treatment of women. Even those depicted as strong figures in their own right (Andromache, Hecuba who is described as ruling Troy alongside her husband, Helen herself) have their good advice ignored, and the war captives are treated as powerless commodities.

Briseis, like Chryseis, Xanthius, the boy Evander and others, gives a non-elite perspective on the siege and sack, and more particularly on its costs. She is one of a number of central *TFOAC* characters who are either not prominent in myth (Pandarus, Thersites) or invented (Litos, Xanthius, Evander). Thersites is seen as an unpleasant and unpopular man, beaten by Odysseus in *Iliad* 2.211–77 to teach him his place, and killed by Achilles in the *Aethiopis* for his ill-timed abuse about Achilles' love for Penthesileia. In *TFOAC*, he has a similar gift for saying the wrong thing at the wrong moment and is also the first choice for any task that involves deceit, treachery, trickery, and the lack of a moral compass: an expansion of his role in the *Iliad* but not a change in his character. Pandarus, on the other hand, is elevated from the treacherous archer of *Iliad* 4.86–140 to a loyal figure in Priam's court with an important and invented subplot: he has little in common with his Iliadic prototype outside their names. Xanthius is also invented, though he may owe something to the episode in the *Little Iliad* in which Odysseus disguises himself, sneaks into Troy, and comes to an agreement with Helen, who recognizes him, about the taking of the city (compare Episode 7; the story is also in part in *Odyssey* 4.242–64).

Farr often includes sideways nods to his mythical sources to warm the heart of the Classics geek. Hector drops his helmet on the ground when he first catches sight of the new-born Astyanax (Episode 6; *Iliad* 6.472–3). There is a nice moment when Paris in Sparta brushes away the plaster from a newly painted wall to find a Mycenean fresco of a woman underneath (Episode 1). Achilles, though Thetis is not mentioned, wonders what the sea would think of the fighting which is everything to him (Episode 3). The drug Helen smokes in Sparta to calm herself (Episode 1) is reminiscent of the one she gives Menelaus and Telemachus in *Odyssey* 4.219–32. In the duel between Paris and Menelaus, when Menelaus has Paris at his mercy, Aphrodite saves him—by telling him to run (Episode 4), whereas in *Iliad* 3.380–2 she shrouds him in mist and sets him down in his own bedroom. Penthesileia tells Aeneas she is not interested in men (Episode 7). Paris makes Aeneas hide under a heap of bodies during the sack of Troy so that he can escape

Epilogue: *Troy: Fall of a City* and Its Ancient Sources

(Episode 8). Oenone's baby son, whom she is quick to keep from Paris in Episode 5, is a reminder of the story in which Paris and Oenone have a child (Conon's *Narratives* 26F1.23).

Achilles' invulnerability, or lack of it, is another such nod. Dual traditions of Achilles' invulnerability existed in antiquity. In the *Iliad*, there is no hint of it; Achilles is even wounded at one point (21.166–7). While the invulnerability is first evident in Statius (*Achilleid* 1.480–1), it is almost certainly older. In *TFOAC*, it makes an appearance as a rumor rather than fact. Achilles himself mentions his mother (who is never named, though he confirms that he is the son of a goddess) dipping him in the river, "fearing that she would drown me even as she sought to make me invincible" (Episode 6). No wonder Hector, in their brutal duel, seems surprised to realize that Achilles can be wounded: "you bleed like the rest of us." The death of Achilles begins with an arrow to the ankle, but that is not what kills him.

Achilles' death provides a particularly interesting mix of tradition and innovation. In myth, Achilles dies at the arrows of Paris, Apollo, or both; the famous arrow in the ankle appears in Apollodorus (*Epitome* 5.3) but was certainly earlier.[11] In *TFOAC*, however, Priam plays a central role in Achilles' death. Achilles is shot through the ankle by Paris from horseback, as he attacks Priam (Episode 7) in anger at the breaking of the truce that they have agreed on for the burial of Hector. Priam then stabs him in the side before Paris shoots him again, this time through the throat. The context for this startling but effective variation is that Achilles agreed with Priam on a twelve-day truce to bury Hector (*Iliad* 24.656–67; Episode 7). But whereas in the *Iliad* the truce stands, in *TFOAC* Odysseus, taking a momentous step on the slippery slope away from his own sense of honor, engineers a trick (carried out by the repulsive Thersites) to make Achilles think the Trojans have broken the truce. The reconciliation scene between Priam and Achilles over Hector's body is thus belied. This scene in Wolfgang Petersen's *Troy*, like that in the *Iliad* itself (24.476–676), was a depiction of two men finding common ground in sympathy with each other, resulting in a convincing reconciliation, whereas the one in *TFOAC* feels far less secure—but perhaps that was deliberate. Like the *Iliad*, the scene (Episode 7) was based on Priam's recognition of Achilles' anger and their mutual grief for those they hold dear. Although Achilles and Priam find a temporary forgiveness, it is not deeply rooted, and the mutual trust that they achieve is shaky—thus enabling Achilles to believe Priam has broken the truce and to attack him, and Priam in turn to stab Achilles. The changed scene does not match the *Iliad*'s theme of redemption for Achilles' character; instead, it fits *TFOAC*'s theme of undermining any chance at such redemption for any character in the end. Achilles, for all his desire for honor, dies knowing that his own side has deceived him into breaking the truce: "tell Odysseus, to him the glory, this always was a shabby war" (Episode 7).

A similar set of changes takes place during the sack itself. Priam is usually killed by Neoptolemus—Hector's father killed by Achilles' son—but in *TFOAC* it is Agamemnon who kills him. Hecuba commits suicide at the same moment (she is usually allocated to Odysseus as his slave, though she does not always make it as far as his ship). Paris is killed during the sack by Menelaus, which makes a rather more satisfying ending than his usual death by Philoctetes' arrows ahead of the sack. The scene offers a definitive final look at the interactions of three crucial figures and also allows Helen to remain faithful to Paris (in the ancient sources she is married to Deiphobus after Paris' death) and allows Paris to make clear to Menelaus how hollow his victory is. Depictions of the sack in ancient art were markedly sympathetic toward the Trojans, showing the Greeks as sacrilegious and violent and drawing the viewer's sympathies to Troy, whose men are depicted fighting desperately and without arms while the women offer hopeless resistance or cower in fear.[12] The sacrilege is not part of *TFOAC*'s sack, but the callous violence is, and the fate of the women in particular brings home the heartbreaking effect of the war.

Overall, the series offers a version of the myth which often follows ancient versions and is fundamentally true to the characters depicted by the ancient sources. Farr has drawn on a wide range of mythical sources, filling out storylines for which we have only a quick sketch. It would be easy to reduce the series to a game of identifying ancient sources, but the choices made by *TFOAC* are also effective in heightening the tension and ultimately in depicting the heartbreaking effect of the war on all those caught up in it, both Greek and Trojan. It is too simple to look at the result of the Trojan War as victorious Greeks and defeated Trojans, as the warriors in the *Iliad* exult over their fallen foes. But the aftermath depicted by sources such as Euripides' *Trojan Women* and Aeschylus' *Agamemnon* offers a bleak picture of the suffering and moral cost paid by the Greek side as well, and that is something that *TFOAC* brings out particularly clearly. Many of the series' innovations focus on minor characters, to bring out the effects of the war on the non-elite figures caught up in it, and on the sack itself, in order to drive home the dire meaning of defeat for all those involved. In the spirit of classical art and mythmaking, *TFOAC* exhibits tradition and originality in its rendering of the cosmic and human misfortune of the Trojan War.

Notes

1. I am grateful to the editors for their patience, to my colleagues for their esoteric knowledge, to my students for their enthusiastic discussion, and to Jeff Tatum for his sensible suggestions.
2. Farr 2018. See also Solomon 2007: 487–8 on these issues in Wolfgang Petersen's *Troy* (2004).
3. Protocorinthian olpe (Chigi Vase), *c.* 640 BC; Rome, Villa Giulia 22679. Hermes approaches Paris with Hera, Athena, and Aphrodite following him.
4. E.g., Attic black-figure krater by Lydos, *c.* 550 BC; London, British Museum 1948.10-15.1. Paris runs off, looking back over his shoulder while Hermes raises a hand to stop him.
5. Substitution: Euripides' *Iphigenia among the Taurians*; Apollodorus' *Epitome* 3.22. No substitution: Aeschylus' *Agamemnon* 228–49; Pindar's *Pythian Ode* 11.17–25. The substitution in Euripides' *Iphigenia at Aulis* 1582–95 was very likely a later addition. On Iphigenia, see Burns and Norgard in this volume.
6. Griffin 1977: 48.
7. Austin 1994; Maguire 2009.

8. Lycophron: see Hornblower 2015: 160–3. Helen in Achilles' cult in the Black Sea: Ochotnikov 2006: 70–1.
9. Griffin 1986: 50–6, especially 53–4.
10. See, among others, Burns, Prince, and Stafford in this volume.
11. See Gantz 1993: 625–8; Burgess 2009: 9–15, 38–9.
12. E.g., Attic red-figure kylix by Onesimos, c. 480 BC; Rome, Villa Giulia 121110 (formerly Malibu, Getty Museum); see Anderson 1997: 197–264 for discussion and other examples.

BIBLIOGRAPHY

Adler, Eric (2016). *Classics, the Culture Wars, and Beyond*. Ann Arbor, MI: University of Michigan Press.
Ahl, Frederick (2007). "*Troy* and the Memorials of War," in Martin M. Winkler (ed.), *Troy: From Homer's* Iliad *to Hollywood Epic*. Oxford: Blackwell, 163–85.
Alarie, Milaine and Carmichael, Jason T. (2015). "The 'Cougar' Phenomenon: An Examination of the Factors That Influence Age-Hypogamous Sexual Relationships Among Middle-Aged Women." *Journal of Marriage and Family* 77.5: 1250–65.
Anderson, Michael J. (1997) *The Fall of Troy in Early Greek Poetry and Art*. Oxford: Clarendon Press.
Appiah, Kwame Anthony (2018). *The Lies that Bind: Rethinking Identity*. New York: Profile Books.
Åström, B. (2011). "Referred Pain: Privileging Male Emotions in Narrative Instances of Female Physical Suffering." *Journal of Gender Studies* 20.2: 125–37.
Augoustakis, Antony (2015). "Dystopian Amazons: Fantasies of Patriarchy in *Le Gladiatrice* (1963)," in Monica S. Cyrino and Meredith Safran (eds.), *Classical Myth on Screen*. New York: Palgrave Macmillan, 63–73.
Augoustakis, Antony and Cyrino, Monica S. (eds.) (2017). *STARZ Spartacus: Reimagining an Icon on Screen*. Edinburgh: University of Edinburgh Press.
Augoustakis, Antony and Raucci, Stacie (2018). "Introduction: The Reinvention of the Ancient Hero," in Antony Augoustakis and Stacie Raucci (eds.), *Epic Heroes on Screen*. Edinburgh: Edinburgh University Press, 1–10.
Austin, Norman (1994). *Helen of Troy and Her Shameless Phantom*. Ithaca, NY: Cornell University Press.
Ayotte, Kevin J. and Husain, Mary E. (2005). "Securing Afghan Women: Neocolonialism, Epistemic Violence, and the Rhetoric of the Veil." *NWSA Journal* 17.3: 112–33.
Bakogianni, Anastasia (2013a). "Who Rules this Nation? (Ποιός κυβερνά αυτόν τον τόπο;): Political Intrigue and the Struggle for Power in Michael Cacoyannis' *Iphigenia* (1977)," in Anastasia Bakogianni (ed.), *Dialogues with the Past: Classical Reception Theory and Practice*. London: Institute of Classical Studies, 225–49.
Bakogianni, Anastasia (2013b). "Annihilating Clytemnestra: The Severing of the Mother-Daughter Bond in Michael Cacoyannis' *Iphigenia* (1977)," in Konstantinos P. Nikoloutsos (ed.), *Ancient Greek Women in Film*. Oxford: Oxford University Press, 207–33.
Bakogianni, Anastasia (2015). "The Anti-War Spectacle: Denouncing War in Michael Cacoyannis' Euripidean Trilogy," in Anastasia Bakogianni and Valerie M. Hope (eds.), *War as Spectacle: Ancient and Modern Perspectives on the Display of Armed Conflict*. London: Bloomsbury, 291–311.
Bakogianni, Anastasia (2017). "The Ancient World is Part of Us: Classical Tragedy in Modern Film," in Arthur J. Pomeroy (ed.), *A Companion to Ancient Greece and Rome on Screen*. Malden, MA: Wiley-Blackwell, 467–90.
Bakogianni, Anastasia (2018). "Shades of Ajax: In Search of the Tragic Hero in Modern War Movies," in Ricardo Apostol and Anastasia Bakogianni (eds.), *Locating Classical Receptions on Screen: Masks, Echoes, Shadows*. New York: Palgrave Macmillan, 147–71.
Bakogianni, Anastasia (2020). "Performing Violence and War Trauma: Ajax on the Silver Screen," in Irene Berti, Maria G. Castello, and Carla Scilabra (eds.), *Ancient Violence in the Modern Imagination: Fear and Fury*. London: Bloomsbury, 57–72.

Bibliography

Banks, Daniel (2019). "The Welcoming Table: Casting for an Integrated Society," in Claire Syler and Daniel Banks (eds.), *Casting a Movement: The Welcome Table Initiative*. London: Routledge, 12–30.
Barsam, Richard (2010). *Looking at Movies: An Introduction to Film*. London: W. W. Norton.
Bashi, Vilna (2004). "Globalized Anti-Blackness: Transnationalizing Western Immigration Law, Policy, and Practice." *Ethnic and Racial Studies* 27: 584–606.
Beard, Mary and Henderson, John (1995). *Classics: A Very Short Introduction*. Oxford: Oxford University Press.
Beardsley, Grace Hadley (1929). *The Negro in Greek and Roman Civilization: A Study of the Ethiopian Type*. New York: Russell & Russell.
Beazley, J. D. (1931–1932). "Groups of Sixth-Century Black-Figure." *The Annual of the British School at Athens* 32: 1–22.
Beazley, J. D. (1963). *Attic Red-Figure Vase-Painters*. 2nd ed. Oxford: Clarendon Press.
Belfiore, Elizabeth S. (1992). *Tragic Pleasures: Aristotle on Plot and Emotion*. Princeton, NJ: Princeton University Press.
Berlinerblau, Jacques (1999). *Heresy in the University: The Black Athena Controversy and the Responsibilities of American Intellectuals*. New Brunswick, NJ: Rutgers University Press.
Berger, Stefan and Conrad, Christopher (2015). *The Past as History: National Identity and Historical Consciousness in Modern Europe*. New York: Palgrave Macmillan.
Bergren, Ann (2008). *Weaving Truth: Essays on Language and the Female in Greek Thought*. Washington, DC: Center for Hellenic Studies.
Berti, Irene (2020). "The Thrill of Ancient Violence: An Introduction," in Irene Berti, Maria G. Castello, and Carla Scilabra (eds.), *Ancient Violence in the Modern Imagination: Fear and Fury*. London: Bloomsbury, 1–12.
Bettini, Maurizio (2016). *Radici: Tradizione, identità, memoria*. Bologna: Il Mulino.
Blok, Josine H. (1995). *The Early Amazons: Modern and Ancient Perspectives on a Persistent Myth* (Trans. Peter Mason). Leiden: Brill.
Blondell, Ruby (2005). "How to Kill an Amazon." *Helios* 32.2: 183–213.
Blondell, Ruby (2009). "Third Cheerleader from the Left." *Classical Receptions Journal* 1: 4–22.
Blondell, Ruby (2013a). *Helen of Troy: Beauty, Myth, Devastation*. Oxford: Oxford University Press.
Blondell, Ruby (2013b). "'Third Cheerleader from the Left': From Homer's Helen to *Helen of Troy*," in Konstantinos P. Nikoloutsos (ed.), *Ancient Greek Women in Film*. Oxford: Oxford University Press, 51–72.
Blundell, Sue (1995). *Women in Ancient Greece*. Cambridge, MA: Harvard University Press.
Blundell, Sue (2002). "Clutching at Clothes," in Lloyd Llewellyn-Jones (ed.), *Women's Dress in the Ancient Greek World*. Swansea: Classical Press of Wales, 143–69.
Boitani, Piero (2020). *A New Sublime: Ten Timeless Lessons On the Classics* (Trans. Ann Goldstein). New York: Europa Editions.
Bonfante, Larissa (1989). "Nudity as a Costume in Classical Art." *American Journal of Archaeology* 93.4: 543–70.
Bonnet, Alastair (2004). *The Idea of the West*. New York: Palgrave Macmillan.
Boyle, A. J. (1994). *Seneca's Troades: Introduction, Text, Translation and Commentary*. Leeds: Francis Cairns.
Bradley, Marion Zimmer (2003). *The Firebrand*. New York: Simon & Schuster.
Britton, Piers D. G. (1999). "Dress and the Fabric of the Television Series: The Costume Designer as Author in *Dr. Who*." *Journal of Design History* 12.4: 345–56.
Bruzzi, Stella (1997). *Undressing Cinema: Clothing and Identity in the Movies*. London: Routledge.
Buck, Amber M. and Plothe, Theo (2019). "Introduction: Netflix at the Nexus," in Amber M. Buck and Theo Plothe (eds.), *Netflix at the Nexus: Content, Practice, and Production in the Age of Streaming Television*. New York: Peter Lang, 1–9.

Bibliography

Burgess, Jonathan S. (2001). *The Tradition of the Trojan War in Homer and the Epic Cycle.* Baltimore, MD: Johns Hopkins University Press.

Burgess, Jonathan S. (2009). *The Death and Afterlife of Achilles.* Baltimore, MD: Johns Hopkins University Press.

Burke, Liam (2018). "'A Bigger Universe': Marvel Studios and Transmedia Storytelling," in Julian C. Chambliss, William L. Svitavsky, and Daniel Fandino (eds.), *Assembling the Marvel Cinematic Universe: Essays on the Social, Cultural and Geopolitical Domains.* Jefferson, NC: McFarland, 32–51.

Butchart, Amber (2016). *The Fashion of Film: How Cinema Has Inspired Fashion.* London: Mitchell Beazley.

Carpenter, Edward. (1915). *Ioläus: An Anthology of Friendship.* 3rd ed. London: Allen & Unwin.

Carter, Lance (2018). "Interview: Bella Dayne on Survival Jobs, Auditioning and Playing Helen of Troy in *Troy: Fall of a City*." *Dailyactor*, April 26, www.dailyactor.com.

Chason, Rachel (2017). "Hollywood Director James Cameron Attacks 'Wonder Woman' and Pays the Price." *The Washington Post*, August 25, www.washingtonpost.com.

Chrisman-Campbell, Kimberly (2017). "Confessions of a Costume Curator." *The Atlantic*, August 18, www.theatlantic.com.

Christensen, Joel (2017). "Addiction and Self-Restraint: Are The Scholia Wrong About Drugs?" *Sententiae Antiquae*, April 8, www.sententiaeantiquae.com.

Clark, Travis (2019). "Netflix Loves 10-Episode TV Seasons and Reportedly Doesn't See the Value in Longer Original Shows." *Business Insider*, March 10, www.businessinsider.com.

Clarke, Stewart (2017a). "Hakeem Kae-Kazim to Play Zeus in BBC and Netflix Series *Troy*." *Variety*, July 31, www.variety.com.

Clarke, Stewart (2017b). "BBC and Netflix Release First Look at *Troy: Fall of a City*." *Variety*, December 20, www.variety.com.

Clarke, Stewart (2018). "*Troy: Fall of a City* Team Talk Casting and Diversity in the BBC and Netflix Epic." *Variety*, February 23, www.variety.com.

Cocca, Caroline (2014). "Negotiating the Third Wave of Feminism in *Wonder Woman*." *Political Science & Politics* 47.1: 98–103.

Cohen, Beth (2012). "The Non-Greek in Greek Art," in Tyler Jo Smith and Dimitris Plantzos (eds.), *A Companion to Greek Art.* Malden, MA: Blackwell, 456–79.

Cole, Emma (2019). "Post-Traumatic Stress Disorder and the Performance Reception of Sophocles' *Ajax*," in David Stuttard (ed.), *Looking at Ajax.* London: Bloomsbury, 151–60.

Collard, Christopher and Morwood, James (eds.) (2017). *Euripides Iphigenia at Aulis.* 2 vols. Liverpool: Liverpool University Press.

Collins, Richard (2004). "'Ises' and 'Oughts': Public Service Broadcasting in Europe," in Robert C. Allen and Annette Hill (eds.), *The Television Studies Reader.* London: Routledge, 33–41.

Conklin, Alice (2013). *In the Museum of Man: Race, Anthropology, and Empire in France, 1850–1950.* Ithaca, NY: Cornell University Press.

Conlan, Tara (2020). "Netflix Pledges to be 'Force For Good' By Diversifying its Programming." *The Guardian*, December 13, www.theguardian.com.

Cook, Erwin (forthcoming). *Omero Iliade. Vol. 1, Libri I–IV. Traduzione della poesia di Piero Boitani.* Turin: Fondazione Lorenzo Valla.

Csapo, Eric and Slater, William J. (1994). *The Context of Ancient Drama.* Ann Arbor, MI: University of Michigan Press.

Cuklanz, Lisa M. (2000). *Rape on Prime Time Television, Masculinity, and Sexual Violence.* Philadelphia, PA: University of Pennsylvania Press.

Cyrino, Monica S. (2005a). *Big Screen Rome.* Malden, MA: Blackwell.

Cyrino, Monica S. (2005b). "She'll Always Have Paris: Helen in Wolfgang Petersen's *Troy*." *Amphora* 4.1: 10–11, 18.

Bibliography

Cyrino, Monica S. (2007). "Helen of *Troy*," in Martin M. Winkler (ed.), *Troy: From Homer's Iliad to Hollywood Epic*. Oxford: Blackwell, 131–47.
Cyrino, Monica S. (ed.) (2008). *Rome Season One: History Makes Television*. Malden, MA: Blackwell.
Cyrino, Monica S. (2010). *Aphrodite*. London: Routledge.
Cyrino, Monica S. (ed.) (2015). *Rome, Season Two: Trial and Triumph*. Edinburgh: Edinburgh University Press.
Daly, Helen. (2018). "*Troy: Fall of a City* Viewers in Horror over Extremely Brutal Sacrifice Scene 'B****y Hell!'" *Express*, February 25, www.express.co.uk.
Davies, Malcolm (2001). *The Greek Epic Cycle*. 2nd ed. Bristol: Bristol Classical Press.
Davies, Malcolm (2019). *The Cypria*. Washington, DC: Center for Hellenic Studies.
Day, Kirsten (2022). "Looking a Gift Horse in the Mouth: Helen of Troy and the Trojan Horse," in Amanda Potter and Hunter Gardner (eds.), *The Ancient Epic in Film and Television*. Edinburgh: Edinburgh University Press, 98–115.
De Cesari, Chiara and Kaya, Ayhan (eds.) (2019). *European Memory in Populism: Representations of Self and Other*. London: Routledge.
Doran, Sarah (2018). "*Troy: Fall of a City*'s Dodgy Dialogue Divided Viewers but Everybody Loved the Ostrich." *Radio Times*, February 18, www.radiotimes.com.
Dover, Kenneth James (1989). *Greek Homosexuality*. Cambridge, MA: Harvard University Press.
Dowden, Ken (1989). *Death and the Maiden: Girls' Initiation Rites in Greek Mythology*. London: Routledge.
Dowell, Ben (2018). "Scripts Are Already Being Developed for a Sequel to *Troy: Fall of a City*." *Radio Times*, February 24, www.radiotimes.com.
Drake, Robert (1998). *The Gay Canon*. New York: Anchor Books.
Drexler, Peggy (2011). "When Mothers Leave." *Psychology Today*, August 8, www.psychologytoday.com.
Drexler, Peggy (2013). "Why There Are More Walk-away Moms." *CNN*, May 6, www.cnn.com.
Eckardt, Stephanie (2017). "Fashion is Suddenly Flocking to Feathers." *W Magazine*, October 6, www.wmagazine.com.
Elley, Derek (1984). *The Epic Film: Myth and History*. London: Routledge.
Ellinas, Antonis A. (2013). "The Rise of Golden Dawn: The New Face of the Far Right in Greece." *South European Society and Politics* 18: 543–65.
Esposito, Stephen (trans.) (2010). *Odysseus at Troy: Ajax, Hecuba, and Trojan Women*. Indianapolis, IN: Hackett.
Eyring, Teresa (2016). "Standing Up for Playwrights and Against 'Colorblind' Casting." *American Theatre*, January 2, www.americantheatre.org.
Famurewa, Jimi (2018). "Yes, Achilles in *Troy: Fall of a City* is Black, and Yes It's a Big Deal." *Digital Spy*, February 17, www.digitalspy.com/tv.
Fantham, Elaine (1982). *Seneca's Troades: A Literary Introduction with Text, Translation, and Commentary*. Princeton, NJ: Princeton University Press.
Farr, David (2018). "*Troy: Fall of a City* Writer David Farr Reveals How He's Putting a New Spin on the Ancient Myth." *Radio Times*, February 17, www.radiotimes.com.
Felson, Nancy (1994). *Regarding Penelope: From Character to Poetics*. Norman, OK: University of Oklahoma Press.
Feltman, Rachel (2016). "A Famous Physicist's Simple Experiment Showed the Inevitability of the *Challenger* Disaster." *Washington Post*, January 27, www.washingtonpost.com.
Ferguson, Niall (2011). *Civilization: The West and the Rest*. New York: Penguin.
Feynman, Richard P. (1974). "Cargo Cult Science." http://calteches.library.caltech.edu/51/2/CargoCult.pdf.
Fields, Karen E. and Fields, Barbara J. (2012). *Racecraft: The Soul of Inequality in American Life*. London: Verso.

Finkelberg, Margalit (2006). "Aristotle and Episodic Tragedy." *Greece & Rome* 53: 60–72.
Fioretti, Julia (2018). "EU Strikes Deal Forcing Netflix, Amazon to Fund European Content." *Reuters*, April 26, www.reuters.com.
Fitton, J. Lesley (2007). "*Troy* and the Role of the Historical Advisor," in Martin M. Winkler (ed.), *Troy: From Homer's* Iliad *to Hollywood Epic*. Malden, MA: Blackwell, 99–106.
Fitton, J. Lesley, Villing, Alexandra, and Donnellan, Victoria (2019). "Troy: Enduring Stories," in Alexander Villing, J. Lesley Fitton, Victoria Donnellan, and Andrew Shapland (eds.), *Troy: Myth and Reality*. London: British Museum/Thames & Hudson, 184–271.
Flowers, Betty Sue (ed.) (1988). *Joseph Campbell: The Power of Myth with Bill Moyers*. New York: Doubleday.
Foley, Helene P. (1985). *Ritual Irony: Poetry and Sacrifice in Euripides*. Ithaca, NY: Cornell University Press.
Foley, Helene P. (2015). *Euripides: Hecuba*. London: Bloomsbury.
Fowler, Don P. (1989). "First Thoughts on Closure: Problems and Prospects." *Materiali e discussioni per l'analisi dei testi classici* 22: 75–122.
Fra-Lopéz, Patricia (2010). "From Jezebel to the Southern Belle: (Mis)Representations of the Female in Classic Hollywood Film: *Jezebel* and *Gone With the Wind*," in Andrea Ruthven and Gabriela Mádlo (eds.), *Illuminating the Dark Side: Evil, Women and the Feminine*. Leiden: Brill, 159–66.
Friedman, May (2014). "Unpacking MILF: Exploring Motherhood, Sexuality and Feminism." *Atlantis: Critical Studies in Gender, Culture & Social Justice* 36.2: 49–60.
Fröhner, W. (1871). *Deux peintures de vases grecs de la nécropole de Kameiros*. Paris: J. Baur et Détaille.
Gantz, Timothy (1993). *Early Greek Myth*. Baltimore, MD: Johns Hopkins University Press.
García, Alberto N. (2016). "Moral Emotions, Antiheroes and the Limits of Allegiance," in Alberto N. García (ed.), *Emotions in Contemporary TV Series*. New York: Palgrave Macmillan, 52–70.
Garcia, Lorenzo F., Jr. (2019). "The Temporality of Aphrodite in Early Greek Epic: Sexuality, Maternity, Mourning." Paper delivered at the annual meeting of the Classical Association of the Middle West and South at the University of Nebraska in Lincoln, April 5.
Gibson, Valerie (2002). *Cougar: A Guide for Older Women Dating Younger Men*. Richmond Hills, ON: Firefly Books.
Gill, James (2017). "British Drama, Global Budgets: How Co-productions Are Changing the Way TV Gets Made." *Radio Times*, March 23, www.radiotimes.com.
Goff, Barbara (2009). *Euripides: Trojan Women*. London: Duckworth.
Gogou, Elena, Stivaktis, Steve, Yatras, Dennis, and Zachari, Georgia (2019). *Greek Love*. Self-published.
Gough, Owen (2018). "*Troy: Fall of a City* Season 2 Release: When Will It Be Released on Netflix?" *Express*, April 14, www.express.co.uk.
Gourgouris, Stathis (1996) *Dream Nation: Enlightenment, Colonization, and the Institution of Modern Greece*. Stanford, CA: Stanford University Press.
Graindor, P. (1908). "Le vases au nègre." *Musée Belge* 12: 25–33.
Grant, Michael (1991). *The Founders of the Western World*. New York: Scribner.
Gregory, Justina (1999). *Euripides, Hecuba: Introduction, Text, and Commentary*. Atlanta, GA: Scholars Press.
Griffin, Jasper (1977). "The Epic Cycle and the Uniqueness of Homer." *Journal of Hellenic Studies* 97: 39–53.
Griffin, Jasper (1986). "Homeric Words and Speakers." *Journal of Hellenic Studies* 106: 36–57.
Griffin, Jasper (2010). "Greek Epic," in Catherine Bates (ed.), *The Cambridge Companion to the Epic*. Cambridge: Cambridge University Press, 13–30.
Griswold, Charles L. and Konstan, David (eds.) (2012). *Ancient Forgiveness*. Cambridge: Cambridge University Press.

Bibliography

Günsberg, Maggie (2004). *Italian Cinema: Gender and Genre*. New York: Palgrave Macmillan.

Hall, Edith (2004). "Why Greek Tragedy in the Late Twentieth Century?," in Edith Hall, Fiona Macintosh, and Amanda Wrigley (eds.), *Dionysus Since 69: Greek Tragedy at the Dawn of the Third Millennium*. Oxford: Oxford University Press, 1–46.

Hall, Jonathan (1997). *Ethnic Identity in Greek Antiquity*. Cambridge: Cambridge University Press.

Halliwell, Stephen (1987). *The Poetics of Aristotle: Translation and Commentary*. Chapel Hill, NC: University of North Carolina Press.

Hamilakis, Yannis (2007). *The Nation and Its Ruins: Antiquity, Archaeology, and National Imagination in Greece*. Oxford: Oxford University Press.

Hanink, Johanna (2017). *The Classical Debt: Greek Antiquity in an Era of Austerity*. Cambridge, MA: Harvard University Press.

Hannelly, Molly (2018). "Trend Report: Feathers in 2018." *Mood Fabrics*, May 3, www.moodfabrics.com/blog.

Hansen, William (2002). *Ariadne's Thread: A Guide to International Tales Found in Classical Literature*. Ithaca, NY: Cornell University Press.

Hanson, J. O. de G. (1974). "The Myth of the Libyan Amazons." *Museum Afircum* 3: 38–43.

Hanson, Victor Davis (1989). *The Western Way of War: Infantry Battle in Classical Greece*. New York: Alfred A. Knopf.

Harrison, A. Cleveland (1969). "Negro Actors: The Added Dimensions of Color." *Southern Journal of Communication* 35: 16–27.

Haywood, Jan and Mac Sweeney, Naoíse (2019). *Homer's Iliad and the Trojan War: Dialogues on Tradition*. London: Bloomsbury.

Heath, Malcolm (1989). *Unity in Greek Poetics*. Oxford: Oxford University Press.

Heiden, Bruce (1998). "The Placement of 'Book Divisions' in the *Iliad*." *The Journal of Hellenic Studies* 118: 68–81.

Heim, S. Mark (2016). "In What Way Is Christ's Death a Sacrifice? Theories of Sacrifice and Theologies of the Cross," in Carrie Ann Murray (ed.), *Diversity of Sacrifice: Form and Function of Sacrificial Practices in the Ancient World and Beyond*. Albany, NY: State University of New York Press, 255–69.

Herrera, Brian E. (2017). "Miranda's Manifesto." *Theater* 47: 23–33.

Hiltunen, Ari (2002). *Aristotle in Hollywood: The Anatomy of Successful Storytelling*. Bristol: Intellect Books.

Hinsley, Curtis M. (1981). *Savages and Scientists: The Smithsonian Institution and the Development of American Anthropology, 1846–1910*. Washington, DC: Smithsonian Institution Press.

Holland, Steve (2018). "At Las Vegas Rally, Trump Backs Kavanaugh, Treads Carefully Around Accusations." *Reuters*, September 20, www.reuters.com.

Hornblower, Simon (2015). *Lykophron: Alexandra*. Oxford: Oxford University Press.

Hughes, Dennis D. (1991). *Human Sacrifice in Ancient Greece*. London: Routledge.

Hughes, Sarah (2018a). "*Troy: Fall of a City* Recap – Series One, Episode One: Black Blood." *The Guardian*, February 17, www.theguardian.com.

Hughes, Sarah (2018b). "*Troy: Fall of a City* Recap – Series One, Episode Two: Conditions." *The Guardian*, February 24, www.theguardian.com.

Hughes, Sarah (2018c). "*Troy: Fall of a City* Recap – Series One, Episode Seven: Twelve Days." *The Guardian*, March 31, www.theguardian.com.

Hughes, Sarah (2018d). "Enter the Wooden Horse. But This Time the Trojans Tell Their Side of Fall of Troy." *The Guardian*, January 27, www.theguardian.com.

Hughes, Sarah (2018e). "*Troy: Fall of a City* Recap – Series One, Episode Four: Spoils of War." *The Guardian*, March 10, www.theguardian.com.

Hughes, Sarah (2018f). "*Troy: Fall of a City* Recap – Series One, Episode Six: Battle on the Beach." *The Guardian*, March 24, www.theguardian.com.

Bibliography

Ilkay, Hilary (2018). "The Madwoman in the Attic Tradition: Netflix's *Troy: Fall of a City* Misses Cassandra's #MeToo Moment." *Eidolon*, May 17, www.eidolon.pub.

Inness, Sherrie A. (1999). *Tough Girls: Women Warriors and Wonder Women in Popular Culture.* Philadelphia, PA: University of Pennsylvania Press.

James, Alan (2004). *The Trojan Epic Posthomerica*. Baltimore, MD: Johns Hopkins University Press.

Jebb, Richard Claverhouse, Headlam, W.G., and Pearson, A.C. (eds.) (2010). *The Fragments of Sophocles*. Cambridge: Cambridge University Press.

Jenkins, Thomas (2015). *Antiquity Now: The Classical World in the Contemporary American Imagination*. Cambridge: Cambridge University Press.

Jenner, Mareike (2018). *Netflix and the Re-invention of Television*. New York: Palgrave Macmillan.

Johnson, Amy (2018). "*Troy: Fall of a City* in 'Blackwashing' Row – Zeus Star Hakeem Kae-Kazim SHUTS DOWN Critics." *Daily Express*, March 3, www.express.co.uk.

Johnson, James Franklin (2016). *Acts of Compassion in Greek Tragic Drama*. Norman, OK: University of Oklahoma Press.

Johnston, Sarah Iles (2008). *Ancient Greek Divination*. Malden, MA: Blackwell.

Jolles, Marjorie (2007). "Knowing for Sure: Epistemologies of the Autonomous Self in O. the Oprah Magazine," in Jennifer Harris and Elwood Watson (eds.), *The Oprah Phenomenon*. Lexington, KY: University of Kentucky Press, 259–76.

Jonason, Peter K., Webster, Gregory D., Schmitt, David P., Li, Norman P., and Crysel, Laura (2012). "The Antihero in Popular Culture: Life History Theory and the Dark Triad of Personality Traits." *Review of General Psychology* 16.2: 192–9.

Kadare, Ismail (2006). *Agamemnon's Daughter*. New York: Arcade.

Karlen, Arno (1988). *Threesomes: Studies in Sex, Power, and Intimacy*. Sag Harbor, NY: Beech Tree Books.

Kearns, Emily (2006). "The Gods in the Homeric Epics," in Robert Fowler (ed.), *The Cambridge Companion to Homer*. Cambridge: Cambridge University Press, 59–73.

Kennedy, George A. (1986). "Helen's Web Unraveled." *Arethusa* 19.1: 5–14.

Kennedy, Rebecca F. (2019). "On the History of Western Civilization, Pt 1." *Classics at the Intersections*, April 3, www.rfkclassics.blogspot.com.

Kennedy, Rebecca F. (forthcoming). "White Supremacism and Myths of a Greco-Roman Past," in Elizabeth Niklasson (ed.), *Polarized Pasts*. Chicago, IL: University of Chicago Press.

Kindt, Julia (2012). *Rethinking Greek Religion*. Cambridge: Cambridge University Press.

Kitto, H. D. F. (2002). *Greek Tragedy: A Literary Study*. 2nd ed. London: Routledge.

Knox, Bernard (1993). *The Oldest Dead White European Males and Other Reflections on the Classics*. London: W. W. Norton.

Knust, Jennifer Wright and Várhelyi, Zsuzsanna (2011). *Ancient Mediterranean Sacrifice*. Oxford: Oxford University Press.

Kofler, Wolfgang and Schaffenrath, Florian (2015). "Petersen's Epic Technique: *Troy* and its Homeric Model," in Martin M. Winkler (ed.), *Return to Troy: New Essays on the Hollywood Epic*. Leiden: Brill, 86–107.

Kokkinidis, Tasos (2018). "Controversy Looms as Mythical Achilles is Played by Black Actor in New BBC Epic." *Hollywood Greek Reporter*, January 2, www.hollywood.greekreporter.com.

Konstan, David (2010). *Before Forgiveness: The Origins of a Moral Idea*. Cambridge: Cambridge University Press.

Kovacs, George Adam (2010). *Iphigenia at Aulis: Myth, Performance, and Reception*. Ph.D. diss., University of Toronto.

Kyle, Chris (2012). *American Sniper: The Autobiography of the Most Lethal Sniper in U.S. Military History* (co-authored with Scott McEwen and Jim DeFelice). New York: William Morrow.

Larsen, A. E. (2018). "*Troy: Fall of a City*: Meh." *An Historian Goes to the Movies: Exploring History on the Screen*, June 14, www.aelarsen.wordpress.com.

Bibliography

Lattimore, Richmond (1953). "Aeschylus' Agamemnon," in David Greene and Richard Lattimore (trans.), *Greek Tragedies: Volume 1*. 2nd ed. Chicago, IL: University of Chicago Press, 1–60.

Lawrence, John Shelton and Jewett, Robert (2017). "The Mythic Shape of *American Sniper* (2015)," in Terence McSweeney (ed.), *American Cinema in the Shadow of 9/11*. Edinburgh: Edinburgh University Press, 23–47.

Lee, K. H. (1976). *Euripides: Troades*. London: Duckworth.

Lee, Mireille M. (2015). *Body, Dress, and Identity in Ancient Greece*. Cambridge: Cambridge University Press.

Lee, Tae Kyoung and Shapiro, Michael A. (2014). "The Interactions of Affective Dispositions, Moral Judgments, and Intentionality in Assessing Narrative Characters: Rationalist and Intuitionist Sequences." *Communication Theory* 24.2: 146–64.

Leitao, David (2018). "Achilles in Love: Politics and Desire in Aeschylus' *Myrmidons*," in Louise Pratt and C. Michael Sampson (eds.), *Engaging Classical Texts in the Contemporary World: From Narratology to Reception*. Ann Arbor, MI: University of Michigan Press, 51–70.

Lenker, Maureen Lee (2017). "The *Marvelous Mrs. Maisel* Costume Designer Takes Us Inside the Marvelous Looks." *Entertainment Weekly*, December 4, www.ew.com/tv.

Lewis, Matt. (2019). "How Steve King's Idiotic and Odious Words Help the Left Destroy Western Civilization." *The Daily Beast*, January 11, www.thedailybeast.com.

Ling, Thomas (2018a). "No, the BBC Is Not 'Blackwashing' *Troy: Fall of a City*." *Radio Times*, May 25, www.radiotimes.com.

Ling, Thomas (2018b). "*Troy: Fall of a City*'s Hakeem Kae-Kazim Calls Out 'Deep Insecurity' of 'Blackwashing' Critics." *Radio Times*, March 10, www.radiotimes.com.

Littler, Jo (2013). "The Rise of the 'Yummy Mummy': Popular Conservatism and the Neoliberal Maternal in Contemporary British Culture." *Communication, Culture and Critique* 6.2: 227–43.

Llewellyn-Jones, Lloyd (2003). *Aphrodite's Tortoise: The Veiled Woman of Ancient Greece*. Swansea: Classical Press of Wales.

Llewellyn-Jones, Lloyd (2005). "The Fashioning of Delilah. Costume Design, Historicism and Fantasy in Cecil B. DeMille's *Samson and Delilah* (1949)," in Liza Cleland, Mary Harlow, and Lloyd Llewellyn-Jones (eds.), *The Clothed Body in the Ancient World*. Oxford: Oxbow Books, 14–29.

Llewellyn-Jones, Lloyd (2007). "Gods of the Silver Screen," in Daniel Ogden (ed.), *A Companion to Greek Religion*. Malden, MA: Blackwell, 423–38.

Llewellyn-Jones, Lloyd (2009). "Hollywood's Ancient World," in Andrew Erskine (ed.), *A Companion to Ancient History*. Malden, MA: Blackwell, 564–79.

Llewellyn-Jones, Lloyd (2013a). *King and Court in Ancient Persia 559 to 331 BCE*. Edinburgh: Edinburgh University Press.

Llewellyn-Jones, Lloyd (2013b). "Ray Harryhausen and Other Gods: Greek Divinity in *Jason and the Argonauts* and *Clash of the Titans*." Animating Antiquity: Harryhausen and the Classical Tradition. New Voices in Classical Reception Studies, Conference Proceedings 1: 3–20.

Llewellyn-Jones, Lloyd (2018). *Designs on the Past: How Hollywood Created the Ancient World*. Edinburgh: Edinburgh University Press.

Lloyd-Jones, Hugh (1962). "The Guilt of Agamemnon." *Classical Quarterly* 12.2: 187–99.

Lobato, Ramon (2019). *Netflix Nations: The Geography of Digital Distribution*. New York: New York University Press.

Lombardo, Stanley (1997). *Homer: Iliad*. Indianapolis, IN: Hackett.

Lombardo, Stanley (2000). *Homer: Odyssey*. Indianapolis, IN: Hackett.

Loraux, Nicole (1987). *Tragic Ways of Killing a Woman* (Trans. Anthony Forster). Cambridge, MA: Harvard University Press.

Lotz, Amanda D. (2014). *Cable Guys: Television and Masculinities in the 21st Century*. New York: New York University Press.

Bibliography

Louden, Bruce (2015). "Odysseus in *Troy*," in Martin M. Winkler (ed.), *Return to Troy: New Essays on the Hollywood Epic*. Leiden: Brill, 80–90.

Mac Sweeney, Naoíse (2018). *Troy: Myth, City, Icon*. London: Bloomsbury.

Mac Sweeney, Naoíse *et al.* (2019). "Claiming the Classical: The Greco-Roman World in Contemporary Political Discourse." *CUCD Bulletin* 48, www.cucd.blogs.sas.ac.uk.

Maguire, Laurie (2009). *Helen of Troy: From Homer to Hollywood*. Malden, MA: Blackwell.

Malamud, Margaret (2013). "Consuming Passions: Helen of Troy in the Jazz Age," in Pantelis Michelakis and Maria Wyke (eds.), *The Ancient World in Silent Cinema*. Cambridge: Cambridge University Press, 330–46.

Maurice, Lisa (2016). "Building a New Ancient Rome in STARZ *Spartacus*," in Antony Augoustakis and Monica Cyrino (eds.), *STARZ Spartacus: Reimagining an Icon on Screen*. Edinburgh: Edinburgh University Press, 111–30.

Maurice, Lisa (2019). *Screening Divinity*. Edinburgh: Edinburgh University Press.

Mayor, Adrienne (2014). *The Amazons: Lives and Legends of Warrior Women Across the Ancient World*. Princeton, NJ: Princeton University Press.

McCabe, Janet and Akass, Kim (2007). *Quality TV: Contemporary American Television and Beyond*. London: I. B. Tauris.

McCoskey, Denise E. (2012). *Race: Antiquity and its Legacy*. London: I. B. Tauris.

McEwan, Cameron K. (2018). "*Troy: Fall of a City* Series 2 – Release Date, Cast, Plot and Everything You Need to Know." *Digital Spy*, March 8, www.digitalspy.com/tv.

McLaren, Clemence (2004). *Waiting for Odysseus*. New York: Simon & Schuster.

Meltzer, Marisa (2013). "Costume Designers for TV Have a Big Impact on Fashion." *New York Times*, September 18, www.nytimes.com.

Mendelsohn, Daniel (2004). "A Little Iliad." *New York Review of Books*, June 24, www.nybooks.com.

Michelakis, Pantelis (2006). *Euripides: Iphigenia at Aulis*. London: Duckworth.

Michelakis, Pantelis (2013). "Homer in Silent Cinema," in Pantelis Michelakis and Maria Wyke (eds.), *The Ancient World in Silent Cinema*. Cambridge: Cambridge University Press, 145–65.

Miller, Madeline (2012). *The Song of Achilles*. New York: Harper Collins.

Miller, Madeline (2018). *Circe*. Boston, MA: Little, Brown.

Mills, Charles W. (2015). "Global White Ignorance," in Matthias Gross and Linsey McGoey (eds.), *Routledge International Handbook of Ignorance Studies*. London: Routledge, 217–27.

Mittell, Jason (2015). *Complex TV: The Poetics of Contemporary Television Storytelling*. New York: New York University Press.

Monteiro, L. (2016). "Race-Conscious Casting and the Erasure of the Black Past in Lin-Manuel Miranda's Hamilton." *The Public Historian* 38: 89–98.

Montiglio, Silvia (2011). *From Villain to Hero: Odysseus in Ancient Thought*. Ann Arbor, MI: University of Michigan Press.

Morford, Mark, Lenardon, Robert, and Sham, Michael (2013). *Classical Mythology*. 9th ed. Oxford: Oxford University Press.

Morley, Neville (2018). *Classics: Why It Matters*. Malden, MA: Polity Press.

Morris, Ian (2003). "Archaeology and Gender Ideologies in Early Archaic Greece," in Mark Golden and Peter Toohey (eds.), *Sex and Difference in Ancient Greece and Rome*. Edinburgh: Edinburgh University Press, 264–75.

Morwood, James (trans.) (2008). *Bacchae and Other Plays*. Oxford: Oxford University Press.

Moyers, B. (1999). "The Mythology of Star Wars with George Lucas." *Moyers on Democracy*, June 18, www.billmoyers.com.

Mueller, Melissa (2010). "Helen's Hands: Weaving for *Kleos* in the *Odyssey*." *Helios* 37.1: 1–21.

Mulvey, Laura (1975). "Visual Pleasure and Narrative Cinema." *Screen* 16: 8–18.

Munich, Adrienne (ed.) (2011). *Fashion in Film*. Bloomington, IN: Indiana University Press.

Murray, A. T. and Wyatt, William F. (1999). *Homer, Iliad*. 2 vols. Cambridge, MA: Harvard University Press.

Bibliography

Murray, Jackie (forthcoming). "Race and Sexuality: Racecraft in the *Odyssey*," in Denise McCoskey (ed.), *Cultural History of Race*. London: Bloomsbury.

Nadoolman Landis, Deborah (2007). *Dressed: A Century of Hollywood Costume Design*. New York: Harper Collins.

Nadoolman Landis, Deborah (2018). "Character and Costume in Cinema: The *Hollywood Costume* Exhibition." *Studies in Costume and Performance* 3.1: 91–6.

Nagy, Gregory (1996). *Homeric Questions*. Austin, TX: University of Texas Press.

Neils, Jennifer (1980). "The Group of the Negro Alabastra: A Study in Motif Transferal." *Antike Kunst* 23: 13–23.

Newman, Michael Z. and Levine, Elana (2012). *Legitimating Television: Media Convergence and Cultural Status*. New York: Routledge.

Ngangura, Tari (2018). "'Jack Ryan' Introduces a New Archetype: The Guilty White Saviour." *Vice*, September 27, www.vice.com.

Nikoloutsos, Konstantinos P. (2015). "From Text to Screen: Celluloid Helens and Female Stardom in the 1950s." *The Cambridge Classical Journal* 61: 70–90.

Nikoloutsos, Konstantinos P. (2016). "Helen's Semiotic Body: Ancient and Modern Representations." *Nuntius Antiquus* 12.1: 187–213.

Nisbet, Gideon (2008). *Ancient Greece in Film and Popular Culture*. 2nd ed. Exeter: Bristol Phoenix Press.

Nussbaum, Martha C. (2001). *The Fragility of Goodness: Luck and Ethics in Greek Tragedy and Philosophy*. New York: Cambridge University Press.

Ochotnikov, Sergej B. (2006). "Achilleus auf der Insel Leuke," in Joachim Hupe (ed.), *Der Achilleus-Kult im nördlichen Schwarzmeerraum vom Beginn der griechischen Kolonisation bis in die römische Kaiserzeit*. Rahden: Leidorf, 49–87.

Onyeani, Chika (2009). "Contemptuousness of Sub-Saharan Africa." *Worldpress*, July 16, www.worldpress.org.

Ormand, Kirk (1999). *Exchange and the Maiden: Marriage in Sophoclean Tragedy*. Austin, TX: University of Texas Press.

Pasin, Burkay (2016). "A Critical Reading of the Ottoman-Turkish Hammam as a Representational Space of Sexuality." *Metu Journal of the Faculty of Architecture* 33.2: 121–38.

Penrose, Walter D., Jr. (2016). *Postcolonial Amazons: Female Masculinity and Courage in Ancient Greek and Sanskrit Literature*. Oxford: Oxford University Press.

Penrose, Walter D., Jr. (2019). "The Unwanted Gaze? Feminism and the Reception of the Amazons in *Wonder Woman*." *Eugesta* 9: 176–224.

Pomeroy, Arthur J. (2008). *Then It Was Destroyed by the Volcano: The Ancient World in Film and on Television*. London: Duckworth.

Pomeroy, Sarah B. (1975). *Goddesses, Whores, Wives, and Slaves: Women in Classical Antiquity*. New York: Schocken Books.

Prakash, Neha (2020). "Jodie Comer on Playing TV's Chicest (and Cheekiest) Assassin." *Marie Claire*, April 26, www.marieclaire.com.

Preece, Caroline (2018). "*Troy: Fall of a City* – Flipping the Script on the *Iliad*." *Den of Geek*, February 13, www.denofgeek.com/tv.

Purves, Alex (2006). "Falling into Time in Homer's *Iliad*." *Classical Antiquity* 25: 179–209.

Rabel, Robert J. (1984). "Agamemnon's Empire in Thucydides." *Classical Journal* 80.1: 8–10.

Rabinowitz, Nancy (1993). *Anxiety Veiled: Euripides and the Traffic in Women*. Ithaca, NY: Cornell University Press.

Rehm, Rush (1994). *Marriage to Death: The Conflation of Wedding and Funeral Rituals in Greek Tragedy*. Princeton, NJ: Princeton University Press.

Roediger, David R. (2005). *Working Toward Whiteness: How America's Immigrant Became White. The Strange Journey from Ellis Island to the Suburbs*. New York: Basic Books.

Rogers Commission Report (1986). "Report of the Presidential Commission on the Space Shuttle *Challenger* Accident." https://history.nasa.gov/rogersrep/genindex.htm.

Roisman, Hanna (2008). "Helen and the Power of Erotic Love: From Homeric Contemplation to Hollywood Fantasy." *College Literature* 35.4: 127–50.

Ruden, Sarah (trans.) (2008). *The Aeneid: Vergil*. New Haven, CT: Yale University Press.

Safran, Meredith E. and Cyrino, Monica S. (2015). "Introduction. Cinemyths: Classical Myth on Screen," in Monica S. Cyrino and Meredith E. Safran (eds.), *Classical Myth on Screen*. New York: Palgrave Macmillan, 1–11.

Saini, A. (2019). *Superior: The Return of Race Science*. Boston, MA: Beacon Press.

Savage, Michael (2020). "BBC Chief Says TV Streaming Services 'Squeeze Out British Culture.'" *The Guardian*, March 15, www.theguardian.com.

Scaife, Ross (1995). "The 'Kypria' and Its Early Reception." *Classical Antiquity* 14.1: 164–92.

Schippers, Mimi (2016). *Beyond Monogamy: Polyamory and the Future of Polyqueer Sexualities*. New York: New York University Press.

Schwab, Katherine A. and Rose, Marice (2015). "Fishtail Braids and the Caryatid Hairstyling Project: Fashion Today and in Ancient Athens." *Catwalk* 4.2: 1–24.

Seidel, Linda (2013). *Mediated Maternity: Contemporary American Portrayals of Bad Mothers in Literature and Popular Culture*. Lanham, MD: Lexington.

Settis, Salvatore (2006). *The Future of the Classical* (Trans. Allan Cameron). Malden, MA: Polity Press.

Shay, Jonathan (1994). *Achilles in Vietnam: Combat Trauma and the Undoing of Character*. New York: Scribner.

Sherwin, Adam (2018). "'Vapid Bitch' Helen of Troy is Empowered, Feminist Icon in New BBC Epic." *i News*, February 2, www.inews.co.uk.

Sheth, Falguni A. (2009). *Toward a Political Philosophy of Race*. Albany, NY: SUNY Press.

Sidebottom, Harry (2004). *Ancient Warfare: A Very Short Introduction*. Oxford: Oxford University Press.

Simons, Meredith (2016). "100 Times a White Actor Played Someone Who Wasn't White." *Washington Post*, January 28, www.washingtonpost.com.

Siraj, Ahmed (1997). "La Libyenne dans la mythologie antique: À propos du mythe des Amazones." *Antiquités africaines* 33: 67–73.

Skouroumouni Stavrinou, Aspasia (2016). "Hermione's Spartan Costume: The Tragic *skeue* in Euripides' *Andromache*." *Illinois Classical Studies* 41.1: 1–20.

Snowden, Frank M., Jr. (1970). *Blacks in Antiquity: Ethiopians in the Greco-Roman Experience*. Cambridge, MA: Harvard University Press.

Solomon, Jon (2001). *The Ancient World in the Cinema*. 2nd ed. New Haven, CT: Yale University Press.

Solomon, Jon (2007). "The Vacillations of the Trojan Myth: Popularization & Classicization, Variation & Codification." *International Journal of the Classical Tradition* 14: 482–534.

Solomon, Jon (2015). "Homer's *Iliad* in Popular Culture: The Roads to *Troy*," in Martin M. Winkler (ed.), *Return to Troy: New Essays on the Hollywood Epic*. Leiden: Brill, 224–54.

Spivey, Nigel (2016). *The Classical World: The Foundations of the West and the Enduring Legacy of Antiquity*. London: Thames & Hudson.

Stafford, Emma J. (2017). "Hercules' Choice: Vice, Virtue and the Hero of the Modern Screen," in Eran Almagor and Lisa Maurice (eds.), *Beauty, Bravery, Blood and Glory: Ancient Virtues and Vices in Modern Popular Culture*. Leiden: Brill, 140–66.

Stafford, Emma J. (2022). "'Mighty Saga of the World's Mightiest Man': Is There Such a Thing as a Modern Hercules Epic?," in Amanda Potter and Hunter Gardner (eds.), *The Ancient Epic in Film and Television*. Edinburgh: Edinburgh University Press, 49–65.

Stanford, W. B. (1976). *The Ulysses Theme: A Study in the Adaptability of a Traditional Hero*. 2nd ed. Ann Arbor, MI: University of Michigan Press.

Bibliography

Stewart, Dan (2020). "Veep Creator Armando Iannucci Says These Times Call for Charles Dickens." *Time*, August 20, www.time.com.
Storey, Ian (2017). "Andromache," in Laura K. McClure (ed.), *A Companion to Euripides*. Malden, MA: Wiley-Blackwell, 122–35.
Street, Sarah (2001). *Costume and Cinema: Dress Codes in Popular Film*. London: Wallflower Press.
Strong, Dawsonne Melancthon (trans.) (1902). *The Udana Or The Solemn Utterances Of The Buddha*. London: Luzac.
Stutesman, Drake (2011). "Costume Design, or, What is Fashion in Film," in Adrienne Munich (ed.), *Fashion in Film*. Bloomington, IN: Indiana University Press, 17–39.
Syler, Claire and Banks, Daniel (eds.) (2019). *Casting a Movement: The Welcome Table Initiative*. London: Routledge.
Tally, Margaret (2016). *The Rise of the Anti-Heroine in TV's Third Golden Age*. Newcastle: Cambridge Scholars Publishing.
Tate, Gabriel (2018). "*Troy: Fall of a City*, BBC1." *Broadcast*, March 16, www.broadcastnow.co.uk.
Thimme, Jürgen (1970). *Griechische Salbgeässe mit libyshen Motiven*. Munich: Deutscher Kunsterverlag.
Thompson, Ayanna (2006). *Colorblind Shakespeare: New Perspectives on Race and Performance*. London: Routledge.
Thompson, Ayanna (2019). "The Chasm Between," in Claire Syler and Daniel Banks (eds.), *Casting a Movement: The Welcome Table Initiative*. London: Routledge, 33–5.
Thompson, Richard J. (1997). *Television's Second Golden Age: From Hill Street Blues to ER*. New York: Syracuse University Press.
Tierno, Michael (2002). *Aristotle's Poetics for Screenwriters: Storytelling Secrets from the Greatest Mind in Western Civilization*. New York: Hyperion.
Tomasso, Vincent (2018). "Ancient (Anti)Heroes on Screen and Ancient Greece Post-9/11," in Antony Augoustakis and Stacie Raucci (eds.), *Epic Heroes on Screen*. Edinburgh: Edinburgh University Press, 206–21.
Torgovnick, Marianna (2009). "Rereading *The Iliad* in a Time of War." *Proceedings of the Modern Language Association* 124.5: 1838–41.
Toscano, Margaret (2008). "Gowns and Gossip: Gender and Class Struggle in *Rome*," in Monica S. Cyrino (ed.), *Rome Season One: History Makes Television*. Malden, MA: Blackwell, 153–67.
Tran, Diep (2015). "On the Rights of Playwrights and White Tears." *American Theatre*, November 15, www.americantheatre.org.
Trivers, Robert (2011). *The Folly of Fools: The Logic of Deceit and Self-Deception in Human Life*. New York: Basic Books.
Trusty, Debra (2018). "Blog: A Classicist Reviews *Troy: Fall of a City*." Society for Classical Studies, April 15, www.classicalstudies.org/scs-blog/.
Tyrrell, William Blake (1984). *Amazons: A Study in Athenian Mythmaking*. Baltimore, MD: Johns Hopkins University Press.
Vaage, Margrethe Bruun (2013). "Fictional Reliefs and Reality Checks." *Screen* 54.2: 218–37.
Vaage, Margrethe Bruun (2016). *The Antihero in American Television*. London: Routledge.
Valverde García, Alejandro (2017). "Visual Poetry on Screen: Sets and Costumes for Ancient Greek Tragedy," in Arthur Pomeroy (ed.), *A Companion to Ancient Greece and Rome on Screen*. Malden, MA: Wiley-Blackwell, 385–402.
Van Vorhis, Genevieve (2018). "This Epic Netflix Series Will Reawaken Your Obsession With Greek Mythology." *Bustle*, April 5, www.bustle.com.
Veness, Ruth (2002). "Investing the Barbarian? The Dress of Amazons in Athenian Art," in Lloyd Llewelyn-Jones (ed.), *Women's Dress in the Ancient Greek World*. Swansea: Classical Press of Wales, 95–110.
Vann, Darah (2016). "Helen of Troy: Unwomanly in Her Sexuality." *Classical Inquiries: Studies on the Ancient World from the Center for Hellenic Studies*, May 3, www.classical-inquiries.chs.harvard.edu.

Verreth, Herbert (2008). "Odysseus' Journey Through Film," in Irene Berti and Marta García Morcillo (eds.), *Hellas on Screen*. Stuttgart: Franz Steiner, 65–73.
Vivante, Bella (2013). "Gazing at Helen," in Konstantinos Nikoloutsos (ed.), *Ancient Greek Women on Screen*. Oxford: Oxford University Press, 19–50.
Voller, Pete (2018). "How Accurate is *Troy: Fall of a City*?" *Historiai*, April 12, www.historiaiweb.wordpress.com.
von Bothmer, Dietrich (1957). *Amazons in Greek Art*. Oxford: Clarendon Press.
Warner, Helen (2009). "Style over Substance? Fashion, Spectacle and Narrative in Contemporary US Television." *Popular Narrative Media* 2.2: 181–93.
Warner, Sam (2018). "*Troy: Fall of a City* FINALLY Delivers the Moment We've All Been Waiting For." *Digital Spy*, July 4, www.digitalspy.com/tv.
Webster, T. B. L. (1947). "Three Interpretations of Greek Vases." *Memoirs & Proceedings of the Manchester Literary and Philosophical Society* 89: 5–14.
Weller, R. C. (2017) "'Western' and 'White Civilization': White Nationalism and Eurocentrism at the Crossroads," in R. C. Weller (ed.), *21st-Century Narratives of World History*. New York: Palgrave Macmillan, 35–80.
West, Martin L. (1981). "Tragica V." *Bulletin of the Institute of Classical Studies* 28: 61–78.
West, Martin L. (2010). "Book Division," in Margalit Finkelberg (ed.), *The Homer Encyclopedia*. Malden, MA: Wiley-Blackwell, 140–2.
White, Peter (2018). "The *Night Manager*'s David Farr Explores Complex Characters in Netflix & BBC Fantasy Drama *Troy: Fall of a City*." *Deadline*, January 30, www.deadline.com.
Whitmarsh, Tim (2018). "Black Achilles: The Greeks Didn't Have Modern Ideas of Race. Did They See Themselves as White, Black – or as Something Else Altogether?" *Aeon*, May 9, www.aeon.co/essays.
Wilson, August (2016). "The Ground on Which I Stand." *American Theatre*, June 20, www.americantheatre.org.
Wilson, Emily (2014). "Slut-Shaming Helen of Troy." *New Statesman*, April 29, www.newstatesman.com.
Wilson, Emily (2017). *Homer, The Odyssey*. London: W. W. Norton.
Winkler, John J. (1990). *The Constraints of Desire: The Anthropology of Sex and Gender in Ancient Greece*. New York: Routledge.
Winkler, Martin M. (ed.) (2007a). *Troy: From Homer's* Iliad *to Hollywood Epic*. Oxford: Blackwell.
Winkler, Martin M. (2007b). "Greek Myth on the Screen," in Roger D. Woodard (ed.), *The Cambridge Companion to Greek Mythology*. Cambridge: Cambridge University Press, 453–79.
Winkler, Martin M. (2009). *Cinema and Classical Texts: Apollo's New Light*. Cambridge: Cambridge University Press.
Winkler, Martin M. (ed.) (2015a). *Return to Troy: New Essays on the Hollywood Epic*. Leiden: Brill.
Winkler, Martin M. (2015b). "Troy and the Cinematic Afterlife of Homeric Gods," in Martin M. Winkler (ed.), *Return to Troy: New Essays on the Hollywood Epic*. Leiden: Brill, 108–64.
Winkler, Martin M. (2016). "Helene Kinematographike; or, Is This the Face that Launched a Thousand Films?" *Nuntius Antiquus* 12.1: 215–57.
Wiltz, Teresa (2007). "A Part Colored by History." *Washington Post*, June 23, www.washingtonpost.com.
Wohl, Victoria (1998). *Intimate Commerce: Exchange, Gender, and Subjectivity in Greek Tragedy*. Austin, TX: University of Texas Press.
Wollersheim, Ruth (2015). *Retrograde Returns of the American Housewife: Reimagining an Old Character in a New Millennium*. Ph.D. diss., University of Wisconsin-Milwaukee.
Wood, Michael (1996). *In Search of the Trojan War*. 2nd ed. Berkeley, CA: University of California Press.
Worman, Nancy (2001). "This Voice Which is Not One: Helen's Verbal Guises in Homeric Epic," in André Lardinois and Laura McClure (eds.), *Making Silence Speak: Women's Voices in Greek Literature and Society*. Princeton, NJ: Princeton University Press, 19–37.

Bibliography

Wright, Robert (1995). *The Moral Animal: Why We Are, The Way We Are. The New Science of Evolutionary Psychology.* New York: Vintage.

Yeazell, Ruth Bernard (2000). *Harems of the Mind: Passages of Western Art and Literature.* New Haven, CT: Yale University Press.

Yglesias, Matthew (2016). "The (((echo))), Explained." *Vox*, June 6, www.vox.com.

Young, Harvey (2013) *Theatre and Race.* New York: Palgrave Macmillan.

FILMOGRAPHY

Feature Films

A Beautiful Mind (2001). Directed by Ron Howard. Universal Pictures.
A Mighty Heart (2007). Directed by Michael Winterbottom. Paramount Vantage.
Alexander (2004). Directed by Oliver Stone. Warner Bros. Pictures.
American Pie (1999). Directed by Paul Weitz. Universal Pictures.
American Sniper (2015). Directed by Clint Eastwood. Warner Bros. Pictures.
Avengers: Infinity War (2018). Directed by Joe Russo and Anthony Russo. Marvel Studios.
Clash of the Titans (1981). Directed by Desmond Davis. Charles H. Schneer Productions.
Coco Before Chanel (2009). Directed by Anne Fontaine. Warner Bros. Pictures.
Dr. No (1962). Directed by Terence Young. Eon Productions.
Elektra (1962). Directed by Michael Cacoyannis. Finos Film.
Eye in the Sky (2016). Directed by Gavin Hood. Entertainment One Films.
Exodus: Gods and Kings (2014). Directed by Ridley Scott. Twentieth Century Fox.
Gone with the Wind (1939). Directed by Victor Fleming. Selznick International Pictures, Metro-Goldwyn-Mayer.
Hercules (Le fatiche di Ercole) (1958). Directed by Pietro Francisci. Embassy Pictures, Galatea Film, Lux Film, Warner Bros. Pictures.
Hercules Unchained (Ercole e la regina di Lidia) (1959). Directed by Pietro Francisci. Galatea Film, Lux Film, Lux Film and Warner Bros. Pictures.
Hercules (2014). Directed by Brett Ratner. Paramount Pictures.
Helen of Troy (1956). Directed by Robert Wise. Warner Bros. Pictures.
History of the World: Part I (1981). Directed by Mel Brooks. Twentieth Century Fox.
Immortals (2011). Directed by Tarsem Singh. Relativity Media.
Iphigenia (1977). Directed by Michael Cacoyannis. Greek Film Center.
Jason and the Argonauts (1963). Directed by Don Chaffey. Columbia Pictures.
Jezebel (1938). Directed by William Wyler. Warner Bros. Pictures.
L'île de Calypso (1905). Directed by Georges Méliès. Star Film Company.
Noah (2014). Directed by Darren Aronofsky. Paramount Pictures.
Oh, God! (1977). Directed by Carl Reiner. Warner Bros. Pictures.
Oh, God! Book II (1980). Directed by Gilbert Cates. Warner Bros. Pictures.
Percy Jackson and the Lightning Thief (2010). Directed by Chris Columbus. Fox 2000 Pictures.
Percy Jackson and the Sea of Monsters (2013). Directed by Thor Freudenthal. Fox 2000 Pictures.
Spartacus (1960). Directed by Stanley Kubrick. Bryna Productions.
The Devil Wears Prada (2006). Directed by David Frankel. Twentieth Century Fox.
The Fall of Troy (La caduta di Troia) (1911). Directed by Luigi Romano Borgnetto and Giovanni Pastrone. Itala Film.
The Killing of the Sacred Deer (2017). Directed by Yorgos Lanthimos. Curzon Artificial Eye.
The Matrix (1999). Directed by Lana Wachowski and Lilly Wachowski. Warner Bros. Pictures.
The Private Life of David Copperfield (2019). Directed by Armando Iannucci. Searchlight Pictures.
The Private Life of Helen of Troy (1927). Directed by Alexander Korda. First National Pictures.
The Trojan Women (1971). Directed by Michael Cacoyannis. Josef Shaftel Productions, Inc.
The 7th Voyage of Sinbad (1958). Directed by Nathan H. Juran. Columbia Pictures.

Filmography

The Golden Voyage of Sinbad (1973). Directed by Gordon Hessler. Columbia Pictures.
Troy (2004). Directed by Wolfgang Petersen. Warner Bros. Pictures.
Ulysses (1955). Directed by Mario Camerini. Lux Film/Paramount Pictures.
Wonder Woman (2017). Directed by Patty Jenkins. Warner Bros. Pictures.

Short Films

Achilles (1995). Directed by Barry Purves. First Run Features.

Television Movies and Series

Avatar: The Last Airbender (2005–2008). Created by Michael Dante DiMartino and Bryan Konietzko. Nickelodeon Animation Studios.
Blood of Zeus (2020–). Created by Charley and Vlas Parlapanides. Powerhouse Animation Studios.
Breaking Bad (2008–2013). Created by Vince Gilligan. High Bridge Productions, Gran Via Productions, Sony Pictures Television.
Cougar Town (2009–2015). Created by Kevin Biegel and Bill Lawrence. Doozer, Coquette Productions, ABC Studios.
Dexter (2006–2013). Created by James Manos, Jr. Showtime Networks, John Goldwyn Productions, The Colleton Company.
Dominion (2014–2015). Created by Vaun Wilmott. SyFy Network.
Dr. Who (1963–1989, 2005–). Created by Sydney Newman, C.E. Webber, Donald Wilson. BBC.
Ellen (1994–1998). Created by Neal Marlens, Carol Black, and David S. Rosenthal. ABC Studios.
Helen of Troy (2003). Directed by John Kent Harrison. USA Network.
Hercules: The Legendary Journeys (1995–1999). Created by Christian Williams. Renaissance Pictures/MCA Television.
Hercules and the Amazon Women (1994). Directed by Bill L. Norton. USA Network.
In Search of the Trojan War (1985). Written by Michael Wood. BBC Two.
Jack Ryan (2018–). Created by Carlton Cuse, Graham Roland. Genre Arts, Push, Boot., Platinum Dunes.
Joseph Campbell and the Power of Myth (1988). Created by Bill Moyers. PBS.
Killing Eve (2018–). Created by Phoebe Waller-Bridge. Sid Gentle Films for BBC America.
Lost (2004–2010). Created by J.J. Abrams, Jeffrey Lieber, Damon Lindelof. Bad Robot, Touchstone Television, ABC Studios.
Mad Men (2007–2015). Created by Matthew Weiner. Lionsgate Television, Weiner Bros., AMC.
Modern Family (2009–2020). Created by Christopher Lloyd and Steven Levitan. ABC Studios.
On the Ropes (2018). Created by Courtney Wise. SBS Network.
Out of the Blue (2008–2009). Created by John Edwards and Julie McGauran. Network Ten.
Rome, Season One (2005). Created by Bruno Heller, William J. MacDonald, and John Milius. HBO–BBC.
Rome, Season Two (2007). Created by Bruno Heller, William J. MacDonald, and John Milius. HBO–BBC.
Schitt's Creek (2015–2020). Created by Dan and Eugene Levy. Canadian Broadcasting Corporation.
Sex and the City (1998–2004). Created by Darren Star. Darren Star Productions/HBO.
Spartacus: Blood and Sand (2010). Created by Steven S. DeKnight. STARZ.

Spartacus: Gods of the Arena (2011). Created by Steven S. DeKnight. STARZ.
Spartacus: Vengeance (2012). Created by Steven S. DeKnight. STARZ.
Spartacus: War of the Damned (2013). Created by Steven S. DeKnight. STARZ.
The Alienist: Angel of Darkness (2018–2020). Created by Caleb Carr. TNT.
The Book of Boba Fett (2021–). Created by Jon Favreau and Dave Filoni. Lucasfilm.
The Fosters (2013–2018). Created by Bradley Bredeweg and Peter Paige. Freeform Original Productions.
The Gamechangers (2015). Directed by Owen Harris. BBC Two/PBS.
The Good Lord Bird (2020). Created by Ethan Hawke and Mark Richard. Showtime.
The Handmaid's Tale (2017–). Created by Bruce Miller. MGM Television.
The Marvelous Mrs. Maisel (2017–). Created by Amy Sherman-Palladino. Amazon Studios.
The Odyssey (1997). Directed by Andrei Konchalovsky. Hallmark Entertainment.
The Passion (2008). Directed by Michael Offer. BBC/HBO/Deep Indigo Productions.
The Secret Circle (2011–2012). Developed by Andrew Miller. CW Network.
The Shield (2002–2008). Created by Shawn Ryan. Fox Television Network, Sony Pictures Television, The Barn Productions.
The Sopranos (1999–2007). Created by David Chase. HBO, Brillstein Entertainment Partners, The Park Entertainment.
The Wire (2002–2008). Created by David Simon. Blown Deadline Productions, HBO.
The X-Files (1993–2002). Created by Chris Carter. 20th Century Fox Television.
Troy: Fall of A City (2018). Created by David Farr. BBC One/Netflix.
Xena: Warrior Princess (1995–2001). Created by Rob Tapert. Renaissance Pictures.

Theater

Dr. Faustus (1968). Directed by Clifford Williams. Royal Shakespeare Company.
Hamilton (2015). Musical by Lin-Manuel Miranda. The Public Theater.
Odyssey (2004). Created by David Farr. Bristol Old Vic.
Oresteia (2015). Directed and adapted by Robert Icke. The Almeida Theatre.
The War of the Roses (2009). Created by Tom Wright and Benedict Andrews. Sydney Theater Company.
Troilus and Cressida (1991). Directed by Sam Mendes. Royal Shakespeare Company.

INDEX

This index is selective for terms such as Homer, Troy, Trojan War, and the series *Troy: Fall of a City*.

#MeToo 97, 133

Achilles 14–15, 20, 60, 69–71, 155, 157–8, 162, 164, 171, 173, 175, 177, 184, 186, 205, 207, 219, 226–7, 229
   and Helen 121–2
   and Patroclus 131–2
   as blond 135
   as gay 111–25
   Black 79–95
   polyqueer threesome with Patroclus and Briseis 116–21
   racist reaction to 79–95
   see also Gyasi, David
Aeneas 44, 48, 79, 133, 228
   see also Enoch, Alfred
Aeolus 73
Aeschines 131
Aeschylus 117, 131–2, 189, 225
Aithiopis 20, 128, 130–1, 135
Africa 135
Agamemnon 14, 32, 34–5, 60, 67, 69–71, 100, 102, 118, 132, 155, 158, 160, 169, 171–6, 178, 184, 190–1, 194, 197, 200–4, 207–8, 225
   see also Harris, Johnny
Ajax 155–68, 199
   see also Breytenbach, Garth
Alexander
   see also Paris
Amazons 127–39
   multiracial 134–7
   see also Penthesilea
Anat 30
Andrews, Harry 15
Andromache 32, 59–60, 105, 113, 144, 148, 176–9, 205, 215, 224, 227
   see also Pirrie, Chloe
Anticlea 66
antiheroes
   TV 51–3
Aphrodite 15, 26–30, 37–50, 128, 144, 146–7, 156, 212
   see also King, Lex; Paris
Apollo 31, 229
Apollonius Rhodius 17, 20

Arctinus 128, 130, 135
arete 157
Aristogeiton 117
Aristotle 13, 16, 19, 22
Armstrong, Jonas
   as Menelaus 4, 73, 143, 189
Artemis 31–2, 34, 37, 79, 172, 184, 203
Assante, Armand 66
Astarte 30
Astyanax 59, 149, 159, 178–9, 224
Athena 26–7, 37, 43, 47, 79, 156, 212
   see also Miller, Shamilla
Athenian tragedy 14, 160, 165–7, 223
Aulis 31, 67, 73, 159, 171, 184

Bactria 66
Baker, Stanley 15, 162
Beckmann, Inge
   as Hera 29
Black Athena 92–3
Blackness
   in antiquity 91
Bloom, Orlando 15, 39
Breytenbach, Garth
   as Ajax 6, 98, 156
Briseis 100, 111–25, 175, 183, 223
   see also Achilles; Wilson, Amy Louise
Butler, Peter
   as Nestor 67

Cacoyannis, Michael 51, 99, 167, 180
Cadmus 18
Calchas 28, 31, 163, 172, 177–8, 203
Calypso 73
Campbell, Joseph 211
Caryatids 134
Cassandra 28, 33, 106, 144, 180, 194, 217, 225, 228
   see also Edwards, Aimee-Ffion
Catalog of Ships
   in Homer 14, 21
Charybdis 73
Child, Emily
   as Clytemnestra 97
Chryseis 159, 179, 183, 194, 227–8
   see also Money, Jamie-Lee

Index

Cilicia 31, 60, 69, 100, 102, 159
Cilliers, Diana 142, 150
Circe 73
Clytemnestra 60, 173, 185–6, 190–1, 202–3
  see also Child, Emily
Coe, Lauren
  as Iphigenia 18, 97, 187
costume design 141–52
cycles
  in epic 19–23, 128–30, 136, 160, 225
Cyclops 73
Cypria 20, 99, 198, 226–7

Dayne, Bella
  as Helen 4, 15, 54, 73, 98, 184
Deiphobus 226, 230
Diodorus Siculus 135
Diomedes 44, 69, 98, 169–70, 199, 206, 224
diversity
  in casting in TV, theater, film 82–5
Dolon 70, 175

Eastwood, Clint 101–2
Edwards, Aimee-Ffion
  as Cassandra 98
Eetion 31–2
Enoch, Alfred
  as Aeneas 5, 8, 43
Eros 31
Ethiopia 135–6
Euripides 51, 61, 99, 165–7, 172–3, 177–8, 180, 183–5, 189, 200, 223–5, 228, 230
Europa 18
Evander 228
  see also Norman, Woody
Exekias 134

Fall of Troy 128–9, 134
  see also *Posthomerica*
Farr, David 1, 17, 25, 27, 65, 79, 164, 185
Feynman, Richard 220

gods
  anthropomorphic 27, 35
  see also *Troy: Fall of a City* (series)
Gogou, Elena 120
Golden Dawn 81–2
Greekness 80
Guillory, Sienna 163
Gyasi, David
  as Achilles 5, 16, 26, 43, 82, 90, 97, 149

Harmodius 117
Harris, Johnny
  as Agamemnon 18, 97, 190, 200
Harrison, Kent 51, 99

Harryhausen, Ray 25
HBO *Rome 2*, 32, 55
Hector 15, 21, 27–8, 30, 59, 71, 105, 113, 171, 177, 179, 205, 213–15, 219, 224, 227, 229
  see also Weston-Jones, Tom
Hecuba 27–8, 53, 58–9, 102, 113–16, 144, 148–9, 165, 178–9, 185, 215–16, 224
  see also O'Connor, Frances
Hedlund, Garrett 117
Helen 28, 30, 100–5, 111–16, 156, 161, 171, 173, 204–5, 212–13, 225
  as antihero 51–64
  dressing 141–52
  teichoskopeia 21
  see also Achilles; Dayne, Bella; Iphigenia
Helen of Troy (1956) 2, 15, 39, 51, 66–7, 71, 114, 162, 204
Helen of Troy (2003) 39, 51, 99, 114, 163, 174, 202, 204
Hera 26, 29, 37, 46–7, 156, 212
  see also Beckmann, Inge
Hercules and the Amazon Women 133
Hermes 26, 37, 41, 199
  see also Murtagh, Diarmaid
Hermione 56–8, 60, 144, 183, 193, 204–7
  see also Hogg-Robinson, Grace
Hesion
  see also Lee-Williams, Deon
Hippolyta 129
Hogg-Robinson, Grace
  as Hermione 192
Homer
  Iliad 20, 69, 99, 104, 128, 132, 135, 163, 166, 185, 194, 219, 225, 227, 229
  Odyssey 20–1, 65, 112, 155, 200, 228
Hunter, Louis
  as Paris 4, 15, 38–9, 98
Hyginus 170, 198–9

Icke, Robert 201
Iliou persis 20
Iphigenia 32, 159, 163, 169, 172–3, 176, 197
  and Helen 184–8
  sacrifice of 183–96, 200–3
  see also Coe, Lauren
Ithaca 66

Jason 17
Jesebel 62–3

Kadare, Ismail 201
Kae-Kazim, Hakeem
  as Zeus 4–5, 8, 26, 41
King, Lex
  as Aphrodite 4, 26, 38, 41–8

Konchalovsky, Andrei 66
Knossos 143
Kruger, Diane 15

Lawless, Lucy
    as Xena 134
Lee-Williams, Deon
    as Hesion 8
Leto 31
Libya 135
Litos 31, 228
Lucas, George 211

McLaren, Clemence 199
Mane, Tyler 163
Marsden, Matthew 39
Mawle, Joseph
    as Odysseus 4, 7–8, 98, 189
Medea 17
Memnon 135–6
Menelaus 27, 32, 44, 53–6, 59, 69–71, 100, 102, 111, 118, 122, 128, 146–7, 155, 159, 161–2, 171, 175–6, 184, 189, 192–3, 197, 204–8, 228–9
    see also Armstrong, Jonas
Miller, Madeleine 118, 199
Miller, Shamilla
    as Athena 5
Milner, Nina
    as Penthesilea 6, 45, 127–39
Money, Jamie-Lee
    as Chryseis 18, 97, 193
Murtagh, Diarmaid
    as Hermes 40
Mycenae 122
Myrina 135
Myrmidons 70–1, 86–7, 118, 123, 129, 159, 164, 185, 227

Neoptolemus 177, 205, 229
Nestor 79
    see also Butler, Peter
Norman, Woody
    as Evander 8
Nostoi 20–1

O'Connor, Frances
    as Hecuba 45, 100, 184
Odysseus 32, 34, 61, 65–75, 155, 159, 169–82, 197, 201–2, 204, 207–8, 216, 227–9
    daughter of 198–200
    as *polytropos* 68–72
    and women and children 175–6
    see also Mawle, Joseph
Odyssey, The 66–7, 71, 199
Oenone
    see also Slabber, Lise

Orestes 117, 205
Orientalism 111, 114
Ovid 18, 223

Palamedes 170, 199
Panathenaic festivals 16
Pandaros 79, 103
Pappas, Irene 66
Paris 28, 30–1, 37–50, 53–4, 57–8, 102, 111, 113, 128, 159, 173, 179, 185, 188, 192, 206, 212–14, 223–5, 229
    Aphrodite and 38–40
    birth of 34
    Judgment of 27–8, 40–4, 211–12, 223
    see also Hunter, Louis
Patroclus 69, 79, 111–25, 128, 131, 228
    see also Achilles; Tsipa, Lemogang
Pelops 203
Penelope 66, 99, 169–71, 174, 178, 199
    see also Wessels, Erica
Penthesilea 20, 101–2, 127–39, 228
    see also Milner, Nina
Persian Wars 165
Petersen, Wolfgang 2, 51, 65, 97, 127, 143, 229
Pirrie, Chloe
    as Andromache 98
Pitt, Brad 117, 143
Plato 131–2
Podestà, Rossana 15
polyamory 120
    see also Achilles
Polyxena 178
Poseidon 14, 25, 226
Posthomerica
    see also Fall of Troy
Priam 15, 33, 53, 100–3, 105–6, 113–16, 149, 165, 179, 194, 212–17, 219, 224, 229
    see also Threlfall, David
Proclus 128
Psiax 136
Pylades 117
Pyrrhus
    see also Neoptolemus

Quintus of Smyra 128, 131, 134

racecraft 83
Reed, Maxwell 162
rhapsodes 17, 21

Sarandos, Ted 164
Scacchi, Greta 66
Schultz, Waldemar
    as Thersites 6, 67, 159
Scylla 73
Seneca 177–8

Index

seriality
   of ancient epic 13–23
Sernas, Jacques 15
Shay, Jonathan 166
Singh, Tarsem 25
Sirens 73
Slabber, Lise
   as Oenone 40
Sophocles 156, 176, 199, 223
Sparta 56–8, 111, 141–51, 179, 192, 228
STARZ *Spartacus* 2
Supreme Court 107
Swing Painter 136

Talthybius 177
Tantalus 203
Telemachus 73, 170, 198, 228
Themiscyra 130, 133
Thersites 71, 73, 131, 155, 158, 165, 176
   see also Schultz, Waldemar
Threlfall, David
   as Priam 16, 100, 143
Trojan Horse 20, 33, 73, 150, 217–18, 226
Troy (2004) 2, 15, 28, 37, 39, 51, 65–7, 72, 97,
      117–18, 127, 143–4, 163, 202, 204, 229
Troy: Fall of a City (series)
   ancient sources for 223–31
   and anti-Blackness 89–92
   Black actors in 79
   costumes in 141–52
   gods and religion in 25–36
   patriarchy 97–109

queering and sexuality 111–25
racist reactions to 79–95
social media 79–95
white supremacy 87–9
women and power 97–109
Tsipa, Lemogang
   as Patroclus 5–6

Ulysses
   see also Odysseus
Uranus 26

Vergil 17, 40, 44, 48, 185, 199, 219

Wax, Derek 17, 25, 28, 80, 82
Wayne, John 101
Wessels, Erica
   as Penelope 98
Weston-Jones, Tom
   as Hector 16, 43, 102
Wilson, Amy Louise
   as Briseis 6, 8, 97
Wise, Robert 2, 51
Wonder Woman 6, 129, 133
Wood, Michael 1
World War One 157

Xanthius 61, 73, 103, 159, 169–70, 176, 225, 228

Zeus 25–6, 29, 37, 46, 55, 79, 147, 179, 212, 225
   see also Kae-Kazim, Hakeem

www.ingramcontent.com/pod-product-compliance
Lightning Source LLC
Chambersburg PA
CBHW051806230426
43672CB00012B/2647